Economic and Financial Law & Policy – Shifting Insights & Values

Volume 9

This book series focuses on presenting critical legal and interdisciplinary research regarding the tools and instruments of free-market-driven societies and their economies.

For the last few decades, the world markets have been in turmoil, to a large extent is a result of value and policy choices which have been made since the late middle ages. As a result, on a global scale, economies and the legal systems giving form to them, have mainly if not exclusively become based on selfishness and greed, a reality which is moreover explicitly propagated by the theories of economic neo-liberalism.

It has nevertheless become clear in the recent past that said free market tools and mechanisms – such as private money creation by banks, next to the way huge corporations in general function and determine the outcome of economic processes – result in disastrous consequences, especially when remaining uncorrected by law and when not being submitted to clear public policy intervention measures.

Despite the evidence and growing understanding of the causes and consequences of neoliberal policy, few alternatives for the capitalist model as currently implemented, have so far been proposed.

In order to meet these concerns, this book series aims at offering an outlet for various forms of scientific research output, both monographs and edited collections.

The objective of every book of the series will hereby be to look critically at the legal methods and mechanisms shaping the free markets, and even to suggest alternatives for these.

Although the book series is initiated by legal scholars, it nevertheless aims to be truly multi- and interdisciplinary. The books series therefor welcomes and will incorporate all relevant disciplines, including law, economics, philosophy, ethics, religion, psychology, sociology, anthropology etc.

José Grabiel Luis Cordova

Theoretical and Legal Dimensions of the Right to Energy

From the Global Context to Cuba as Case Study

Springer

José Grabiel Luis Cordova
Energy Law Section and Security Technology
and e-Privacy Research Group, Faculty of Law
University of Groningen
Groningen, The Netherlands

ISSN 2522-5243 ISSN 2522-5251 (electronic)
Economic and Financial Law & Policy – Shifting Insights & Values
ISBN 978-3-032-33251-6 ISBN 978-3-032-33252-3 (eBook)
https://doi.org/10.1007/978-3-032-33252-3

This Springer imprint is published by the registered company Springer Nature Switzerland AG
The registered company address is: Gewerbestrasse 11, 6330 Cham, Switzerland

This book is dedicated to my mom, who remained by my side until the end.

Foreword

When I first began collaborating with researchers in Latin America on questions of energy vulnerability and resilience, it became clear how often the topic of a "right to energy" was missing—not only from legal frameworks, but from wider academic and policy debates. Despite growing interest in energy poverty, there was very little work that approached energy access as a legal entitlement or considered its relationship with other rights.

Over the last 5 years, through the *Energy Solidarity in Latin America* project, I worked with colleagues across the region to map out existing legislative and policy frameworks, and to conduct in-depth, multi-scalar assessments of energy vulnerability. José Grabiel Luis Cordova, as part of the Cuban team, contributed significantly to this shared effort, particularly through his legal perspective on energy access and its intersection with national rights frameworks. Our collective work underscored how fragmented the picture remains, and how vital it is to develop more coherent, rights-based understandings of energy vulnerability.

It is a privilege to introduce this important and timely contribution by José, which continues that agenda in a focused and detailed way. It traces the evolution of the right to energy in international law and then brings that lens to the Cuban context—one that is often overlooked in English-language (and indeed Spanish) scholarship. Cuba offers a rich case study, both because of its longstanding emphasis on universal service provision and because of the structural constraints it faces in delivering reliable, affordable, and sustainable energy. In particular, the book draws attention to the diverse ways the right to energy is named and framed across contexts—a fragmentation that complicates comparative analysis and conceptual clarity. I was especially struck by the observation that "the concept of energy is not fixed or immutable; rather, it is societies that shape the definition of this category"—an important reminder of how socially embedded and contested this field is. Through this lens, the book offers a comprehensive and carefully considered delimitation of the right to energy, contributing much-needed structure to a field often characterised by doctrinal dispersion.

What this book contributes is a clear, doctrinally grounded account of how the right to energy might be constructed, interpreted, and defended within a specific legal system. Its emphasis on constitutional frameworks, legal guarantees, and normative instruments helps to illuminate what is—and is not—currently possible within the Cuban legal tradition.

In earlier work I co-authored about the COVID-19 pandemic, we noted how many emergency energy measures taken around the world to keep energy available and affordable seemed to reflect an implicit recognition of energy as a basic right. Yet these measures were often ad hoc, lacking in legal grounding. The kind of legal scaffolding that this book provides could help ensure that such recognition is not just momentary, but part of a lasting shift towards more equitable and resilient energy systems.

For practitioners, policymakers, and researchers interested in how the right to energy might be understood and implemented within national systems, this book offers an important reference point—one that invites further engagement, debate, and development.

It is both a scholarly achievement and a call to action.

Glasgow, United Kingdom
May 2025

Harriet Thomson

Preface

Humankind's history is the history of the constant search for energy sources to satisfy growing needs. The imperiousness of satisfying the energy needs of the human species, as a fundamental needs, has led to decisions regarding energy sources at every stage of history. Such decisions throughout human evolution have resulted in the current energy context at the global, regional, national, and local levels. A deep dependence on non-renewable energy sources marks this context. Such dependence constitutes a risk to economic development and the full realisation of the right to energy.

This book starts from the following premise: meeting energy needs is not a luxury but fundamental to human dignity. Therefore, energy cannot be understood only as a mere resource or a commodity, but as a human and fundamental right.

From this perspective, the growing claim for a right to energy is not an isolated event but a response to unjust energy systems and legal gaps due to the expansion of neoliberal globalisation. Hence, energy has become an instrument of power and not of empowerment through human and fundamental rights. The consequences of this are visible today through the growth of energy poverty, social exclusion, and environmental degradation. This is therefore the context that this book challenges.

By analysing the energy history of humanity, this book argues for the legal recognition and protection of the right to energy as a human and fundamental right. To this end, it analyses how public international law has laid the foundations for the recognition of the right to energy as a human right and how regional and selected national legal frameworks in the European Union and Latin America and the Caribbean have addressed its protection as a fundamental right. Additionally, this book places Cuba under the microscope. This Caribbean nation, with a highly complex geopolitical and energy context, presents limitations to the realisation of the right to energy. Through a critical analysis of the Cuban legal framework, from the Constitution to development norms, this book identifies gaps and opportunities for recognising and configuring the right to energy.

This work is not a mere academic exercise. It is a legal-theoretical proposal for the recognition and legal configuration of the right to energy as a premise for fulfilling other rights. This book is a call to reimagine law not as a reflection of the market but as a tool to empower and protect. If this book, however modestly, can contribute to that, it will have served its purpose.

Groningen, Netherlands
16 April 2025

José Grabiel Luis Cordova

Acknowledgements

This book is the result of a doctoral journey developed within a joint doctoral programme framework between the Vrije Universiteit Brussel and the Universidad Central "Marta Abreu" de Las Villas. I am deeply grateful to these two institutions for the support they have provided and for fostering a collaborative environment that made this work possible.

The research that underpins this book was supported by funding from the Universitas 2020 scholarship, awarded by Vrije Universiteit Brussel within the framework of development cooperation. I express my sincere gratitude for the support of international research cooperation.

Additionally, I am grateful for the support received from the Economic and Social Research Council (United Kingdom) through the project "UKRI-GCRF Energy Solidarity in Latin America: generating inclusive knowledge and governance to address energy vulnerability and energy systems resilience" (ES/T006382/1), which contributed to disseminate the main findings of this research.

I would like to extend my most sincere appreciation to Prof. Dr Harriet Thomson, whose foreword offers invaluable insights and adds immense value to this work. Her insight and longstanding commitment to studying energy vulnerability and poverty have contributed to this work. I sincerely appreciate her support and encouragement.

When I started on this path, I never imagined that it would be full of many challenges, for which solutions were found, or so many sad moments that were overcome with joy. Five years ago, I began an arduous journey without imagining it, which has marked me for life. Without a doubt, I have had the opportunity to count on the extraordinary support of my family and friends, many of whom are now my chosen family, because, without you, this achievement would not have been possible. Thank you all, and especially:

To my parents, for always guiding me and supporting all my decisions,
To my aunt, who has always been my second mother,

To my grandparents for all their infinite love,

To my brother and uncles, for always being by my side,

To my wife, for her unconditional love and endless strength, for illuminating every day of my life and for pushing me forward,

To my chosen siblings, Freddy, for his advice, his scolding, and his unconditional friendship, and Anaely and Carlitos, because no matter the place, the time, or the distance, they have never left me alone,

To Indirita and Camilo because, although we are not blood-related, we are family.

Of course, to Ro and Eli for proving that there are no cultural or blood barriers, because wherever I go, I know they will be with me,

To Koen and Kim, thank you for always finding a solution, even when "*es complicado*". Where there is a will, there is a way.

To Yane for always being the push I needed to keep going,

To friends who are also, today, my family, Roberto, Maha, Katarzyna, and María Eugenia,

To my guardian angel, Rita, who has always treated me like a son,

To Serge and Jenneke, because they are just extraordinary,

To Stefano and Gioia, because I only regret not having shared more time with them.

To Yaniel, David, Erick, Fernando, and Isaac, for the debate nights,

To Gwen and Paola for their support, understanding, and friendship,

To Tony, for overcoming all the impossible situations,

To Eddy Van Driesche and Sonia Beckmans, for all their experience and every moment shared,

To IRMO for always having a place for me, to Karen, Jacqueline, Francoise, and Anne Martine for always thinking of solutions, to Cailin, Steven, John, Ingrid, Carin, and Yann,

To Olga, Patrick, and Cirelda for welcoming me into their family,

To Yuri, not only for taking care of my health but also for being a great person,

To Yunior and María Elena for their help and joy,

To Karen, Avinash, and Anas, "*De Musketeers*",

To the UCLV Law Department, and especially to Rei, Yulier, Alex, and Betty, for all their support and guidance,

To the professors, researchers, and administrative staff of the Faculty of Law and Criminology at VUB,

To Richard Alexander for welcoming me with open arms at the SOAS University of London,

To Francisco Javier Valenzuela and Gabriel Balles, for their kind welcome to the Universidad de Granada,

To all those people I have had the privilege to meet, because each one of them has left a mark on me,

Thank you very much!

Competing Interests The author has no competing interests to declare that are relevant to the content of this manuscript.

Contents

List of Figures

Chapter 1
General Introduction

1.1 Introduction

1.1.1 Introductory Remarks

Throughout history, access to energy has been an essential pillar for the development of human life and society. For this reason, advances in energy use have facilitated progress from one economic and social formation to another. For this reason, obtaining energy has become a vital sustenance that has marked the evolution of the human species since its earliest origins.[1]

Energy is at the heart of the functioning of contemporary society and the market. It is unquestionably an inescapable prerequisite for progress in a general sense. Thus, the development of humankind is inescapably linked to energy, from systems as old as the traditional exploitation of biomass and animal traction to more sustainable practices such as the use of renewable sources.[2]

Access to energy is currently highly contentious due to multiple factors, such as monopolisation and liberalisation[3] of the energy market. These trends jeopardise the affordability of energy supply by increasing energy prices in the market. Globally, access to energy is a controversial reality, where a large part of the population remains energy-deprived.[4]

In this regard, the United Nations identifies as challenges: inadequate development and/or sub-optimal implementation of enabling policy and legal frameworks that promote and protect energy access; incomplete socio-economic inclusiveness

---

[1] Cunningham (2003).

[2] Rhodes (2018).

[3] Cf. Bedi (2018).

[4] International Energy Agency et al. (2023).

J. G. Luis Cordova, *Theoretical and Legal Dimensions of the Right to Energy*, Economic and Financial Law & Policy – Shifting Insights & Values 9,
https://doi.org/10.1007/978-3-032-33252-3_1

in energy access; misaligned costs; reliability; quality and affordability of energy services; and inefficient or misdirected financing for energy access.[5] This situation generates a growing concern in market regulation, considering the constant increase in energy demand and the energy sector's volatility, which are subject to multiple variables.

Many countries, faced with constant energy crises and market complexities due to the lack of availability, affordability and overexploitation of fossil fuels, have promoted sustainable policies aimed at energy security and sovereignty and democratisation of energy.[6] They have also become aware that energy accessibility is an invariable element for the functioning of all internal processes of society, reorienting their legal systems to offer protection for the right to energy based on international standards.

1.1.2 International Overview

The concern to connect access to energy with human rights can find one of its most remote antecedents in the twentieth century, with the Universal Declaration of Human Rights. The right to energy can be deduced from this international legal instrument when an extensive analysis of the norm is made in the formulation of Article 25.[7] Despite its unspoken recognition, its protection today has been on the rise.

Following this Declaration, the International Covenant on Economic, Social and Cultural Rights was adopted.[8] For part of the doctrine,[9] this instrument establishes in an unspoken manner the need to improve cooking, lighting, and heating conditions, constituting an indirect reference to the right to energy.

One of the primary antecedents of the juridification process of the right to energy at the international level is the Convention on the Elimination of All Forms of Discrimination against Women.[10] This instrument establishes the first legal reference for the right in question, empowering women in productive processes through access to energy. Another international legal norm that expressly recognises this

---

[5] Department of Economic and Social Affairs (2021).

[6] The International Bank for Reconstruction and Development/The World Bank (2018).

[7] Cf. Article 25, Organización de Naciones Unidas (1948).

[8] Article 11.1, Organización de Naciones Unidas (1976).

[9] Garcia and Mundó (2014), p. 15, Bradbrook and Gardam (2006), Solis (2018), Durán and Condorí (2015).

[10] Cf. Article 14.1 (h) "States Parties shall take all appropriate measures to eliminate discrimination against women in rural areas in order to ensure, on a basis of equality of men and women, their equal participation in and benefit from rural development, and in particular shall ensure to them the right (…) to enjoy adequate living conditions, particularly in the areas of housing, (…) electricity (…)". Convention on the Elimination of All Forms of Discrimination against Women. Organización de Naciones Unidas (1979).

right is the Universal Declaration of Emerging Human Rights.[11] Both instruments result from states' awareness of the need for energy for human development.

Subsequently, the 2015 United Nations Conference adopted the Framework Convention on Climate Change. In its preamble, it recognises the need to promote access to energy from sustainable sources.[12] Like this, access to energy begins to be qualified with sustainability because such access must be based on renewable energy sources. In this way, the impact of climate change is highlighted in the decision-making of States in the interests of energy transition and sustainable development.[13]

In the same year, the Sustainable Development Goals of the United Nations Organisation came into being and are closely related to the subject of Goal 7.[14] This sustainable development goal aims to combat the adverse effects of the lack of access to energy on three levels: the satisfaction of basic needs, directly affecting the full realisation of human beings and society; productive processes, on which economic development depends; and the satisfaction of the needs of modern societies, such as education, communication, recreation, among other elements that affect individual and social development.[15]

From a theoretical-legal perspective, access to energy has also been a recurring theme in human rights and has even been explained as a premise for tackling poverty.[16] According to B. Ki-moon: "Energy is crucial for achieving almost all of the Sustainable Development Goals, from its role in the eradication of poverty (…)".[17]

The value of recognising this right is also underpinned by the essence of sustainable development, especially concerning health, education, food security, gender equality, and climate change, among many others.[18] In this way, the right to energy derives from the need to be supported by substantive and adjective law as a possibility for action.

This scenario is why part of the doctrine is based on recognising the right to energy as a human right. Examples include Owoeye,[19] Tully,[20] Olawuyi,[21] Shyu,[22]

---

[11] Cf. Article 1.1, Institut de Drets Humans de Catalunya (2010).

[12] Organización de Naciones Unidas (2015).

[13] Milian Gómez et al. (2023).

[14] "Ensuring access to affordable, reliable, sustainable and modern energy for all". Comisión Económica para América Latina y el Caribe (2016).

[15] De la Vega (2015), p. 3.

[16] Garcia and Mundó (2014).

[17] Economic and Social Council (2016).

[18] International Bank for Reconstruction and Development/The World Bank (2017), p. 11.

[19] Owoeye (2016).

[20] Tully (2006, 2009).

[21] Olawuyi (2018).

[22] Shyu (2021).

Bradbrook and Gardam,[23] Acuña Zepeda and Díaz Zepeda,[24] Frigo et al.,[25] Solis,[26] Sovacool and Dworkin,[27] Schiano,[28] Aviles,[29] Clemson,[30] Wewerinke-Singh,[31] Ambihaipahar,[32] Sin-Hang Ngai,[33] Akizu et al.[34] and Hesselman et al.[35]

Therefore, the scientific construction of the right to energy would provide the legal basis for determining its content and scope. In this way, the guidelines for shaping this right in the legal system of each country would be established, taking into consideration theoretical-legal shaping elements such as principles, subjects, content, and guarantees.[36]

For his part, Schiano considers sustainability to be the way forward regarding the right to energy, expressed when he says: "If access to energy is a human right, then renewable energy and the more efficient distribution of energy is clearly advancing this cause (…) Access to energy is critical for the reduction of poverty and is listed as Goal 7 of the 16 United Nations Sustainable Development Goals".[37]

This statement presents using renewable sources as underpinning the right to energy, a controversial reality in multiple scenarios. Although there is a significant international movement towards energy transition as an initiative consistent with sustainable development, this reality is different in other contexts.[38]

The realisation of the content of the right to energy requires an energy source, regardless of its nature, as a necessity that cannot be postponed. Although using

---

[23] Bradbrook and Gardam (2006).

[24] Acuña Zepeda and Díaz Zepeda (2017).

[25] Frigo et al. (2021).

[26] Solis (2014, 2018).

[27] Sovacool and Dworkin (2014).

[28] Schiano (2017).

[29] Aviles (2012).

[30] Clemson (2012).

[31] Wewerinke-Singh (2022).

[32] Ambihaipahar (2014).

[33] Sin-Hang Ngai (2012).

[34] Akizu et al. (2017), 18,059.

[35] Hesselman et al. (2021).

[36] Peces-Barba et al. (1995).

[37] Schiano (2017), p. 2.

[38] Energy transition as a global trend is a priority for sustainable development. However, while the global North is extremely concerned about the need to reform the energy sector by increasing the share of renewable sources in the energy mix, this concern is different in the global South. The concerns of developing countries are related to issues of energy availability and affordability, which have major implications for the development capacity of nations in the global South.

At the same time, the accelerated energy transition in these countries is extremely difficult by the existence of barriers. These barriers include: the existence of centralised energy systems, limited investment capital, high technology costs for energy transition and others. Energy is, without a doubt, an essential element for social and economic development, which is why the process of energy transition requires adequate design and planning to minimise the impacts on the economies of the global south without neglecting the just transition. Cf. Goldthau et al. (2020).

renewable sources is the way towards sustainability, this must not compromise the realisation of the right to energy by depriving its subjects of an energy supply.

The analysis of the evolution of thinking on energy in the global legal framework has highlighted the international community's growing concern in the recognition and protection of the right to energy. This evolution has been reflected within states, both at the factual and normative levels, taking into consideration the increasing levels of poverty, social inequalities, as well as inequity concerning the right to development at the international, regional, and national levels.[39] The major trends in protecting the right to energy are oriented towards its indirect protection.

An example of this is the protection of the right to energy in the framework of the right to adequate housing, health, and education, among others. This trend is adopted by Constitutions such as those of Honduras, Chile, France, and Belgium, among many others.[40]

This trend is not considered correct by this author, as it results in the subordination imposed by restricting the content of the right to energy. In this case, how is access to energy outside the home protected? How is energy access guaranteed to ensure productive processes' functioning in the most vulnerable sectors, such as small producers?

This scenario and others will generate legal vulnerability in the face of the subordination of the right to energy and the disaggregation of its content within the framework of other rights. This disaggregation would subject the right to the legal regimes of other rights. The right to energy can bring together an accumulation of coherently structured claims to substantiate multiple conflict situations, obeying principles that inform it.

Another trend in national law has been including the right to energy in the consumer rights framework.[41] However, although there are examples of its express recognition at the constitutional level,[42] this trend has been slowly gaining ground in legislative initiatives of this nature.[43]

This research considers the constitutional recognition of the right to energy as its first legal guarantee. The need for such recognition is reinforced by the indispensable relationship between the right to energy and the realisation of other human rights, recognised in international legal instruments, as well as with the fundamental rights included in the Constitutions, given that the right in question is a right of a human and fundamental nature.[44] In addition to its recognition as a right, other defence mechanisms of various kinds must be provided for its materialisation. In

---

[39] Organización Latinoamericana de Energía and Sistema de Información Energética-Legal (2011).

[40] De Belgische Grondwet (1994), Constitution de la République française (1958), Constitución de la República de Honduras (1982), Constitución Política de la República de Chile (2010).

[41] Cf. European Parliament and European Council (2019), Parlamento Europeo 2009.

[42] Constitución Política de la República de Nicaragua (2014), Constitución Política del Estado de Bolivia (2009).

[43] Convención Constitucional (2022).

[44] Chakraborty (2016), p. 5.

this order, a system of guarantees must be set up to allow the full realisation of the content of the right to energy.

1.1.3 Preliminary Analysis of the Cuban Context

In that sense, in Cuba, we should not ignore factors that have a direct negative impact on availability as one of the integral elements of the content of the right to energy. Among them are the economic and financial sanctions imposed by the United States in the framework of its blockade policy since the 1960s.

The tightening of the US blockade of Cuba[45] has caused damages in the order of 136 million 6,300,043 dollars to the Cuban mining-energy sector, which has exacerbated Cuba's financial limitations to invest in the national energy sector. Such damage includes the effects on Cuban companies that play a significant role in the country's energy development. Examples of this are the enterprises Unión Cuba-Petróleo and Moa NICKEL S.A., which have lost all or a significant part of their suppliers due to the persecution of companies that trade with Cuba.[46]

The damage caused by the sanctions imposed on Cuba and the impact of the global economic crisis, which will become even more acute between 2022 and 2026, among other causes, means that the Cuban energy sector has not evolved sufficiently. At the same time, the constant rise in oil prices constitutes a critical limit for the energy sector due to the high dependence on oil and the limited availability of this type of resource in the country.

This situation harms energy generation. Such dependence on fossil fuels has forced Cuba to exploit domestic fossil fuels, especially when acquiring this resource is challenging. This measure has affected the proper functioning of the generation systems due to the high sulphur content of national crude oil and has shortened the planned maintenance cycles.[47] Financial limitations and demanding access to material resources have caused the national energy system to present a complex situation, which has led to power outages throughout the Cuban archipelago.

Such conditions undermine two of the integral elements of the content of the right to energy. First and foremost, availability is a crucial factor that directly impacts the fulfilment of the right to energy, as it is a fundamental prerequisite for its satisfaction.

The reliability of the electrical energy service is also compromised due to voltage fluctuations occurring during the connection and disconnection of electrical circuits, thereby impacting one of the essential elements of the service. Furthermore, the accessibility of the network is hindered by the damage inflicted by adverse

[45] U.S. Department of the Treasury (2022).

[46] Cf. Ministerio de Relaciones Internacionales de Cuba (2022).

[47] Figueredo Reinaldo and Carmona Tamayo (2022).

weather events that impact the country. All the above has undoubtedly harmed the realisation of the right to energy in the national context.

Despite the above, Cuba's progress in the right to energy has been palpable, with high levels of electrification and the adoption of public policies that advocate for energy security.[48] However, the high percentage of electrification cannot be identified with full access to electricity, given that in many isolated areas, it is only received partially, so full accessibility to energy is negatively affected. In these areas, energy is obtained from renewable sources such as solar photovoltaic (PV).

This source per se depends on two aspects: equivalent peak solar hours[49] and the limited storage system.[50] Another element that undermines access to energy is the low levels of supply quality in certain specific time-space situations[51] due to technical generation factors. As a result of the above, there is an affectation on the reliability that should characterise energy services.[52]

There has also been an increase in national energy demand. This increase is clearly related to the strengthening of the private sector in the domestic market and the opening of the economy. This context requires greater availability of energy to increase production processes. The private sector provides the national economy with essential goods and services and the corresponding taxation according to the profits received.

Similarly, the residential sector has increased its electricity consumption by 19.22% between 2011 and 2021.[53] In turn, high temperatures, as a consequence of climate change and self-insulation due to COVID-19, have been some of the triggers for overconsumption between 2020 and 2021.[54] In addition to the above, another factor at the practical level directly undermines the right to energy: the low share of renewable energy sources in the national electricity generation matrix.[55]

Also, since 2019, a series of events have become evident in Cuba that have resulted in a national energy crisis affecting all sectors of the economy, especially the residential sector.[56]

The conditions mentioned above collectively create a context in which the complete fulfilment of the right to energy has been compromised. In this sense, the legal framework plays a fundamental role in the recognition and protection of the right to energy by establishing a system of guarantees. In response to this call, regulatory

---

[48] Partido Comunista de Cuba (2021), p. 50.

[49] Cf. Martínez et al. (2017).

[50] "The average solar generation that Cuba receives during a year is (…) an average of about 5 hours per day." Stolik Novygrod (2014).

[51] At present, distributed generation systems in Cuba present negative elements that threaten the quality of the energy generated. Francisco Fernández et al. (2010). At present, distributed generation systems in Cuba have negative elements that threaten the quality of the energy generated.

[52] Peña Pupo et al. (2020).

[53] Oficina Nacional de Estadística e Información (2022a).

[54] Ramos (2020).

[55] Oficina Nacional de Estadística e Información (2022b).

[56] Redacción Digital (2019).

responses have sought to alleviate the negative consequences of the energy crisis from a legal perspective through the promotion of renewable energy sources, both in the state and private spheres and the creation of incentive mechanisms.[57]

However, the incentives created by the national legal system are hindered by the current economic reality, where credits are granted in Cuban pesos (CUP), a currency whose convertibility is limited by the availability of foreign currency in the national market. This reality affects the acquisition of technologies for the exploitation of renewable energy sources in the international context. At the same time, the national production of this type of equipment and the exercise of energy prosumerism initiatives[58] are still not significant.[59]

Despite the existence of normative initiatives that promote the realisation of the content of the right to energy, no relevant studies have been systematised concerning the configuration of the right under investigation from the national legal framework, where it is not expressly recognised. This scenario determines the novelty of the present research, given that there is little research on this right, a factor that leads to the lack of a solid and developed doctrine. Examples are Delgado Triana and Fariñas Wong,[60] Peña Pupo et al.,[61] Luis Cordova et al.,[62] and Delgado Triana et al.[63] The lack of a clear theoretical and normative framework hinders the regulation, implementation, and legal safeguarding of the right to energy.

From the objective Cuban reality, the need to recognise the right to energy is based on protecting human beings[64] in the framework of availability, accessibility, affordability, and reliability. In this context, energy should not be understood in a restrictive sense as electrical energy but should include other forms and sources. In this same line of thought, it is considered that the recognition of this right would offer legal guarantees of protection to holders in situations such as service interruptions, changes in tariffs, voltage variations, and access to information, among other circumstances that could place them in situations of energy vulnerability.

Those elements determine the need to base the right to energy on doctoral research to construct a theoretical doctrine based on its constituent elements:

---

[57] Consejo de Estado (2019), Banco Central de Cuba (2019), Ministerio de Finanzas y Precios (2021a, 2021b), Ministerio de Energía y Minas (2021b, 2021a).

[58] Energy prosumerism is a phenomenon where consumers evolve from a passive to an active position in the energy need satisfaction. Within this context, "active customer means a final customer, or a group of jointly acting final customers, who consumes or stores electricity generated within its premises located within confined boundaries or, (…), within other premises, or who sells self-generated electricity or participates in flexibility or energy efficiency schemes, provided that those activities do not constitute its primary commercial or professional activity. European Parliament and European Council (2019), Kotilainen (2020), Cseres (2018).

[59] Martín López (2022).

[60] Delgado Triana and Fariñas Wong (2016).

[61] Peña Pupo et al. (2020).

[62] Luis Cordova et al. (2022).

[63] Delgado Triana et al. (2019).

[64] Ministerio del Comercio Interior (2018).

subjects, principles, content, and guarantees. The proposed study will be based on constitutional precepts, as they are the supreme norm that marks the country's fundamental structure and legal dynamics, as well as on the system of guarantees that enable the realisation and effective exercise of the right to energy.

The recognition of the right to energy is also based on the interconnectivity and interdependence of rights. In this sense, other rights recognised in the Cuban Constitution depend on the right to energy, such as health, education, and food. The materialisation of guiding principles such as sustainable development, progressiveness, equality, and non-discrimination also depends on the right to energy.

Therefore, for the protection of this right, its constitutional recognition would be unavoidable, mainly due to the existence of a Socialist State based on the rule of law, democracy, and social justice, which is committed to sustainable development and the improvement of people's quality of life. This way of thinking and acting would be coherent with the projection of the Conceptualisation of the Cuban Economic and Social Model of Socialist Development and the Guidelines of the Economic and Social Policy of the Cuban State,[65] as well as with the Tarea Vida.[66]

When analysing the Cuban Constitution of 2019,[67] the right to energy finds its basis in several articles, although not expressly.[68] However, we wish to highlight the relationship between the right to energy and the right to a healthy environment, provided for in Article 75 of the supreme law.[69] In this sense, sustainability emerges as a nexus for energy generation through the exploitation of renewable sources, minimising the environmental impact of the national energy sector, and the rational use of energy resources.

Concerning the jurisdictional protection of fundamental rights, the Constitution of the Republic of Cuba of 2019 provides in Article 99[70] for the possibility of appealing to the competent jurisdictional instance when constitutional rights are violated, which is complemented by Law 153, "On the Process of Protection of Constitutional Rights"[71]; but what jurisdictional protection will be granted to the right to energy, when the Cuban legislative body has not expressly recognised it?

Once the Constitution of the Republic of Cuba of 2019 has been analysed, the conclusion that the right to energy is not expressly reflected, even though its regulation can be deduced, stands out. Therefore, it would be pertinent to analyse other Cuban legal provisions to find out if there are any precepts related to the legal protection of the right to energy.

---

[65] Partido Comunista de Cuba (2021).

[66] Ministerio de Ciencia Tecnología y Medio Ambiente (2021).

[67] Cf. Article 1, 11 b), 13 e) f), 16 and 46. Constitución de la República de Cuba (2019).

[68] An analogous situation occurs with other rights such as the right to adequate housing. In this context, housing is indispensable for "cooking, heating, lighting and food preservation or waste disposal". Oficina del Alto Comisionado para los Derechos Humanos (2010).

[69] Cf. Article 75 Constitución de la República de Cuba (2019).

[70] Cf. Article 99 Constitución de la República de Cuba (2019), Asamblea Nacional del Poder Popular (2022).

[71] Asamblea Nacional del Poder Popular (2022).

Continuing the analysis of the legal framework for energy in Cuba, we can cite the current Electricity Law.[72] Despite the date of its entry into force, this body of law governs electricity generation, distribution, and commercialisation. This law does not foresee complaint mechanisms for the suspension of service or any other violation of the right under analysis; the only form of complaint foreseen would be in the case of Article 11 for undue payments and debts.

Another regulatory provision resulting from shaping the legal framework for energy in Cuba is Decree-Law No. 345, "On the development of renewable sources and the efficient use of energy,"[73] dated 23 March 2017, which came into force on 28 November 2019. Although this Decree-Law does not provide legal protection for the right to energy, it supports the realisation of the right to energy. It promotes energy generation from renewable sources and energy efficiency, elements that positively impact the realisation of the right to energy. It also encourages the use of renewable energy sources, both by natural and legal persons, through bank credits and tax benefits.

In 2021, the Cuban legal system underwent an opening concerning the importation of technologies associated with the exploitation of renewable sources. As part of this opening, a series of tax benefits were conceived for this import type.[74] These measures promoted energy democracy within the country through energy prosumerism practices. Despite these regulations, acquiring this type of equipment in Cuba is difficult due to its scarce availability, costs and the technical specificities that must be met.

The Cuban legal system leaves questions unanswered for the interested party due to the scarce regulation of such a specific matter as the right to energy. The Cuban government's will[75] to guarantee access to clean and stable energy has not kept pace with the legislation, and the latter has lagged. Therefore, there is a great need to improve the existing regulations for the protection and realisation of the right to energy.

The novelty and importance of the subject lie in the contribution, from a doctrinal approach, of the foundation of the theoretical-legal bases for the recognition and configuration of the right to energy in Cuba, contributing to the improvement of constitutional regulation, complementary regulations, and ways to defend it. The protection of the right to energy favours, among other elements, its effective protection and legal security and constitutes an indispensable prerequisite for sustainable development in contemporary times.

---

[72] Poder Ejecutivo del Consejo de Ministros (1975).

[73] Consejo de Estado (2019).

[74] Ministerio de Finanzas y Precios (2021a, 2021b); Ministerio de Energía y Minas (2021b, 2021c).

[75] Access to electricity has reached most of the country using alternatives in the most intricate areas such as Distributed Generation Systems understood as systems "comprising localised electricity generation, close to the load centre with storage and management, which can work in isolation or integrated to the electricity grid, to provide multiple benefits on both sides of the meter". Francisco Fernández et al. (2010), p. 42.

1.2 Research Questions and Objectives

Therefore, following the rationale developed above, the scientific research question to be answered is determined as follows: What essential theoretical-legal elements should underpin the right to energy in Cuba to sustain its recognition and configuration?

In line with this research question, this book aims to lay the foundations of the essential theoretical-legal elements on which the right to energy must be based, recognised, and configured in Cuba.

The essential theoretical-legal elements that should underpin the right to energy are widely scattered in modern legal doctrine. This right has not undergone a solid doctrinal systematisation and structuring, as it is a subject that is still hesitantly analysed by the legal academy. This situation is reflected in the limited literature on the topic. For this reason, the present research will provide the essential bases that will fill the scientific gaps concerning the essential theoretical-legal elements that should underpin the right to energy.

This research will adopt a transdisciplinary approach to achieve the general objective since its results will not be limited to the study of the legal field alone. It will include historical, economic, social, political, and doctrinal elements, among other aspects. This approach will contribute to advancing doctrine, which is still sectorial and dispersed. It will also serve as a basis for raising awareness at the national and international levels of the need to recognise and protect the right to energy. It will provide a solid basis for including the right to energy in international legal instruments and national legal frameworks.

The specific objectives are set as follows to achieve the general objective of this research. The first of those objectives is to systematise the essential theoretical-legal elements that underpin the recognition and configuration of the right to energy from a doctrinal, legal, and comparative approach. Then, this research will be focused on assessing the scope of the normative provisions on energy in Cuba to recognise and configure the right to energy. After developing these objectives, this research will argue the essential theoretical-legal elements of the right to energy, in light of the current Cuban legal system, for its recognition and configuration.

In light of the general objective outlined, the first specific objective is to systematise the essential theoretical elements that underpin the configuration of the right to energy from a legal, doctrinal, and comparative approach. For this reason, historical, economic, social, political, and other milestones that form the backdrop of the right to energy and thus have influenced its origin and development will be considered. Furthermore, this research will draw on the normative background of the right to energy at the international, regional, and national levels in the selected cases in the European Union as well as in Latin America and the Caribbean. On this basis, the main theoretical elements that should underpin the recognition and configuration of the right to energy will be systematised. For this systematisation, the existing doctrine on the right to energy and other related categories will be studied in order to understand the origin and evolution of the aforementioned right. The theoretical and legal elements that should underpin the recognition and configuration of the right to energy will then be substantiated based on the results of this study.

The second specific objective will be to assess the scope of the normative provisions on energy in Cuba in order to recognise and configure the right to energy. This objective will pursue a thorough exegetical analysis of the Cuban legal framework, starting with the Constitution of the Republic of Cuba of 2019 and then examining the norms that govern the energy sector in the Caribbean country. This analysis will be systematic in nature so that the legal framework of the energy sector will be analysed according to temporal and hierarchical logic, given the wide regulatory dispersion that exists in the regulatory ecosystem of the energy sector.

The analysis derived from the fulfilment of the second objective will be used as a basis for the theoretical development of the right to energy. In addition, the third objective will draw on the findings of the previous chapters and sections. This third objective will aim to argue the essential elements of the right to energy in light of the current Cuban legal system, with a view to its recognition and configuration. This objective will contribute to filling the gnosciological and scientific gaps in order to serve as a theoretical basis for the future legal recognition and configuration of the right to energy in Cuba.

This research will have a target audience at three levels. First, the results of this research will be of interest at the international level, with potential implications for international bodies responsible for the approval and implementation of binding and non-binding legal instruments.

At the regional level, this research will be relevant to regional integration organisations in the European, Latin American, and Caribbean contexts. However, the potential impact of this research will not be limited to the aforementioned regions, as many of its findings are generalisable to other regions. Despite this generalisability, further research may be necessary to optimise the legal-theoretical postulates of this research.

Finally, considering the above context, the national level is also reached. The results of this research will also be relevant at the national level for legislators, public decision-makers, and administrative bodies with regulatory powers. In addition to these actors, this research will be valuable for legal practitioners in the judiciary, public prosecution, lawyers, legal academics, and university students in fields of study related to this research. However, given the transdisciplinary nature of this research, the target audience is not limited to the fields mentioned above. Examples are professionals in sociology, economics, geography, and other sciences with related fields of study.

The limits of the scope of this research will be considered. These limits will partially or totally affect the scientific results. Without implying any order of priority or hierarchy, the first of the limitations of this research is the temporality of its information sources. The consulted information sources (bibliography, reports, legislation, etc.) are limited to November 2023. Such a limitation implies that the research topic is based on precedents that will evolve over time. Similarly, the legislation consulted may be subject to reform, replacement, or repeal, which will have an impact on the exegetical analyses developed.

The second limit to the scope of this research will be its disciplinary nature. Although a transdisciplinary approach will be encouraged for the production of scientific results, there are technical aspects that require interdisciplinary groups for their analysis. An example of such a reality is the quantitative determination of energy affordability, in addition to other matters of exact sciences, natural sciences and social sciences other than Law.

The third limit to the scope of the research will be multilingualism. The main sources of information consulted are in English and Spanish. Although other sources have been consulted in languages such as French, Polish, Portuguese and Dutch, there will still be a body of knowledge that will not be used in this research. This limitation implies a gap in the information consulted, which can be exploited in future research on the right to energy.

The fourth and final limit of the scope of this research is its legal-theoretical nature. This limitation implies that the main results of this research will focus on the foundation of the essential theoretical and legal elements on which the right to energy must be based to be recognised and configured in Cuba. For these reasons, this research does not have a practical component where the scientific results are implemented. An example of this absence is the possible impact on the Cuban legal academy but not on legislation since the legislative faculty is still in the hands of competent bodies. For these reasons, the effectiveness of the implementation of the scientific contributions of this research will not be validated qualitatively or quantitatively.

1.3 Research Methods and Techniques

The following research methods and techniques are used to achieve the scientific objectives.[76]

First, through the historical-legal method, this research aims to reveal the genesis and historical development of the right to energy. This method will be used to evaluate the existing historical knowledge in order to identify the causes and conditions that led to the birth of the right to energy in the international legal framework and to support the need for its recognition in Cuba. The research will begin with the study of the evolution of humanity from the perspective of energy, progressing through each of the historical periods. Similarly, the historical-legal method will be used in Chap. 7 to identify the main historical milestones before and after the triumph of the Revolution that support the need to recognise the right to energy in Cuba.

In addition, through the legal-doctrinal method, different doctrinal publications related to the right to energy will be analysed, obtaining a broad spectrum of knowledge on the subject and thus allowing the objectives of this research to be fulfilled. This method will provide the research with a solid theoretical-conceptual basis.

[76] Pérez Hernández (2011), Del Río Hernández (2012).

This basis will be constituted by a set of coherently organised theoretical foundations that will constitute the theoretical underpinning of the right to energy in this research. This method will allow us to take a position on the debate around the right to energy. For this purpose, the legal-doctrinal method will be used in Chaps. 5, 6 and 10. The application of this research method in Chaps 5 and 6 will not be limited to the analysis of the right to energy but also to other interconnected categories such as energy security, energy poverty, energy justice, energy democracy, energy citizenship and energy sovereignty. Subsequently, through the legal-doctrinal method, the essential theoretical elements that will underpin the configuration of the right to energy will be grounded. This method will be used again in Chap. 10 to adapt those essential theoretical elements defined in Chap. 6 to the Cuban legal system in order to support the legal recognition and configuration of the right to energy.

Moreover, the analytical-legal method will also be used in Chaps. 3, 4, 8 and 9 to analyse international, regional, and national legal norms related to energy, considering the recognition and protection of the right to energy. This method will be used in Chaps. 3 and 4 to determine the meaning and scope of international and regional legal instruments in Europe, Latin America, and the Caribbean. In turn, the legal-analytical method will be the tool for the critical assessment of national legal norms in the selected case studies. Moreover, the analytical legal method will allow the analysis of the systemic functioning of the legal system as a result of this historical-concrete moment, where the realisation of the right to energy is an essential condition for the full development of the personality, as well as the realisation of the rights associated with it. Finally, in Chaps. 8 and 9, the analytical-legal method will be used to analyse the Cuban Constitution of 2023 and the rest of the complementary norms that make up the legal framework governing the energy sector in Cuba.

Furthermore, the legal comparison method will allow for the systematisation of trends in recognising the right to energy and its essential elements in foreign legal systems. Besides, its use will facilitate the identification of points of convergence and divergence in the positivisation of the right to energy in each State to contribute to its recognition and configuration in Cuba. The method of legal comparison is first applied in Chap. 4 through an external comparison by analysing the similarities and differences in the constitutional regulation of the right to energy in the selected case studies in the European, Latin American, and Caribbean regions. This external comparison will make it possible to identify regularities in recognising and configuring the right to energy. Subsequently, in Chaps. 8 and 9, the research method mentioned above will be used with an internal comparison approach to compare Cuban national norms from a systemic approach to substantiate the essential theoretical-legal elements that should underpin the legal recognition and configuration of the right to energy in Cuba.

Additionally, the document-analysis method will be used to evaluate documents such as reports, public policy plans or programmes, public archives, speeches, press, and other documents issued by international and regional bodies related to the right to energy as the object of study of this research. The analysis of documents also allows for the study of documents at the national level with information related to the realisation of the content of the right to energy, including national statistical yearbooks, reports issued by the Cuban government, digital and printed press articles, the programme of the Cuban electricity generation matrix until 2030, among other documents issued by national organisations and institutions.

1.4 Research Roadmap and Expected Results

This research is structured in 11 chapters. From Chap. 2 to Chap. 6, this book will set up the essential theoretical foundations for configuring the right to energy. Because of that, Chap. 2 starts by studying humanity's energy problems to determine the historical foundations of the current energy situation, which led to the recognition and protection of the right to energy, both in the international framework and in national legal systems. As a result, Chap. 2 of this research will address the first specific objective. For this reason, this chapter will focus on the essential theoretical elements that underpin the recognition and configuration of the right to energy from a doctrinal, legal, and comparative perspective. In order to achieve this objective, Chap. 2 will be structured around the following three sections.

In this sense, sect. 2.1 offers introductory ideas that set the path for sects. 2.2 and 2.3. Section 2.2, being the nuclei of Chap. 2, will then focus on a comprehensive analysis of humanity's energy problem in order to substantiate the historical basis for the need for legal recognition and protection of the right to energy. In order to develop this analysis, this study will start from the most remote stages of humanity to the present day, with the aim of characterising the different historical stages of human history from the point of view of the right to energy. This analysis will consider the main social, economic, and political milestones in the energy field that have brought humanity to the present day.

Subsequently, the international framework is systematised in Chap. 3 to determine the recognition and protection of the right to energy in the leading international and regional legal instruments. For that reason, Chap. 3 will examine the legal treatment of the right to energy at the international and regional levels in sects. 3.1 and 3.2. For this purpose, the relevant international legal instruments will be thoroughly examined in light of the right to energy. The research will then focus on the regional legal frameworks of the European Union, Latin America, and the Caribbean. For this purpose, the main regional legal instruments will be identified and exegetically analysed in order to determine their significance and scope in the recognition and legal protection of the right to energy.

This systematisation is followed by Chap. 4. This chapter will then focus on analysing the legal-constitutional systems in Latin America, the Caribbean, and the European Union in order to identify and substantiate the main trends in the positivisation of the right to energy. Based on this analysis, the best regulatory practices at the legal-constitutional level in regulating the right to energy will be identified. This identification will make it possible to determine the elements that make up the right to energy in the foreign legal systems identified.

Then, Chap. 5 then turns to the conceptual delimitation of the right to energy. For this purpose, sects. 5.1 and 5.2 will begin with analysing energy as a transdisciplinary category full of complexity. The conceptual delimitation of energy is essential for defining the right to energy and determining its meaning and scope. Next, to establish the theoretical and conceptual foundations of the right to energy, six doctrinal reference concepts are examined in sect. 5.3: energy security, energy poverty, energy justice, energy democracy, energy citizenship and energy sovereignty. Finally, this section will outline the conceptualisation of the right to energy in the context of this research.

Once the right to energy has been conceptually delimited, this study will identify the legal-theoretical elements underpinning the recognition and formulation of the right to energy in Chap. 6. For this purpose, the legal nature of the right to energy will be determined in sect. 6.1 from a human and fundamental rights perspective. This research will then establish the essential principles that should underpin the right to energy by identifying and substantiating specific principles in sect. 6.2. Subsequently, the study will focus on identifying the subjects of the right to energy in sect. 6.3, taking into consideration current normative trends from a critical perspective.

After Chap. 6, from Chaps. 7, 8, 9 and 10, the research aims to assess the scope of the normative provisions on energy in Cuba and the basis of the essential elements of the right to energy, in light of the current Cuban legal system, for its recognition and configuration. In that sense, Chap. 7 begins with the study of the relevant historical, economic, political, and legal contributions that motivated the construction of the right to energy in Cuba, starting with the most important milestones of two periods: before 1959 and after the Triumph of the Cuban Revolution.

Then, the current Cuban constitutional framework is analysed in Chap. 8 to determine to what extent it responds to the recognition and configuration of the right to energy based on the constitutional system itself. Later, the national norms associated with the content of the right to energy are analysed in Chap. 9 to identify how the national legal system responds to the recognition and configuration of the right to energy from a systemic and intersectoral approach.

After this analysis, the theoretical-legal bases for recognising and configuring the right to energy in Cuba are argued in Chap. 10 based on its legal regulation, conceptual definitions, principles that inform it, subjects, content and guarantees. In that sense, Chap. 10 sets out the elements that should underpin the recognition of the right to energy in Cuba. To this end, it will combine the theoretical elements defined in the first chapter of this research with the elements resulting from the political and legal framework (constitutional and infra-constitutional). Based on the above, the conceptual premises of the future right to energy in Cuba, its subjects, the elements that make up its content and the guarantees (legal and material) that must ensure its effective realisation will be identified.

Finally, Chap. 11 of this research will conclude this book by presenting the conclusions. In order to structure the conclusions, the three specific objectives outlined in the methodological design of the research will be followed. Thus, Chap. 11 will explain how the research objectives were implemented and what the main scientific contributions or contributions to the state of the art will be. Within Chap. 11, sect. 11.2 will present the essential legal-theoretical elements that should underpin the recognition and configuration of the right to energy in Cuba. It will then outline some of the areas that need to be studied in the future in order to ensure the scientific development of the theory of the right to energy.

This research has three main results. The first of those results is the systematisation of the essential theoretical elements that underpin the recognition and configuration of the right to energy from a doctrinal, legal, and comparative approach. Secondly, another research result is the assessment of the scope of the normative provisions on energy in Cuba to recognise and configure the right to energy. Finally, another research result is the argumentation of the essential elements of the right to energy, in light of the current Cuban legal system, for its recognition and configuration.

References[77]

Acuña Zepeda MS and Díaz Zepeda JE (2017) Energy and human rights: a perspective from Mexico. J Energy Nat Resour Law 35(4):377–380. https://www.tandfonline.com/doi/full/10.1080/02646811.2017.1355512. Accessed 28 Feb 2025

Akizu O, Urkidi L, Bueno G, Lago R, Barcena I, Mantxo M, Basurko I, and Lopez-Guede JM (2017) Tracing the emerging energy transitions in the Global North and the Global South. Int J Hydrog Energy 42(28):18045–18063. https://linkinghub.elsevier.com/retrieve/pii/S0360319917317913. Accessed 28 Feb 2025

Ambihaipahar A (2014) Access to energy: a human right? International Development Law. https://www.academia.edu/29424868/Access_to_Energy_A_Human_Right. Accessed 28 Feb 2025

Asamblea Nacional del Poder Popular (2022) Ley 153 'Del Proceso de Amparo de los Derechos Constitucionales'. Gaceta Oficial No. 74 Ordinaria de 15 de julio. Cuba: Gaceta Oficial de la República. https://www.gacetaoficial.gob.cu/sites/default/files/goc-2022-o74.pdf. Accessed 28 Feb 2025

Aviles LA (2012) Electric energy access in European law: a human right? SSRN Electron J 217(2008):1–8. http://www.ssrn.com/abstract=2008887. Accessed 28 Feb 2025

Banco Central de Cuba (2019) Instrucción 6. Gaceta Oficial No. 95 Ordinaria de 28 de noviembre. Gaceta Oficial de la República de Cuba. https://www.gacetaoficial.gob.cu/es/instruccion-6-de-2019-de-banco-central-de-cuba. Accessed 28 Feb 2025

Bedi HP (2018) 'Our energy, our rights': National extraction legacies and contested energy justice futures in Bangladesh. Energy Res Soc Sci 41(April):168–175. doi:https://doi.org/10.1016/j.erss.2018.04.009. Accessed 28 Feb 2025

Bradbrook AJ, Gardam JG (2006) Placing the access to energy services within a human rights framework. Hum Rights Quart 28(2):389–415. https://www.jstor.org/stable/pdf/20072742.pdf?refreqid=excelsior%3A43476d5b7137fdcb80d186deeef37e29&ab_segments=&origin=&acceptTC=1. Accessed 28 Feb 2025

Chakraborty SK (2016) The 'fundamental' right to access energy: issues, opportunities and challenges in India. In: Energy Law Policy India. National Law School of India University, Begaluru, pp 3–22. https://papers.ssrn.com/sol3/papers.cfm?abstract_id=3687914. Accessed 28 Feb 2025

[77] All links to the cited websites were operational as of 28 February 2025.

Clemson M (2012) Human rights and the environment: access to energy. New Zealand J Environ Law 16:39–81. https://search.informit.org/doi/10.3316/informit.319036289897776. Accessed 28 Feb 2025
Comisión Económica para América Latina y el Caribe (2016) Agenda 2030 y los Objetivos de Desarrollo Sostenible Una oportunidad para América Latina y el Caribe. Organización de Naciones Unidas https://repositorio.cepal.org/bitstream/handle/11362/40155/24/S1801141_es.pdf. Accessed 28 Feb 2025
Consejo de Estado (2019) Decreto Ley 345 "Del Desarrollo de las Fuentes Renovables y el Uso Eficiente de la Energía". Gaceta Oficial No. 95 Ordinaria de 28 de noviembre. Gaceta Oficial de la República de Cuba, Cuba.
Constitución de la República de Cuba (2019) Gaceta Oficial No. 5 Extraordinaria de 10 de abril de 2019. Gaceta Oficial de la República de Cuba, Havana, Cuba. https://www.gacetaoficial.gob.cu/sites/default/files/goc-2019-ex5.pdf. Accessed 28 Feb 2025
Constitución de la República de Honduras (1982) Honduras: La Gaceta. Diario Oficial de la República de Honduras. https://www.se.gob.hn/media/files/leyes/LC_BTf7DGE.pdf. Accessed 28 Feb 2025
Constitución Política de la República de Chile (2010) Chile. https://www.camara.cl/camara/doc/leyes_normas/constitucion_politica.pdf. Accessed 28 Feb 2025
Constitución Política de la República de Nicaragua (2014) Nicaragua. https://www.asamblea.gob.ni/assets/constitucion.pdf. Accessed 28 Feb 2025
Constitución Política del Estado de Bolivia (2009) Bolivia: Gaceta Oficial de Bolivia. http://www.gacetaoficialdebolivia.gob.bo/normas/verGratis_gob1/36208. Accessed 28 Feb 2025
Constitution de la République française (1958) Francia. https://www.conseil-constitutionnel.fr/sites/default/files/as/root/bank_mm/constitution/constitution.pdf. Accessed 28 Feb 2025
Convención Constitucional (2022) Propuesta de Constitución Política de la República de Chile. Santiago de Chile, Chile. https://archive.org/details/propuestaconstitucionchile2022/page/24/mode/2up?q=electr. Accessed 28 Feb 2025
Cseres KJ (2018) The active energy consumer in EU law. Eur J Risk Regul 9(2):227–244. https://www.cambridge.org/core/product/identifier/S1867299X18000077/type/journal_article. Accessed 28 Feb 2025
Cunningham RE (2003) La energía, historia de sus fuentes y transformación. Petrotecnia, pp 52–60. https://www.scribd.com/document/113461584/Historia-de-La-Energia. Accessed 28 Feb 2025
De Belgische Grondwet (1994) De Kamer.Be, België. https://www.dekamer.be/kvvcr/pdf_sections/publications/constitution/GrondwetUK.pdf. Accessed 28 Feb 2025
De la Vega Navarro A (2015) El acceso a la energía. Encyclopédie de l'energie. https://www.encyclopedie-energie.org/wp-content/uploads/2018/09/art044_DeLaVegaNavarro-Angel_Acceso-energia.pdf. Accessed 28 Feb 2025
Del Río Hernández MA (2012) La Investigación Jurídica en Opción a Grados Científicos. Rev Cubana Derecho 39:90–102. https://cuba.vlex.com/vid/jura-dica-grados-cienta-ficos-437405766
Delgado Triana Y and Fariñas Wong EY (2016) Derecho de acceso a la energía. Protección constitucional en Cuba. Caribeña de Ciencias Sociales. https://www.eumed.net/rev/caribe/2016/04/energia.html. Accessed 28 Feb 2025
Delgado Triana Y, Fariñas Wong EY, Luis Cordova JG (2019) El derecho de acceso a la energía en Cuba. Necesidad del uso de un SIG para el fomento de este derecho. In: Aragão A, Gomes dos Santos J (eds) Sistemas sociais complexos e integração de geodados no Direito e nas políticas. Instituto Jurídico da Faculdade de Direito da Universidade de Coimbra, Coimbra, pp 111–136. https://estudogeral.uc.pt/handle/10316/95914. Accessed 28 Feb 2025
Department of Economic and Social Affairs (2021) Energy Access: Towards the Achievement of SDG 7 and Net-Zero Emissions. United Nations https://www.un.org/sites/un2.un.org/files/2021-twg_1-061921.pdf. Accessed 28 Feb 2025
Durán R, Condorí M (2015) El acceso a la energía desde la óptica de los derechos humanos. Su medición y relación con el acceso a otros derechos elementales en Salta, Argentina.

Avances Energías Renovables Medio Ambiente 19:57–67. https://sedici.unlp.edu.ar/handle/10915/143520#:~:text=En%20la%20presente%20contribuci%C3%B3n%20se%20aborda%20la%20problem%C3%A1tica,concepci%C3%B3n%20de%20la%20energ%C3%ADa%20como%20un%20derecho%20elemental. Accessed 28 Feb 2025

Economic and Social Council (2016) Progress towards the Sustainable Development Goals. United Nations https://unstats.un.org/sdgs/files/report/2016/secretary-general-sdg-report-2016%2D%2Den.pdf. Accessed 28 Feb 2025

European Parliament, European Council (2019) Directive 2019/944 on common rules for the internal market for electricity and amending Directive 2012/27/EU. Official Journal of European Union, Brussels. https://eur-lex.europa.eu/legal-content/EN/TXT/PDF/?uri=CELEX:32019L0944&from=EN. Accessed 28 Feb 2025

Figueredo Reinaldo O, Carmona Tamayo E (2022) Cuba en Datos: Apuntes necesarios sobre las termoeléctricas que debes conocer. Cubadebate Havana http://www.cubadebate.cu/especiales/2022/09/14/cuba-en-datos-apuntes-necesarios-sobre-las-termoelectricas-que-debes-conocer/. Accessed 28 Feb 2025

Francisco Fernández M, Díaz Fuentes R, Castro Fernández M, Costa Montiel A (2010) Calidad de la energía y generación distribuida en Cuba. Rev Cubana Ingeniería 1(3):41–50. https://rci.cujae.edu.cu/index.php/rci/article/view/28/29. Accessed 28 Feb 2025

Frigo G, Baumann M, Hillerbrand R (2021) Energy and the Good Life: Capabilities as the Foundation of the Right to Access Energy Services. J Hum Dev Capabilit 22(2):218–248. https://www.tandfonline.com/doi/full/10.1080/19452829.2021.1887109. Accessed 28 Feb 2025

Garcia M, Mundó J (2014) La energía como derecho. Cómo afrontar la pobreza energética. Taula d'entitats del Tercer Sector Social de Catalunya, Barcelona, España. https://www.eapn.es/ARCHIVO/documentos/documentos/1411457073_dossier_la_energia_como_derecho._como_afrontar_la_pobreza_energetica.pdf. Accessed 28 Feb 2025

Goldthau A, Eicke L, Weko S (2020) The global energy transition and the global south. Lect Notes Energy 73:319–339. http://link.springer.com/10.1007/978-3-030-39066-2_14. Accessed 28 Feb 2025

Hesselman M, Varo A, Guyet R, Thomson H (2021) Energy poverty in the COVID-19 era: mapping global responses in light of momentum for the right to energy. Energy Res Soc Sci 81(September):102246. https://doi.org/10.1016/j.erss.2021.102246. Accessed 28 Feb 2025

Institut de Drets Humans de Catalunya (2010) Declaración Universal de los Derechos Humanos Emergentes. Barcelona, España. https://www.idhc.org/wp-content/uploads/DUDHE.pdf. Accessed 28 Feb 2025

International Bank for Reconstruction and Development/The World Bank (2017) State of Electricity Access Report. Washington DC. https://documents1.worldbank.org/curated/en/364571494517675149/pdf/114841-REVISED-JUNE12-FINAL-SEAR-web-REV-optimized.pdf. Accessed 28 Feb 2025

International Energy Agency, International Renewable Energy Agency, United Nations Statistics Division, The International Bank for Reconstruction and Development/The World Bank, World Health Organization (2023) Tracking SDG 7 | Progress towards sustainable energy 2023. https://trackingsdg7.esmap.org/. Accessed 28 Feb 2025

Kotilainen K (2020) Energy prosumers' role in the sustainable energy system. In: Leal Filho W, Marisa Azul A, Brandli L, Gökcin Özuyar P, Wall T (eds) Affordable and clean energy, Springer International Publishing, Cham, pp 1–14. http://link.springer.com/10.1007/978-3-319-71057-0_11-1. Accessed 28 Feb 2025

Luis Cordova JG, Dueñas Rodríguez A, Byttebier K, Delgado Triana Y (2022). Energy and law. A critical approach to the Cuban context. Global Jurist 22(2):413–432. https://www.degruyter.com/document/doi/10.1515/gj-2021-0085/html. Accessed 28 Feb 2025

Martín López L (2022) Instalar un panel solar… ¿o ser financista? Tribuna de La Habana. Havana. http://www.tribuna.cu/ciencia/2022-07-10/instalar-un-panel-solar-o-ser-financista. Accessed 28 Feb 2025

Martínez MP, Clemente-Morales Rodríguez I, Castro E (2017) The hour equivalent solar pick, definition, and interpretation. Rev Ingeniería Energética 38(2):124–131. https://www.redalyc.org/pdf/3291/329151462006.pdf. Accessed 28 Feb 2025

Milian Gómez JF, Luis Cordova JG, Delgado Triana Y (2023) Energy transition in Latin-American countries, example Cuba: looking for interconnections with food sovereignty. In: Gromek-Broc K (ed) Regional approaches to the energy transition. Springer International Publishing, Cham, pp 187–203. https://link.springer.com/10.1007/978-3-031-19358-3_12. Accessed 28 Feb 2025

Ministerio de Ciencia Tecnología y Medio Ambiente (2021) Tarea Vida. Havana. https://www.citma.gob.cu/wp-content/uploads/2021/11/proyecciones-tarea-vida.pdf. Accessed 28 Feb 2025

Ministerio de Energía y Minas (2021a) Resolución 206. Gaceta Oficial No. 67 Extraordinaria de 28 de julio. Cuba: Gaceta Oficial de la República de Cuba. https://www.gacetaoficial.gob.cu/sites/default/files/goc-2021-ex67.pdf. Accessed 28 Feb 2025

Ministerio de Energía y Minas (2021b) Resolución 208. Gaceta Oficial No. 69 Extraordinaria de 30 de julio. Cuba: Gaceta Oficial de la República de Cuba. https://www.gacetaoficial.gob.cu/sites/default/files/goc-2021-ex69.pdf. Accessed 28 Feb 2025

Ministerio de Energía y Minas (2021c) Resolución 242. Gaceta Oficial No. 111 Extraordinaria de 30 de diciembre. Gaceta Oficial de la República de Cuba, Cuba. https://www.gacetaoficial.gob.cu/sites/default/files/goc-2021-ex111_0.pdf. Accessed 28 Feb 2025

Ministerio de Finanzas y Precios (2021a) Resolución 319. Gaceta Oficial No. 67 Extraordinaria de 28 de julio. Gaceta Oficial de la República de Cuba, Cuba. https://www.gacetaoficial.gob.cu/sites/default/files/goc-2021-ex67.pdf. Accessed 28 Feb 2025

Ministerio de Finanzas y Precios (2021b) Resolución 322. Gaceta Oficial No. 69 Extraordinaria de 30 de julio. Gaceta Oficial de la República de Cuba, Cuba. https://www.gacetaoficial.gob.cu/sites/default/files/goc-2021-ex69.pdf. Accessed 28 Feb 2025

Ministerio de Relaciones Internacionales de Cuba (2022) Informe de Cuba en virtud de la resolución 75/289 de la Asamblea General de las Naciones Unidas, titulada "Necesidad de poner fin al bloqueo económico, comercial y financiero impuesto por los Estados Unidos de América contra Cuba". Havana. https://cubaminrex.cu/es/informe-de-cuba-en-virtud-de-la-resolucion-75289-de-la-asamblea-general-de-las-naciones-unidas. Accessed 28 Feb 2025

Ministerio del Comercio Interior (2018) Resolución No. 54 'Indicaciones para la organización y ejecución de la protección al consumidor en el sistema de comercio interno'. Gaceta Oficial de la República, Cuba. https://www.gacetaoficial.gob.cu/sites/default/files/goc-2018-ex26_mincin.rar. Accessed 28 Feb 2025

Oficina del Alto Comisionado para los Derechos Humanos (2010) El derecho a una vivienda adecuada. Organización de Naciones Unidas, Ginebra. https://www.ohchr.org/sites/default/files/Documents/Publications/FS21_rev_1_Housing_sp.pdf. Accessed 28 Feb 2025

Oficina Nacional de Estadística e Información (2022a) Anuario Estadístico de Cuba 2021. Havana. https://www.onei.gob.cu/anuario-2021#:~:text=La%20presente%20publicaci%C3%B3n%20Anuario%20Estad%C3%ADstico%20de%20Cuba%202021,situaci%C3%B3n%20demogr%C3%A1fica%2C%20econ%C3%B3mica%20y%20social%20de%20los%20cubanos. Accessed 28 Feb 2025

Oficina Nacional de Estadística e Información (2022b) Electricidad en Cuba. Indicadores seleccionados 2021. Cuba. https://onei.gob.cu/electricidad-en-cuba-indicadores-seleccionados-enero-diciembre-2021. Accessed 28 Feb 2025

Olawuyi DS (2018) Energy (and human rights) for all: addressing human rights risks in energy access projects. In: Energy justice. Edward Elgar Publishing, pp 73–104. https://www.elgaronline.com/view/edcoll/9781786431752/9781786431752.00011.xml. Accessed 28 Feb 2025

Organización de Naciones Unidas (1948) Declaración Universal de los Derechos Humanos. https://www.ohchr.org/sites/default/files/UDHR/Documents/UDHR_Translations/spn.pdf. Accessed 28 Feb 2025

Organización de Naciones Unidas (1976) Pacto Internacional de Derechos Económicos, Sociales y Culturales. https://www.ohchr.org/es/instruments-mechanisms/instruments/international-covenant-economic-social-and-cultural-rights. Accessed 28 Feb 2025

Organización de Naciones Unidas (1979) Convention on the elimination of all forms of discrimination against women. Oficina del Alto Comicionado para los Derechos Humanos. https://www.ohchr.org/en/instruments-mechanisms/instruments/convention-elimination-all-forms-discrimination-against-women. Accessed 28 Feb 2025

Organización de Naciones Unidas (2015) Convención Marco sobre el Cambio Climático. Organización de Naciones Unidas. https://documents-dds-ny.un.org/doc/UNDOC/LTD/G15/283/22/PDF/G1528322.pdf?OpenElement. Accessed 28 Feb 2025

Organización Latinoamericana de Energía, Sistema de Información Energética-Legal (2011) Situación de la normativa energética nacional en América Latina y el Caribe. Quito, Ecuador. http://biblioteca.olade.org/opac-tmpl/Documentos/old0306.pdf. Accessed 28 Feb 2025

Owoeye O (2016) Access to energy in Sub-Saharan Africa. Environ Law Rev 18(4):284–300. http://journals.sagepub.com/doi/10.1177/1461452916678521. Accessed 28 Feb 2025

Parlamento Europeo (2009) Carta Europea de los Derechos de los Consumidores de Energía. Diario Oficial de la Unión Europea. https://eur-lex.europa.eu/legal-content/ES/TXT/PDF/?uri=CELEX:52008IP0306. Accessed 28 Feb 2025

Partido Comunista de Cuba (2021) Conceptualización del modelo económico y social cubano de desarrollo socialista. Lineamientos de la política económica y social del Partido y la Revolución para el período 2021-2026. Havana. https://www.mined.gob.cu/wp-content/uploads/2021/09/CONCEPTUALIZACION-DEL-MODELO-ECONOMICO-Y-SOCIAL-CUBANO-DE-DESARROLLO-SOCIALISTA-y-LINEAMIENTOS-DE-LA-POLITICA-ECONOMICA-Y-SOCIAL-DEL-PARTIDO-Y-LA-REVOLUCION-PARA-EL-PERIODO-2021.pdf. Accessed 28 Feb 2025

Peces-Barba G, de Asís Roig R, Llamas Cascón A (1995) Cursos de derechos fundamentales. Teoría general. Editorial Universidad Carlos III, Madrid. https://www.corteidh.or.cr/tablas/17289.pdf. Accessed 28 Feb 2025

Peña Pupo L, Fariña Wong EY, Luis Cordova JG, Delgado Triana Y (2020) Quality of energy, energy access and law within the Cuban hydropower context. Global Jurist 20(3). https://www.degruyter.com/document/doi/10.1515/gj-2020-0012/html. Accessed 28 Feb 2025

Pérez Hernández L (2011) Algunas consideraciones a debate sobre la ciencia jurídica y sus métodos. Rev Cubana Derecho 38. https://cuba.vlex.com/vid/consideraciones-debate-juridica-metodos-345011718. Accessed 28 Feb 2025

Poder Ejecutivo del Consejo de Ministros (1975) Ley 1287 'Ley Eléctrica'. Gaceta Oficial de la República de Cuba, Havana, Cuba. https://www.unionelectrica.cu/wp-content/uploads/2018/11/ley-electrica.pdf. Accessed 28 Feb 2025

Ramos GL (2020) Ahorrar electricidad para evitar los apagones. Granma. https://www.granma.cu/file/pdf/2020/04/20/G_2020042005.pdf. Accessed 28 Feb 2025

Redacción Digital (2019) Presidente de Cuba anuncia medidas para la coyuntura energética del país. Granma, Havana. https://www.granma.cu/cuba/2019-09-11/en-vivo-presidente-de-cuba-anuncia-medidas-para-la-coyuntura-energetica-del-pais-video-11-09-2019-15-09-41. Accessed 28 Feb 2025

Rhodes R (2018) Energy: a human history. Simon & Schuster, New York. https://www.goodreads.com/book/show/36373616-energy. Accessed 28 Feb 2025

Schiano A (2017) Human rights and renewable energy: a critical link. LSE Human Rights. https://eprints.lse.ac.uk/80101/1/Human%20Rights%20and%20Renewable%20Energy_%20A%20Critical%20Link%20_%20LSE%20Human%20Rights.pdf. Accessed 28 Feb 2025

Shyu CW (2021) A framework for 'right to energy' to meet UN SDG7: policy implications to meet basic human energy needs, eradicate energy poverty, enhance energy justice, and uphold energy democracy. Energy Res Soc Sci 79(December):102199. https://www.sciencedirect.com/science/article/pii/S2214629621002929?via%3Dihub. Accessed 28 Feb 2025

Sin-Hang Ngai, J (2012) Energy as a human right in armed conflict: a question of universal need, survival, and human dignity. Brooklyn J Int Law 37(2):579–622. https://core.ac.uk/download/pdf/228597477.pdf. Accessed 20 November 2021. Accessed 28 Feb 2025

Solis MPS (2014) From right to light: a human rights-based approach to universal access to modern energy services. Adelaide University. https://digital.library.adelaide.edu.au/dspace/bitstream/2440/92548/3/02whole.pdf. Accessed 28 Feb 2025

Solis MPS (2018) Legal perspectives on a human rights-based approach to energy access in the Philippines. Ateneo LJ 62(3):669. https://papers.ssrn.com/sol3/papers.cfm?abstract_id=3280057. Accessed 28 Feb 2025

Sovacool BK, Dworkin MH (2014) Global energy justice. Problems, principles, and practices. Cambridge University Press, Reino Unido. https://www.cambridge.org/us/universitypress/subjects/politics-international-relations/political-theory/global-energy-justice-problems-principles-and-practices. Accessed 28 Feb 2025

Stolik Novygrod D (2014) La energía FV: oportunidad y necesidad para Cuba. Econ Desarrollo 152(2):69–86. http://scielo.sld.cu/scielo.php?script=sci_arttext&pid=S0252-85842014000200005#:~:text=En%20este%20art%C3%ADculo%20se%20presenta%20un%20an%C3%A1lisis%20de,econ%C3%B3micos%20y%20los%20pron-%C3%B3sticos%20de%20la%20energ%C3%ADa%20FV Accessed 28 Feb 2025

The International Bank for Reconstruction and Development/The World Bank (2018) Policy matters: regulatory indicators for sustainable energy. Washington DC. https://documents1.worldbank.org/curated/en/553071544206394642/pdf/132782-replacement-PUBLIC-RiseReport-HighRes.pdf. Accessed 28 Feb 2025

Tully SR (2006) The contribution of human rights to universal energy access. Northwest J Int Hum Rights 4(3). https://scholarlycommons.law.northwestern.edu/cgi/viewcontent.cgi?article=1043&context=njihr. Accessed 28 Feb 2025

Tully SR (2009) The human right to access clean energy. J Green Build 2(1):140–148. https://www.scienceopen.com/document_file/c3efa42a-b169-4440-bf3b-42335b42ee2f/API/i1943-4618-3-2-140.pdf. Accessed 28 Feb 2025

U.S. Department of the Treasury (2022) Cuba sanctions. https://home.treasury.gov/policy-issues/financial-sanctions/sanctions-programs-and-country-information/cuba-sanctions. Accessed 28 Feb 2025

Wewerinke-Singh M (2022) A human rights approach to energy: realizing the rights of billions within ecological limits. Rev Eur Comparat Int Environ Law 31(1):16–26. https://onlinelibrary.wiley.com/doi/10.1111/reel.12412. Accessed 28 Feb 2025

Chapter 2
The Historical Energy Odyssey of Human Evolution

2.1 Introduction

Energy is a category that transcends time and space; the functioning of any process depends on it. From its very origins as a species, humanity has depended on obtaining energy from the metabolisation of food, where chemical energy is transformed into other energy necessary for life. According to Lotka, in all cases considered, natural selection will operate in such a way that the evolution of an organism will depend on the energy available for it.[1]

The relationship of energy to the human environment is confirmed in Kostic's thinking when he says:

> The historical picture of energy intrinsically includes the chronological (…) social (human) development. The view of the world from the inside out is figuratively and literally possible through the energetic prism. From the shining stars to the spinning planets, through the global cycles of water, atmosphere, and life, to the evolution, industrialisation and modernisation of civilisation, energy is the cause and measure of all that has existed, exists, and will exist.[2]

Given the above, increasing levels of development imply an increase in energy demand. For this reason, since the energy crisis following the Industrial Revolution,[3] states have shown increasing concern for the energy sector.[4] By 1800, global energy consumption was only 5653 TWh. This consumption increased over time, reaching 28,526 TWh in 1950, after which the growth curve steadily peaked, reaching an

[1] Lotka (1922).

[2] Kostic (2014), p. 1.

[3] Coyle and Simmons (2014).

[4] The International Bank for Reconstruction and Development/The World Bank (2020).

J. G. Luis Cordova, *Theoretical and Legal Dimensions of the Right to Energy*, Economic and Financial Law & Policy – Shifting Insights & Values 9,
https://doi.org/10.1007/978-3-032-33252-3_2

energy consumption of 177,340 TWh in 2019.[5] Over 83% of this consumption is covered by traditional biomass, coal, oil, and gas. According to Our World in Data statistics, energy demand has been rising over the years, indicating that energy needs have steadily increased.[6]

Despite the above, access to energy at a global level is not a universal and equitable phenomenon because vulnerability and energy poverty are present in many regions, threatening people's development and typical development.[7] The affectation of the satisfaction of energy needs harms life in conditions of dignity and the capacity to respond to the rest of human needs.

Throughout history, energy needs have diversified with the level of development, which in turn has generated a constant increase in energy demand. The main reason for this phenomenon is that energy availability determines the amount of activity that can be carried out, and controlling these energy flows establishes power in human affairs and its influence on nature.[8] For these reasons, the energy issue has transcended every stage of human history.

2.2 Energy Issues in Human History: Between the Solution and the Problem

Humanity's energy problems go back to the most remote moments of human history. The very beginning of the human species, according to Cipolla, seemed like another biological energy converter in addition to the existing ones (plants and animals). Everything that the human species consumes is the result of a process of energetic transformation, including food. This context sets the stage for humanity's biggest energy problem, which still plagues human society today. This problem lies in the control of energy and its economic transformation into useful forms of energy when energy needs arise. One of the essential elements in this transformation process is what Cipolla defines as a "converter". Understanding and assimilating this idea sheds light on the energy debacle of humanity in each of its stages.[9]

To illustrate this, one of the oldest examples is the energetic use of wood. Through photosynthesis, plants convert solar energy into chemical energy. This accumulation of energy results in a useful energy source to satisfy certain energy needs such as lighting, heat energy for cooking food and many others. Another example is the use of animal traction, where animals function as energy converters by ingesting plants, which implies a constant cycle of energy transformation.[10]

---

[5] Ritchie et al. (2023).

[6] Ritchie et al. (2023).

[7] The International Bank for Reconstruction and Development/The World Bank (2020).

[8] Odum (1971), p. 34.

[9] Cipolla (1961), p. 523.

[10] Cipolla (1961), p. 524.

Following the previous contexts, the search for and exploitation of new energy sources have been among the priority objectives of people and, at a higher level, states through energy policies and regulations.[11] In this regard, many alternatives have been used to guarantee the energy necessary for the evolution and development of humanity. The constant search for energy to satisfy energy demand is supported by Cunningham, who divides human history evolutionarily, under the prism of energy, into six models: pre-agricultural, agricultural, advanced agricultural, pre-industrial, industrial, and advanced industrial.[12]

The first phase began 300,000 years ago, with the origin of Homo sapiens, until settled societies were developed 10,000 years earlier. In this phase, needs were initially satisfied with thermal energy from the sun and mechanical energy obtained by humans from food metabolisation as an energy transformation process. The latter was initially used to develop food-gathering processes and some primitive forms of hunting. In this context, energy consumption was determined by the activities' difficulty level.[13]

With the discovery of fire from the combustion of energy carriers in their natural state, man took a step forward in his energetic development. Valavanidis and Vlachogianni describe the discovery of fire and the use of energy as mediating elements in the history of humankind.[14]

This discovery implied an evolutionary leap with multiple applications: in defence against wild animals, clearing large areas for cultivation, and even developing social relations.[15] In this sense, according to Brown et al., the controlled use of fire was a great advance in the evolution of humankind. From the combustion of wood or other energy carriers like peat, cut turf, animal dung, animal bone, seaweed, and straw,[16] fire enabled the generation of light and heat, allowed the cooking of food, and became a mechanism of protection against predators.[17] Regarding this last element, Clark and Harris allude to the transport of fire as a deterrent mechanism against the threat posed by large animals, especially carnivores.[18]

In addition to using fire to clear large areas, such practices were useful in increasing the productivity of these areas. According to Mellars, the burning of vegetation in Africa may have involved the use of controlled fire to increase the production of certain crops. This would attribute to energy a significant role in the management of plant food production.[19]

---

[11] Smil (1994).

[12] Cunningham (2003).

[13] Smil (2004).

[14] Valavanidis and Vlachogianni (2013).

[15] Smil (2017).

[16] Hirst (2019).

[17] Brown et al. (2009), p. 861.

[18] Clark and Harris (1985), p. 21.

[19] Mellars (2006), p. 9383.

In addition, the use of fire for burning woodlands also had certain food motivations in primitive populations. According to Mason, these included increasing the productivity and nutritional quality of forage for animals. This led to an increase in hunting animal populations and thus increased food availability. After the burning of vegetation, new plant shoots became an attraction for animals in certain areas, making them easier to hunt. Another food motivation for burning wooded areas was to improve visibility for hunting.[20] These implications denote the usefulness of thermal energy in the form of fire for food production in the initial stages of humanity.

At the same time, the discovery of fire impacted people's diet, from the cooking of food, a vital component in the evolution of the human species. Cooking food by fire allowed the elimination of toxins and bacteria that endangered human health. Thus, the heat energy from the combustion of wood influenced food safety.[21] This practice of using wood was used as traditional biomass implied increased wood consumption.[22]

The development of social relations was also illuminated by the practice of grouping around the fire, both for heat energy and as a means of defence. This consolidated social ties and, thus, the basis of human society. At the same time, humans resorted to the domestication of wild animals and their use for traction to guarantee the functioning of productive processes.[23] The use of mechanical energy from animals was one of the forms of energy that served as the driving force behind the still-incipient productive processes.

The beginnings of experiences associated with animal domestication can be framed in the Middle East between the tenth and seventeenth century BC in Egypt and the present-day region of Palestine.[24] The use of animals as biological energy converters has accompanied humankind ever since to satisfy some energy needs, especially in the productive sector.

With the growth of the human population and its needs, the agricultural phase came into being. Instead of wasting energy on food gathering, humans leapt to mastering the surrounding natural resources to secure their livelihoods.[25] The survival needs of human societies at this stage forced them to evolve. In addition to population growth, the environmental stress caused by the exploitation of the surrounding environment (flora and fauna) brought with it limits to the satisfaction of basic needs. Therefore, the beginning of agriculture represented an efficient way to increase and maintain human settlements with a stable supply of food.[26]

In the beginning, agricultural practices did not show a significant increase in energy demand compared to gathering and hunting societies. However, as more

[20] Mason (2000), p. 140.

[21] Clark and Harris (1985), pp. 20–21.

[22] Smil (2017).

[23] Penna (2020).

[24] Cipolla (1961), p. 526.

[25] Díaz et al. (2014).

[26] Smil (1994), pp. 22–23.

productive processes were put in place, the need for energy increased, and the exploitation of all available energy sources increased.[27]

During this phase, energy sources such as biomass and animal traction continued to be used. The increased use of animals as an energy source required increased energy consumption to ensure their feeding and reproduction. However, using draft animals facilitated the speeding up of agricultural production and transportation.[28] Wind and waterpower also began to be used incipiently.

Wind and water power, as forms of solar energy, replaced people and animals as biological energy converters with others of an artificial nature: windmills and watermills. Although these two renewable sources of energy depended on certain variables not subject to human control (availability of sufficient water resources or the necessary wind power), they boosted the development of humankind.[29]

As time passed, social and productive relations became more complex and required more energy for their development. The development of productive relations gave way to the advanced agricultural phase, where the energy sources used up to this historical moment continued to be used. Wind power continued to diversify as a driving force for navigation. New natural resources, such as iron, were exploited, which allowed for greater use of wood as an energy carrier.[30] In this context, the availability of timber resources began to be reduced because of excessive logging due to their multiple uses.

The impact on the availability of timber resources in pre-industrial societies was closely related to population growth. The increase in population meant that larger areas of land could contain a larger number of people, which led to the deforestation of large areas of forest. Added to this was the fact that population growth brought with it an increase in needs. Such a context required the clearing of land for agriculture, as noted earlier in this research. In turn, the versatility of timber meant that meeting the needs of growing human populations resulted in a detriment to the availability of such resources. Among the needs that wood helped to satisfy were the energy needs of the population. For this reason, timber resources were further affected by the use of wood as a fuel.[31]

Within that context, the reduction of timber resources ushered in the pre-industrial energy period. In this energy era, innovations for using the energy sources of the time were widely disseminated. An example of this is the wheel and hydraulic and wind-powered mills.[32]

The exploitation of hydropower was used during the medieval period, mainly for grain grinding, ore crushing and smelting, stone and wood sawing, wood turning, oil pressing, paper making, tanning, wire pulling, stamping, cutting, metal grinding,

[27] Smil (1994), p. 23.

[28] Smil (2017).

[29] Penna (2020), p. 27.

[30] Rhodes (2018).

[31] Kaplan et al. (2009), pp. 3018–3019.

[32] Gimpel (2002).

blacksmithing, glazing and majolica polishing. In some cases, English waterwheels were also used to pump water into underground mines.[33] Hydraulic power, harnessed through waterwheels, was more energy efficient than mechanisms for exploiting animal or human traction as a source of power.

While hydropower served as a driving force in territories with abundant water resources, in other contexts, given the scarcity of this type of resource, wind energy took centre stage. Examples of this were the Netherlands, Denmark, and England. The wind was used as an energy carrier for grinding cereals, chalk, sugar cane, mustard, and cocoa, as well as for papermaking, sawing, metalworking, pumping water and extracting salt, among many others.[34]

In addition, animal traction and wood remained the predominant energy sources in production processes. Wood, as a type of biomass due to its energy content, both in its natural state and in the form of charcoal, was used inside the home for heating, cooking, and lighting. It was used in small and medium-sized enterprises to manufacture bricks, ceramics, glass, and metalworking. Because of extractive practices, the decline of wood resources at the time was once again a limit to development, given the scarcity of this biomass as an energy resource.[35]

The Industrial Revolution ushered in a different energy period for humanity. This period's cause and distinguishing feature is that the energy matrix changed from using free energy sources such as wind and hydropower to one with a commercial value: coal.[36] The scarcity of wood, as one of the primary energy carriers of the time, put human ingenuity to the test. The need for sufficient energy to meet the growing energy demand due to population growth and the diversification of production processes made coal the energy source to be used. This structural change brought about transformations in all spheres.

The prominence assumed by coal as "the largest source of solid fuel in the world"[37] implied the energy transition of humankind to fossil fuels. The emergence of this energy carrier was not an event unique to the beginning of the industrial revolution. Long before that, there were precedents for the use of coal in many regions of the ancient world. Examples of such antecedents include China, where it was used in 1000 BC. In this country, coal became the main source of energy in AD 1000. At the same time, the societies of ancient Greece and Rome used coal, although in their beginnings, the exploitation of this mineral was minor. This situation changed later with the mining and use of coal by the Roman Empire in Britain during the early Christian era.[38]

However, the expansion of coal mining in the United Kingdom during the eighteenth century led to the Industrial Revolution from 1750 to 1850. With the scarcity

[33] Smil (2017), Langdon and Watts (2005).

[34] Smil (2017), pp. 157–158, 161.

[35] Grebner et al. (2013).

[36] Cunningham (2003).

[37] Miller (2011), p. 1.

[38] Elliott (1981), p. 5.

of wood as one of the main energy carriers at this time, coal became the only fuel available in England to meet the growing energy demand. This context led to the rise of coal to become the main source of energy to meet the energy needs of the domestic sector and small businesses.[39]

Within this context, coal could gradually displace the use of charcoal as an energy generation source. The abundance of coal and the accelerated increase in its efficiency meant more affordable prices for satisfying energy demand. Thus, low coal prices caused other energy carriers, such as charcoal, to experience an increase in market prices around the 1750s.[40]

With the expansion of coal in the 1800s, its energy uses diversified. Among these uses, coal gas production developed. In 1832, the first coal gas producer was created to ensure the production of this energy carrier. One of its main purposes was to obtain thermal energy at a low production cost until it was replaced by natural gas as a cheaper energy carrier.[41]

The relevance of coal as an energy carrier forced the regulation of the means and routes of transportation to ensure the success of the developing Industrial Revolution.[42] This path resulted in the fact that, over the course of history, coal became the primary source of energy in the form of heat, steam, and electricity for decades,[43] playing an essential role in the development of the Industrial Revolution.[44]

The use of coal, which had a specific commercial value, led to an increase in the cost of energy generation. According to de Zeeuw, this led to the flourishing of the Netherlands due to the discovery of peat deposits in the country.[45] This new energy carrier had lower prices than others on the market. As a non-renewable resource, its sources were gradually depleted, and its excessive mining caused innumerable environmental damages, including soil erosion. As the resource became scarce, the price of other energy carriers, such as coal and wood, became competitive again.

The use of coal accelerated industrial development in this historical period, together with the invention of the steam engine. The use of coal as an energy carrier to drive large steam engines revolutionised production processes. This fossil fuel made the production of goods at levels unprecedented in history possible. It also drove the establishment of networks, accelerated the operation of processes, and remained at the heart of the Industrial Revolution.[46]

In addition, there was a leap in the evolution of the metallurgical enterprise due to the energetic superiority of coal over other carriers used up to that time. The energy contained in coal, which was transformed into mechanical energy through

---

[39] Miller (2011), p. 4.

[40] Deane (1979), p. 104.

[41] Miller (2011), p. 5–6.

[42] Miller (2011), p. 4.

[43] Finkelman et al. (2021), p. 99.

[44] Silva and Wolfe (2021), p. 1.

[45] de Zeeuw (1978).

[46] Osterhammel (2014), p. 62.

steam engines, opened up a number of opportunities for ironmasters. By restricting any productive limits imposed by the old methods of ironworking, ironmasters began to move into areas where coal was more readily available. The availability of this resource made the metallurgical enterprise flourish as never before and became a driving force in the economy of the time.[47]

The innovative movement around steam engines continued to provide high energy efficiency, reducing energy carrier consumption. Similarly, the application of this invention enjoyed a multiplicity of applications in the transport sector as an energy source, both on land and at sea.[48]

The development of steam engines responded to the interest of capitalist entrepreneurs in increasing productivity, for which they needed a source of energy independence for individual producers. By prioritising capitalist relations of production above all ecological interests, the steam engine industry was able to strengthen itself at the cost of CO_2 emissions into the atmosphere.[49] Despite the advantages of steam engines, they were still too large and cumbersome. Moreover, the development of internal combustion engines put their power at a disadvantage.

Also, the availability of coal as a non-renewable source declined over the years. The development of industry and the improvement of steam engines resulted in an increased demand for coal. As a result, coal mines became more profound and more dangerous.[50] The increasing dangers of mining activity led to the start of numerous strikes by mine workers around the world. Examples of such demonstrations took place in the USA, Britain, and China.[51] The shortage of coal as a primary energy carriers of the time once again put human ingenuity to the test. Reliance on non-renewable energy sources has provided a time-limited solution to energy demand.

The decline in demand for coal became more widespread over the years. It was only in extreme emergencies, such as the First World War, that the coal industry enjoyed growth again. Despite the importance of coal up to this time, it was quickly displaced by other energy carriers. By the 1970s, the demand for coal experienced a growth of only 1%, while crude oil and natural gas began their rise of 662% and 2589%, respectively.[52]

This context represented the beginning of the advanced industrial energy period. The extraction of crude oil, a new carrier with a higher energy value, characterised this new stage in human history. Even though, in its beginnings, oil had multiple uses since 2500 BC, this natural resource gradually gained prominence in the energy matrix until it became the primary source of energy for contemporary society.[53]

---

[47] Miller (2011), pp. 4–5.

[48] Smil (2017), pp. 161–167.

[49] Cutter (2020), p. 368.

[50] Valavanidis and Vlachogianni (2013).

[51] Penna (2020), p. 74.

[52] Savage (1990), p. 11.

[53] International Renewable Energy Agency (2021).

Oil, also known as black gold, drove the flourishing society of the twentieth century but consolidated the dependence on non-renewable sources, which humanity still faces today. The first obstacle to using oil as the primary energy source came in the 1970s due to armed conflicts in the Middle East.

The origins of the energy crisis of the 1970s lay in the strategic interest in oligarchic control over oil reserves in the Middle East. Following the beginning of the withdrawal of the United Kingdom's imperial presence in the Persian Gulf, the United States of America began to express concern over the control of the region's large oil reserves. The shift in the balance of power in the Middle East led governments in the region that had previously expressed dissatisfaction with the domination and unfair practices of oil companies to take action to manage the control of oil prices.[54]

For this purpose, the Organisation of Petroleum Exporting Countries (OPEC) was created in 1960 with the agreement of many of the major oil producers in the Middle East. The organisation became more effective in the 1970s with the nationalisation of oil companies. These nationalisations brought control over oil production in the region. Control of energy (oil in this case) gave OPEC the power to confront the geopolitical actions of the United States, a nation that has demonstrated staunch support for Israel in its foreign policy. Following Egypt's attack on Israeli forces to recapture the Sinai Peninsula, the US contributed to Israel's military build-up to confront Egyptian forces.[55]

In response to this scenario, OPEC unleashed an oil embargo in retaliation for US support for Israel.[56] With direct control over oil production and oil prices on the international market, OPEC had at its disposal a powerful weapon to dissuade the United States and other Western nations from meddling in Middle Eastern affairs. This embargo was a long-term strategy to control prices by withholding oil. This practice led to a three-dollar increase in the value of a barrel of oil.

Especially in the United States, the oil embargo had a strong impact. By 1973, the United States was the world's largest oil consumer. The United States consumed a third of the oil produced at this time despite having a small population relative to the rest of the world. Among the impacts of America's dependence on oil exports and the crisis of the 1970s was the rising unemployment rate. At least 1 million people found themselves unable to find work in the US labour market. The energy crisis caused massive inflation in the US economy, with the Consumer Price Index rising to 12.2% and the Wholesale Price Index to 20.9% in 1975. Inflation was also characterised by a rise in labour costs to 11.4%. The oil embargo negatively impacted emerging economic sectors, such as the automobile industry, among others.[57]

[54] Jones (2012), p. 210.

[55] Jones (2012), p. 210.

[56] Bösch and Graf (2014).

[57] Zulkifli and Haqeem (2022), pp. 137, 139–143.

As described above, the impact of the measure implemented by the leading oil producers was not long in coming on the United States domestic market. Long lines at fuel stations and rising gasoline and home heating oil prices meant the inflationary process was underway. This energy crisis seriously threatened the United States economy, and it became a "power source" for OPEC members. From that moment on, the rise in the price of a barrel of oil became the trend for regulating the international market.[58]

Between 1973 and 1974, the price of crude oil increased four times its value. Such a runaway rise in the value of crude oil affected national economies irrespective of their level of development. The United Kingdom can be cited as an example of the impact of the price increase. One of the direct consequences of the OPEC oil embargo was the proliferation of energy poverty.[59]

Although fuel poverty was analysed in 1982 by Lewis,[60] the term evolved over time to energy poverty. However, such a phenomenon was defined initially by Lewis and later developed by Boardman[61] as "the inability to afford adequate warmth in the home."[62] Of course, such a vision was intended to describe the reality in the United Kingdom in the aftermath of the energy crisis of the 1970s.

The precipitous increase in energy prices at this time placed people in deep budgetary difficulties. This situation particularly affected the low-income section of the population, whose energy consumption accounted for a substantial proportion of expenditure. This context resulted in an average of 150,000 households losing access to electricity and gas supplies since 1970, and in 1975, this total rose to 176,000 households. Among the worst affected were the elderly due to their increasing debts and thus their disconnection from these energy services.[63]

In response to the growing rates of fuel poverty and the effects of this phenomenon on people's health (e.g. hypothermia), public pressure was not long in coming. This is why, in 1975, the National Right to Fuel Campaign was launched in the UK. This movement focused on:

> The single aim of ensuring that every household was able to afford adequate heat, light, and power, to end fuel poverty by securing a warm, dry, well-lit home for all, regardless of income and location. Energy is vital to life, health, and well-being and not something that we can live without and remain part of society.[64]

Naturally, the increase in energy prices following the OPEC oil embargo was not the source of fuel poverty, as its roots can be traced back in time to different energy efficiency conditions of UK households.[65] However, this energy crisis undoubtedly

[58] Penna (2020), p. 105.

[59] Boardman (1991), p. 18.

[60] Lewis (1982).

[61] Boardman (1991).

[62] Li et al. (2014), p. 477.

[63] Boardman (1991), pp. 21–22.

[64] National Right to Fuel Campaign (2007).

[65] Cf. Boardman (1991), pp. 11–18.

aggravated fuel poverty to unprecedented levels in the UK and thus magnified its negative consequences on people's lives.

This moment is one of the most severe energy crises that humanity has ever faced. The growing energy demand of the world's population and rising energy market prices were significantly affected. This increase in energy prices highlighted national economies' dependence on non-renewable energy sources, especially oil producers. This energy dependence was a brake on development but opened the door to new energy sources.

Alongside using oil as an energy carrier, the penetration of the nuclear industry into the electricity sector began in the 1950s. Nevertheless, nuclear studies began in 1789 with the discovery of uranium.[66] Nuclear energy sources were initially presented as inexhaustible, bringing lower power generation costs. By 1960, nuclear power had declared itself a technically proven and commercially viable energy source; thus, nuclear power generation steadily increased in the energy markets.[67]

After World War II, nuclear energy was conceived for war purposes in the nuclear programmes of the United States, the United Kingdom, France, and the Soviet Union. By the 1970s, however, nuclear technologies were extended to Asia, Africa, and Latin America. At the same time, the use of nuclear generation became a key aspect of the US discourse to promote the use of nuclear generation under the slogan "atoms for peace."[68]

With the oil crisis of the 1970s, the impact on generation costs was not long in coming, so nuclear generation also became markedly more expensive. Although nuclear generation involves lower costs compared to fossil fuel generation, the construction of nuclear plants has higher costs. This is compounded by the need to maximise safety conditions in energy generation to avoid major accidents.[69]

In addition, the nuclear events at Three Mile Island in 1979 and Chernobyl in 1986 created global anti-nuclear awareness. These events demonstrated the dangers of nuclear power generation. Another damaging and hazardous element of the nuclear industry is the waste it generates. The management, transportation and storage of nuclear waste are among the most lethal challenges facing the contemporary energy industry.[70]

Another major event that raised public concern about nuclear power generation was the Fukushima nuclear accident. At this time, the threats posed by nuclear generation were once again highlighted. The impact of a magnitude nine tsunami at the Fukushima Nuclear Power Plant released 16.5 times the amount of energy of the atomic bomb dropped on Hiroshima and was only matched by the Chernobyl nuclear disaster. The consequences of a nuclear disaster of global proportions led to the displacement of more than 80,000 people. Thus, once again, nuclear generation

[66] Hore-Lacy (2007), p. 1.

[67] Char and Csik (1987).

[68] Elliott (2013), p. 2.

[69] Elliott (2013), p. 2.

[70] Char and Csik (1987).

proved not to be the way forward because of the danger it poses to humanity and the environment.[71]

It is not only the above that discourages the use of nuclear power generation. Although the development of nuclear power generation for peaceful purposes has satisfied part of the global energy demand, its multiple applications have also made it a significant player in the arms industry. Examples of this are the detonation by the United States of America of two atomic bombs in Hiroshima and Nagasaki around 1945.[72] These nuclear-destructive events led to the international community's concern to ensure the non-proliferation of nuclear weapons.[73]

States began to realise the need to develop the transition to renewable energy sources. Considering the effects of the energy crisis of the 1970s and the potential negative consequences of the use of nuclear generation. Penna refers to this new phase as the renewable energy regime.[74] As a result of the search for energy sources to respond to the growing energy demand and its transition, renewable sources emerged as an answer.

Even though humankind has been using renewable sources such as solar, wind, and hydroenergy, the mechanisms for exploiting these sources have been modernised to make them more effective and efficient. This initiative went hand in hand with the awareness of nations on climate issues and sustainable development. Although energy demand had to be met to ensure the functioning of society, the market and the state, the negative impact on the environment of the non-renewable energy sources used up to that time was increasing.[75]

Since the Brundtland Report Our Common Future,[76] sustainable development has been at the top of the international and national debate agenda. Today, renewable energy sources make up 29% of the global energy matrix.[77] The development of these energy sources has demonstrated numerous strengths. Especially in 2020, with the COVID-19 pandemic, the demand for fossil fuels decreased due to the shutdown of energy-intensive economic activities. Renewable sources have proven to lower energy generation costs compared to conventional sources. Moreover, energy demand can be met through their use with decreased CO_2 emissions into the atmosphere.[78]

In 2018, REN21 defined three main uses of the total energy generated: thermal energy, transportation, and electricity generation. That same year, 10.2% of the thermal energy generated worldwide was produced from renewable sources, 3.4% of the energy consumed in the transport sector and 27.1% of the electricity produced.

---

71 Kim et al. (2013), p. 822.

72 Hore-Lacy (2007).

73 Cf. Tratado de No Proliferación de Armas Nucleares (1970).

74 Penna (2020).

75 Foster and Bedrosyan (2014).

76 Organización de Naciones Unidas (1987).

77 REN21 (2021).

78 REN21 (2021).

In 2020, USD 303.5 billion was invested in developing renewable energy sources, reflecting the state's efforts for energy transition.[79]

The incentive for renewable sources has been reinforced since the approval of the 2030 Agenda in 2015.[80] Although it is not binding, nations have agreed to its progressive fulfilment in the interests of sustainable development. It sets out 17 Sustainable Development Goals (SDGs) and 169 targets to promote dignity and equality among people. Specifically, SDG #7 states, "Ensure access to affordable, secure, sustainable and modern energy for all".[81] This SDG represents the manifestation of the political will of States to ensure access to energy through the prism of sustainability, security, and accessibility based on modern forms of generation.

Today, the constant search for energy continues to be a priority, but access to energy has become a challenge for states to combat poverty, energy vulnerability, and the negative phenomena associated with them.[82] Throughout history, it has been proven impossible to satisfy basic human needs without guaranteeing the energy necessary as a vital premise.

At times in history when energy availability has been affected, processes in all areas have come to a standstill, and thus, development has come to a halt. Despite this immutable reality, access to energy is not a universal process, and nations' development levels vary, as does energy availability in each nation.

In 2019, 10% of the world's population lacked access to electricity, today's predominant form of energy, to meet energy needs. The lowest levels of electrification are found in developing countries. Despite a mere 83% electrification rate 10 years ago, the percentage of the world's population without access to electricity is still far too large. The increase in the level of electrification globally denotes unequal progress in energy access, which affects the development of nations. Among the three countries with the most significant deficits are Nigeria, the Democratic Republic of Congo and Ethiopia.[83]

While the energy access gap is narrowing globally, energy poverty and vulnerability surface in multiple contexts. While many nations are undergoing complex technological transformation and planning processes for the sustainable development of their energy systems for energy transition, many other nations must focus their efforts and limited financial resources on securing at least enough energy to meet their domestic demand.

[79] REN21 (2021), p. 37.

[80] Comisión Económica para América Latina y el Caribe (2016).

[81] Comisión Económica para América Latina y el Caribe (2016).

[82] Penna (2020).

[83] Tracking SDG7 (2021).

2.3 Conclusion

The energy problem has accompanied human beings since their very origins as a species. From the earliest times of the human species, the constant search for energy sources has been perpetuated as a priority and *conditio sine qua non* for survival. The analysis carried out so far shows that humanity and states are becoming increasingly aware of the importance of energy. At the same time, it highlights the need for energy sovereignty to guarantee energy security.

However, the history of humankind has revolved around satisfying energy needs, and numerous alternatives have been used to respond to the growing levels of energy consumption. For this purpose, humankind has used different energy sources. Since ancient times, the energy evolution of the human species has been based on exploiting available energy sources with a growing dependence on non-renewable sources, where fossil fuels have taken a leading role. This context has been nothing more than the result of the urgent and imperative need to satisfy a growing energy demand.

Then, as a consequence, the realisation of the right to energy has been determined by dissimilar variables that have put it at constant risk, placing its rightholders in situations of vulnerability and energy poverty and also threatening the state's functioning, economic development, and even political stability. An example of such variables is the strengthening of energy dependence, not only on external suppliers but also on energy sources that are finite in time.

Nevertheless, energy dependence has promoted scientific and technological development to guarantee access to energy for all people with the least negative environmental impact. This context has led to the adoption of legal instruments that support protecting the right to energy at both international and national levels.

References[84]

Boardman B (1991) Fuel poverty: from cold homes to affordable warmth. Belhaven Press. https://biblio.vub.ac.be/iguana/www.main.cls?surl=search&p=f88fe9ec-2425-11e7-a7e4-90084dd7a2c4#recordId=3.240219. Accessed 28 Feb 2025

Bösch F, Graf B (2014) Reacting to anticipations: energy crises and energy policy in the 1970s. An introduction. Hist Soc Res 39(4):7–21. https://www.ssoar.info/ssoar/bitstream/handle/document/40658/ssoar-hsr-2014-4-bosch_et_al-Reacting_to_anticipations__energy.pdf?sequence=1&isAllowed=y&lnkname=ssoar-hsr-2014-4-bosch_et_al-Reacting_to_anticipations__energy.pdf. Accessed 28 Feb 2025

Brown KS, Marean CW, Herries AIR, Jacobs Z, Tribolo C, Braun D, Roberts DL, Meyer MC, Bernatchez J (2009) Fire as an engineering tool of early modern humans. Science 325(5942):859–862. https://www.science.org/doi/10.1126/science.1175028. Accessed 28 Feb 2025

[84] All links to the cited websites were operational as of 28 February 2025.

Char NL, Csik BJ (1987) Nuclear power development: history and outlook. Int Atomic Energy Agency Bull 29(3):19–23. https://www.iaea.org/sites/default/files/publications/magazines/bulletin/bull29-3/29304781925.pdf. Accessed 28 Feb 2025

Cipolla CM (1961) Sources d'énergie et Histoire de l'Humanité. Ann Hist Sci Soc 3:521–534. https://www.jstor.org/stable/pdf/27575601.pdf?refreqid=excelsior%3A714467ff1ae0be33ccbf1db5d5a6da61&ab_segments=&origin=&initiator=&acceptTC=1. Accessed 28 Feb 2025

Clark JD, Harris JWK (1985) Fire and its roles in early hominid lifeways. Afr Archaeol Rev 3:3–27. https://link.springer.com/article/10.1007/BF01117453

Comisión Económica para América Latina y el Caribe (2016) Agenda 2030 y los Objetivos de Desarrollo Sostenible Una oportunidad para América Latina y el Caribe. Organización de Naciones Unidas. https://repositorio.cepal.org/bitstream/handle/11362/40155/24/S1801141_es.pdf. Accessed 28 Feb 2025

Coyle ED, Simmons RA (2014) Understanding the global energy crisis. Purdue University Press West Lafayette, Indiana. https://library.oapen.org/bitstream/id/a79c8a8e-7bae-4c41-9844-2cde33da8c52/649976.pdf. Accessed 28 Feb 2025

Cunningham RE (2003) La energía, historia de sus fuentes y transformación. Petrotecnia: 52–60. https://studylib.es/doc/8656209/historia-de-la-energ%C3%ADa. Accessed 28 Feb 2025

Cutter L (2020) Fossil capital: the rise of steam power and the roots of global warming by Andreas Malm. Environ Polit 29(2):367–369. https://doi.org/10.1080/09644016.2020.1718873. Accessed 28 Feb 2025

de Zeeuw JW (1978) Peat and the Dutch golden age: the historical meaning of energy-attainability. https://www.peatandculture.org/documenten/Zeeuw.pdf. Accessed 28 Feb 2025

Deane P (1979) The first industrial revolution. Cambridge University Press, Cambridge. https://www.cambridge.org/core/books/first-industrial-revolution/56BCD4D8F433A55735432B24E851CE22. Accessed 28 Feb 2025

Díaz LG, Tarifa PG, Gerje FL, Benítez MB, Ercoli PH (2014) Alimentos: Historia, Presente y Futuro. Escritura en Ciencias. http://www.bnm.me.gov.ar/giga1/documentos/EL005266.pdf. Accessed 28 Feb 2025

Elliott MA (1981) Chemistry of coal utilization. second supplementary volumen. John Wiley & Sons, New York. https://searchworks.stanford.edu/view/1453786. Accessed 28 Feb 2025

Elliott D (2013) Fukushima: impacts and implications. Palgrave Macmillan UK, London. http://link.springer.com/10.1057/9781137274335. Accessed 28 Feb 2025

Finkelman RB, Wolfe A, Hendryx MS (2021) The future environmental and health impacts of coal. Energy Geosci 2(2):99–112. doi:https://doi.org/10.1016/j.engeos.2020.11.001. Accessed 28 Feb 2025

Foster V, Bedrosyan D (2014) Understanding CO_2 emissions from the global energy sector. The International Bank for Reconstruction and Development/The World Bank. https://documents1.worldbank.org/curated/en/873091468155720710/pdf/851260BRI0Live00Box382147B00PUBLIC0.pdf. Accessed 28 Feb 2025

Gimpel J (2002) La révolution industrielle au moyen-âge. Éditions du Seuil, Paris. https://archive.org/details/larvolutionindus0000jean. Accessed 28 Feb 2025

Grebner DL, Bettinger P, Siry JP (2013) Introduction to forestry and natural resources. Elsevier. https://linkinghub.elsevier.com/retrieve/pii/C20100649662. Accessed 28 Feb 2025

Hirst KK (2019) The discovery of fire. Thought Co. social sciences section. Dotdash, New York. https://www.thoughtco.com/the-discovery-of-fire-169517. Accessed 28 Feb 2025

Hore-Lacy I (2007) History of nuclear energy. In: Nuclear energy in the twenty-first century. Elsevier, pp 139–151. https://linkinghub.elsevier.com/retrieve/pii/B978012373622250012X. Accessed 28 Feb 2025

International Renewable Energy Agency (2021) World energy transition outlook 1.5 °C pathway. Abu Dhabi. https://www.irena.org/-/media/Files/IRENA/Agency/Publication/2021/Jun/IRENA_World_Energy_Transitions_Outlook_2021.pdf. Accessed 28 Feb 2025

Jones TC (2012) America, oil, and war in the Middle East. J Am Hist 99(1):208–218. https://academic.oup.com/jah/article-lookup/doi/10.1093/jahist/jas045. Accessed 28 Feb 2025

Kaplan JO, Krumhardt KM, Zimmermann N (2009) The prehistoric and preindustrial deforestation of Europe. Quat Sci Rev 28(27–28):3016–3034. doi:https://doi.org/10.1016/j.quascirev.2009.09.028. Accessed 28 Feb 2025

Kim Y, Kim M, Kim W (2013) Effect of the Fukushima nuclear disaster on global public acceptance of nuclear energy. Energy Policy 61:822–828. doi:https://doi.org/10.1016/j.enpol.2013.06.107. Accessed 28 Feb 2025

Kostic MM (2014) Energy: global and historical background. In: Encyclopedia of energy engineering and technology, 2nd edn. CRC Press, pp 644–657. https://www.researchgate.net/publication/268254994_Energy_Global_and_Historical_Background. Accessed 28 Feb 2025

Langdon J, Watts M (2005) Tower windmills in Medieval England: a case of arrested development? Technol Cult 46(4):697–718. https://www.jstor.org/stable/pdf/40060955. Accessed 28 Feb 2025

Lewis P (1982) Fuel poverty can be stopped. National Right to Fuel Campaign, Bardford

Li K, Lloyd B, Liang XJ, Wei YM (2014) Energy poor or fuel poor: what are the differences?. Energy Policy 68:476–481. doi:https://doi.org/10.1016/j.enpol.2013.11.012. Accessed 28 Feb 2025

Lotka AJ (1922) Contribution to the energetics of evolution. Proc Natl Acad Sci USA, 8:147–151. https://www.pnas.org/content/pnas/8/6/147.full.pdf. Accessed 28 Feb 2025

Mason SLR (2000) Fire and Mesolithic subsistence—managing oaks for acorns in northwest Europe? Palaeogeogr Palaeoclimatol Palaeoecol 164(1–4):139–150. https://linkinghub.elsevier.com/retrieve/pii/S0031018200001814. Accessed 28 Feb 2025

Mellars P (2006) Why did modern human populations disperse from Africa ca. 60,000 years ago? A new model. Proc Natl Acad Sci 103(25):9381–9386. https://pnas.org/doi/full/10.1073/pnas.0510792103. Accessed 28 Feb 2025

Miller BG (2011) Coal as fuel. In Clean coal engineering technology. Elsevier, pp 1–51. https://linkinghub.elsevier.com/retrieve/pii/B9781856177108000017. Accessed 28 Feb 2025

National Right to Fuel Campaign (2007) Memorandum submitted by the National Right to Fuel Campaign. UK Parliament website. UK Parliament, London. https://publications.parliament.uk/pa/cm200910/cmselect/cmenergy/424/424we50.htm. Accessed 28 Feb 2025

Odum HT (1971) Environment, power, and society. John Wiley & Sons Inc., New York. http://www.amazon.com/Environment-Society-Environmental-Science-Technology/dp/047165275X. Accessed 28 Feb 2025

Organización de Naciones Unidas (1987) Report of the World Commission on Environment and Development. New York. http://digitallibrary.un.org/record/139811. Accessed 28 Feb 2025

Osterhammel J (2014) The transformation of the world. A global history of the nineteenth century. Camiller P. Princeton University Press, Princeton and Oxford. https://press.princeton.edu/books/paperback/9780691169804/the-transformation-of-the-world. Accessed 28 Feb 2025

Penna AN (2020) A history of energy flows: from human labor to renewable power. Routledge. https://www.routledge.com/A-History-of-Energy-Flows-From-Human-Labor-to-Renewable-Power/Penna/p/book/9780367777067. Accessed 28 Feb 2025

REN21 (2021) Renewables 2021. Global status report. Paris. https://www.ren21.net/wp-content/uploads/2019/05/GSR2021_Full_Report.pdf. Accessed 28 Feb 2025

Rhodes R (2018) Energy: a human history. Simon & Schuster, New York. https://www.goodreads.com/book/show/36373616-energy. Accessed 28 Feb 2025

Ritchie H, Roser M, Rosado P (2023) Energy production and consumption. https://ourworldindata.org/energy-production-consumption. Accessed 28 Feb 2025

Savage L (1990) Thunder in the mountains: the West Virginia Mine War, 1920–21. University of Pittsburgh Press, Pittsburgh. https://www.jstor.org/stable/j.ctt6wrc1c. Accessed 28 Feb 2025

Silva LFO, Wolfe AL (2021) Coal energy and environmental impacts: introduction. Energy Geosci 2(2):87–89. doi:https://doi.org/10.1016/j.engeos.2020.12.001. Accessed 28 Feb 2025

Smil V (1994) Energy in world history. Westview Press. https://openlibrary.org/books/OL1092168M/Energy_in_world_history#:~:text=Vaclav%20Smil%20offers%20a%20comprehensive%20look%20at%20the,to%20preindustrial%20hydraulic%20techniques%20and%20modern%20fossil-fueled%20civilization. Accessed 28 Feb 2025

Smil V (2004) World history and energy. Encyclopedia of energy. Elsevier Inc, p 6. https://www.academia.edu/5209154/2004_Smil_World_History_and_Energy. Accessed 28 Feb 2025

Smil V (2017) Energy and civilization. Energy and civilization. The MIT Press, Cambridge. https://direct.mit.edu/books/book/3576/energy-and-civilizationa-history. Accessed 28 Feb 2025

The International Bank for Reconstruction and Development/The World Bank (2020) Tracking SDG 7: The energy progress report 2020. https://www.irena.org/-/media/Files/IRENA/Agency/Publication/2020/May/SDG7Tracking_Energy_Progress_2020.pdf. Accessed 28 Feb 2025

Tracking SDG7 (2021) The energy progress report 2021. Washington DC. https://trackingsdg7.esmap.org/data/files/download-documents/2021_tracking_sdg7_report.pdf. Accessed 28 Feb 2025

Tratado de No Proliferación de Armas Nucleares (1970). https://www.iaea.org/sites/default/files/publications/documents/infcircs/1970/infcirc140_sp.pdf. Accessed 28 Feb 2025

Valavanidis A, Vlachogianni T (2013) Homo sapiens' energy dependence and use throughout human history and evolution, vol 1. Chem-Tox-Ecotox.Org, pp 1–32. https://www.researchgate.net/publication/303370977_Homo_Sapiens%27_Energy_Dependence_and_Use_Throughout_Human_History_and_Evolution#:~:text=The%20present%20review%20describes%20the%20role%20of%20different,narrated%20by%20different%20energy%20regimes%20throughout%20the%20centuries. Accessed 28 Feb 2025

Zulkifli N, Haqeem D (2022) The Opec oil shock crisis (1973): an analysis. Asian Journal of Research in Business and Management (March). https://myjms.mohe.gov.my/index.php/ajrbm/article/view/17477. Accessed 28 Feb 2025

Chapter 3
International and Regional Normative Treatment of the Right to Energy

3.1 The Right to Energy Under the International Legal Framework

The need to protect the right to energy has been growing. The Universal Declaration of Human Rights, adopted and proclaimed by the United Nations General Assembly through a non-binding Resolution 217 A(III) in 1948, is the first historical precedent.[1] This legal instrument "reaffirms" the international community's commitment to protecting human rights despite its non-binding nature. From its preamble, this international legal instrument declares:

> Whereas the peoples of the United Nations have in the Charter reaffirmed their faith in fundamental human rights, in the dignity and worth of the human person and in the equal rights of men and women and have determined to promote social progress and better standards of life in larger freedom.[2]

In this way, the basic human rights and fundamental rights assumptions are established. Human dignity[3] and equality are presented as universal principles of rights.

> Human dignity has acquired a central and pre-eminent place in the norms of international public law. A dignity that is inviolable and non-derogable, but irresolute (Own translation).[4]

The incorporation of human dignity in the Universal Declaration was not a product of spontaneity. Although dignity as a category has its origins in ancient Rome, its incorporation into international human rights law set a precedent in history. Such a

---

[1] Organización de Naciones Unidas (1948).

[2] Organización de Naciones Unidas (1948), p. 1.

[3] Pacheco-Zerga (2008).

[4] Chueca (2015).

J. G. Luis Cordova, *Theoretical and Legal Dimensions of the Right to Energy*, Economic and Financial Law & Policy – Shifting Insights & Values 9, https://doi.org/10.1007/978-3-032-33252-3_3

precedent has not been accepted free of debate, given the multiplicity of interpretations depending on the approaches of those who have ventured into its analysis.

Although the international human rights debate has focused on the freedoms contained in the so-called first-generation human rights, especially in Western nations,[5] this research assumes human dignity, instead of traditional liberties, as the starting point and endpoint of the right to energy. Notwithstanding the ambiguities that can be attributed to human dignity[6] as a concept emerging from the iusnaturalistic declarations of the Universal Declaration of Human Rights, this supreme value is framed as the underpinning of socio-economic rights. However, this research will not delve into the historical origins of human dignity but rather the analysis of this fundamental principle of human rights as the foundation of the right to energy.

In order to develop the above purpose, it is necessary to understand the context that generated the adoption of human dignity as a precursor principle of human rights. The Second World War brought, perhaps as the only positive element, the awareness on the part of states of the massacres and barbarisms generated in the Nazi extermination camps. From the sad reality of the Second World War onwards, the promulgation of a universal human rights code became a priority on the international agenda.[7]

For this purpose, it was necessary to have a foundation for the existence of human rights and the inalienability of these rights. According to McCrudden, the ideas of the French Catholic philosopher Jacques Maritain offered a solution to the problem of the foundation of human rights. Based on the ideas of Thomas Aquinas, Maritain developed his own conceptualisation of human dignity. From his thinking, beyond basing human dignity on the nature of the human being as an "inherited" condition, Maritain conceived of human dignity, moreover, as a condition further determined by political life and human relations. Such ideals implied the promotion of the common good beyond a mere expression of ethical radicalism.[8]

From Martain's thinking, human dignity implies the development of political, economic, social, and cultural conditions to ensure the development of the human personality and the enjoyment of human rights. Energy is embedded in such ideas, and the creation of conditions would then lead to human rights. For this reason, energy makes up prosperity as a material task of the state and the distribution of the benefits of energy as a support for human dignity.[9]

In addition to this, human dignity is seen as absolute by considering the human being as a whole, regardless of his or her economic status or physical condition. For this reason, dignity is conceived as universal because of the value of the human being.[10] Despite Martain's natural law view, his ideas reflect three manifestations of human dignity that are still reflected in international human rights law today.

---

[5] Cf. Gutwirth and De Hert (2021).

[6] Gutwirth and De Hert (2021), p. 437.

[7] Hughes (2011), pp. 2–3.

[8] McCrudden (2008), p. 662.

[9] Maritain (1951), p. 172.

[10] Maritain (1944), p. 6.

In this respect, McCrudden defines human dignity on the basis of three fundamental pillars, which in turn support the argument for the right to energy in the framework of the Universal Declaration of Human Rights. The first of these pillars is the ontological claim. This pillar is the intrinsic value of every human being as a human being. The second pillar of human dignity is the relational claim. This pillar is based on human relationships and the respectful treatment of all human beings as of equal value. The third pillar of human dignity arises in the relationship between human beings and the state. This relationship is conceived as unidirectional in that the state is obliged to look after the individual welfare of human beings.[11]

The recognition of dignity as a guiding principle of the Universal Declaration of Human Rights is a call for the recognition of the value of every human being, for respectful treatment in accordance with that value, and for the obligation of every state to protect each individual human being. This obligation is made effective on the basis of human rights as enforceable mechanisms against the state.

Within this context, the right to energy becomes a human right, inseparable from the rest for the full realisation of the human personality. The call to ensure the conditions that guarantee the existence of human dignity, including energy, is the only way to materialise the postulates of the Universal Declaration of Human Rights.

That is supported by Article 21.2 of the Declaration. This postulate states:

> Everyone has the right of equal access to public service in his country.[12]

This paragraph of article 21 sheds the first light on the right to energy. Based on the importance of energy services to guarantee the realisation of the right to energy, the conception of such services under the legal regime of public services is a reality that is difficult to erase from the legal system.

The public service character of those services aimed at satisfying energy needs imposes the responsibility of the state for their operation. Even in contexts such as that of the European Union, where the liberalisation of the energy market has had a negative impact on the realisation of the right to energy, member states continue to treat energy services as services of general economic interest. This status implies the application of public service obligations to public energy services.[13]

The Universal Declaration of Human Rights promotes the right to energy on the basis of equal access to public services, as enshrined in Article 21. In this way, this international legal instrument pursues equity in access to energy as provided by public energy services. However, it is important to emphasise that equitable access to energy is promoted from a universality that is limited to the boundaries of a particular state.

Another pronouncement on the right to energy in the Universal Declaration of Human Rights is contained in Article 22. However, this article has been supplemented by subsequent international instruments such as the International Covenant

---

[11] McCrudden (2008), p. 679.

[12] Cf. Article 22.2. Organización de Naciones Unidas (1948).

[13] Krope and Krope (2007).

on Economic, Social and Cultural Rights. Therefore, the right to energy as a socio-economic right[14] is inferred from its wording.

> Article 22. Everyone, as a member of society, has the right to social security and is entitled to realization, through national effort and international co-operation and in accordance with the organization and resources of each State, of the economic, social and cultural rights indispensable for his dignity and the free development of his personality.[15]

The wording of this article directs States to mobilise resources for the fulfilment of economic, social, and cultural rights as a way of guaranteeing human dignity and the free development of the personality. As discussed above, the spirit of Article 22 implies the realisation of these rights and constitutes an advocation of the right to energy, the realisation of which is a sine qua non for the dignity and full development of the human personality.[16]

The importance of energy covers a number of areas in the fulfilment of the human rights set out in the Universal Declaration. Another example is Article 23 on the right to work under fair and satisfactory conditions.

> Article 23.1. Everyone has the right to work, to free choice of employment, to just and favourable conditions of work and to protection against unemployment.[17]

Guaranteeing conditions such as connectivity, communication, lighting, and sanitation, among others, would be almost impossible without a continuous and quality energy supply.

As a complement to the right to work provided for in Article 23, there is a right to rest and leisure.[18] This right would even be affected by the non-fulfilment of the right to energy. There are so many human needs that depend on the fulfilment of what this research defines as the content of the right to energy that without its guarantee, the right to rest and leisure would be affected. Moreover, these needs have grown and diversified over the years, and energy has become a defining element. There are many examples of this. These include indoor air conditioning, lighting, transport, the enjoyment of audiovisual media and connectivity, to name but a few.

At the same time, the Universal Declaration of Human Rights declares a commitment to social progress and raising the quality of life. This commitment is reinforced in Article 25.1.

> Article 25.1. Everyone has the right to a standard of living adequate for the health and well-being of himself and of his family, including food, clothing, housing and medical care and necessary social services, and the right to security in the event of unemployment, sickness, disability, widowhood, old age or other lack of livelihood in circumstances beyond his control.[19]

---

[14] Cf. infra, Sect. 5.2.

[15] Cf. Article 22.2. Organización de Naciones Unidas (1948).

[16] Cf. already supra, Sect. 2.2, pp. 50–51.

[17] Cf. Article 23.1. Organización de Naciones Unidas (1948).

[18] Cf. Article 24. Organización de Naciones Unidas (1948).

[19] Cf. Article 25.1. Organización de Naciones Unidas (1948).

From Article 25.1, the first normative assumptions of the right to energy are derived. It is impossible to fulfil what is stated in Article 25.1 without an energy supply that guarantees adequate living conditions and well-being, among others. Similarly, the full realisation of the rest of the human rights provided for in the Declaration depends on a sufficient energy supply.

As examples where the above is applicable, mention can be made of the right to education, provided for in Article 26: "Everyone has the right to education"[20] The full realisation of this right would be impossible without energy; the existence of a continuous and quality supply conditions many conditions necessary for its development. Among them are lighting conditions for study, access to digital materials and tools, and many others that would be reduced.

Although the Universal Declaration of Human Rights does not recognise the right to energy in an exhaustive manner, it is deduced through an extensive interpretation of its articles. This indirect protection is also motivated by the legal principles of interdependence, indivisibility, and interrelation of human rights.[21]

In 1973, with the non-binding Declaration of the United Nations Conference on the Human Environment, the improvement of the human environment was declared to be a fundamental requirement affecting the well-being of people and the world's economic development.[22] That is endorsed in Principle 1, which states that human beings have the fundamental right to enjoy adequate living conditions in a quality environment that enables them to lead a life of dignity and well-being.

> Principle 1: Man has the fundamental right to freedom, equality, and adequate conditions of life, in an environment of a quality that permits a life of dignity and well-being, and he bears a solemn responsibility to protect and improve the environment for present and future generations. In this respect, policies promoting or perpetuating apartheid, racial segregation, discrimination, colonial and other forms of oppression and foreign domination stand condemned and must be eliminated.[23]

These aspirations would remain a dead letter if there were no way to satisfy the energy demand, a basic human life necessity. Moreover, Principle 1 is complemented by Recommendations 58 and 59 of this international legal instrument. Both recommendations do not ignore the necessity to meet energy needs, but they do express concern for the management of energy sources and the protection of the environment. Despite the pollution caused by energy production, this United Nations Declaration sought to explore alternatives for energy development that would reduce the environmental impact of such development.

Following this analysis, Principle 8 of the Declaration conceives economic and social development as a premise for improving the quality of life, a development which, throughout the history of humanity, has implied an increase in energy demand.

---

[20] Cf. Article 26. Organización de Naciones Unidas (1948).

[21] Solis (2014).

[22] Acuña Zepeda and Díaz Zepeda (2017).

[23] Organización de Naciones Unidas (1972).

> Principle 8: Economic and social development is essential for ensuring a favourable living and working environment for man and for creating conditions on earth that are necessary for the improvement of the quality of life.[24]

As mentioned, recommendation 59 presents a concern regarding the study of energy sources, such as the time and energy consumption patterns, to make progress in efficient energy use. In this way, the Declaration of the United Nations Conference on the Human Environment declares that obtaining energy and its efficient use is a priority for states.

> Recommendation 59: It is recommended that the Secretary-General take steps to ensure that a comprehensive study be promptly undertaken with the aim of submitting a first report, at the latest in 1975, on available energy sources, new technology, and consumption trends, in order to assist in providing a basis for the most effective development of the world's energy resources, with due regard to the environmental effects of energy production and use: such a study to be carried out in collaboration with appropriate international bodies such as the International Atomic Energy Agency and the Organisation for Economic Co-operation and Development.[25]

Another international legal instrument is adopted, moving forward in time. The International Covenant on Economic, Social and Cultural Rights[26] entered into force in 1976. Based on fundamental principles taken from the Universal Declaration of Human Rights, economic, social, and cultural rights are declared to be a direct outgrowth of the inherent dignity of the human person. One element to highlight is the binding character of those nations that ratify the International Covenant. However, it should be noted that its binding character has been reduced, given the number of nations that have not yet ratified it.[27]

Article 1 of the International Covenant links the economic, social, and cultural development of peoples to natural resources.[28] This is why this international instrument empowers people to freely dispose of their natural resources for their development. Such an attribution includes the right to energy in a double dimension: the link between natural energy resources and energy development and the energy availability to support the economic and social development of people. At the same time, it protects natural energy resources under the prohibition of any practice that deprives people of such resources as a means of subsistence.

As discussed above, the realisation of the right to energy is particularly relevant to the right to work. For this reason, the analysis derived from Article 23.1 of the Universal Declaration of Human Rights becomes relevant in Article 7 of the International Covenant, which deals with the conditions of work that depend on the fulfilment of the right to energy. Among other things, Article 7 declares the right of

[24] Cf. Principle 8. Organización de Naciones Unidas (1972).

[25] Cf. Recommendation 59. Organización de Naciones Unidas (1972).

[26] Organización de Naciones Unidas (1976).

[27] Cf. UN (2023).

[28] Cf. Article 1. Organización de Naciones Unidas (1976).

all persons to enjoy decent living conditions for themselves and their families, occupational safety and health, and work rest.[29]

Following the same line of thought, considering energy as a human right because of its essential nature, its fulfilment determines the existence of adequate living conditions. In this sense, Article 11.1 of the International Covenant states:

> Article 11.1. The States Parties to the present Covenant recognize the right of everyone to an adequate standard of living for himself and his family, including adequate food, clothing and housing, and to the continuous improvement of living conditions.[30]

This article recognises everyone's right to an adequate standard of living, as well as the right to adequate housing and the continuous improvement of living conditions. How can this be achieved without satisfying the associated energy demand? It would be impossible.

As needs and activity levels increase, the energy amount required will increase. Therefore, although the right to energy is not yet expressly protected, it is protected under other rights' umbrella. Such rights include the right to food,[31] where energy conditions the production, preservation, and distribution of food.

The right to health is another right recognised by the International Covenant, where measures such as "the reduction of stillbirths and infant mortality, and for the healthy development of the child (…) the creation of conditions which would guarantee to all medical service and medical care in the event of sickness"[32] are envisaged. These conditions depend on the fulfilment of the right to energy, which will be analysed later in this study.[33]

The practice of protecting the right to energy under other rights' umbrella was broken in 1979 with the approval of the Convention on the Elimination of All Forms of Discrimination against Women.[34] This legally binding convention arose from the repeated call for gender equality in the international framework and the solution to women's situations of poverty in terms of access to food, health, education, and many other relevant aspects of life. This instrument is the most remote antecedent of the express recognition of the right to energy, taking women's empowerment as a starting point.

In Article 14, the Convention is concerned with applying its provisions to the protection of the role of women in the rural context.

> Article 14. States Parties shall take into account the particular problems faced by rural women and the significant roles which rural women play in the economic survival of their families, including their work in the non-monetized sectors of the economy, and shall take all appropriate measures to ensure the application of the provisions of the present Convention to women in rural areas.

---

29 Cf. Article 7 ii), b) & d). Organización de Naciones Unidas (1976).

30 Cf. Article 11.1. Organización de Naciones Unidas (1976).

31 Cf. Article 11.2. Organización de Naciones Unidas (1976).

32 Cf. Article 12. Organización de Naciones Unidas (1976).

33 Cf. infra, pp. 60, 266.

34 Organización de Naciones Unidas (1979).

> 2. States Parties shall take all appropriate measures to eliminate discrimination against women in rural areas in order to ensure, on a basis of equality of men and women, that they participate in and benefit from rural development and, in particular, shall ensure to such women the right: (…)
>
> (h) To enjoy adequate living conditions, particularly in relation to housing, sanitation, electricity and water supply, transport, and communications.[35]

Thus, the second paragraph of Article 14 establishes the commitment of the States Parties to ensure certain rights, including the right to enjoy adequate living conditions, including electricity. The most remote normative and international antecedent of the right to energy can be expressly appreciated from this article, even though it only alludes to electrical energy. Authors such as Garcia, Mundó, Bradbrook, Gardam, Solis, Durán and Condorí consider that this legal instrument also protects the right to energy to improve cooking, lighting, and heating conditions.[36]

Despite this progress, the Convention was only a first step in recognising the right to energy. Given the context in which it is recognised, it might seem that only women in rural areas would be the holders of this right, to the exclusion of all other people. This consideration would be misguided, given the universal nature of human rights. At the same time, the right to energy is also seen as restrictive, limiting it only to electricity. The right to energy goes beyond electricity, even though this energy form use is one of the most widespread nowadays.

In 1966, the United Nations Declaration on the Right to Development was not legally binding, but some of its provisions were contained in other international legal instruments with binding force.[37] Article 8 of the Declaration on the Right to Development mandated states to adopt the necessary measures for the realisation of the right to development. In this sense, Article 1 recognises the right to development as an inalienable human right.[38]

Article 1 echoes the Universal Declaration of Human Rights and other international human rights instruments, such as the International Covenant on Economic, Social and Cultural Rights. In this sense, it emphasises the subjection to Human Rights Laws and the exercise of the right to the free disposal of natural resources, including energy resources, in order to realise the right to development.

Another element that underpins the right to energy is the inclusion of the right and duty of the rest in the formulation of national policies with the aim of continuously increasing the well-being of the population. In this context, it is worth noting that "energy is widely recognised as a prerequisite for progress and well-being."[39] For this reason, the development of national public policies aimed at promoting well-being must address energy as an enabler and even a determinant of well-being.[40]

---

[35] Cf. Article 14. Organización de Naciones Unidas (1979).

[36] Garcia and Mundó (2014), Bradbrook and Gardam (2006), Solis (2018), and Durán and Condorí (2015).

[37] Cf. Human Rights Council 2022.

[38] Cf. Article 1. Organización de Naciones Unidas (1986).

[39] Mayer and Smith (2019), p. 2.

[40] Cf. Hernández (2016), p. 7; Frank et al. (2006), Nord and Kantor (2006), and Rao and Min (2018).

In addition, new elements advocating the realisation of the right to energy are integrated in Article 8.1 of the Declaration.

> Article 8.1. States should undertake, at the national level, all necessary measures for the realization of the right to development and shall ensure, inter alia, equality of opportunity for all in their access to basic resources, education, health services, food, housing, employment, and the fair distribution of income. Effective measures should be undertaken to ensure that women have an active role in the development process. Appropriate economic and social reforms should be carried out with a view to eradicating all social injustices.[41]

It also promotes equal opportunities for all regarding primary resources, education, housing, and health, among many others. In this way, the right to development is perpetuated as an inalienable right, and consequently, the right to energy is a vital element which was not left unprotected under this approach. As analysed in Chapter 2 of this research, as development levels increase and the population grows, society's energy needs increase, and a race to meet these needs begins.

In 1990, the Convention on the Rights of the Child came into force, but it should be noted, however, that its binding nature depends on ratification by the Member States.[42] In its preamble, the principles of dignity and inalienability of rights are taken up again, focused on promoting the improvement of the living conditions of children for their development. From its articles, the right to energy is deduced as a sine qua non-requirement for the realisation of the rights provided for in this international legal instrument.

In this sense, Vashchenko argues that the realisation of the right to energy determines the enjoyment of a large part of children's rights. According to Vashchenko, the right to energy has particular implications for:

> Survival rights (the right to life and the right to health); development rights (the right to education, play, leisure, cultural activities, access to information, and freedom of thought, conscience, and religion); protection rights (against all forms of abuse, neglect, and exploitation); and participation rights (the right to the expression of one's own opinion and to participation in decision-making processes at the national, regional, and local levels).[43]

In this context, Vashchenko explains the implications of access to energy for the realisation of children's rights. Such implications include the importance of the right to energy in ensuring children's social, physical, and psychological well-being. This well-being translates into the right to health, which is particularly affected by air pollution, caused in part by the use of polluting energy sources. In turn, the lack of energy affects children, particularly as one of the most vulnerable sectors, as they are unable to meet basic energy needs such as food and access to water, among others. In addition, energy services are essential for the functioning of health services.[44]

In this context, Gómez Bengoechea argues that the non-realisation of the right to energy affects the right to health and other rights, such as the right to adequate food

[41] Cf. Article 8. Organización de Naciones Unidas (1986).

[42] UNICEF (2023).

[43] Vashchenko (2021), p. 77.

[44] Cf. Article 24. Organización de Naciones Unidas (1989); Vashchenko (2021), p. 77.

for children,[45] which can be extended to all age groups. With regard to the right to adequate food, the lack of energy makes it impossible to operate refrigeration systems. This contributes to the increased risk of food poisoning due to inadequate food preservation. This means that access to fresh food is necessary, and when access is affected, adequate food is affected. Inadequate refrigeration also affects the preservation of medicines. In addition, in cold climates, energy deficits increase the risk of hypothermia, especially in children. This risk may lead to the use of polluting energy sources to meet heating needs, but this increases the risk of carbon monoxide poisoning and burns.[46]

Within this context, the right to energy has a palpable impact on the child's normal development, especially to guarantee a decent life.

> Article 23.1. States Parties recognize that a mentally or physically disabled child should enjoy a full and decent life, in conditions which ensure dignity, promote self-reliance and facilitate the child's active participation in the community.[47]
>
> Article 24.1. States Parties recognize the right of the child to the enjoyment of the highest attainable standard of health and to facilities for the treatment of illness and rehabilitation of health. States Parties shall strive to ensure that no child is deprived of his or her right of access to such health care services.[48]

Ensuring the realisation of the right to health depends mainly on the availability of power, equipment, lighting, and refrigeration systems, as described before. These elements would be practically dysfunctional without an electricity supply.

In addition to that context, the vital role of energy in the realisation of the right to an adequate standard of living must be highlighted "for the child's physical, mental, spiritual, moral and social development."[49] Such an adequate standard of living depends on the availability, accessibility, affordability, and reliability of energy.

Another of Vashchenko's arguments for the need to guarantee the right to energy is its link to the right to education,[50] which can be violated in many ways by lack of energy. Lack of energy, in turn, undermines children's education, especially in rural contexts, as they are often responsible for collecting wood to meet the family's energy needs. Such practices undermine the time spent on education.[51]

In the context of the right to education, lack of energy contributes to increased inequality among children. Unequal access to energy is an advantage for some children and a vulnerability for others, undermining access to education, academic performance and even self-esteem at an early age.[52]

---

[45] Cf. Article 24.2 c). Organización de Naciones Unidas (1989).

[46] Gómez Bengoechea (2023), pp. 48–49.

[47] Cf. Article 23. Organización de Naciones Unidas (1989).

[48] Cf. Article 24. Organización de Naciones Unidas (1989).

[49] Cf. Article 27. Organización de Naciones Unidas (1989).

[50] Cf. Article 28. Organización de Naciones Unidas (1989).

[51] Cf. Vashchenko (2021), p. 78.

[52] Gómez Bengoechea (2023), p. 47.

In addition, two other areas in which the right to energy is guaranteed in the Convention on the Rights of the Child stand out. The first of these areas is the right of the child to be protected from all forms of physical or mental violence, injury or abuse, neglect, or negligent treatment, and the second is the right to be heard.[53]

In the first of these areas, the right to energy has special implications, especially with regard to the functioning of lighting systems. For this reason, the lack of energy makes lighting inside homes difficult, which constitutes an obstacle to the identification of domestic violence.[54] The same applies to lighting in public spaces where children are vulnerable to acts of violence. Similarly, children are highly vulnerable to burns, especially when using fossil fuels such as coal for cooking.[55] For this reason, the use of modern technologies could reduce the risk of children being burned as a result of adult negligence.

The second area related to the right to be heard concerns, in particular, the exercise of energy democracy. Within the framework of the Convention on the Rights of the Child, it is, therefore, necessary to create mechanisms for children's participation in decision-making processes in the energy sector. Otherwise, the right to be heard would be undermined. In this context, there are experiences where such participation mechanisms have made it possible for children to be creatively involved in shaping economically viable solutions for the energy transition in their areas of residence.[56]

An examination of the Convention on the Rights of the Child reveals that there is no explicit recognition of the right to energy. However, many of the provisions of this international instrument call for the realisation of the right to energy in order to ensure the effectiveness of the Convention's normative provisions.

Subsequently, and continuing the analysis of the international legal framework, the United Nations Declaration on the Rights of Indigenous Peoples emerged in 2007 without legally binding force. Its Article 21 declared the right to improve economic and social conditions.

> Article 21.1. Indigenous peoples have the right, without discrimination, to the improvement of their economic and social conditions, including, inter alia, in the areas of education, employment, vocational training and retraining, housing, sanitation, health and social security.
>
> 2. States shall take effective measures and, where appropriate, special measures to ensure continuing improvement of their economic and social conditions. Particular attention shall be paid to the rights and special needs of indigenous elders, women, youth, children, and persons with disabilities.[57]

These provisions of the United Nations Declaration on the Rights of Indigenous Peoples have been identified as interrelated to the goal of sustainable

---

[53] Cf. Article 19 and 12 respectively. Organización de Naciones Unidas (1989).

[54] Vashchenko (2021), p. 78.

[55] Kawalec and Pawlas (2020), p. 173.

[56] Hettinga et al. (2021).

[57] Cf. Article 21. Organización de Naciones Unidas (2007).

development, which subsequently became the goal with the adoption of the 2030 Agenda.[58] Wherever the improvement of economic and social conditions is sought, the right to energy becomes relevant. For this reason, this Declaration implicitly endorses the right to energy and the realisation of what this study defines as its content.

In this way, through the United Nations Declaration on the Rights of Indigenous Peoples, States are charged with the mission of adopting measures for the continuous improvement of such conditions. In this sense, Article 43 also refers to the dignity and well-being of Indigenous peoples. Once again, energy is indispensable for materialising these rights and principles. Otherwise, such regulations would be a mere legal formula.

The Universal Declaration of Emerging Human Rights was adopted within the Universal Forum of Cultures framework in the same year as a non-binding manifestation of the international civil society. As recognised in its prologue, this Declaration is the result of recognising human rights as an unfinished process of permanent transformation. This instrument, despite its non-binding character, is aimed at strengthening the integrity and interdependence of human rights.[59]

Article 1 of the Universal Declaration of Emerging Human Rights recognises the macro right to existence in dignity as a fundamental right.

> Article 1. The right to existence under conditions of dignity: All human beings and every community have the right to live under conditions of dignity. This fundamental human right comprises the following rights:
>
> 1. The right to security of life, which entails the right of all human beings and communities, for their survival, to drinking water and sanitation, energy, and adequate basic food, and to not suffer situations of hunger. All individuals have the right to a continuous and sufficient supply of electricity and to free access to drinking water in order to satisfy their basic needs of life. (…).[60]

This policy paper takes human dignity as its starting point from a human rights perspective. In this way, the right to live in conditions of dignity becomes a mega-right that depends on others for its full realisation. Within that context, paragraph 1 declares the right to security of life.

The right to security of life includes the human right to energy, along with other rights such as the right to food, drinking water and sanitation, which are essential for human survival. As a consequence, this provision states that the electricity supply is also a prerequisite for survival. Once again, only electricity is recognised in a restrictive way as it was made in the Convention on the Elimination of All Forms of Discrimination Against Women.[61] Nevertheless, the Universal Declaration of Emerging Human Rights is a step forward in the right to energy, and the so-called right to an electricity supply has been granted universal character.

---

[58] Cf. Indigenous Peoples Major Group (2018).

[59] Institut de Drets Humans de Catalunya (2010).

[60] Cf. Article 1. Institut de Drets Humans de Catalunya (2010).

[61] Organización de Naciones Unidas (1979).

The supply qualification is another novel element in regulating this right, given that it must be continuous and sufficient. In the case of continuity, reference is made to a fundamental principle of public services, which is understood as:

> As the basis on which the provision of the public service is sustained and is based on the fact that a specific activity that has received this consideration is made available to citizens (...) on a permanent or regular basis so that it can satisfy any needs that may arise (Own translation).[62]

In the case of sufficiency of supply, although there is no definition in the Universal Declaration of Emerging Human Rights, it could be understood as the capacity to satisfy energy demand. This demand will depend on objective factors such as the climatic characteristics of a given geospatial context and the level of industrialisation, among others. Due to the above, determining which needs are essential is an aspect that could be widely debated.[63] The continuity and sufficiency of the electricity supply determine its operation.

The same year, the United Nations Secretary-General's Advisory Group on Energy and Climate Change called for transforming national energy systems to ensure energy access by 2030. This report starts with the recognition that:

> Energy is at the heart of most critical economic, environmental and developmental issues facing the world today.[64]

Based on this assumption, prosperity depends on clean, affordable, efficient, and reliable energy services, which play an important role in poverty eradication, human health, productivity, and economic growth. In this context, Energy for a Sustainable Future calls for addressing different challenges related to the right to energy in high-income, middle-income, and low-income countries. Particularly in the latter case, it calls for the expansion of modern energy services to combat energy poverty. This means advocating for progress on accessibility as an integral part of the right to energy. At the same time, there is a call to increase energy efficiency because of the benefits it brings, not only to the government but also to the individual, by positively impacting energy affordability. This is another element of the right to energy that the report focuses on. In this sense, it is ague:

> Affordable in this context means that the cost to end users is compatible with their income levels and no higher than the cost of traditional fuels, in other words what they would be able and willing to pay for the increased quality of energy supply. If the cost of the minimum energy package to end users should be more than a reasonable fraction of their income (10–20 percent), it may be necessary to provide temporary subsidies to reach affordability in the shorter run before economic development accrues.[65]

The Secretary-General's Advisory Group on Energy and Climate Change thus informs basic guidelines for assessing the affordability of energy services. Such a

---

[62] Zegarra Valdivia (2012).

[63] Cf. infra, p. 104.

[64] The Secretary-General's Advisory Group on Energy and Climate Change (2010), p. 7.

[65] The Secretary-General's Advisory Group on Energy and Climate Change (2010), p. 13.

view aligns with the doctrine developed by Broadman, a leading academic, regarding energy affordability and definitional delimitation within energy poverty.[66]

Reliability as a principle of energy services is stated in "Energy for a Sustainable Future." In this respect, it is necessary to define what reliability means. Duque defines reliability or trustworthiness in services as:

> The capacity that the company providing the service must have to offer it in a reliable, safe and careful manner. Within the concept of reliability are included all the elements that allow the client to detect the capacity and professional knowledge of the organisation, which is to say, reliability means providing the service correctly from the first moment (Own translation).[67]

Thus, the reliability of energy services would be the consumers' trust in the energy service provider.

The legally binding Framework Convention on Climate Change will be analysed to continue the analysis of the international legal order. This convention was approved at the United Nations Climate Change Conference held in 2015. Its preamble recognises the need to promote access to energy from renewable sources.

> Acknowledging the need to promote universal access to sustainable energy in developing countries, in particular in Africa, through the enhanced deployment of renewable energy (…).[68]

This statement is not an isolated phenomenon. It aligns the right to energy with the framework of sustainable development. This new vision is developed based on the SDGs contained in the non-legally binding 2030 Agenda.

SDG #7 strengthens the commitment of states to guarantee the right to energy. It was declared as a priority:

> Ensure access to affordable, reliable, sustainable and modern energy for all.[69]

Within this framework, five targets to be achieved by 2030 are declared. The first of these targets is to ensure universal access to affordable, reliable, and modern energy services. This target builds on the spirit of SDG #7 and sets out basic principles that should, therefore, underpin the right to energy, such as affordability, reliability, and modernity.

The second aims to increase the share of renewable sources in energy generation. The third aims at improving energy efficiency. In addition, the fourth goal is to increase international cooperation to facilitate access to clean energy research and technology. The fifth goal is to expand infrastructure and improve technology to provide energy services.

After analysing international legal instruments, this research concludes that the right to energy is not yet widely recognised. Nevertheless, the Convention on the Elimination of All Forms of Discrimination against Women, the Universal

[66] Boardman (1991), p. 199–207.

[67] Duque (2005), p. 69.

[68] Organización de Naciones Unidas (2015).

[69] Comisión Económica para América Latina y el Caribe (2016).

Declaration of Emerging Human Rights and the 2030 Agenda can be examples of recognition and protection of the right to energy. Nevertheless, the right to energy suffers from the same vulnerability as other economic, social, and cultural rights, as it is mostly supported by soft law that does not legally bind states to its fulfilment. This context has been the result of human rights remaining as "an à la carte device".[70]

However, all the regulations analysed result from international political dialogue and the commitment of States, which promote the realisation of the right to energy, without which it would be impossible to achieve many of the goals they pursued. For this reason, in the following section, it is necessary to assess the regional legal instruments that offer protection and recognition of the right to energy. The analysis will begin within the European Union.

3.2 The Right to Energy in the European Regional Framework

The first instrument to consider is the European Charter of Fundamental Rights with legally binding force. This regional regulation does not expressly recognise the right to energy. However, Article 36 of the Charter establishes the right to access services of general economic interest.[71] Services of general economic interest are defined as:

> Services of an economic nature which the Member States or the Community subject to specific public service obligations by virtue of a general interest criterion. The concept of services of general economic interest thus covers in particular certain services provided by the big network industries such as transport, postal services, energy, and communications. However, the term also extends to any other economic activity subject to public service obligations.[72]

In this way, the European Commission determined that public energy services provide services of general economic interest and are therefore assigned universal service obligations.[73] However, following the liberalisation of the EU energy market, energy services have fallen into a regulatory limbo, with Member States being responsible for their organisation and provision. In this sense, public service obligations have been affected by the privatisation of the European energy sector, imposing a vision of consumer protection that restricts the fundamental rights approach to access to services of general economic interest.

Within that context, the European Union's standard-setting instrument that set a precedent for the right to energy was the European Charter for Energy Consumers.

---

[70] Gutwirth and De Hert (2021), p. 432.

[71] Access to services of general economic interest. The Union recognises and respects access to services of general economic interest as provided for in national laws and practices, in accordance with the Treaty establishing the European Community, in order to promote the social and territorial cohesion of the Union. Parlamento Europeo, Consejo Europeo, and Comisión Europea (2000).

[72] Comisión de las Comunidades Europeas (2003).

[73] Aviles (2012); Koukiadaki (2012), p. 2; Clifton et al. (2005), p. 422.

Despite lacking binding force, this initiative is based on recognising energy as a critical element for participation in economic and social life. On this basis, the European Energy Consumers' Charter calls on Member States to strengthen their consumers' protection and guarantee and respect their rights. Among the provisions concerning access to transmission, distribution, and supply networks, it calls for guaranteeing freedom of choice of supplier, the right to connection, transparent, non-discriminatory, clearly comparable prices based on actual consumption, and disconnection as a last resort in the event of non-payment.[74]

The European Energy Consumers' Charter also calls on Member States to:

> Ensure the protection of universal rights, especially in terms of access to energy for different social, economic and regional groups, through stability and security of supply, as well as network efficiency.[75]

At the same time, transparency in the energy consumption process is promoted, considering the flow of information from the contracting process, the deductible tariffs, and energy sources used for energy generation, among many others. In the articles of the European Energy Consumers' Charter, the Member States are called upon to create procedures accessible to energy consumers for handling complaints and for alternative dispute resolution. The role of ombudspersons and consumer organisations in safeguarding the rights of energy consumers is recognised. In this framework, the European Energy Consumers' Charter calls on Member States to guarantee the powers of ombudspersons in dealing with energy-related issues and to ensure that consumer organisations have the necessary resources to function.[76]

Later, in 2017, the EU Pillar of Social Rights was established as a policy instrument designed to guide 'efficient employment and social outcomes when responding to current and future challenges which are directly aimed at fulfilling people's essential needs, and towards ensuring better enactment and implementation of social rights'.[77] Although these guidelines are not legally binding, they represent a step forward in recognising the right to energy. In this regard, Chapter 3 on social protection and inclusion recognises the universal right of access to essential services of good quality, including energy services. In this respect, the EU Pillar of Social Rights highlights accessibility and affordability as essential elements of the right to energy, particularly for 'people in need'.[78] In this way, these policy guidelines promote the reduction of energy poverty in the European Union.[79]

Subsequently, with Directive (EU) 2019/944,[80] the internal electricity market was perfected because of this sector's profound changes. Among other elements, it

---

74 Parlamento Europeo (2009).

75 Parlamento Europeo (2009), p. 3.

76 Parlamento Europeo (2009), p. 6.

77 European Union 2017, p. 8.

78 Ibid., 22.

79 Luis Cordova 2025, pp. 30–31.

80 According to article 288 TFEU, EU Directives "directive shall be binding, as to the result to be achieved, upon each Member State to which it is addressed, but shall leave to the national authori-

establishes the rules for protecting electricity consumers and establishes flexibility, fairness, and transparency as guiding principles.

The aim of the Directive (EU) 2019/944 is to ensure affordable energy prices and costs for consumers, as well as the security of supply and energy transition. It establishes the consumer's free choice of supplier and the possibility of having more than one electricity supply contract.

Member States are given the responsibility to ensure the protection of consumers in situations of energy poverty and vulnerability. To this end, Member States can intervene in setting prices when this situation arises. It is established that the obligations imposed by the States on the service may be related to:

> Security, including the security of supply, regularity, quality and price of supplies and environmental protection, including energy efficiency, energy from renewable sources and climate protection. Such obligations shall be clearly defined, transparent, non-discriminatory, and verifiable, and shall guarantee equality of access for electricity undertakings of the Union to national consumers.[81]

Chapter III, Consumer Empowerment and Protection, sets out basic contractual rights. From the formulation of this chapter, the content of the right to energy is framed as part of these contractual rights. Elements of the supply contract are regulated in this respect, such as the obligation to give prior notice of changes to the terms and conditions and the right to terminate the contract.[82]

Moreover, it also establishes the obligation of the supplier to provide consumers with transparent information on prices, tariffs, and general conditions applicable to access and use of electricity services. It states the free choice of payment method, the right to a satisfactory level of service, the right to lodge complaints, and the right to out-of-court settlement of disputes, among others.[83]

In addition, Articles 28 and 29 contain specific regulations for protecting consumers in situations of vulnerability or energy poverty. Although the EU directives are not mandatory, they constitute a methodological guide for the member states, which will be discussed later.[84]

The European Convention on Human Rights does not expressly refer to the right to energy. Nevertheless, this right is protected under the protective spectrum of the rights declared in this instrument, such as the right to life and the right to education.[85] This trend is evident in other legal instruments analysed so far.

The EU's regional regulatory framework does not explicitly address the right to energy. An extensive and complex legal system offers a protective framework with legal and material guarantees for this right. Despite this, the right to energy is framed

---

ties the choice of form and methods." European Union (2012).

[81] Cf. Article 9. European Parliament and European Council (2019).

[82] Cf. Article 10. European Parliament and European Council (2019).

[83] Cf. Article 10. European Parliament and European Council (2019)

[84] Cf. infra, Chapter 4.

[85] Cf. Article 1 of the Convention, on the right to life. Article 2 of the Additional Protocol, on the right to education. Consejo Europeo (2021).

as a consumer right without being expressly considered at the regional level as a fundamental right.

3.3 The Right to Energy in the Latin American Regional Framework

There are four legal instruments to consider in the Latin American regional context regarding the right to energy. Following a chronological order, the first to be analysed is the 1978 American Convention on Human Rights or Pact of San José, Costa Rica.[86] Although this Pact does not expressly recognise the right to energy, it offers a protective aura from Article 26.

> Article 26. The States Parties undertake to take steps, both internally and through international co-operation, especially economic and technical, to achieve progressively the full realisation of the rights deriving from the economic, social, educational, scientific and cultural standards contained in the Charter of the Organisation of American States, as amended by the Protocol of Buenos Aires, within available resources, by legislation or other appropriate means.[87]

In this sense, the spirit of this article enshrines the commitment of States to developing economic, social, and cultural rights. In this way, the Pact of San José de Costa Rica declares the principle of progressivity, which influences the realisation of socio-economic rights, the right to energy being part of this group.[88] However, the inclusion of the right to energy among socio-economic rights does not imply its categorical and strict affirmation as a second-generation human right. Although the right to energy could be exercised individually, it could also be exercised collectively (third generation of human rights),[89] depending on its legal configuration. For this reason, this study does not take a position on framing the right to energy within the currently criticised classification[90] of human rights generations[91] but reaffirms

[86] The legally binding nature of the American Declaration of Human Rights is subject to ratification by States Parties. Cf. OEA (2006).

[87] Organización de Estados Americanos (1978).

[88] Cf. Walker (2016), p. 1, Graham (2010), Odeku and Gundani (2017), Hesselman (2016), and Tocqué and Rivoalan (2015), p. 22.

[89] Košir and Lakshminarayanan (2021), p. 2.

[90] Domaradzki et al. (2019).

[91] The division of human rights into three generations is attributed to Karel Vasak. He describes the following human rights generations:

> The first-generation concerns "negative" rights, in the sense that their respect requires that the state do nothing to interfere with individual liberties and correspond roughly to the civil and political rights. The second generation, on the other hand, requires positive action by the state to be implemented, as is the case with most social, economic, and cultural rights. The international community is now embarking upon a third generation of human rights which may be called "rights of solidarity" (…) Since these rights reflect a certain concep-

its status as a socio-economic right, the enforceability of which could be exercised individually or collectively.

Because of the Pact of San José, its additional protocol was adopted: El Protocolo del Salvador[92] Its postulates contain several provisions that indirectly protect the right to energy. An example is the right to work, where energy is a prerequisite for satisfactory conditions in the working environment. Within the right-to-work framework, limits to the right to strike are declared when it may affect essential public services, including energy services. The right to a healthy environment deserves special attention in Article 11, which recognises the right to essential public services, including energy services.

> Article 11. Everyone has the right to live in a healthy environment and to have access to basic public services (Own translation).[93]

In 2007, the Declaration of Panama: Energy for Sustainable Development was issued. This instrument recognises the importance of access to energy for economic and social development. In this context, the Declaration highlights the requirements that should characterise access to energy. These requirements include diversification of energy supply, reliability, security, and affordability. Such pronouncements encompass cardinal elements that underpin the right to energy for its configuration in the Americas.

> Recognizing that energy is an essential resource for sustainable development of peoples, and that access to energy that is diverse, reliable, secure, and affordable is of paramount importance to economic growth with equity and social inclusion and contributes to poverty eradication.[94]

At the same time, the Declaration of Panama[95] mandates Member States to increase the coverage of energy services for social development. In this Declaration, Member States commit themselves to developing and investing in energy infrastructure to ensure the availability of energy resources, access to energy and the protection of both elements.[96]

Within this framework, emphasis is placed on the need to use renewable sources to meet present energy demand without compromising the interests of future

---

> tion of community life, they can only be implemented by the combined efforts of everyone: individuals, states, and other bodies, as well as public and private institutions.

Vasak (1977), p. 29.

[92] El Protocolo del Salvador is legally binding on States Parties that have signed and ratified it. Cf. OEA (2023).

[93] Cf. Articles 7, 8.2, 11 and 12. Organización de Estados Americanos (1988).

[94] Organización de Estados Americanos (2007).

[95] According to the guidelines of the Inter-American Juridical Committee on Binding and Non-Binding Treaties, the Panama Declaration is a political commitment of the States Parties without binding legal force. OEA (2021).

[96] Cf. Para. 9. Organización de Estados Americanos (2007).

generations. In this way, intergenerational equity is pursued to satisfy energy needs and promote energy justice.

In paragraph 14, the Panama Declaration recognises the determination of Member States to increase access to efficient energy services in the region.

> Their determination to increase access by citizens of the member states to efficient energy services; and to emphasize that the use of energy for household purposes and for small scale productive activities contributes to improving living conditions and fighting poverty.[97]

This paragraph emphasises the importance of energy use for domestic purposes and small-scale productive activities, which contributes to the improvement of living conditions and the fight against poverty. Although there is no recognition of the right to energy per se, the political will of the member states for its materialisation is clear.

Two years later, in 2009, the Joint Declaration of the VII Summit of the Bolivarian Alliance for the Peoples of Our America—Peoples' Trade Treaty (ALBA—TCP)[98] was adopted. In it, essential postulates of the right to energy were considered.

> 13. In order to generate a real change in access to energy in the world, particularly in developing countries, it is essential to make efforts for cooperation, complementation, and regional integration, in the development of energy efficiency models in generation, transmission and consumption, as well as in the development of renewable energies, guaranteeing access to services for the entire population.
>
> 14. Access to energy is a right of peoples that States must guarantee by strengthening their public policies, defending the right of peoples to their national natural resources, and seeking alternative energy sources, ensuring conservation and development in harmony with nature (Own translation).[99]

Point 13 declares the will of the member states to deepen cooperation, complementation, and regional integration for the development of energy-efficient models in generation, transmission, and consumption, as well as the development of renewable energy sources, guaranteeing the population's access to these services. Point 14 expressly recognises the right to energy as a people's right. It establishes the need for its protection through public policies, the defence of people's right to their natural resources and the constant search for alternative energy sources.

3.4 Conclusion

Throughout the analysis of the historical evolution of the right to energy in the international framework, since the Universal Declaration of Human Rights, there has been a growing interest of the international community in recognising and

[97] Cf. Para. 14. Organización de Estados Americanos (2007).

[98] The ALBA-TCP declarations have no binding force as they are only used as guidelines for decision-making in the member states.

[99] ALBA-TCP (2009).

protecting the right to energy. Although some international legal instruments do not expressly recognise the right to energy, it is protected through the principles of indivisibility, interdependence, and interrelatedness of human rights.

The most remote antecedent of the right to energy is the Convention on the Elimination of All Forms of Discrimination against Women, which includes access to electricity as a right and the first manifestation of the right under study. This normative instrument marked a turning point in recognising the right to energy. From the study carried out, it was found that, before this international legal instrument, there was no other express reference to the right to energy, so its protection was framed in extensive interpretations.

Nevertheless, this legal instrument adopts a restrictive approach to the right in question. Although much remains to be done to improve the international order in the light of the right to energy, it can be seen in the regional frameworks analysed that concrete actions have been developed from the normative point of view for its protection. In the European regional framework, the right to energy is protected through the figure of the energy consumer, while the EU Pillar on Social Rights advocates for an universal right to energy. This right is also recognised as part of the right to access services of general economic interest. The European Union legally reinforces this protection on the rights of energy consumers and Directive 2019/944. In the Latin American regional framework, there is an express recognition of the right to energy as a fundamental right, from which the full realisation of the human rights that depend on it derives.

Based on the analysis of the normative treatment that the right to energy has received in international legal instruments, it is necessary to develop a study of national legal frameworks. In this way, it will be possible to identify the main trends in the positivisation of the right to energy.

References[100]

Acuña Zepeda MS, Díaz Zepeda JE (2017) Energy and human rights: a perspective from Mexico. J Energy Nat Resour Law 35(4):377–380. https://doi.org/10.1080/02646811.2017.1355512

ALBA-TCP (2009) Declaración Conjunta de la Alianza Bolivariana para los Pueblos de Nuestra América—Tratado de Comercio de los Pueblos. Cochabamba. https://www.albatcp.org/acta/declaracion-conjunta-5/. Accessed 28 Feb 2025

Aviles LA (2012) Electric energy access in European law: a human right? SSRN Electr J 217(2008):1–8. http://www.ssrn.com/abstract=2008887. Accessed 28 Feb 2025

Boardman B (1991) Fuel poverty: from cold homes to affordable warmth. Belhaven Press. https://biblio.vub.ac.be/iguana/www.main.cls?surl=search&p=f88fe9ec-2425-11e7-a7e4-90084dd7a2c4#recordId=3.240219. Accessed 28 Feb 2025

Bradbrook AJ, Gardam JG (2006) Placing the access to energy services within a human rights framework. Hum Rights Quart 28(2):389–415. https://www.jstor.org/stable/pdf/20072742.pdf?refreqid=excelsior%3A43476d5b7137fdcb80d186deeef37e29&ab_segments=&origin=&acceptTC=1. Accessed 28 Feb 2025

[100] All links to the cited websites were operational as of 28 February 2025.

Chueca R (2015) Dignidad humana y derecho fundamental. In: Estudios Constitucionales Madrid: Centro de Estudios Políticos y Constitucionales. https://www.researchgate.net/profile/Ricardo-Chueca/publication/277715654_Dignidad_humana_y_derecho_fundamental/links/5bc37c7d299bf1004c5f371c/Dignidad-humana-y-derecho-fundamental.pdf. Accessed 28 Feb 2025.

Clifton J, Comín F, Díaz Fuentes D (2005) 'Empowering Europe's citizens'? Towards a charter for services of general interest. Public Manag Rev 7(3):417–443. http://www.tandfonline.com/doi/abs/10.1080/14719030500181052. Accessed 28 Feb 2025

Comisión de las Comunidades Europeas (2003) Libro Verde sobre los Servicios de Interés General. Bruselas. https://eur-lex.europa.eu/legal-content/ES/TXT/PDF/?uri=CELEX:52003DC0270&from=EN. Accessed 28 Feb 2025

Comisión Económica para América Latina y el Caribe (2016) Agenda 2030 y los Objetivos de Desarrollo Sostenible Una oportunidad para América Latina y el Caribe. Organización de Naciones Unidas. https://repositorio.cepal.org/bitstream/handle/11362/40155/24/S1801141_es.pdf. Accessed 28 Feb 2025

Consejo Europeo (2021) Convenio Europeo de Derechos Humanos. https://www.echr.coe.int/documents/convention_spa.pdf. Accessed 28 Feb 2025

Domaradzki S, Khvostova M, Pupovac D (2019) Karel Vasak's generations of rights and the contemporary human rights discourse. Human Rights Review 20(4):423–443. https://link.springer.com/article/10.1007/s12142-019-00565-x. Accessed 28 Feb 2025

Duque E (2005) Del Servicio Y Sus Modelos De Medición. Rev Innovar 15(25):64–80. https://www.redalyc.org/pdf/818/81802505.pdf. Accessed 28 Feb 2025

Durán R, Condorí M (2015) El acceso a la energía desde la óptica de los derechos humanos. Su medición y relación con el acceso a otros derechos elementales en Salta, Argentina. Avances Energías Renovables Medio Ambiente 19:57–67. https://sedici.unlp.edu.ar/bitstream/handle/10915/143520/Documento_completo.pdf-PDFA.pdf?sequence=1. Accessed 28 Feb 2025

European Parliament, European Council (2019) Directive 2019/944 on common rules for the internal market for electricity and amending Directive 2012/27/EU. Official Journal of the European Union, Brussels. https://eur-lex.europa.eu/legal-content/EN/TXT/PDF/?uri=CELEX:32019L0944&from=EN. Accessed 28 Feb 2025

European Union (2012) Consolidated version of the Treaty on the Functioning of the European Union. Official Journal of European Union. https://eur-lex.europa.eu/legal-content/EN/TXT/PDF/?uri=CELEX:12012E/TXT. Accessed 28 Feb 2025

European Union (2017) European Pillar of Social Rights. European Commission. https://commission.europa.eu/publications/european-pillar-social-rights-booklet_en

Frank DA, Neault NB, Skalicky A, Cook JT, Wilson JD, Levenson S, Meyers AF, Heeren T, Cutts DB, Casey PH, Black MM, Berkowitz C (2006) Heat or eat: the low income home energy assistance program and nutritional and health risks among children less than 3 years of age. Pediatrics 118(5):e1293–e1302. https://publications.aap.org/pediatrics/article-abstract/118/5/e1293/69884/Heat-or-Eat-The-Low-Income-Home-Energy-Assistance?redirectedFrom=fulltext. Accessed 28 Feb 2025

Garcia M, Mundó J (2014) La energía como derecho. Cómo afrontar la pobreza energética. Taula d'entitats del Tercer Sector Social de Catalunya, Barcelona, España. https://www.tercersector.cat/sites/default/files/dossier_la_energia_como_derecho._como_afrontar_la_pobreza_energetica.pdf. Accessed 28 Feb 2025

Gómez Bengoechea B (2023) La luz y la energía como derecho fundamental: el caso de los niños de la Cañada Real. Aposta Rev Ciencias Soc 97:42–62. http://www.apostadigital.com/revistav3/hemeroteca/blancagomez.pdf. Accessed 28 Feb 2025

Graham C (2010) Socio-economic rights and essential services: a new challenge for the regulatory state. In: The regulatory state: constitutional implications. Oxford University Press, Oxford, pp 157–177. https://academic.oup.com/book/8885/chapter/155139497. Accessed 28 Feb 2025

Gutwirth S, De Hert P (2021) Human rights: a secular religion with legal crowbars. From Europe with hesitations. Natl Law School India Rev 33(2):420–462. https://repository.nls.ac.in/nlsir/vol33/iss2/9. Accessed 28 Feb 2025

Hernández D (2016) Understanding 'energy insecurity' and why it matters to health. Soc Sci Med 167:1–10. https://www.sciencedirect.com/science/article/pii/S0277953616304658. Accessed 28 Feb 2025

Hesselman M (2016) Socio-economic human rights in essential public services provision. Human Rights and International Law. Abingdon, Oxon [UK]; New York: Routledge, 2017. |: Routledge. https://www.taylorfrancis.com/books/9781315618081. Accessed 28 Feb 2025

Hettinga S, Boter J, Dias E, Fruijtier S, de Vogel B, Scholten H (2021) Urban energy transition in a gaming context: The role of children. Land Use Policy 111(October 2019):104903. doi:https://doi.org/10.1016/j.landusepol.2020.104903. Accessed 28 Feb 2025

Hughes G (2011) The concept of dignity in the universal declaration of human rights. J Relig Ethics 39(1):1–24. https://www.jstor.org/stable/pdf/23020122.pdf. Accessed 28 Feb 2025

Human Rights Council (2022) Commentary on article 1 (1) of the Declaration on the Right to Development. First draft of the Chair for initial discussion at the fifth session. United Nations. https://www.ohchr.org/sites/default/files/2022-03/A_HRC_EMRTD_5_CRP1.pdf#:~:text=In. Accessed 28 Feb 2025

Indigenous Peoples Major Group (2018) Doing it right! Sustainable energy and indigenous peoples. https://www.indigenouspeoples-sdg.org/index.php/english/all-resources/ipmg-position-papers-and-publications/ipmg-submission-interventions/83-doing-it-right-sustainable-energy-and-indigenous-peoples/file. Accessed 28 Feb 2025

Institut de Drets Humans de Catalunya (2010) Declaración Universal de los Derechos Humanos Emergentes. Barcelona, España. https://catedraunescodh.unam.mx/catedra/CONACYT/04_Docentes_UdeO_ubicar_el_de_alumnos/Contenidos/Lecturas obligatorias/M.5_cont_3_DUDHE.pdf. Accessed 28 Feb 2025

Kawalec A, Pawlas K (2020) Home environment and burns in children. Burns Open 4(4):167–175. doi:https://doi.org/10.1016/j.burnso.2020.05.006. Accessed 28 Feb 2025

Košir S, Lakshminarayanan R (2021) Inclusion of 'generations of human rights' in social science textbooks. Int J Educ Dev 80(October 2020):102295. https://linkinghub.elsevier.com/retrieve/pii/S0738059320304545. Accessed 28 Feb 2025

Koukiadaki A (2012) EU governance and social services of general interest: when even the UK is concerned. EIOP Eur Integr Online Papers 16(1):1–21. http://eiop.or.at/eiop/pdf/2012-005.pdf. Accessed 28 Feb 2025

Krope T, Krope J (2007) Liberalising energy in Europe: public service obligations in the energy sector. In: Krope J, Garbai L, Kozic D, Goricanec Portoroz D (ed) IASME/WSEAS international conference on energy & environment. http://www.wseas.us/e-library/conferences/2007portoroz/papers/555-165.pdf. Accessed 28 Feb 2025

Luis Cordova JG (2025) Energy and sustainability: integrating a rights perspective in EU energy law and policy. In: Tiche F, Squintani L, de Graaf K, Vedder H, Woerdman E, Sustainable energy: still united in diversity? Integrating energy, climate and environmental law in times of geopolitical instability. University of Groningen Press, Groningen, pp 23–48. doi:https://doi.org/10.21827/697ca31999bd0. Accessed 12 December 2025

Maritain J (1944) The rights of man and natural law. The Centenary Press, London. https://archive.org/details/in.ernet.dli.2015.76201/page/n9/mode/2up. Accessed 28 Feb 2025

Maritain J (1951) Man and the state. University of Chicago Press, Chicago. https://archive.org/details/manstate00mari/page/n9/mode/2up. Accessed 28 Feb 2025

Mayer A, Smith EK (2019) Exploring the link between energy security and subjective well-being: a study of 22 nations. Energy Sustain Soc 9(1):34. https://energsustainsoc.biomedcentral.com/articles/10.1186/s13705-019-0216-1. Accessed 28 Feb 2025

McCrudden C (2008) Human dignity and judicial interpretation of human rights. Eur J Int Law 19(4):655–724. https://academic.oup.com/ejil/article-lookup/doi/10.1093/ejil/chn043. Accessed 28 Feb 2025

Nord M, Kantor LS (2006) Seasonal variation in food insecurity is associated with heating and cooling costs among low-income elderly Americans. J Nutr 136(11):2939–2944. https://www.sciencedirect.com/science/article/pii/S0022316622085509. Accessed 28 Feb 2025

Odeku KO, Gundani SR (2017) Ensuring affordable electricity as a vital socio-economic right in South Africa. Probl Perspect Manag 15(3):334–342. https://businessperspectives.org/journals/problems-and-perspectives-in-management/issue-258/ensuring-affordable-electricity-as-a-vital-socio-economic-right-in-south-africa. Accessed 28 Feb 2025

OEA (2006) Ratificaciones de la Convención Americana Sobre Derechos Humanos o Pacto de San José de Costa Rica. Organización de Estados Americanos, Washington, DC. https://www.cidh.oas.org/annualrep/2006eng/ANNEXES/1.Ratifications.pdf. Accessed 28 Feb 2025

OEA (2021) Directrices del Comité Jurídico Interamericano para los Acuerdos Vinculantes y No Vinculantes. Organización de Estados Americanos. https://www.oas.org/es/sla/cji/docs/informes_culminados_recientemente_Acuerdos_Vinculantes_y_No_Vinculantes_DIRECTRICES.pdf. Accessed 28 Feb 2025

OEA (2023) Acerca del Protocolo. Protocolo de San Salvador. https://www.oas.org/es/sadye/inclusion-social/protocolo-ssv/docs/protocolo-san-salvador-es.pdf. Accessed 28 Feb 2025

Organización de Estados Americanos (1978) Convención Americana sobre Derechos Humanos o Pacto de San José de Costa Rica. Tratados multilaterales interamericanos. http://www.oas.org/dil/esp/tratados_B-32_Convencion_Americana_sobre_Derechos_Humanos.pdf. Accessed 28 Feb 2025

Organización de Estados Americanos (1988) Protocolo Adicional a la Convención Américana sobre Derechos Humanos en Materia de Derechos Económicos, Sociales y Culturales o Protocolo del Salvador. Tratados multilaterales interamericanos. https://www.oas.org/dil/esp/protocolo_de_san_salvador_1988.pdf. Accessed 28 Feb 2025

Organización de Estados Americanos (2007) Declaration of Panama: energy for sustainable future. Ciudad de Panamá. https://www.oas.org/dsd/Documents/DECLARATION%20OF%20PANAMA.pdf. Accessed 28 Feb 2025

Organización de Naciones Unidas (1948) Declaración Universal de los Derechos Humanos. https://www.ohchr.org/sites/default/files/UDHR/Documents/UDHR_Translations/spn.pdf. Accessed 28 Feb 2025

Organización de Naciones Unidas (1972) Informe de la Conferencia de Naciones Unidas sobre el Medio Humano. Nueva York. https://documents-dds-ny.un.org/doc/UNDOC/GEN/N73/039/07/PDF/N7303907.pdf?OpenElement. Accessed 28 Feb 2025

Organización de Naciones Unidas (1976) Pacto Internacional de Derechos Económicos, Sociales y Culturales. https://www.ohchr.org/es/instruments-mechanisms/instruments/international-covenant-economic-social-and-cultural-rights. Accessed 28 Feb 2025

Organización de Naciones Unidas (1979) Convention on the elimination of all forms of discrimination against women. Oficina del Alto Comicionado para los Derechos Humanos. https://www.ohchr.org/en/instruments-mechanisms/instruments/convention-elimination-all-forms-discrimination-against-women. Accessed 28 Feb 2025

Organización de Naciones Unidas (1986) Declaración de las Naciones Unidas sobre el Derecho al Desarrollo. https://www.ohchr.org/sites/default/files/Documents/Issues/Development/RTD_booklet_sp.pdf. Accessed 28 Feb 2025

Organización de Naciones Unidas (1989) Convention on the rights of the child. https://www.ohchr.org/sites/default/files/crc.pdf. Accessed 28 Feb 2025

Organización de Naciones Unidas (2007) Declaración de las Naciones Unidas sobre los Derechos de los Pueblos Indígenas. https://www.un.org/development/desa/indigenouspeoples/wp-content/uploads/sites/19/2018/11/UNDRIP_S_web.pdf. Accessed 28 Feb 2025

Organización de Naciones Unidas (2015) Convención Marco sobre el Cambio Climático. Organización de Naciones Unidas. https://documents-dds-ny.un.org/doc/UNDOC/LTD/G15/283/22/PDF/G1528322.pdf?OpenElement. Accessed 28 Feb 2025

Pacheco-Zerga L (2008) WHAT. In: Universidad Católica Santo Toribio de Mogrovejo (ed) 60 años de la Declaración Universal de los Derechos Humanos: Jornadas Universitarias, pp 9–30.

https://www.usat.edu.pe/biblioteca-tienda/jornadas-universitarias-60-anos-de-la-declaracion-universal-de-los-derechos-humanos/. Accessed 28 Feb 2025

Parlamento Europeo (2009) Carta Europea de los Derechos de los Consumidores de Energía. Diario Oficial de la Unión Europea. https://eur-lex.europa.eu/legal-content/ES/TXT/PDF/?uri=CELEX:52008IP0306. Accessed 28 Feb 202.

Parlamento Europeo, Consejo Europeo, Comisión Europea (2000) Carta de los Derechos Fundamentales de la Unión Europea. In: La Europa que viene: el Tratado de Lisboa, pp 405–412. Marcial Pons, ediciones jurídicas y sociales. https://www.europarl.europa.eu/charter/pdf/text_es.pdf. Accessed 28 Feb 2025

Rao ND, Min J (2018) Decent Living standards: material prerequisites for human wellbeing. Soc Indicators Res 138(1):225–244. http://link.springer.com/10.1007/s11205-017-1650-0. Accessed 28 Feb 2025

Solis, MPS (2014) From Right to light: a human rights-based approach to universal access to modern energy services. Adelaide University. https://digital.library.adelaide.edu.au/dspace/bitstream/2440/92548/3/02whole.pdf. Accessed 28 Feb 2025

Solis, MPS (2018) Legal perspectives on a human rights-based approach to energy access in the Philippines. Ateneo LJ 62(3):669. https://papers.ssrn.com/sol3/papers.cfm?abstract_id=3280057. Accessed 28 Feb 2025

The Secretary-General's Advisory Group on Energy and Climate Change (2010) Energy for a sustainable future. United Nations, New York. https://www.undp.org/sites/g/files/zskgke326/files/publications/AGECCsummaryreport.pdf. Accessed 28 Feb 2025

Tocqué F, Rivoalan S (2015) Droit à l'énergie, progrès ou illusion? Projet 344(1):19. http://www.cairn.info/revue-projet-2015-1-page-19.htm. Accessed 28 Feb 2025

UN (2023) UN treaty body database. United Nations Human Rights Treaty Bodies. https://tbinternet.ohchr.org/_layouts/15/TreatyBodyExternal/Treaty.aspx?Treaty=CESCR. Accessed 28 Feb 2025

UNICEF (2023) How the convention on the rights of the child works. Convention on the rights of the child. https://www.unicef.org/child-rights-convention/how-convention-works. Accessed 28 Feb 2025

Vasak K (1977) A thirty-year struggle: the sustained efforts to give force of law to the universal declaration of human rights. In: UNESCO courier. UNESCO, Paris, pp 29–32. https://unesdoc.unesco.org/in/rest/annotationSVC/DownloadWatermarkedAttachment/attach_import_61f5bf04-1c56-4086-a9a2-c38fe56dc62e?_=074816engo.pdf&to=36&from=1#pdfjs.action=download. Accessed 28 Feb 2025

Vashchenko Y (2021) Access to modern energy services through the prism of children's rights: an overview from the perspectives of the convention on the rights of the child and the policy and law approaches of certain EU Member States and Ukraine. Int Compar Jurisprudence 7(1):75–87. https://ojs.mruni.eu/ojs/international-comparative-jurisprudence/article/view/6568. Accessed 28 Feb 2025

Walker G (2016) The right to energy: meaning, specification and the politics of definition. L'Europe Form 378(4):26–38. https://www.cairn.info/revue-l-europe-en-formation-2015-4-page-26.htm?ref=doi. Accessed 28 Feb 2025

Zegarra Valdivia D (2012) Del Servicio Público a los servicios de interés general: la evolución del service public en el sistema. Circ Derecho Admin 12:13–43. https://dialnet.unirioja.es/descarga/articulo/7810135.pdf. Accessed 28 Feb 2025

Chapter 4
Trends in the Constitutional Positivisation of the Right to Energy

4.1 Introduction

From the analysis of the historical evolution of the right to energy at the international level, it can be seen that it has been gaining maturity over time. This trend has directly impacted national legal systems as states have become aware of it. The need for energy for the functioning of society and even the state has prompted the adoption of political, regulatory, and practical measures.

Several approaches to recognising and protecting the right to energy have been identified at the State level. For this analysis, the Constitutions of Latin American and European countries with promising results were chosen according to the indicators of the implementation of SDG #7.[1] In the didactic organisation of these constitutional bodies, this research will present the approaches taken to the right to energy in four main trends: the first: indirect protection of the right to energy; the second: protection of the right to energy in the framework of consumer rights; the third: recognition of energy as a fundamental need; and the fourth: the express recognition of the right to energy as a fundamental right.

Despite this didactic organisation, these trends are not mutually exclusive, but there are points of contact between them in the Constitutions analysed. This distribution is due to the normative reinforcement offered to the content of each of the tendencies in the Constitutions under study. It is important to emphasise that these constitutional approaches to the right to energy do not originate from the regulatory spontaneity of the States but are consistent with international and regional legal dynamics.

---

[1] The indicators defined for monitoring by the custodian agencies are: Access to electricity, Access to clean cooking, Renewable energy, Energy efficiency, Renewable capacity per capita and International financial flows. International Energy Agency et al. (2023).

J. G. Luis Cordova, *Theoretical and Legal Dimensions of the Right to Energy*, Economic and Financial Law & Policy – Shifting Insights & Values 9,
https://doi.org/10.1007/978-3-032-33252-3_4

4.2 Indirect Protection of the Right to Energy

Indirect protection of the right to energy is referred to when it depends on the legal system's recognition and protection of other fundamental rights. Based on the approach adopted in the Universal Declaration of Human Rights, recognising the rights declared in its normative body is presented as a mechanism for indirectly protecting the right to energy. The same is true of many of the legal instruments analysed so far.[2]

There are numerous examples of this approach in Latin American countries. In the Constitution of Belize, the recognition of constitutional rights is limited. There is no express declaration of the right to energy; only the preamble mentions human rights, so there is indirect constitutional support for the right to energy as a human right.[3] This constitutional support is reinforced by the recognition of dignity as a fundamental value, which cuts across human rights,[4] and therefore, it can be asserted that the right to energy has a place.[5]

The Constitution of El Salvador promotes sustainable development, both in the economic and social spheres, placing the person as the origin and end of the State's activity. The Salvadoran Constitution converts international treaties signed by El Salvador into laws of the Republic with their entry into force.[6] An example of this treaty is the Convention on the Elimination of All Forms of Discrimination against Women.[7]

The Constitution of Honduras promotes the fulfilment of individual, economic and social well-being through development. The materialisation of this statement would be impossible without the right to energy, considering it is a basic premise to guarantee development. Like El Salvador, the Honduran Constitution converts international treaties into domestic law only after Congress approves. Article 63 recognises that constitutionally defined declarations, rights, and guarantees do not negate other declarations, rights and guarantees that emanate from sovereignty and democracy, as well as human dignity.[8] This framework opens a spectrum of possibilities in which the right to energy can be embraced.

The Chilean Constitution does not expressly refer to the right to energy; it is subsumed in the recognised constitutional rights. The right to energy, in the Chilean constitutional body, is subsumed within the framework of the human rights contained in current international treaties that have been ratified by this nation. This phenomenon was brought about by Article 1 of the Constitutional Reform Law No. 18.825 of 1989, which modified Constitutional Article 5. Consequently, the Chilean State's

---

[2] Cf. already supra, Chap/ 3.

[3] Cf infra, Sect. 6.1.

[4] Mujica-Johnson and Orellana-Arduiz (2021).

[5] Cf. Article 3. Belize Constitution (2000).

[6] Cf. Articles 1, 101, 118, 114, 183. Constitución de la República de El Salvador (1983).

[7] Organización de Naciones Unidas (1979).

[8] Cf. Articles 1, 2, 16, 63, 151, 183. Constitución de la República de Honduras (1982).

organs were obliged to respect and promote the rights contained in those international treaties. Thus, the Chilean Constitution assumed, as the internal norm, international treaties such as the International Covenant on Civil and Political Rights, the International Covenant on Economic, Social and Cultural Rights and the American Convention on Human Rights. In this way, these human rights are considered fundamental rights. For this reason, the Chilean Constitution accepts the right to energy as a premise for the realisation of its constitutionally recognised human rights.[9]

In addition, within that framework, the right to petition recognised by this body of law can constitute a means of protection by providing a defence mechanism for the subjects of the right to energy in the field of energy services of a public nature.[10]

The Jamaican Constitution subsumed the right to energy under the recognised constitutional rights. Article 13 recognises the State's obligation to promote universal respect for and observance of human rights. In turn, recognising the right to enjoy a productive and healthy environment is closely interrelated with protecting the right to energy by promoting renewable sources.[11]

The Constitution of Guyana protects the right to energy through rights such as the right to the environment. In this regard, article 149, as part of the right to the environment, establishes the State's obligation to ensure sustainable development and the use of natural resources for economic and social development. The Constitution of Guyana, in turn, provides for the existence of the Office of the Ombudsman. The Ombudsman has jurisdiction in circumstances where any person has suffered injustice because of administrative action. Although this does not constitute a form of recognition, it creates a guarantee of realisation of the right under study through a competent body to represent the subjects of the right to energy vis-à-vis the providers of public energy services.[12]

The Puerto Rican Constitution establishes some assumptions that support the right to energy. Article 2 establishes human dignity as inviolable, as well as education and work, among other fundamental rights. As stated above, access to energy is a premise for guaranteeing other constitutional rights. Subsequently, article 19 establishes that the recognised constitutional rights are not exclusive of other rights belonging to the people, leaving the framework open for the inclusion of other rights, such as the right to energy.[13]

In the European context, there are States that adopt the same approach. The French Constitution states in its preamble that the nation ensures the individual and the family the conditions necessary for their development. These conditions include the right to energy, as a matter of general economic interest that enjoys protection.[14]

---

[9] Constitución Política de la República de Chile (2010).

[10] Constitución Política de la República de Chile (2010).

[11] Cf. Articles 13. The Constitution of Jamaica (1962).

[12] Cf. Articles 149, 191–196. Constitution of the Co-operative Republic of Guyana (2003).

[13] Constitución del Estado Libre Asociado de Puerto Rico (1952).

[14] Cf. already supra, pp. 66–67.

The German Constitution recognises, in Article 2, the right to free development of the personality, for which the satisfaction of energy demand is of utmost importance. Article 12 (2) provides a significant element for protecting energy services. It states that the exception to the prohibition of compulsory work is the proper performance of general public services, which includes energy services. Thus, the continuity of the energy supply would be safeguarded.[15]

The Norwegian Constitution declares the state administration responsible for respecting and guaranteeing human rights. The protection of the right to energy under a human rights approach is the alternative followed by this constitutional body.[16]

In the Belgian Constitution, the right to energy is protected by fundamental rights such as the right to a decent life and decent housing.[17] This alternative, followed in other legal systems, limits the content and scope of the right to energy, as only the satisfaction of basic needs within the scope of housing is protected.

The Italian Constitution does not expressly take sides in recognising and protecting the right to energy. Therefore, this right would find protection in the framework of other rights. An example of this is the right to work. In this respect, the Italian Constitution is designed to promote the existence of working conditions that make this right effective so that energy services would be included to guarantee such conditions.[18]

The Danish Constitution also provides some protection for the right to energy. An example is the right to work, which establishes the need for adequate working conditions. In turn, Article 76 recognises the right to education, a fundamental right that depends on energy services for its realisation.[19]

Indirect protection of the right to energy, through other fundamental rights, has been a trend in the legal systems analysed. Although such protection is not the product of express recognition, it offers some protection for the right to energy. The author considers this approach unfinished, given that protecting the right to energy would depend on other rights and would, therefore, be fragmented. In this context, creating the right to energy as a legal subsystem[20] is the way forward for legal systems.

---

[15] Cf. Articles 2 and 12.2. Grundgesetz für die Bundesrepublik Deutschland (1949).

[16] Kongeriket Noregs grunnlov (1814).

[17] Cf. Articles 22 and 23. De Belgische Grondwet (1994).

[18] Cf. Articles 4, 34. Costituzione italiana (1947).

[19] Cf. Articles 75, 76. Danmarks Riges Grundlov (1953).

[20] Cf. infra, citation 24, Sect. 6.1.

4.3 The Protection of the Right to Energy in the Framework of Users' or Consumers' Rights

Following the review of constitutional bodies, a second trend that stands out is protecting the right to energy within the consumer rights framework. Although consumer rights have had constitutional backing, this trend differs from the previous one because it is a more favourable framework for the right to energy, where the consumer figure has special prominence and protection.

Without claiming to deepen the categorical system of Consumer Law, this research considers the trend under analysis to be present in this research when the right to energy finds tutelary support in the framework of services.[21] Although there is a broad debate in the doctrine on the conceptual differentiation of the consumer, user and client categories, this research equates the terms to identify, from a single denomination (consumer), one of the subjects of the energy legal relationship.[22]

To begin the analysis, the Mexican Constitution is taken as a starting point,[23] from which it can be argued a priori that it enjoys indirect protection in the constitutional framework. However, a characteristic element of this body of law is that it attributes the character of public service to electricity, which implies that the subjects of the right to energy are the users or consumers of electricity. This element motivated the inclusion of this Constitution in the trend under analysis. Mexico's Basic Law also provides constitutional support for human rights and international treaties.[24] In this sense, the international legal framework has strengthened the right to energy. At first, tacitly, it was in the Universal Declaration of Human Rights[25] and the International Covenant on Economic, Social and Cultural Rights.[26] Subsequently, it was expressly protected, among other instruments, in the Convention on the Elimination of All Forms of Discrimination against Women[27] and in the sustainable development goals declared by the 2030 Agenda, starting with goal number 7 and its subsequent targets.[28]

The Mexican Constitution recognises universality, interdependence, indivisibility, and progressivity as principles. These principles also support the right to energy,

---

[21] Cf already supra, Chap. 4.

[22] Energy-legal relations are understood to be the social relations that arise in the context of the exploration, generation, distribution, storage, commercialisation, and consumption of energy. These types of social relations are regulated by energy law.

[23] Cf. Articles 1, 2, 4, 8, 15, 27. Constitución Política de los Estados Unidos Mexicanos (1917).

[24] Cf. Article 1: "In the United Mexican States all persons shall enjoy the human rights recognised in this Constitution and in the international treaties to which the Mexican State is a party, as well as the guarantees for their protection, the exercise of which may not be restricted or suspended, except in the cases and under the conditions established by this Constitution." Constitución Política de los Estados Unidos Mexicanos (1917).

[25] Organización de Naciones Unidas (1948).

[26] Asamblea General de la Organización de Naciones Unidas (1976).

[27] Organización de Naciones Unidas (1979).

[28] Comisión Económica para América Latina y el Caribe (2016).

considering that they guarantee the materialisation of other rights, such as the fundamental rights to education, health, adequate housing, and food, among many others supported by the constitutional body. In turn, Mexico's Constitution supports sustainable and integral development and the protection of renewable resources.

In Paraguay, the Constitution sets forth the possibility of individually or collectively claiming before public authorities measures to defend the rights of consumers, as well as the environment and health, among others, which by their legal nature belong to the community and are related to the quality of life and the collective patrimony. Such diffuse rights,[29] as they are called, open the spectrum so that the right to energy finds a place and protection in the legal system. The provision of energy is recognised as a competence of departmental governments.[30]

In Costa Rica, the Constitution promotes sustainable development and human dignity. However, Costa Rica's supreme law recognises the rights of consumers with constitutional status. In addition, through a constitutional mandate, the state will support consumer protection organisations. In this framework, energy consumers would be protected.[31]

The protection of the right to energy in the consumer rights framework is also reflected in the Panamanian constitutional order. Article 49 of the Constitution recognises the right to obtain quality services, as well as truthful, clear, and sufficient information on goods and services, freedom of choice, and fair and dignified treatment. The figure of the ombudsman and the right to petition are established as defence mechanisms for the protection of the fundamental rights and guarantees enshrined in the Constitution, as well as the rights provided for in international agreements. At the same time, constitutional rights and guarantees are declared as a minimum but not exclusive of others that affect fundamental rights and human dignity. Article 40 includes the right to make individual or collective petitions to the authorities, which means that the governing authorities of the energy sector are susceptible to receiving petitions from energy consumers.[32]

The right to energy in the Uruguayan constitutional framework is subsumed under the protection of public services. In this way, energy consumers are protected against the authorities or concessionaires that administer services of this nature, guaranteeing their continuity. The Uruguayan Constitution also provides for the right to petition, a trend prevalent in the rest of the region. This right is regulated in Article 30, which recognises the right of every inhabitant to petition all the authorities of the Republic. This provision opens the spectrum of complaints to the

[29] According to Elizalde Castañeda and Bonzo Morales Arzate, diffuse rights constitute interests of a supra-individual nature. These rights transcend the individual sphere of persons to be unified in the interest of the common good. The aforementioned diffuse rights protect the general or community interest. Elizalde Castañeda and Bonzo Morales Arzate (2018), pp. 30–32.

[30] Cf. Articles 38, 163. Constitución de Paraguay (2011).

[31] Cf. Articles 27, 46, 50, 56. Constitución Política de la República de Costa Rica (2009).

[32] Cf. Articles 17, 40, 49, 129. Constitución Política de la República de Panamá (2016).

competent authorities in the energy services field, thus establishing a tool for protecting the right to energy.[33]

The Guatemalan Constitution grants, ab initio, indirect protection to the right to energy, based on the recognition of rights such as education and health, as well as the promotion of integral development and the raising of the standard of living. Despite this, the protection of consumers or users stands out. The Guatemalan Basic Law recognises the country's electrification as a national urgency. This statement shows the government's interest in guaranteeing the right to energy.[34]

> Article 129. "Electrification. The electrification of the country shall be declared a national emergency, on the basis of plans drawn up by the State and the Municipalities, in which private initiative may participate." (Own translation)[35]

Colombia has also taken up the regional trend of protecting the right to energy through consumer rights. Colombia's supreme law regulates the judicial protection of these rights as a legal guarantee through a preferential and summary procedure. It also regulates the existence and action of consumer protection organisations.[36]

Principles such as dignity and general welfare protect the right to energy in the Venezuelan Constitution. The rights of users and consumers and the Ombudsman's Office are recognised with constitutional rank to watch over fundamental rights and guarantees. Like other legal systems, the Venezuelan Constitution incorporates the right to petition and the right of Amparo as protection mechanisms. Treaties, covenants, and conventions relating to human rights signed and ratified by Venezuela, are also recognised as having constitutional status.[37]

The Ecuadorian Constitution also assumes this approach, where the constitutional and human rights recognised in international instruments are directly applicable.[38] Concerning Ecuador's legal-constitutional system, it is crucial to highlight its consistency with SDG #7.[39] In this sense, renewable energy sources are promoted, both in the public and private sectors. The constitutional text orients economic and trade policy towards energy sovereignty, which will be analysed later.[40] At the same time, it makes the State responsible for the public electricity service and, within the framework of the right to work, it prohibits the paralysis of this service, which ensures the continuity of the energy supply.

In the Ecuadorian Constitutional context, there is an empowerment of the defence of users and consumers in Article 52. This article establishes all persons' right to access services of optimum quality, with freedom of choice. Reference is also made

---

[33] Cf. Articles 30, 45. Constitución de la República del Uruguay (2004).

[34] Cf. Articles 2, 28, 119. Constitución Política de la República de Guatemala (1986).

[35] Cf. Article 129. Constitución Política de la República de Guatemala (1986).

[36] Cf. Articles 16, 23, 78, 86. Constitución Política de Colombia (2016).

[37] Cf. Articles 1, 3, 20, 23, 23, 27, 30, 51, 75, 117, 178. Constitución de la República Bolivariana de Venezuela (2009).

[38] Cf. Articles 3, 15, 284, 304, 314, 326. Constitución de la República del Ecuador (2008).

[39] Comisión Económica para América Latina y el Caribe (2016).

[40] Cf. infra, Sect. 5.3.2.6.

to the right to receive accurate information. As protection mechanisms, the law regulates control mechanisms, as well as the defence of consumers, the establishment of sanctions for the infringement of consumer rights and the corresponding reparation and compensation for the damages caused by this type of behaviour. The interruption of public services is framed in this area, which protects the continuity and stability of energy services.[41]

In the case of Peru, the right to energy is not expressly recognised. The constitutional articles make local governments responsible for the provision of public services. This body of law constitutionally protects energy users and consumers. Chapter 11 recognises the institution of the Ombudsman's Office to defend the constitutional and fundamental rights of the individual and the community and to supervise the fulfilment of the duties of the state administration and the provision of public services to the citizens.[42]

The Brazilian Constitution favours the creation of an international human rights court. Considering the recognition of the right to energy as a human right, recognised in the international framework, this would be susceptible to jurisdictional protection. In turn, it declares the creation of a Consumer Defence Code, which would create the normative bases for the protection of consumer rights. In this way, the figure of the energy consumer would be protected.[43]

The Dominican Republic does not have express protection of the right to energy in its Constitution. Despite this, Article 53 of the Constitution recognises the rights of consumers, including the right to quality goods and services, objective, truthful and timely information, and compensation for damages. With the recognition of these rights, the right to energy would have the effective judicial protection offered by Article 69. The principles of universality, accessibility, efficiency, transparency, responsibility, continuity, quality, reasonableness, and tariff equity constitutionally strengthen the public energy service. Similarly, compliance with SDG #7 is guaranteed by promoting renewable sources in the public and private sectors.[44]

In the case of Argentina, the right to energy is protected in Article 42. This precept recognises the rights of consumers in a consumption relationship to protect their health, safety, and economic interests, as well as adequate and truthful information, freedom of choice, and conditions of fair and dignified treatment. The right to energy is framed within this broad content of consumer rights. Article 43 provides an expeditious and rapid recourse to the competent court for acts or omissions by public or private authorities violating these rights. In this way, Amparo's remedy is manifested as a mechanism for effectively protecting rights.[45]

On the other hand, in the European context, the first example to analyse is the Spanish Constitution. Article 51.1 decrees the obligation of public authorities to

[41] Cf. Article 52. Constitución de la República del Ecuador (2008).

[42] Cf. Articles 1, 3, 55, 65, 69, 162, 195, Constitución Política de Perú (1993).

[43] Cf. Articles 7, 48. Constituição da República Federativa do Brasil (1988).

[44] Cf. Articles 53, 67, 69. Constitución Dominicana (2010).

[45] Cf. Articles 42, 43. Constitución Nacional Argentina (1994).

guarantee the defence of consumers and users through effective procedures to protect their safety, health, and legitimate economic interests. The general approach of this constitutional provision allows energy consumers to be included in the framework. Of course, this constitutional mandate is aligned with Directive (EU) 2019/944.[46] Like other constitutions analysed, the Spanish Constitution provides for rights that demand energy for their materialisation, such as the right to decent housing. The constitutional body also projects itself towards promoting favourable conditions for social and economic progress, which entails the availability of the necessary energy.[47]

Article 60 of the Portuguese Constitution refers to the rights of consumers. In this way, the rights provided for therein apply to energy consumers. These include the right to quality in the goods and services consumed, the prohibition of fraudulent advertising, and the role of consumer associations. Article 81 declares that the state's priorities are the promotion of social and economic welfare and the quality of life of the people within the framework of sustainable development. These are aspects that serve as the basis for the right to energy.[48]

Although the Swiss Confederation is not a member of the European Union, the Constitution places the right to energy within the consumer rights framework. Article 97 establishes consumer protection provisions and recognises consumer organisations' role. In turn, Article 89 declares the promotion of a sufficient, diversified, secure, economically optimal, and environmentally friendly energy supply.[49]

Although the right to energy in many constitutional legal systems finds a home in consumer rights, this approach can be improved. The consumer rights framework offers too broad a spectrum, which can lead to minimising the fundamental nature of the right to energy. Therefore, an express recognition of the right to energy is the first step towards its protection and guarantee.

4.4 Recognition of Energy as a Fundamental Human Need

Energy services are considered essential services par excellence for improving human well-being, economic development, and social inclusion.[50] As part of state awareness raising, their constitutional bodies have highlighted energy as a fundamental human need.

In this sense, article 24 of the Surinamese Constitution declares the State's responsibility to ensure the creation of conditions that guarantee the optimal satisfaction of fundamental needs, including energy.

---

[46] European Parliament and European Council (2019).

[47] Cf. Articles 37, 45, 51.1. Constitución del Reino de España (1978).

[48] Cf. Articles 60, 81. Constitución de la República Portuguesa (2005).

[49] Cf. Articles 89 and 97. Constitución Federal de la Confederación Suiza (1999).

[50] Bombaerts et al. (2020).

> Article 24: "The State is responsible for creating conditions that ensure the optimal satisfaction of basic needs in the areas of work, food, healthcare, education, energy, clothing, and communication. (Own translation)"[51]

This recognition opens the framework for claims before the Constitutional Court for violations of the right to energy, and thus, judicial protection appears.[52]

A particular situation arises in the Maldives. Although it is not a self-governing territory, it is essential to note that its constitutional text provides for the progressive realisation of the right to energy. To this end, it provides for the adoption of reasonable measures following the availability of resources.

> Article 23: "(…) State undertakes to achieve the progressive realisation of these rights by reasonable measures within its ability and resources: (…)
>
> g) the establishment of an electricity system of a reasonably adequate standard on every inhabited island that is commensurate to that island."[53]

In this sense, the Constitution of this territory projects the development of electricity systems, with an adequate standard in the inhabited islands, as a fundamental condition for the realisation of constitutionally recognised rights. In turn, this Constitution declares human dignity, equality, and freedom as values to be considered by the judicial system in interpreting and applying constitutional rights.[54]

4.5 Express Recognition of the Right to Energy as a Right

Express constitutional recognition is the maximum reflection of the fundamental nature of a right. In this sense, legal-constitutional systems have evolved, progressively incorporating new rights. Such is the case of the right to energy; although there are many examples where there is no express recognition, others have managed to condense the spirit of international instruments, referring to the right to energy in their Constitutions. Some examples of this trend will be analysed in this section.

The Nicaraguan Constitution, in Article 105, establishes the obligation of the State to promote, facilitate and regulate the provision of public energy service. It goes on to declare access to energy as an inalienable right.

> Article 105. "It is an obligation of the State to promote, facilitate and regulate the provision of basic public energy services (...) to the population, and an inalienable right of the population to access them. Private investments and their modalities and exploitation con-

[51] Cf. Article 24. Grondwet Suriname (1987).

[52] Cf. Article 144. Grondwet Suriname (1987).

[53] Cf. Article 23. Constitution of the Republic of Maldives (2008).

[54] Cf. Article 68. "When interpreting and applying the rights and freedoms contained within this Chapter, a court or tribunal shall promote the values that underlie an open and democratic society based on human dignity, equality and freedom, and shall consider international treaties to which the Maldives is a party" Constitution of the Republic of Maldives (2008).

> cessions to private parties in these areas shall be regulated by law in each case." (Own translation)[55]

This express recognition of the right in question breaks with the constitutional trends addressed in this research until now. This constitutional regulation also shows interest in regulating private initiatives in the energy sector in order to safeguard the fundamental right to energy.

Furthermore, the progressive position of the Nicaraguan Constitution is reinforced by the inclusion of human dignity as a constitutional principle and the declaration of sustainable development and the improvement of the living conditions of the population as functions of the State. The right to a healthy environment and adequate housing, among other human rights, reinforce the fundamental right to energy.[56]

Bolivia's Constitution sets one of the most relevant legislative precedents for the right to energy. Article 378 recognises the forms and energy sources as strategic resources. It declares access to them as a fundamental and essential right for the integral and social development of the country.

> Article 378. "The various forms of energy and their sources constitute a strategic resource, access to which is a fundamental and essential right for the full and social development of the country and must be governed by the principles of efficiency, continuity, adaptability and respect for the environment." [57]

Furthermore, this article establishes the principles that should underpin access to energy, efficiency, continuity, adaptability, and environmental preservation. Article 379 makes the State responsible for guaranteeing energy generation for internal consumption, which must be considered for the export of surpluses. The protection of the right to energy is not only in the constitutional text; the existence of the Plurinational Constitutional Tribunal reinforces the protection of the right to energy.[58]

Despite the analysis made regarding the Chilean Constitution,[59] a particularly relevant initiative regarding the right to energy is the Proposed Political Constitution of the Republic of Chile, to be put to a referendum in September 2022. Article 59 declared a fundamental right to a vital minimum of affordable and safe energy.[60]

At the same time, it made the State responsible for guaranteeing equitable and non-discriminatory access to energy and for regulating and promoting a distributed, decentralised, and diversified energy matrix based on renewable energies with low environmental impact through the participation of energy cooperatives and the practice of energy prosumerism. This constitutional legislative initiative considered energy infrastructure to be in the public interest.[61]

---

[55] Cf. Article 105. Constitución Política de la República de Nicaragua (2014).

[56] Cf. Articles 5, 60, 46, 52, 64, 98. Constitución Política de la República de Nicaragua (2014).

[57] Cf. Article 378. Constitución Política del Estado de Bolivia 2009.

[58] Cf. Articles 378 and 379. Constitución Política del Estado de Bolivia 2009.

[59] Cf. already supra, pp. 82–83.

[60] Cf. Article 24. Convención Constitucional (2022).

[61] Convención Constitucional (2022).

The Chilean constitutional initiative of 2022 could have become one of the most advanced Constitutions regarding the right to energy, but it did not obtain a majority of votes in the constitutional referendum. Despite this precedent, the new proposed Chilean constitution excludes the right to energy, which is a major step backwards. Only Article 100 (r) refers to the obligation to protect critical infrastructure (including energy) in the event of serious or imminent danger. In addition, Article 210 merely states that the state has a duty to 'promote an energy matrix compatible with environmental protection, sustainability and development, as well as waste management, in accordance with the law'.[62] (Own translation)

4.6 Conclusion

The constitutional recognition of the right to energy is a development process. Most of the constitutions analysed in this research do not recognise this right. Consequently, national legal frameworks have assumed different trends towards the recognition and protection of the right to energy. Whereby four main trends have been identified: the trend of indirect protection, the trend of protection of the right to energy within the framework of the rights of users or consumers, the recognition of energy as a fundamental need and the trend of express recognition of the fundamental right to energy.

Indirect protection is manifested in several of the legal systems analysed, and it is crystallised through the recognition of other constitutional rights that need energy for materialisation. This trend includes Belize, El Salvador, Honduras, Chile, Jamaica, Guyana, Puerto Rico, France, Germany, Norway, Belgium, Italy, and Denmark.[63]

There is a growing trend in the constitutional protection of the right to energy through users' and consumers' rights. This trend includes Mexico, Paraguay, Costa Rica, Panama, Uruguay, Guatemala, Colombia, Venezuela, Ecuador, Peru, Brazil, Dominican Republic, Argentina, Spain, Portugal, and Switzerland.[64]

---

[62] Consejo Constitucional (2023).

[63] Belize Constitution (2000); Constitución de la República de El Salvador (1983); Constitución de la República de Honduras (1982); Constitución Política de la República de Chile (2010); The Constitution of Jamaica (1962); Constitution of the Co-operative Republic of Guyana (2003); Constitución del Estado Libre Asociado de Puerto Rico (1952); Constitution de la République française (1958); Grundgesetz für die Bundesrepublik Deutschland (1949); Kongeriket Noregs grunnlov (1814); De Belgische Grondwet (1994); Costituzione italiana (1947); Danmarks Riges Grundlov (1953).

[64] Constitución Política de los Estados Unidos Mexicanos (1917); Constitución de Paraguay (2011); Constitución Política de la República de Costa Rica (2009); Constitución Política de la República de Panamá (2016); Constitución de la República del Uruguay (2004); Constitución Política de la República de Guatemala (1986); Constitución Política de Colombia (2016); Constitución de la República Bolivariana de Venezuela (2009); Constitución de la República del Ecuador (2008); Constitución Política de Perú (1993); Constituição da República Federativa do

Suriname and the Maldives are part of the third trend of recognising energy as a fundamental human need.[65] While these are the only constitutions identified in this trend, recognising energy as a fundamental need lays the foundation for recognising energy as a right of equal nature.

Examples of states with express recognition of the right to energy in their constitutions include Nicaragua and Bolivia,[66] not to mention the Chilean constitutional project, which, despite not being approved, adopted a vanguard stance.[67] Based on the trends examined, the Bolivian Constitution is considered the most advanced of the Constitutions analysed[68] for its express recognition of the right to energy, the establishment of a system of principles and the creation of mechanisms for effective protection through the creation of a Plurinational Constitutional Tribunal.

The ombudspersons' offices and consumer rights organisations, such as consumer associations, protect the right to energy. These entities, in many of the cases analysed, have constitutional recognition. The regulation of these institutions has been a step forward in protecting rights and, consequently, the right to energy. Given this regulatory trend, the right to energy must have an adequate conceptual basis to understand and delimit its scope.[69]

References

Asamblea General de la Organización de Naciones Unidas (1976) Pacto Internacional de Derechos Económicos, Sociales y Culturales. https://www.ohchr.org/es/instruments-mechanisms/instruments/international-covenant-economic-social-and-cultural-rights. Accessed 28 February 2025

Belize Constitution (2000) Belize: The National Committee for Families and Children. https://www.ncfc.org.bz/download/the-constitution-of-belize/?wpdmdl=1876&refresh=6172c177ab7741634910583. Accessed 28 February 2025

Bombaerts G, Jenkins K, Sanusi YA, Guoyu W (2020) Energy Justice Across Borders. Edited by Bombaerts G, Jenkins K, Sanusi YA, Guoyu W. Energy Justice Across Borders. Cham: Springer. https://link.springer.com/10.1007/978-3-030-24021-9. Accessed 28 February 2025.

Comisión Económica para América Latina y el Caribe (2016) Agenda 2030 y los Objetivos de Desarrollo Sostenible Una oportunidad para América Latina y el Caribe. Organización de Naciones Unidas. https://repositorio.cepal.org/bitstream/handle/11362/40155/24/S1801141_es.pdf. Accessed 28 February 2025

Consejo Constitucional (2023) Constitución política de la República de Chile. Santiago de Chile: Gobierno de Chile. https://s3.amazonaws.com/gobcl-prod/public_files/Plebiscito-

Brasil (1988); Constitución Dominicana (2010); Constitución Nacional Argentina (1994); Constitución del Reino de España (1978); Constitución de la República Portuguesa (2005); Constitución Federal de la Confederación Suiza (1999).

[65] Grondwet Suriname (1987); Constitution of the Republic of Maldives (2008).

[66] Constitución Política de la República de Nicaragua 2014; Constitución Política del Estado de Bolivia (2009).

[67] Convención Constitucional (2022).

[68] Luis Cordova (2023), pp. 101.

[69] All links to the cited websites were operational as of 28 February 2025

constitucional/PROPUESTA-DE-NUEVA-CONSTITUCION-POLITICA-DE-LA-REPUBLICA.pdf. Accessed 28 February 2025
Constitución de la República Bolivariana de Venezuela (2009) Venezuela: Consejo Electoral Nacional de Venezuela. https://www.cgr.gob.ve/assets/pdf/leyes/Constitucion.pdf. Accessed 28 February 2025
Constitución de la República de El Salvador (1983) El Salvador. https://www.asamblea.gob.sv/sites/default/files/documents/decretos/171117_072857074_archivo_documento_legislativo.pdf. Accessed 28 February 2025
Constitución de la República de Honduras (1982) Honduras: La Gaceta. Diario Oficial de la República de Honduras. https://www.se.gob.hn/media/files/leyes/LC_BTf7DGE.pdf. Accessed 28 February 2025
Constitución de la República del Ecuador (2008) Ecuador: Biblioteca: Juan León Mera. https://www.asambleanacional.gob.ec/sites/default/files/private/asambleanacional/filesasambleanacionalnameuid-20/transparencia-2015/literal-a/a2/Const-Enmienda-2015.pdf. Accessed 28 February 2025
Constitución de la República del Uruguay (2004). https://parlamento.gub.uy/documentosyleyes/documentos/11/HTML. Accessed 28 February 2025
Constitución de la República Portuguesa (2005) Portugal. https://www.parlamento.pt/Legislacao/Paginas/ConstituicaoRepublicaPortuguesa.aspx. Accessed 28 February 2025
Constitución de Paraguay (2011) Paraguay: Biblioteca y Archivo del Congreso de la Nación. https://www.bacn.gov.py/archivos/9580/CONSTITUCION_ORIGINAL_FIRMADA.pdf. Accessed 28 February 2025
Constitución del Estado Libre Asociado de Puerto Rico (1952) Portal Oficial del Gobierno de Puerto Rico. https://poderjudicial.pr/Documentos/Leyes-Reglamentos/Constitucion-Estado-Libre-Asocicado-PR.pdf. Accessed 28 February 2025
Constitución del Reino de España (1978) Spain. https://www.boe.es/buscar/pdf/1978/BOE-A-1978-31229-consolidado.pdf. Accessed 28 February 2025
Constitución Dominicana (2010) hhttps://www.dgcp.gob.do/transparencia/documentos/base_legal_institucional/Constituci%C3%B3n%20Dominicana%202015.pdf. Accessed 28 February 2025
Constitución Nacional Argentina (1994). https://www.casarosada.gob.ar/images/stories/constitucion-nacional-argentina.pdf. Accessed 28 February 2025
Constitución Política de Colombia (2016) Colombia: Sistema Único de Información Normativa. http://www.suin-juriscol.gov.co/viewDocument.asp?ruta=Constitucion/1687988. Accessed 28 February 2025
Constitución Política de la República de Chile (2010) Chile. https://www.camara.cl/camara/doc/leyes_normas/constitucion_politica.pdf. Accessed 28 February 2025
Constitución Política de la República de Costa Rica (2009) Costa Rica: Revista Parlamentaria. https://www.tse.go.cr/pdf/normativa/constitucion.pdf. Accessed 28 February 2025
Constitución Política de la República de Guatemala (1986) Guatemala. https://mingob.gob.gt/wp-content/uploads/2020/10/GUATEMALA-Constitucion.pdf. Accessed 28 February 2025
Constitución Política de la República de Nicaragua (2014) Nicaragua. https://www.asamblea.gob.ni/assets/constitucion.pdf. Accessed 28 February 2025
Constitución Política de la República de Panamá (2016) Panamá: Ministerio Público. Procuraduría General de la Nación. https://ministeriopublico.gob.pa/wp-content/uploads/2016/09/constitucion-politica-con-indice-analitico.pdf. Accessed 28 February 2025
Constitución Política de los Estados Unidos Mexicanos (1917) México: Diario Oficial de la Federación. https://www.gob.mx/cms/uploads/attachment/file/627005/CPEUM_11_03_2021.pdf. Accessed 28 February 2025
Constitución Política de Perú (1993) Peru. https://www.congreso.gob.pe/Docs/constitucion/constitucion/index.html. Accessed 28 February 2025
Constitución Política del Estado de Bolivia (2009). Bolivia: Gaceta Oficial de Bolivia. http://www.gacetaoficialdebolivia.gob.bo/normas/verGratis_gob1/36208. Accessed 28 February 2025

Constituição da República Federativa do Brasil (1988). https://www.planalto.gov.br/ccivil_03/Constituicao/Constituicao.htm. Accessed 28 February 2025

Constitution de la République française (1958) France. https://www.conseil-constitutionnel.fr/le-bloc-de-constitutionnalite/texte-integral-de-la-constitution-du-4-octobre-1958-en-vigueur. Accessed 28 February 2025

Constitution fédérale de la Confédération suisse (1999) Switzerland. https://www.fedlex.admin.ch/eli/cc/1999/404/fr#tit_1. Accessed 28 February 2025

Constitution of the Co-operative Republic of Guyana (2003) Co-operative Republic of Guyana. http://www.parliament.am/library/sahmanadrutyunner/gayana.pdf. Accessed 28 February 2025

Constitution of the Republic of Maldives (2008) Maldives: The President's Office of the Republic of Maldives. https://storage.googleapis.com/presidency.gov.mv/Documents/ConstitutionOfMaldives.pdf. Accessed 28 February 2025

Convención Constitucional (2022) Propuesta de Constitución Política de la República de Chile. Santiago de Chile, Chile. https://archive.org/details/propuestaconstitucionchile2022. Accessed 28 February 2025

Costituzione italiana (1947) Italia: Senato della Repubblica. https://www.senato.it/sites/default/files/media-documents/Costituzione.pdf. Accessed 28 February 2025

Danmarks Riges Grundlov (1953) Denmark. https://www.grundloven.dk/. Accessed 28 February 2025

De Belgische Grondwet (1994) België: De Kamer.Be. https://www.dekamer.be/kvvcr/pdf_sections/publications/constitution/GrondwetUK.pdf. Accessed 28 February 2025

Elizalde Castañeda RR, Bonzo Morales Arzate C (2018) Los derechos difusos en México. Una mirada desde el Derecho Comparado. Revista de investigación en Derecho, Criminología y Consultoría Jurídica 12(23):27–50. https://revistas-colaboracion.juridicas.unam.mx/index.php/dike/article/viewFile/37042/33949. Accessed 28 February 2025

European Parliament, European Council (2019) Directive 2019/944 on common rules for the internal market for electricity and amending Directive 2012/27/EU. Brussels: Official Journal of the European Union.. https://eur-lex.europa.eu/legal-content/EN/TXT/PDF/?uri=CELEX:32019L0944&from=EN. Accessed 28 February 2025

Grondwet Suriname (1987) Surinam: De Nationale Assemblée van de Republiek Suriname. https://www.dna.sr/wetgeving/surinaamse-wetten/geldende-teksten-tm-2005/grondwet-suriname/. Accessed 28 February 2025

Grundgesetz für die Bundesrepublik Deutschland (1949) Germany. https://www.bundestag.de/gg. Accessed 28 February 2025

International Energy Agency, International Renewable Energy Agency, United Nations Statistics Division, The International Bank for Reconstruction and Development/The World Bank, and World Health Organization (2023) Tracking SDG 7|Progress Towards Sustainable Energy 2023. https://trackingsdg7.esmap.org/. Accessed 28 February 2025

Kongeriket Noregs grunnlov (1814) Lovdata. https://lovdata.no/dokument/NL/lov/1814-05-17-nn#KAPITTEL_5. Accessed 28 February 2025

Luis Cordova JG (2023) Right to energy: good practices in the constitutional Latin-American context. In: Public C (ed) Law, edited by ali Saiyed A, Ayat Ansari F. Harshwardhan, Maharashtra, pp 92–108

Mujica-Johnson FN, Orellana-Arduiz NC (2021) El respeto a la dignidad humana: Un valor fundamental para promover los derechos humanos. Revista de Educación de Puerto Rico 4(1):1–13. https://revistas.upr.edu/index.php/educacion/article/view/17131/16116. Accessed 28 February 2025

Organización de Naciones Unidas (1948) Declaración Universal de los Derechos Humanos. https://www.ohchr.org/sites/default/files/UDHR/Documents/UDHR_Translations/spn.pdf. Accessed 28 February 2025

Organización de Naciones Unidas (1979) Convention on the elimination of all forms of discrimination against women. Oficina del Alto Comicionado para los Derechos Humanos. https://

www.ohchr.org/en/instruments-mechanisms/instruments/convention-elimination-all-forms-discrimination-against-women. Accessed 28 February 2025

The Constitution of Jamaica (1962) Jamaica: Jamaica Information Service. https://jis.gov.jm/media/Ja-Constitution-Order-in-Council-1962-full.pdf. Accessed 28 February 2025

Chapter 5
Towards a Conceptual Delimitation of the Right to Energy

5.1 The Genesis of the Concept of the Right to Energy

While it has been proven that the adoption of the right to energy by legal systems is a gradual process, legal doctrine, for its part, has faced a similar process. Society[1] and the law increasingly clamour for a right to energy, but its theoretical foundations are still forming.

Different denominations of this right can be found in the legal doctrine of the right to energy. It has been called the right to energy,[2] right of access to energy,[3] right to electricity,[4] right to electricity,[5] right of access to electricity,[6] right of access to electricity,[7] right of access to clean energy,[8] right of access to energy services[9] and right to universal access to modern energy services.[10]

Although this fragmentation makes the conceptual analysis of the right to energy difficult, each author presents critical aspects for understanding this right. Therefore, this research will develop the theoretical contributions of the doctrine to arrive at a conceptual definition of the right to energy.

---

[1] Right to Energy Coalition | Take Action to End Energy Poverty in Europe (2022).

[2] Walker (2016a); Hesselman et al. (2021); Azad and Chakraborty (2020); Shyu (2021); Przybojewska (2017); Sin-Hang Ngai (2012).

[3] Delgado Triana and Fariñas Wong (2016); Durán and Condorí (2015).

[4] Löfquist (2020); Peña Pupo et al. (2020).

[5] Comité de Desarrollo Campesino (2014).

[6] Cf. Tully (2006), p. 530.

[7] Aviles (2012).

[8] Tully (2009).

[9] Frigo et al. (2021).

[10] Solis (2014).

J. G. Luis Cordova, *Theoretical and Legal Dimensions of the Right to Energy*, Economic and Financial Law & Policy – Shifting Insights & Values 9, https://doi.org/10.1007/978-3-032-33252-3_5

Before entering the theoretical disquisition associated with the conceptualisation of the right to energy, it is vital to consider the impact that the complex definition of energy has had on the framework of the right under study. This complexity has led to diverse doctrinal positions regarding the denomination and content of the right to energy.

5.2 Energy as an Unresolved Concept for a Right to Energy

Understanding energy as a core category plays an indispensable role in determining the meaning and scope of the law under study. The conceptualisation of energy is still an unresolved scientific element made more complex by its transdisciplinary nature. Its doctrinal approach has been developed from multiple sides of science, among which the social and legal fields, for example, are taking on an increasingly relevant role.

In that sense, it is worth noting that the linguistic origin of this category dates to the Aristotelian period, with the denomination of *energeia* associated with an action or work.[11] This remote energy denomination constituted the first antecedent for conceptual approaches derived in multiple fields.

The most commonly accepted definition of energy in the physical sciences is: "Energy is the capacity to produce work".[12] Despite being the most commonly used definition, it is not entirely accurate since work is only one of the manifestations of energy, among which are electrical, magnetic, and thermal energy, among others, energy forms.[13]

Illich approached the work as a physical category in his scientific paper titled: "The social construction of the Energy".[14] In this article, Illich takes a challenging position by analysing energy not as a mere concept derived from science but as the result of a deep social construction process. The fact that scientific thought focuses on the analysis of energy as a quantitative category overlooks a very different reality. Energy is a category inextricably linked to social norms, cultural attitudes, and economic systems.

Such a context means that the understanding of energy and its use is defined by social factors. This means that the concept of energy is not fixed or immutable; rather, it is societies that shape the definition of this category according to their interests and ideologies. Therefore, it is society that determines the value of energy and its use according to its objective needs and defined priorities.

In "The social construction of the Energy", Illich argues that work meant work, task, effort, or duty when energy was charged with new meanings. It always referred

[11] Yepes Stork (2018).

[12] U.S. Energy Information Administration (2020).

[13] Pirstner-Ebner (2019).

[14] Illich (2013).

to a concrete action or its result. Towards the middle of the eighteenth century, work could mean, for the first time, the set of these actions.[15]

According to Illich, the category energy is only a verbal symbol that does not have a simple, immediate, or singular form.[16] Such a consideration derives from the assumption that the understanding and use of energy are phenomena shaped by language and discourse. Illich, therefore, interprets energy as the result of cultural processes influenced by linguistic and social factors. Nevertheless, energy cannot be understood as an abstract category but as a phenomenon present in all areas of the universe.

The economic sciences have also taken sides in defining energy as a category. In this field, the conceptualisation of energy includes all energy commodities and energy resources, which contain significant amounts of physical energy and, therefore, offer the capacity to do work.[17]

In that sense, Sweeney defines energy commodities as natural gas, gasoline, propane, and coal. Such energy commodities act as resources to ensure the provision of energy services that meet the energy needs of human society. These include cooking, lighting, heating, and many other human needs that depend on energy for their satisfaction.[18] At the same time, energy resources include crude oil, biomass, wind, and sunlight, among other resources. In this way, energy resources are the starting point for meeting energy needs. They can be used for energy production by transforming them into energy commodities and then into useful energy forms.[19]

The legal notion of energy, offered by Walker, presents it as a resource that can be accessed and consumed but also brings together different forms of material substances and energy flows, which have a high potential and are susceptible to transformation for useful purposes.[20] Although this is a broad definition, simultaneously capable of describing energy from a legal approach, energy sources and, as a result, energy services can be included in this conceptualisation. Examples could be coal, wind, water, solar radiation, and services such as electricity and gas.

Having presented the above conceptions, this research, without entering a technical-conceptual definition of energy, will define it based on two central elements, on which the core of powers that make up the content of the right to energy fall. The first is energy sources, and the second is energy services.

Energy sources have sufficient energy potential to be converted into energy services.[21] The conceptualisation of energy sources is linked to energy carriers, which are:

---

[15] Illich (2013), p. 98.

[16] Illich (2013), p. 92.

[17] Sweeney (2001), p. 4513.

[18] Timilsina (2019), p. 14.

[19] Sweeney (2001).

[20] Walker (2016b).

[21] Colino Martínez and Caro (2010); International Institute for Applied Systems Analysis (2012).

> The resources used to obtain energy, which can be natural or the result of a transformation. Among them are those that are obtained directly, such as hydraulic, wind and solar energy; those that go through a mining process, such as oil, natural gas, coal, fusible minerals, and geothermal energy; those that are generated through photosynthesis, such as firewood and other fuels of plant or animal origin. Those resulting from a transformation process include electricity, the full range of petroleum derivatives, charcoal, denatured alcohol, and manufactured gas

(Own translation).[22]

Renewable energy sources are those derived from natural processes that are replenished at a faster rate than they are consumed.[23] For this reason, renewability rests with the energy carrier in question. Conversely, non-renewable energy sources are those whose energy potential cannot be replenished or would take prolonged periods to replenish. Despite these conceptualisations, the normative definition of energy sources, both renewable and non-renewable, is still a pending task for the law.

The difficulty in defining what is meant by renewable or non-renewable energy stems from Illich's approach to energy as a social construct. In this sense, Crossley, after analysing the definitions of renewable energy in different jurisdictions, highlights the importance of establishing a comprehensive and consistent understanding of this type of energy. This is based on the absence of a universally accepted definition of renewable energy, which has led to a diversification of interpretations and normative implications around the world. This tendency corresponds to Illich's view of energy as a cultural, social, and linguistic element. The ambiguity of the term energy (renewable or non-renewable) merits the interdisciplinary collaboration of energy experts, legal scholars, and public policy makers.[24]

After analysing the first energy component as a didactic category, in the framework of the present research, a second element would be energy services. There is a wide and varied debate in academia on the definition of energy services, with a variety of conceptual approaches.[25] Such a debate is analysed by Fell, who considers that definitions of energy services are associated with benefits, energy provision, services demanded and delivered to people, which are results (at least partially) of energy conversion combined with technology.[26]

In this sense, energy services are understood as the result of the combined operation of primary or secondary energy sources, energy-related technologies, labour, materials, and infrastructure.[27] Nevertheless, it is important to highlight the link

[22] Ministerio de Energía y Minas (2018).

[23] Sustainable Energy for All (2013).

[24] Crossley (2022).

[25] Cf. Barnett (1986), p. 426; Bertoldi et al. (2006), p. (1820); Cravioto et al. (2014), p. 11; Greening et al. (2000), p. 389; Haas et al. (2008), p. 4012; Kowsari and Zerriffi (2011), p. 7013.

[26] Fell (2017), p. 136.

[27] Bradbrook and Gardam (2006), pp. 2–3.

between such services and human well-being[28] as these services result in the satisfaction of human energy needs.

With this definition of energy services, the need to have an energy source, the necessary technology for the generation, as well as a distribution network that guarantees the transmission of the energy supply to the place of consumption and its maintenance actions to contribute to the functioning of the energy system is noted.

The conceptualisation of the third Energy Plan of the Government of Navarre can support the above elements. In this plan, the energy service is defined as:

> The set of services including the carrying out of immaterial investments, works or supplies necessary to optimise the quality and reduction of energy costs. This action may include, in addition to the construction, installation or transformation of works, equipment and systems, their maintenance, updating or renovation, their operation or management resulting from the incorporation of efficient technologies

(Own translation).[29]

In this definition, it is essential to highlight elements such as quality of service, energy efficiency and reduction of generation costs. These elements are the responsibility of the energy service provider and contribute to the security of the energy supply and its affordability. Within this framework, Sovacool differentiates between energy services used in five primary sectors: residential, commercial, transport, agriculture, and industry.[30] Such diversity in energy services makes them the driving force in many sectors of everyday life.

5.3 The Right to Energy Between Denominations and Concepts

5.3.1 The Right to Energy, the Beginning of a Definition

The need to conceptually delimit energy has strongly impacted the naming and definition of the right to energy. This research considers that the scope authors have marked the denomination of the right to energy have given to energy as a didactic category. Following the bibliographic review, three doctrinal approaches to the right to energy can be identified. A first approach would be the limitation of the content of this right, where only the right to electricity would be subject to protection by the State.[31] A second approach would be the right to energy as a right of access to energy, where accessibility is the object of protection. Finally, the third approach would be the right to energy itself.

---

[28] Sovacool (2011a), p. 1660; Modi et al. (2005), p. 9.

[29] Gobierno de Navarra (2020).

[30] Cf. Sovacool (2011b); Sovacool (2011a).

[31] Tully (2006).

The first approach focuses on electricity as an essential energy form in society, given its widespread use by the global population. This approach has led even international bodies to include the percentage of electrification as an indicator. However, when referring to energy as a right, it would be a restrictive approach to limit its scope to this spectrum.

Therefore, with SDG#7 and its targets in the 2030 Agenda,[32] indicators beyond electrification have been enunciated. The Tracking SDG7: The Energy Progress Report states indicators for measuring SDG7 concerning electrification, access to clean cooking fuels and technologies, renewable energy performance and energy efficiency, and international public financial flows to developing countries supporting clean energy.[33]

While understanding energy sheds light on the conceptual delimitation of the right to energy, it is crucial to consider its purpose: energy services, which can be a material guarantee[34] of the right in question. Thanks to this, energy needs can find a sufficient and timely response when safeguarded by the right to energy. Cooking food, lighting, heating, and mobility, among many others, are the fundamental foundations of the need for the recognition and protection of the right to energy.

These needs vary depending on the geographical and climatic context. Therefore, the meaning and scope of recognising the right to energy will also be motivated by material sources of law, such as economic, social, and political factors.[35] While in the Nordic countries, there is a growing concern for heating systems, in tropical countries, such as Cuba, such a concern does not make sense. Other types of air-conditioning systems and other needs of various kinds can also be used as examples.

According to Walker, the definition of the right to energy has two main complexities. The first complexity is that energy is not a thing itself, and the second is its multi-functionality. The first of these complexities set intangibility as an essential characteristic of energy. This complexity is because the conceptualisation includes multiple forms and sources, so when we talk about the right to energy, are we talking about all of them? According to the international framework, clean and sustainable forms of energy obtained from modern sources stand out. Are these forms more important than others?[36]

A second complexity would be the multifunctional character of energy, given that it supports multiple services, so it is generally not an end itself but a means to ensure the functioning of other services. How would it be possible to define which services are vital?[37] Many of these questions do not have a simple answer, as it would depend on multiple factors: geographical, cultural, political, climatic, economic, and social, among many others.

[32] Comisión Económica para América Latina y el Caribe (2016).

[33] International Energy Agency et al. (2023).

[34] Prieto Valdés (2016), p. 171.

[35] Ramírez (2020), p 82.

[36] Walker et al. (2015).

[37] Walker et al. (2015).

This research assumes that using energy forms and sources to satisfy the right to energy should not have a restrictive approach if they provide a valuable outcome and do not result in profound negative consequences for the public interest and the environment. Special attention needs to be paid to prioritising renewable sources over non-renewable ones. While it is true that renewable sources are environmentally friendly and have a long-life span, in many contexts, objective conditions prevent their further penetration into the energy matrix.

Against this backdrop, one invariant element is energy demand, and the need to meet it is unstoppable. While many nations have opted for energy policies based on renewable sources, many others can barely meet the demand.[38] Sustainability is the way forward in the energy sector, but without compromising the satisfaction of energy demand, since the existence of human beings and the functioning of society, the state and the economy depend on it.

In the conceptual approaches to the right to energy analysed above,[39] there is a tendency in the doctrine to conceive of the right to energy as a right to access energy. This tendency constitutes the second approach mentioned above.[40] While accessibility is a core element of the right to energy, this term is ambiguous to a certain extent. Energy consumers need access, not to the energy itself but to the services that depend on it.[41] Energy only becomes an end itself within the framework of its generation process. Once generated, it is transmitted and consumed to satisfy the needs that depend on energy services.

Hence, Walker, as an exponent of the third approach, defines the right to energy from a dual perspective: the right to have access and the right to be able to use it.[42] The necessary infrastructure is required to guarantee the right to have access. Moreover, quality standards are required to establish a connection point between the central network and the consumption place. In this sense, energy accessibility would be part of the realisation of the right to energy.

The energy supply must be accessible to consumers to achieve the intended purpose (meeting energy demand). Energy accessibility will depend on factors such as the affordability of the service, whereby costs must be consistent with the consumer's income. If energy costs substantially affect the economic capacity of the consumer, this may be a partial realisation of the right to energy but not a full realisation. This partial realisation is because the satisfaction of the consumer's energy needs may be reduced to use part of the economic resources to satisfy other vital needs.

Shyu defines the right to energy from three levels and eight dimensions. He calls the first level fundamental, which includes two dimensions: the right of access to energy and the right of access to energy services, as priority tasks for satisfying basic needs, poverty eradication and improving energy justice. The second level is

[38] International Energy Agency et al. (2023).

[39] Cf. already supra, pp. 103–105.

[40] Cf. already supra, pp. 103–104.

[41] Shove and Walker (2014).

[42] Walker (2016b).

called incremental. Once the right of access to energy is secured, the incremental level is declared, consisting of three dimensions: the right of access to energy-efficient products, the right to the affordability of energy use and the right of access to energy information. Shyu calls the last level a supplement. At this level, dimensions such as the right to select the type of energy and supplier, the right to negotiate or refuse payment of embedded costs, and the right to participate in energy policy-making are declared.[43] This last right is considered a manifestation of energy democracy.

Bradbrook and Gardam define the right to energy as access to products and lifestyle changes provided by adequate modern energy services availability.[44] They focus their definition of the right to energy on the positive impact of the availability of energy services on the quality of life. It also refers to modern energy services, a condition in SDG #7. This modernity, which is called for, aims to banish the use of traditional sources, such as wood, as an energy source, given its adverse effects on human health.[45]

Hesselman et al. define the right to energy as all human beings' right to enjoy access to the energy services necessary for health, well-being, social inclusion, and full participation. It also recognises the duties of suppliers and the state in ensuring these rights. Hesselman et al. explain the right to energy through access, affordability, and energy democracy. The first of these three spheres envisages access to specific energy resources and supplies, energy services, and reliable supply with zero risk of disconnection due to the inability to pay. Affordability, as the second sphere, is conceived as being oriented towards people's income and current needs, energy efficiency of housing and electrical equipment, and an energy market free of discriminatory billing practices. Energy democracy, as the third area of the right to energy, aims to promote the right to participate in energy decision-making and energy policies, the right to participate in energy communities,[46] the right to energy information and energy rights, and access to justice.[47]

5.3.2 *Reference Doctrinal Concepts for the Right to Energy*

5.3.2.1 Energy Security

The arguments presented above lead this research to delve into several reference concepts that constitute part of the doctrinal basis of the right to energy. Among these concepts emerge some that are traditionally established in academia, such as energy security and energy poverty, and other relatively recent concepts, such as

[43] Shyu (2021).

[44] Bradbrook and Gardam (2006).

[45] Cf. Cabrera et al. (2015); Organización Mundial de la Salud (2014).

[46] Luis Cordova et al. (2023).

[47] Hesselman et al. (2017).

energy justice, democracy, citizenship, and sovereignty. These categories constitute the background and foundations for the configuration of the right to energy by shedding light on a series of aspects that impact the basic structure of the right to energy, which will be defined later.

According to Ngai, four elements must be considered in formulating the right to energy: availability, regularity, continuity, and reliability.[48] These elements are closely related to the so-called four As of energy security: availability, affordability, accessibility, and acceptability.[49] This context establishes energy security as a reference concept for the right to energy as a fundamental right.

The term energy security first appeared in 1961 in Lubell's "Security of Supply and Energy Policy in Western Europe". At that time, Lubell explained in detail the need to ensure a reliable and secure energy supply in the face of growing energy demand and the repercussions that the geopolitical context could have on this supply. Although this was a first approximation of what is now called energy security, it set the first academic precedents. Western European countries began implementing measures to ensure energy security as early as the early 1960s.[50]

Since the emergence of energy security as a scientific category, academia has incorporated and shaped it from various approaches. Yergin took up the concept associated with oil supply as a primary element of state security, especially in military preparedness for wartime.[51] The association of energy security with oil supply security was reinforced in the aftermath of the 1970s energy crisis.[52]

Despite what has been described above, the energy crisis of 1970 was a determining factor in the revolution around the definition of energy security. This energy crisis ushered in a new era of economic power based on the dominance of natural energy resources. Since the OPEC oil embargo, energy security has been strengthened as a priority for states due to the divorce between military power and economic and political power caused by the dominance of oil as the leading energy carrier of the time.[53]

For his part, after experiencing the energy crisis of the 1970s, Deese ventured to define energy security as:

> a condition in which a nation perceives a high probability that it will have adequate energy supplies (including traditional sources such as firewood, and plant and animal residues that are frequently not traded in the marketplace) at affordable prices.[54]

In defining energy affordability, Deese explained that energy prices are affordable when they do not cause severe social and economic impacts. It, therefore, attributes to the state the responsibility to provide affordable energy prices in the short term,

---

[48] Sin-Hang Ngai (2012).

[49] Cherp and Jewell (2014).

[50] Lubell (1961).

[51] Esakova (2012), p. 36.

[52] Yergin (1991), p. 410.

[53] Biresselioglu (2011), pp. 10–11.

[54] Deese (1979), p. 140.

keeping the balance between society and the economy. To complement this vision of energy security, Deese defines two other elements that makeup energy security. On the one hand, it identifies actions that can undermine the quantity and reliability of the national energy supply and, on the other hand, external phenomena that can threaten the energy supply.[55]

This vision is also a consequence of the energy crisis of the 1970s. For this reason, according to Biresselioglu, energy security became an object of national and international strategy underpinned by political, economic, and military pillars. The consequence of the post-crisis phase continued to be accompanied by the primary goal of ensuring reliable and affordable energy supplies.[56]

Despite the broad academic movement around energy security during the 1970s and 1980s, the debate ceased during the 1990s. Crooks, in his article "Security of supply: Delusional dream of independence", argues:

> Energy security, a dead issue during the 1990s, has emerged as a pressing concern of governments and businesses.[57]

According to Cherp and Jewell, the term energy security re-emerged in the early 2000s in association with the growth of energy demand in Asia, gas supply disruptions in Europe and the campaign for decarbonisation of energy systems.[58] As a first example of this, Fergin takes a different stance on energy security than Yegrin did in 1991.

In this regard, Fergin considered that energy security is not limited to oil as an energy carrier with a long-established tradition in energy systems. Power outages in the US, Europe, Russia, and China underpinned this consideration. This context was compounded by increased demand for gas in North America, which caused the United States to enter the international gas market due to its inability to meet the growing demand for this energy carrier.[59] In this way, the understanding of energy security was extended to other forms of energy that had hitherto not been considered in this area.

However, the conceptual essence of energy security set out in 1976 by Desse as the adequate supply of energy at an affordable price[60] was accepted by Haghighi in 2007. In this context, Haghighi adds an essential element to satisfy the energy supply: energy availability.[61] Energy availability is an invariant element that sustains the functioning of the supply.

In addition to the above, other more recent approaches to energy security consider its growing intertwining with states' foreign policy, giving rise to energy

---

[55] Deese (1979), p. 140.

[56] Biresselioglu (2011), pp. 12, 15.

[57] Crooks (2007).

[58] Cherp and Jewell (2014), p. 415.

[59] Yergin (2006), p. 70.

[60] Cf. already supra, p. 108.

[61] Haghighi (2007), p. 14.

democracy.[62] This intertwining is based on the projection of energy security within state energy policy, which is focused on guaranteeing access to energy sources and reducing the risks of energy dependence.[63]

Willrich proposed a different and forward-looking approach for its time when he considered energy security from a dual perspective. During the energy crisis of the 1970s, while the main concern at the global level was focused on the security of supply, Willrich also emphasised the security of demand. On the one hand, this dual perspective is taken by energy-importing countries that focus on guaranteeing access to energy by purchasing energy carriers at affordable prices[64] and, on the other hand, by energy-exporting countries. The latter's concern focuses on the existence of demand for obvious reasons.[65] The international energy market is based on the existence of energy supply and demand in a symbiotic relationship where any change at either end represents a change for the other.

However, despite the significance of Willrich's approaches to energy security, according to Jakstas, in academia and among public decision-makers, the main concern has focused on the diversification of supply, its uninterruption and the affordability of energy. As a result, supply continues to dominate the definition of energy security, with new dimensions such as sustainability, energy efficiency, reduction of greenhouse gas emissions, and energy accessibility and affordability as determinants of energy poverty.[66]

As has been seen, the understanding of energy security has moved from its definition as security of supply threatened by geopolitical factors that have triggered embargoes and price spikes to more encompassing perspectives.[67] In this sense, the evolution of thinking around energy security has implied a call to link it to energy access and climate change as associated issues.[68] As such, a thorough understanding of energy security has implications for shaping the right to energy.

Within that context, Esakova considers energy security an umbrella term that links energy with economic growth and political power. She explains energy security in terms of vulnerability to disconnection due to multiple factors, energy prices during non-emergency periods, and national security and welfare.[69] Similarly, energy security has been explained in terms of security of supply, security of demand, reliability of supply and physical security of facilities and personnel.[70] In

[62] Hancock and Vivoda (2014), p. 206.

[63] Hughes and Lipscy (2013), p. 461.

[64] Dannreuther (2010), p. 145.

[65] Willrich (1976), pp. 751–752.

[66] Jakstas (2020), p. 100.

[67] Cherp and Jewell (2014), p. 415.

[68] Goldthau (2011), p. 215.

[69] Esakova (2012).

[70] Biresselioglu (2011).

this context, energy security has also been defined as the low vulnerability of vital energy systems and the sustained supply of modern energy services.[71]

Understanding energy security is not a simple process of reasoning. In this sense, Dannreuther says:

> Energy security is a multifaceted and complex phenomenon. At its heart, it is about ensuring that there are sufficient energy supplies at reasonable prices to meet the socio-economic needs of society.[72]

In this broad definition, several essential elements determine the configuration of the right to energy. The first of these elements is securing the supply of energy. For this reason, it is necessary to guarantee energy availability through the resources available in a given territory or by importing them from foreign suppliers.

In addition to the above, the sufficiency of supply is essential to guarantee the satisfaction of energy demand. Otherwise, a context of energy insecurity arises where human energy needs would be only partially satisfied. The use of supply as a scientific trend in the energy security doctrine requires a definition. In this sense, Hasanuzzaman and Kumar State:

> Energy supply is the quantity of energy that suppliers/resources have available to provide to end users.[73]

According to Hasanuzzaman and Kumar, this definition of energy supply encompasses processes such as extraction, transmission, generation, distribution and storage or energy consumption. Such processes imply the existence of three components of the energy supply chain. The first of these elements is energy commodities, where electricity, natural gas or landfill gas could be included as examples. The second element is network services. These involve the transmission and transformation of energy from the point of generation to the point of final consumption. Finally, the third element of the energy supply chain is retail services. These services include energy billing.[74]

Taking up Dannreuther's definition, the affordability of energy is another crucial element. While availability and accessibility are basic premises for ensuring energy security and the right to energy, affordability is a vital element for people to be able to afford the costs involved in meeting their energy needs as fundamental human needs.

Energy security, as a multi-, inter-, and trans-disciplinary category, has proven to be a highly complex category. In this regard, Sovacool et al. identify 16 dimensions of energy security:

- "Securing a supply of fossil fuels and uranium;
- bolstering trade in energy fuels and commodities;
- minimising depletion of domestically available fuels;

---

[71] Laldjebaev et al. (2018).

[72] Dannreuther (2010), p. 152.

[73] Hasanuzzaman and Kumar (2020), p. 91.

[74] Hasanuzzaman and Kumar (2020), pp. 91–92.

- providing predictable and clear price signals;
- enabling affordably priced energy services;
- providing equitable access to energy services;
- decentralising to small-scale energy supply;
- lowering energy intensity (energy use per unit of Gross Domestic Product);
- researching and developing new energy technologies;
- ensuring transparency and participation in project siting and decision-making;
- offering energy education and information;
- preserving land and forests;
- enhancing the availability and quality of water;
- minimising air pollution;
- responding to climate change/adaptation;
- reducing greenhouse gas emissions/mitigation".[75]

These dimensions highlight numerous elements that link to what this research will define as the structure of the right to energy. These include energy availability, security of supply, energy affordability, universal access, energy democracy, energy literacy, renewable energy generation and climate change mitigation.

More recent views of energy security, such as those offered by Jones and Dodds, reinforce the reliability of energy by expressing:

> Energy security is not just about ensuring a reliable supply of fuel, but also ensuring that there is reliable infrastructure in place to carry energy to the end user.[76]

The call to highlight energy reliability as a component of energy security is not an innovative element but the result of the pronouncements of academics and public decision-makers.[77] It is not enough for energy to be available, accessible, and affordable if it is unreliable.

Energy reliability is an element that determines the satisfaction of energy needs, which implies that the stability of the energy system and its resilience to adverse events allows the satisfaction of such needs when they exist. In this sense, Jasiūnas et al. explain:

> All sources distinguish reliability as a static concept with time-averaged metrics from resilience, which addresses dynamics during a disruption event. (...) reliability as operation within desired system state boundaries under high probability threats, while the resilience focus is described in terms of less likely threats that knock the system outside the desired system state.[78]

Such requirements respond to people's expectation that energy services will be available when demanded.[79] Hence, such expectations are not a mere hope but a

---

[75] Sovacool et al. (2012a), pp. 45–46.

[76] Jones and Dodds (2017), p. 22.

[77] Cf. Department of Energy & Climate Change (2012); Mitchell and Watson (2013); Checchi et al. (2009); Cox (2018).

[78] Jasiūnas et al. (2021), p. 3.

[79] Mitchell and Watson (2013), p. 61.

fundamental human need that must be satisfied; otherwise, energy security would be affected.

Within this research, the concept of energy security rests on four essential pillars: availability, affordability, accessibility, and reliability.[80] If one of these pillars were to be affected, there would be a direct impact on the realisation of the right to energy, and adverse effects would be generated.

As the first of the components of energy security, availability has had multiple definitions, ranging from more restrictive to more comprehensive positions. In this sense, with the evolution of energy security itself, energy availability has been restricted to the availability of energy resources, which have been included from oil, natural gas, and coal with fossil resources to others of a renewable nature such as wind, solar and hydro energy, among others.[81] In this sense, Kruyt et al. estimate that energy availability is based on the physical existence of resources of this nature.[82]

However, energy availability cannot be limited to the availability of energy resources. Although this is a vital requirement to guarantee energy security, energy resources may be available and not be used sufficiently to meet energy demand. Such a reality could occur for multiple reasons, such as instability of the energy system, insufficient energy generation, and financial limitations for energy investment, among many others.

For this reason, energy availability encompasses energy supply. In this context, Couder defines the availability of supply as:

> Total supply available on the market divided by the consumption needs of the country considered.[83]

Without sufficient energy supplies, the proper functioning of energy services as the basis of energy security would not be able to meet the human needs that depend on them. For this reason, availability as the first pillar of energy security must be built on the availability of energy resources and the availability of energy supply.[84] In this sense, Sovacool and Mukherjee State:

> Availability includes having sufficient energy resources, stockpiles, and fuels, as well as the appropriate infrastructure to transform these reserves into energy services.[85]

Hence, energy security depends on the availability of energy resources and the infrastructure capable of carrying out the energy transformation processes to obtain useful energy. Without this, energy availability encompasses the energy flow from

[80] Cf. Couder (2015).

[81] APERC (2007), p. 1.

[82] Kruyt et al. (2009), p. 2179.

[83] Couder (2015), p. 23.

[84] APERC (2007), p. 91.

[85] Sovacool and Mukherjee (2011), p. 5346.

energy generation to energy consumption,[86] where accessibility is the second component of energy security.

For its part, accessibility has been considered an element subsumed under energy availability.[87] This situation is because the close relationship between the two elements makes it a problematic task to separate them in the energy flow. However, from a theoretical approach, it is essential to establish such a disquisition.

While energy availability is the primary element for energy security, accessibility becomes one of the biggest challenges for meeting the growth in energy demand. In this sense, seen from a macroeconomic approach, accessibility faces barriers due to economic, political, and technological factors.[88] This approach responds to the assumption that energy security is strictly related to state security.

For this reason, in this research, while recognising the importance of energy security for state security, energy security will be analysed from a perspective oriented towards the right to energy, given that this approach is not incompatible with the previous one and seeks complementarity.

An important aspect to highlight is that, when discussing accessibility in this research, reference is not made to energy as an abstract category but to the energy services that derive from it and its sources. In this way, it is emphasised that access to energy is aimed at the enjoyment of the benefits it represents, given that, in the framework of the right to energy, energy is not an end in itself but a means to satisfy specific human needs.[89]

Lehr, in his analysis of accessibility, states:

> The import/domestic sources distribution is part of the accessibility question, such as technological development within a country and the development of human resources for energy questions.[90]

Following this line of thought, it is necessary to highlight that energy accessibility is associated with the fair and equitable distribution of its benefits.[91] Thus, Jones and Dodds define energy accessibility as focusing on ensuring that all people have access to energy universally, which is ensured by a reliable infrastructure in such a way that low energy prices are maintained to minimise energy poverty.[92] Such a statement presents energy affordability and reliability as two other elements of energy security. While not novel, given the theoretical evolution of energy security, these elements need to be explained.

As with the other components of energy security, there is no consensus on the definition of energy affordability. According to Couder, this term can refer to:

---

[86] Hughes (2012), p. 224.

[87] Cf. Sovacool and Saunders (2014), p. 642.

[88] APERC (2007), p. 18.

[89] Cf already supra, p. 105.

[90] Lehr (2009), p. 2.

[91] Sovacool and Mukherjee (2011), p. 346; Sovacool and Saunders (2014), p. 644; Cherp and Jewell (2014), p. 100.

[92] Jones and Dodds (2017), p. 23.

> Profitability of energy investments,[93] low energy prices for consumers[94]or government accounts in terms of subsidy levels and import/export balance.[95,96]

However, this research partially affiliates with the definition of energy affordability as:

> The ability of households to purchase a necessary quantity of energy or level of energy services without suffering undue financial hardship.[97]

Despite the above definition, two elements need to be clarified. Energy affordability is a variable that cannot be standardised globally. For its determination, it is necessary to develop interdisciplinary research in order to have a comprehensive approach to the context where it is to be assessed. The affordability of energy, although it has an essentially economic content, is also conditioned by social, political, and legal factors that must be assessed as a whole.

In addition, energy affordability should not only be assessed when purchasing energy (payments for energy services) but also be applicable to the field of energy prosumerism. In this field, energy affordability refers to the technological provisioning necessary for independent producers or collectives organised in energy communities to meet the self-sufficiency of energy needs.

In this sense, it is necessary to encourage the commercialisation of technologies for the self-generation of energy (mainly from renewable sources) by people at affordable prices. For this purpose, alternatives should be explored, including the reorientation of subsidies that may be aimed at subsidising energy generation from fossil fuels.

The fourth element of energy security is reliability. This fourth pillar has enjoyed prominence in academia, where it has been referred to as energy acceptability (the fourth pillar of energy security). From its analysis, this element referred to the social and environmental acceptance of energy generation and consumption by the local population, States, NGOs, and industries.[98]

To illustrate the above, the elements that Ren and Sovacool define to measure energy acceptability are briefly mentioned. The proposed indicators include the environmental impacts of energy generation, public attitudes and perceptions of energy systems, energy governance at national and international levels, transparency of energy information, efficiency in measuring levels of energy consumption and losses, progress in technological innovation, and finally, investment and job creation in the energy sector.[99]

93 APERC (2007), p. 35–39.

94 Kruyt et al. (2009), p. 2176.

95 Sharifuddin (2014), pp. 576, 579.

96 Couder (2015), p. 11.

97 Kessides et al. (2009), p. 3; Dubois and Meier (2016), p. 22.

98 Hughes and Shupe (2010), p. 283; Couder (2015), p. 11.

99 Ren and Sovacool (2014), p. 841.

Although there is divergence in academia regarding this denomination, "energy reliability" has gained prominence. In this regard, Baarsma and Hop define energy reliability as:

> The ability of a power system to provide an adequate and secure supply of electrical energy at any point in time.[100]

This definition refers to a permanently adequate and secure supply as a requirement. Therefore, any interruption, regardless of the causes, implies a reduction in the reliability of energy services. However, due to the approach taken, these authors limit reliability to the field of electricity. Pan maintains this restrictive approach, but it refers to the sufficiency of generation by stating that electricity generation must be able to meet demand.[101]

For their part, Sovacool and Mukherjee, in defining energy reliability indicators, mention the frequency of the electricity grid, voltage control, continuity of supply, accidents and failures in the electricity sector, among others.[102] Despite the constant reference to electric power service, the diversity of energy services imposes the obligation to extend reliability to its domains in order to achieve energy security. This affirmation is supported by Mitchell and Watson by also including gas service within the definition of reliability.[103]

Hernandez further expands the conceptualisation of reliability as follows:

> Reliability includes a condition where the sources of energy are relatively stable and the country's access to these sources is relatively assured by stable relations with the authorities governing these sources, and supply routes relatively safe from disruptions caused by both state and non-state actors.[104]

Despite broadening the scope of the conceptualisation, the reference to "relative stability" opens the framework to the manifestation of certain disturbances that result in a detriment to reliability. Vine also acknowledges this tendency when he considers reliability as the provision of power with minimal interruptions.[105] Therefore, allowing for relative power stability could denote "relative" reliability.

Hence, Hughes and Shupe establish as indicators of reliability the existence of A robust, diversified energy value chain, Adequate reserve capacity, protection from attacks and disruptions and adequate access to energy information.[106] In this way, energy reliability closes the cycle of energy security as an elementary condition for the realisation of the right to energy.

Following that debate, it is clear that any impact on the availability, accessibility, affordability, and reliability of energy as pillars of energy security implies

---

[100] Baarsma and Hop (2009), p. 1378.

[101] Pan (2020), p. 14.

[102] Sovacool and Mukherjee (2011), p. 5349.

[103] Mitchell and Watson (2013), p. 221.

[104] Hernandez (2008), pp. 218–219.

[105] Vine (2012), pp. 401–402.

[106] Hughes and Shupe (2010), p. 10.

undermining the right to energy. This situation can lead to the existence and proliferation of energy poverty.[107] For this reason, it is necessary to understand energy poverty as a concept that has evolved historically and theoretically as another reference concept for the right to energy.

5.3.2.2 Energy Poverty

Without wishing to enter a deep conceptual debate on what is meant by fuel poverty, it is essential to highlight that this term arose in the United Kingdom, developed by Brenda Boardman around 1991.[108] This year, her 1989 doctoral thesis began to be rapidly distributed,[109] highlighting a phenomenon virtually unknown in the academic and political sphere. In this way, energy poverty was studied from households in developed countries without heating. Despite that, these studies, taken up by geography and statistics academics, did not immediately gain widespread political recognition.[110]

The context in which Boardman's studies took place shaped the definition of fuel poverty based on the ideas offered by Lewis[111] to conceptualise this phenomenon as follows:

> (...) The inability to afford adequate warmth because of the energy efficiency at the home.[112]

In order to understand the reasons that led Boardman to develop this definition, it is necessary to understand the underlying conditions of her study. Contrary to what might be thought, the emergence of fuel poverty was not a response to the energy crisis of 1970, even though this crisis strengthened the phenomenon. In the United Kingdom, the causes that led to the advent of fuel poverty went back well before 1970.

Due to regulatory misjudgements, the Public Health Act of 1845, concerning environmental health standards and British dwellings, prioritised other aspects such as structural stability, lighting, and ventilation, among others, leaving the obligation of adequate heating unreinforced. In this way, the British regulatory framework concentrated on keeping houses dry rather than warm. However, fireplaces were frequently used in all rooms and were considered part of the structure. With the transition to coal, heating systems ceased to be part of the structure of the dwelling, and there began to be adequate heating provision in the United Kingdom,[113] given

---

[107] Luis Cordova and Milian Gomez (2025, pp. 207–208).

[108] Boardman (1991).

[109] Liddell (2012), p. 2.

[110] Bouzarovski and Petrova (2015), p. 31.

[111] Lewis (1982), p. 1.

[112] Boardman (1991), p. 219.

[113] Boardman (1991), p. 11.

systems that only allowed some rooms to be heated, reducing the living space of the dwelling.

The very architectural structure of English houses prevented them from being kept warm, making them energy inefficient,[114] an issue that remained ignored in the political and legal sphere. This phenomenon became evident in 1919 when subsidies were granted for social housing construction, where conditions such as space, lighting and fresh air were prioritised without paying attention to the need to create heating systems.[115] This need was only realised in 1946 by the Fuel and Power Advisory Committee, highlighting the need for thermal insulation in English homes. However, such recommendations had no impact on improving home energy efficiency. Despite this, it remained a recurring theme in 1961 in the Parker-Morris Report.[116]

It was not until 1970 that some thermal insulation standards slowly began to manifest themselves in the United Kingdom. The effects of the non-existence of heating standards meant that hypothermia began to affect vulnerable sections of the British population, such as children and seniors, especially in the extremely cold winter of 1963.[117]

With the advent of the energy crisis in 1970, the resulting inflation only aggravated the situation in the United Kingdom.[118] Boardman thus theoretically developed fuel poverty, which public decision-makers resisted by equating it with poverty.

Having briefly analysed the context that generated the rationale for fuel poverty, three pillars that have transcended over time can be identified. According to Thomson, fuel poverty has been explained by low household income, high market prices, and energy inefficiency in housing.[119]

These aspects highlight an essential element in determining the existence of fuel poverty: the affordability of energy. In this sense, Boardman's operationalisation of fuel poverty determined that energy expenses should not exceed the threshold of 10% of the household budget and, if they did, additional assistance should be provided. This percentage was the basic threshold defined for households to be able to have adequate energy services, including heating.[120]

In this way, Boardman established a relationship between energy expenditures and household income. This relationship was supported generally by the fact that household disposable income to cover energy expenditures increases with family

[114] Osbaldeston (1984).

[115] Rudge (2012), pp. 7–9.

[116] Boardman (1991), pp. 12–13.

[117] Boardman (1991), pp. 16–17.

[118] Cf. supra, pp. 38–41.

[119] Thomson et al. (2017).

[120] Boardman (1991), p. 201.

size. In turn, Boardman considered the equivalent relationship between the number of cohabitants and the living space of dwellings.[121]

In this way, Boardman's ideas took root over time and in academia.[122] Nevertheless, despite its initial name (Fuel Poverty), it is now more commonly called energy poverty.[123] Thus, the denomination "energy poverty" has spread as a more often-used denomination to describe energy deprivation in housing.[124] What was once a tiny academic movement around this phenomenon has become a prolific interdisciplinary research field.

This context has led to an understanding of fuel poverty that has moved beyond focusing on the lack of income to cover energy services (energy affordability).[125] Today, research associated with fuel poverty has diversified from one-dimensional perspectives to multidimensional approaches.[126] Although such progress makes this field of research more complex, fuel poverty can only be assessed as a phenomenon caused by a multi-causality.

A political maturation at the international and regional levels around energy poverty has accompanied this evolution. Since 2005, the United Nations Development Programme has defined energy poverty as:

> Inability to cook with modern cooking fuels and the lack of a bare minimum of electric lighting to read or for other household and productive activities at sunset.[127]

This approach highlights two metrics of energy poverty that were commonly used globally. The first of these metrics is lack of electricity, and the second is dependence on solid biomass fuels such as wood for cooking and heating.[128] While this approach is insufficient given the multiplicity of forms of energy and energy services on which human energy needs depend, in 2007, the Asian Development Bank defined energy poverty as:

> The absence of sufficient choice in accessing adequate, affordable, reliable, high-quality, safe and environmentally benign energy services to support economic and human development.[129]

However, the energy ladder framework used to measure energy poverty continued to focus on access to electricity and clean cooking. In this regard, the Asian Development Bank, through the energy ladder framework, classifies household

---

[121] Boardman (1991), p. 201.

[122] Cf. Romero et al. (2018); Galvin (2020); Sokołowski et al. (2020); Deller et al. (2021); Lin and (2020).

[123] Cf. Sovacool et al. (2012b); Apergis et al. (2022); Day et al. (2016); Brugger (2016); Bazilian et al. (2013); Spreng and Pachauri (2003); Thomson et al. (2017); Simcock et al. (2016).

[124] Thomson et al. (2017), p. 879; Thomson et al. (2016).

[125] Pereira et al. (2021), p. 3.

[126] Nussbaumer et al. (2012), p. 232.

[127] Gaye (2007), p. 4.

[128] Sovacool and Dworkin (2012), p. 15.

[129] Masud et al. (2007), p. 47; Reddy (2000), p. 44.

fuels in a broad spectrum. In this context, the use of simple biomass fuels, fossil household fuels such as paraffin and electricity as a modern form of energy are assessed.[130]

In the European Union, concern about energy poverty began to be noted in 2007, when the term was discussed more frequently in EU policy documents.[131] However, it was not until 2008 that the European Union ventured to give a concept of energy poverty as follows:

> "40. "Energy poverty" means the situation where the members of a household cannot afford to heat their home to an acceptable standard, based on the levels recommended by the World Health Organisation.
>
> 41. "affordable price" means a price defined by Member States at national level in consultation with national regulatory authorities, social partners and relevant stakeholders while taking account of the definition of energy poverty provided for in point 40".[132]

These provisions offered by the European Union took up the idea of energy affordability as the sole determinant of energy poverty. This approach only mentions heating services to maintain a temperature following World Health Organisation standards. While home heating generated the debate around fuel poverty, energy services have diversified to meet specific human needs. For this reason, this result responded to its historical moment by leaving out many of the energy services that underpin the lives of EU citizens. Nevertheless, the understanding of energy poverty at the regulatory level has continued to evolve over the years.[133]

However, it is worth noting that this definition takes a broad approach by giving autonomy to member states to define the affordable price. This approach is a step forward given that the economic and social reality of each EU Member State is different and, therefore, energy prices and energy consumption patterns may vary from one State to another.

Currently, the European Union determines that fuel poverty exists when energy bills represent a high percentage of consumers' income, which affects their ability to cover other expenses. It can also occur when consumers are forced to reduce their household energy consumption.[134] This situation would affect the ability to use energy, as described by Walker.[135]

Although, from a conceptual perspective, energy affordability remains one of the leading indicators of fuel poverty, many indicators are now used to measure it. Such indicators include arrears on utility bills; inability to keep the house warm; high share of energy expenditure in household income; low absolute energy expenditure; the risk of poverty or social exclusion; household prices of electricity, gas, biomass,

---

[130] Sovacool (2012), p. 273; Reddy (2000), p. 64.

[131] Thomson et al. (2016), p. 16.

[132] European Parliament (2008), p. 9.

[133] Cf. European Commission (2020)

[134] Energy Poverty Advisory Hub (2022).

[135] Cf. already supra, p. 105–106.

fuel oil, coal; district heating; energy efficiency of housing; excess mortality in winters, air conditioning (heating and air-conditioning) among other indicators.[136]

The academic debate around fuel poverty has taken on various dimensions. An interesting perspective is presented by Day, Walker and Simcock when analysing energy poverty using a capabilities framework. Such an approach responds to the analysis of the relationship between energy consumption, energy services and what these services generate in terms of people's well-being. This approach highlights the importance of energy in ensuring the full realisation of the human personality.[137]

For this approach, Day, Walker and Simcock start from the capability theory developed by Sen and Nussbaum.[138] In this sense, the analysis of energy poverty is based on two central elements defined by Sen: functionings and capabilities.

The first of these elements (functionings) is understood as beings and doings that lead to each person's achievements: enjoyment of a good diet, health, and education, among many others. On the other hand, capabilities are the opportunities to materialise functions in order to facilitate the possibility of choosing one type of life or another.[139] Based on this reasoning, Day, Walker and Simcock define energy poverty as follows:

> An inability to realise essential capabilities as a direct or indirect result of insufficient access to affordable, reliable and safe energy services, and taking into account available reasonable alternative means of realising these capabilities.[140]

This definition refers to the adverse effects of energy poverty on the human personality's full realisation. It highlights the limits that energy poverty imposes on people's capacity for development, making it difficult to access material living conditions that support human dignity and the realisation of the desires and aspirations of the population affected by this phenomenon.

Although assuming this definition may harm the measurement and monitoring of energy poverty on a large scale, it presents energy as an indispensable element to support capabilities, especially in the Global South. In developing countries, energy poverty affects many areas, such as employment, education, social participation, and other elements necessary to ensure a dignified life.[141]

The above leads this research to address the approach to energy poverty developed by Bouzarovski and Petrova. In this respect, it is relevant to highlight the divergent elements concerning energy poverty in developing and developed countries. In the former, energy poverty refers to insufficient infrastructure to meet energy needs such as cooking, lighting, household appliances, cooling, and heating systems. Meanwhile, in developed countries, energy poverty refers to the adequacy

[136] Cf. Gouveia et al. (2022).

[137] Day et al. (2016), p. 255.

[138] Cf. Nussbaum and Sen (1993); Sen (1992); Sen (1999); Nussbaum (2001).

[139] Sen (1992), pp. 39–40.

[140] Day et al. (2016), p. 260.

[141] Day et al. (2016), pp. 260–261.

of home heating and other systems, such as refrigeration and lighting, among other relevant elements.[142]

Recognising this divergent reality concerning energy poverty, Bouzarovski and Petrova define this category as:

> As a set of domestic energy circumstances that do not allow for participating in the lifestyles, customs and activities that define membership of society.[143]

In this way, the social dimension of fuel poverty is described beyond any fouling of indicators for its measurement. Although monitoring fuel poverty is a necessary process, identifying its causes and consequences is essential to raise awareness of the need to protect people affected by this phenomenon. This identification is the first step in implementing mechanisms to measure, monitor, and take effective actions to reduce and eliminate energy poverty.

In this context, it is necessary to define energy vulnerability as the factors leading to energy poverty.[144] Therefore, determining these factors leads to identifying the causes and conditions that generate energy poverty. In this respect, Bouzarovski and Petrova define the factors that determine the existence of energy vulnerability and the circumstances that determine it.

The first of these factors is access to energy. This first factor of energy vulnerability is determined by the low availability of energy carriers to meet household energy needs. This factor relates to energy accessibility as one of the pillars of energy security as a *conditio sine qua non* for eradicating energy poverty, establishing energy security and the satisfaction of the right to energy. In this context, accessibility depends on internal circumstances regarding energy needs and consumption patterns manifested in the household and external circumstances (political, social, economic, or infrastructural conditions).[145]

The second factor of energy vulnerability is energy affordability. This factor, already discussed above as a pillar of energy security, responds to the relationship between energy price and household income.[146] In turn, energy affordability depends on market prices and the efficiency and costs of the equipment needed to use it. Moreover, according to Pachauri and Spreng, energy affordability is not only a function of monetary value, as some energy carriers may not have a commercial value, such as fuelwood. In these cases, the costs depend on several factors, such as the time taken for collection, processing and the energy efficiency of the specific energy carrier used.[147]

The statement above indicates that flexibility is the third factor contributing to energy vulnerability. Flexibility refers to the ability to choose the energy or energy

---

[142] Bouzarovski and Petrova (2015), p. 32.

[143] Bouzarovski and Petrova (2015); Buzar (2016), pp. 9–10.

[144] Bouzarovski (2018), p. 18; Bouzarovski and Petrova (2015), p. 35; Bouzarovski (2014).

[145] Bouzarovski and Petrova (2015), p. 37.

[146] Walker and Day (2012).

[147] Spreng and Pachauri (2003), pp. 273–274; Freund and Wallich (1996).

service used to meet intra-household needs.[148] In this sense, choice can be affected by, among other factors, the availability and affordability of energy. These limits may force people to use a specific type of energy carrier or service because it is the only one available or the most affordable.

Another factor determining energy vulnerability is the energy efficiency of households. In dwellings with low energy efficiency, there are higher energy losses due to transforming useful energy into non-useful forms of energy.[149] This situation leads to higher energy and economic costs. Reducing energy losses can motivate people to change the type of energy used and opt for more energy-saving energy systems.[150]

The last two energy vulnerability indicators that Bouzarovski and Petrova identified are human needs and practices.[151] Needs become a factor of energy vulnerability when a mismatch between the needs of people in their dwellings and the energy services available becomes apparent. This situation implies that a set of needs may not be met due to the unavailability of the necessary energy services. This reality harms people's well-being due to the appearance of social, economic, and cultural disparities.

In turn, people's practices can be another factor that can generate energy vulnerability, leading to energy poverty. The lack of knowledge regarding national support programmes and energy use has been identified in this sense.[152] Low levels of energy literacy determine this factor. For this reason, it is crucial to equip people with the necessary knowledge to prevent energy vulnerability as a breeding ground for fuel poverty. In turn, promoting energy literacy settles a path to reduce energy poverty by providing people with the necessary tools to escape such a situation.[153]

The reality described until now frames the phenomenon of energy poverty in the household context. While the right to energy covers this context, it is not the only one to be considered. According to the United Nations Advisory Group on Energy and Climate Change, three incremental levels of energy access are described. The first level consists of basic human needs, including electricity for lighting, health, and many others, as well as modern fuels and technologies for cooking and air conditioning. The second level addresses using energy for productive purposes, such as agriculture and transport. The third level described by the Advisory Group relates to the needs of modern societies to ensure the use of many other modern household equipment, such as those associated with communication and air conditioning, as well as private transportation, among others.[154]

---

148 Bouzarovski and Petrova (2015), p. 37.

149 Bouzarovski and Petrova (2015), p. 37.

150 Milne and Boardman (2000), p. 413.

151 Bouzarovski and Petrova (2015), p. 37.

152 Bouzarovski and Petrova (2015), p. 37; Thomson et al. (2017), p. 880.

153 Adams et al. (2022).

154 The Secretary-General's Advisory Group on Energy and Climate Change (2010).

Energy poverty, as well as energy poverty in multiple contexts, has attracted the attention of states, taking into consideration its negative impact on both the development of nations and the quality of life of the population. The negative consequences of energy poverty can be divided into direct and indirect. Direct consequences include the cooling of houses during the winter or their extreme heating during the summer, poor indoor air quality, the impact on energy bills and, consequently, disconnection from the central grid. Indirect effects on physical and mental health, social exclusion, air pollution, and reduced family economic capacity, among others, could occur.[155]

Although the consequences mentioned above occur in the family context, the lack of energy also affects the productivity of economic sectors, especially the case of small businesses, and the normal development of the rest of the services and price increases. The lack of sufficient energy to cover demand will harm the development of any process.

This phenomenon has led to an essential level of concern on the part of States, which has led to the creation of mechanisms to protect energy consumers. Based on the above, the recognition of the right to energy and its protection through a system of guarantees[156] has been constantly analysed by the States. On this path, such recognition is the most significant legal conquest achieved in national legal systems.

For these reasons, the right to energy has been reflected at the political level in national energy policies through the priority given to energy security. For this purpose, public policies must consider energy justice and democracy as two other core concepts of the right to energy.

In this context, it is worth noting that the intersection between energy and poverty offers many possibilities for seeking justice and equity between people. It is, therefore, essential to understand the links between energy vulnerability and poverty and energy justice[157] as a core concept of the right to energy.

5.3.2.3 Energy Justice

The energy justice debate has been raging in academia for over two decades. In 2010, Guruswamy defined energy justice as a combination of justice and energy for applying basic principles. In this sense, Guruswamy argued that energy justice pursues the application of fairness to the manifestations of injustice among people deprived of sustainable energy.[158]

However, according to Jenkins, the first precursors of energy justice as a policy-oriented term[159] were McCauley, Heffron, Stephan and Jenkins in 2013 with their

[155] Thomson et al. (2017).

[156] Cf. infra, Sect. 6.5.

[157] Hernández (2015), p. 152.

[158] Guruswamy (2010), p. 233.

[159] Jenkins (2018), p. 117.

publication "Advancing Energy Justice: The Triumvirate of Tenets."[160] Thus, in the work of the authors, as mentioned earlier, energy justice was constituted by taking Campbell's conceptualisation of justice as a starting point:

> (...) is a combination of ensuring and recognising the basic equal worth of all human beings together with a commitment to the "distribution of good and bad things.[161]

Taking into consideration this approach and that of many other authors,[162] the definition of energy justice took advantage of the established doctrine of environmental justice[163] and climate or atmospheric justice.[164] However, in Jenkins' view, energy justice surpassed its predecessors by being more specific in its subject matter and having a systemic approach. Moreover, it is not the result of anti-establishment social movements and is supported by a solid methodological tradition with applications in academia and politics.[165]

In this context, since energy justice took root in academia, it has been oriented towards:

> To provide all individuals, across all areas, with safe, affordable and sustainable energy. The focus here is firmly on energy policy and the key theme of energy systems.[166]

From this declaration, energy justice directly addresses energy policy and energy systems in order to highlight social justice within energy systems. With the shaping of energy justice, social issues within the energy field are highlighted to ensure universal access to energy and reduce the disparities that may arise in this field.

In 2014, Sovacool and Dworkin defined energy justice as everyone's right to access energy services, regardless of whether they are citizens of developed or developing economies. They also see the term as encompassing how energy-related negative environmental and social impacts are distributed in space and time, including human rights abuses and the access that disadvantaged communities have or should have to solutions. Energy justice ensures that energy permitting and siting do not infringe on fundamental civil liberties and that communities are informed and meaningfully represented in energy decisions.[167]

One year later, Sovacool and Dworkin, to bring more clarity to the definition of energy justice, pointed to three key elements:

- "Costs, or how the hazards and externalities of the energy system are imposed on communities unequally, often the poor and marginalised.
- Benefits, or how access to modern energy systems and services, are highly uneven.

---

[160] McCauley et al. (2013).

[161] Campbell (2010).

[162] Cf. McCauley et al. (2013), p. 1.

[163] Schlosberg (2007).

[164] Dawson (2010); Vanderheiden (2008); Sovacool and Linnér (2016), p. 19.

[165] Jenkins (2018), p. 120.

[166] McCauley et al. (2013), p. 1.

[167] Sovacool and Dworkin (2014), p. 5.

- Procedures, or how many energy projects proceed with exclusionary forms of decision-making that lack due process and representation".[168]

Based on these elements, energy justice is associated with well-being, equity, due process, happiness, and freedom for both the subjects involved, on the one hand, the energy suppliers and, on the other, the people who use it. In this way, energy justice promotes the reduction of environmental and social risks that may arise from the energy sector, guarantees equitable access to energy and information related to this sector, and promotes the empowerment of people through participation in decision-making processes in this field.[169]

By 2016, Sovacool continued this line of thinking on energy justice by stating that it can be understood as:

> A global energy system that fairly disseminates both the benefits and costs of energy services and one that contributes to more representative and impartial energy decision-making.[170]

This definition further strengthens this position by linking energy justice to the fair distribution of energy services costs and benefits with an inclusive and impartial decision-making system. This position opened a second pathway for determining the principles underpinning energy justice.[171] The first of these pathways was established by energy justice pioneers in 2013, laying out a triumvirate of principles, including distributive, procedural and recognition justice..[172]

The second pathway was established by Sovacool et al. in 2016, stating eight basic energy justice principles. These principles are energy availability, energy affordability, due process, transparency and accountability, sustainability, intragenerational equity, intergenerational equity, and accountability.[173]

As mentioned, energy justice orbits on a triumvirate of principles for McCauley, Heffron, Stephan, and Jenkins. These principles include distributive as the first tenant. This principle is inherently spatial and includes sharing the energy sector's costs, risks, and externalities, as well as the benefits and access to the energy system by all members of society[174] beyond resource distribution and proximity.[175]

According to Fuller and McCauley, within the energy justice framework, distributive justice focuses on the two extremes of the energy supply chain. The first is energy generation, with the unfair distribution and development of energy infrastructure, such as the nuclear industry, being debated from a geospatial perspective

168 Sovacool and Dworkin (2015), p. 437.

169 Sovacool and Dworkin (2015), p. 437.

170 Sovacool et al. (2016), p. 4.

171 Heffron and McCauley (2017), p. 659.

172 McCauley et al. (2013).

173 Sovacool et al. (2016).

174 McCauley et al. (2013), p. 2.

175 Walker (2009).

for specific communities.[176] On the other hand, distributive justice has focused on energy consumption, specifically affordable access to energy.[177] Since Boardman's work was published, there has been a broad debate on energy poverty and vulnerability globally.[178]

In this regard, Walker and Day state:

> Fundamentally, fuel poverty is a matter of distributive injustice in access to energy services which is produced through the interaction between underlying inequalities related to income, energy prices and housing.[179]

From the scenario described above, distributive justice essentially pursues fair energy distribution. Such distribution pursues the primary objective of eradicating injustices related to the disproportionate distribution and disproportionate costs and benefits among energy end-users.[180]

The second principle of energy justice is procedural justice, which includes access to energy information, participation in decision-making processes and access to justice mechanisms.[181] Given the doctrinal heritage of environmental justice, the procedural justice principle of energy justice is also based on the fair treatment and meaningful participation of all persons[182] in an impartial manner through appropriate and sympathetic engagement mechanisms.[183]

A cardinal element of procedural justice as a principle of energetic justice relates to:

> Fairness in decision-making processes, including those that develop and deliver policies that impact people's ability to secure energy services.[184]

In this sense, Simcock states that the pillars of fair decision-making processes involve three essential elements. The first element is inclusion, which refers to allowing the participation of the people affected by the energy decision to be evaluated. The second of these elements is influence, which is determined by the ability of the results of people's participation to shape the decision.[185]

Finally, the third element is access to information to ensure transparency, effective participation, and informed consent of those affected by the decision to be taken. The observance of these three elements defines how the expectations of the people affected by the outcomes of the decision-making process will be realised.[186]

---

176 Endres (2009).

177 Fuller and McCauley (2016), p. 2.

178 Cf. supra, pp. 118–120.

179 Walker and Day (2012), p. 73.

180 Paškevičius (2020), p. 172.

181 McCauley et al. (2013), p. 2.

182 Davies (2006), pp. 710–711.

183 McCauley et al. (2013), p. 2.

184 Hernández et al. (2022), p. 132.

185 Simcock (2016), pp. 468–470.

186 Simcock (2016), pp. 468–470.

Huhta highlights the multiple implications of energy decisions on fulfilling human rights, access to information, public participation, access to justice, and many other areas.[187] This reality is most evident in the right to energy, the realisation of which depends on energy decisions. For this reason, procedural justice reinforces the need for people's empowerment to ensure the full realisation of the right to energy and other human rights that depend on energy.

Creating such empowerment mechanisms provides legal protection for the holders of the right to energy. For this purpose, the universal recognition of people as subjects of the right to energy, especially those living in energy poverty, is essential. This situation brings up the third principle of energy justice: recognition justice.

The recognition justice principle involves identifying and respecting those affected by energy decision-making. This principle implies the satisfaction of energy-related needs, rights, and experiences, as well as special attention to neglected social sectors.[188]

While according to McCauley et al., recognition justice aims at fair representation with equal political rights in a context free of degrading and disrespectful treatment, this context was later expanded.[189] No human rights are more important than others, so giving civil and political rights a preponderance over economic, social, and cultural rights is unacceptable.

This reality is irrefutable when we consider that existence in conditions of dignity depends on the latter. In this respect, Heffron states:

> Recognition justice is concerned with the recognition of rights of different groups and in particular local and/or indigenous communities.[190]

This definition leaves the framework open for including all human rights, especially the right to energy, as a legal mechanism to safeguard against energy injustices. Thus, recognition justice involves identifying social groups that have been ignored, marginalised, or misrepresented in energy systems and recognising different sociocultural perspectives[191] around specific energy needs and vulnerabilities of different social groups.[192] For this reason, recognition justice aims to give respect to all people who have not been valued[193] within energy systems and have, therefore, been disadvantaged compared to the rest of society.

McCauley and Heffron added another principle to these three traditional energy justice principles.[194] This principle is restorative justice directed at energy suppliers regarding the obligation to restore environmental damage. Heffron and McCauley first substantiated this principle of energy justice in 2017. According to the authors

---

[187] Huhta (2023), p. 10.

[188] McCauley et al. (2013), p. 2.

[189] McCauley et al. (2013), p. 2.; Salter et al. (2018), p. 6.

[190] Heffron (2022), p. 2.

[191] Vågerö and Zeyringer (2023), p. 2.

[192] Lee and Byrne (2019), p. 2.

[193] Wood and Roelich (2020), p. 147.

[194] McHarg (2020), p. 21.

mentioned above, restorative justice with doctrinal origins in criminal law[195] aims to repair damage to people, society, or nature. For this reason, this principle is fully applicable within the energy justice framework. An example of this is accidents in the energy sector.[196]

In this context, restorative justice becomes a policy tool to ensure energy justice in practice. This principle complements the three principles described above to restore distributive justice. In turn, procedural justice provides the necessary cause to urge the competent bodies to restore the harm that may have occurred as part of the functioning of the energy system or decision-making processes. In addition, recognition justice is particularly important for implementing restorative justice, as specific social sectors that need special attention and protection are neglected.[197]

Finally, Sovacool proposed cosmopolitan justice as a principle in 2016. This author argues that:

> Cosmopolitan justice accepts that all human beings have equal moral worth and that our responsibilities to others do not stop at borders.[198]

Therefore, the principles of energy justice, especially distributive justice and procedural justice, are universally applicable to all human beings regardless of the physical borders of states or citizenship. That leads to the realisation that the application of energy justice is not limited to specific geographical areas or communities but should benefit all of humanity.[199]

Cosmopolitan justice promotes "global citizenship", where all people have an obligation to themselves and the rest of the world's people concerning the enforceability of States to meet energy and climate objectives in the interests of intergenerational justice. In this way, a link is evident between this principle of energy justice and intergenerational equity that integrates environmental law. Thus, the principle of cosmopolitan justice pursues environmental protection and safeguards energy resources to enable future generations to meet their energy needs as fundamental human needs.[200]

These energy justice principles underpin the need to recognise and protect the right to energy. Regarding distribution, the right to energy must ensure fair and equitable access to energy. This access must be safeguarded through procedural justice by establishing mechanisms for public participation in energy decision-making processes and by creating effective enforcement systems.

For this purpose, it is imperative to determine who is entitled to demand the obligations derived from the content of the right to energy, with preferential protection for those people in energy vulnerability or poverty. Binding mechanisms complement the above to restore the full enjoyment of the right to energy based on

---

[195] Cf. Galaway and Hudson (1996).

[196] Heffron and McCauley (2017), pp. 660–661.

[197] Hazrati and Heffron (2021), p. 4.

[198] Sovacool (2016), p. 548.

[199] Luis Cordova 2026, p. 5.

[200] Heffron and De Fontenelle (2023), p. 145.

control bodies that allow for the enforceability of this right. Finally, implementing the principle of cosmopolitan justice leads to an energy transition to mitigate climate change and ensures energy availability for future generations.

This vision is complemented by the set of principles of energy justice proposed by Sovacool et al.[201] Without implying a break with the theory advanced by McCauley et al.,[202] Sovacool et al. propose new principles that serve as a background and a required study for understanding the right to energy. Many of these new principles relate to the doctrine analysed in this research regarding energy security and poverty. In this sense, the availability and affordability of energy stand out.

The first of these principles establishes the need for sufficient high-quality energy resources. This principle refers to elements explained earlier, such as energy sufficiency. To this are added qualifiers concerning energy resources, which must be able to provide a significant amount of energy with increased energy efficiency.[203] Added to this is the principle of energy affordability, which promotes that energy costs do not constitute a financial burden for individuals, especially those on low incomes.[204]

Another proposed principle related to the principle of procedural justice is due process. This principle is fundamental in linking human rights and energy justice.[205] This affirmation involves all human rights, particularly the right to energy, which must be safeguarded through effective protection mechanisms to ensure its legal protection and enjoyment.

The principle of due process gives way to the transparency and accountability principle. This principle promotes access to quality information on energy and the environment and the implementation of transparent and accountable decision-making mechanisms.[206] This principle is related to the principle of restorative justice, especially in the field of decommissioning and waste management actions derived from the energy generation process.[207] In addition, the transparency and accountability principles become the basis for good energy governance.[208]

In addition to these principles, Sovacool et al. defined sustainability from a perspective that has been described as restrictive and anthropocentric.[209] In this sense, these authors limit themselves to proposing that natural energy resources not be depleted rapidly. They, therefore, propose the creation of mechanisms to ensure the availability of energy to meet the energy needs of future generations.[210]

---

201 Sovacool et al. (2016).

202 McCauley et al. (2013).

203 Hiteva and Sovacool (2017), p. 633.

204 Sovacool et al. (2016), p. 5.

205 Redgwell and Rajamani (2020), p. 53.

206 Sovacool et al. (2016), p. 5.

207 Heffron (2022), p. 6.

208 Ciplet (2021), p. 10.

209 Wood and Roelich (2020), p. 147.

210 Sovacool et al. (2016), p. 5.

Based on the above, Sovacool et al. propose two further principles called intra- and intergenerational equity. The intra-generational equity principle aligns with Sustainable Development Goal 7 by addressing the universal right to fair access to energy services. Meanwhile, the principle of intergenerational justice is to enjoy a good life that is not affected by the negative environmental impact of energy systems on the environment.[211]

Although, a priori, the principle of intergenerational equity seems to be oriented only towards environmental protection, it also applies to the management of natural resources. The extractivist nature of today's energy systems threatens the availability of non-renewable natural resources on Earth. Therefore, such practices threaten future generations by depriving them of energy resources that can contribute to meeting future energy needs. This threat means that the principle of intergenerational equity can be oriented towards preserving the energy interests of future generations by eradicating the uncontrolled consumption of non-renewable natural energy resources.

Of course, this line of thinking goes hand in hand with environmental protection. This link is reinforced by responsibility, as the last principle was put forward by Sovacool et al. This last principle reinforces the State's responsibility for environmental protection and, especially, for threats from the energy sector to meet the climate goals set out in the global agenda.[212]

The principles of energy justice described above have taken root in contemporary academia. For example, Fløytrup et al. explain the energy justice framework along five main axes that relate to the pillars of energy security and determine the conceptual delimitation of the right to energy. The first of these axes is energy availability, which is the primary aspect of energy justice.[213]

This axis is the starting point for the realisation of the right to energy. Energy availability materialises from each country's physical resources and technical facilities. The second axis of energy justice is accessibility and reliability for fair access to energy services under the intergenerational equity prism.[214]

Affordability is the third axis of energy justice through stable and equitable prices that do not imply the use of a disproportionately large share in satisfying energy needs. The fourth element is sustainability, which is based on managing natural resources without affecting intergenerational equity. The fifth element is good governance, which is divided into three areas: the State's responsibility for the sustainable management of natural resources, the accountability of the energy system for democratic decision-making and the creation of mechanisms for participation in energy-related decision-making.[215]

---

[211] Sovacool et al. (2016), p. 5.

[212] Sovacool et al. (2016), p. 5.

[213] Fløytrup et al. (2022).

[214] Sovacool and Dworkin (2015).

[215] Fløytrup et al. (2022).

5.3.2.4 Energy Democracy

That context leads to the emergence of energy democracy in the literature and on public agendas due to humanity's energy problems. The energy crises that have plagued humanity have imposed challenges that have become opportunities for transforming energy systems for the sake of energy sovereignty. One example of such opportunities is the promotion of energy democracy in public policy, which has motivated a relatively recent and developing debate dating back to 2012.

According to James, Kunze and Becker, the concept of energy democracy emerged within the framework of the environmental justice movement in Germany. In this framework, the 2012 Lausitz Climate Camp declared:

> Energy democracy means that everybody is ensured access to sufficient energy. Energy production must thereby neither pollute the environment nor harm people. More concretely, this means that fossil fuel resources must be left in the ground, the means of production need to be socialised and democratised, and that we must rethink our overall attitude towards energy consumption.[216]

This definition set a precedent in academia that aligns with several postulates on energy security, poverty, and justice. Such a definition integrates several relevant spheres that influence the development of the right to energy, among which universal access can be highlighted. In this area of thought, reference is made to energy sufficiency as an element that makes it possible to ensure access to energy from an environmental sustainability perspective.

For this reason, the definition of energy democracy initially calls for an energy transition from fossil fuels due to their profoundly negative environmental impact to renewable energy sources. To this end, it calls for the socialisation of the means of production, the democratisation of energy generation and a paradigm shift in energy consumption.

This perspective on energy democracy prompted Kunze and Becker to divide, didactically, energy democracy into four essential areas. The first of these areas is democratisation and participation. The approach to this area is closely related to the procedural justice principle of energy justice, which promotes popular participation in energy decision-making processes and energy policy.[217]

The second area refers to the ownership regime within energy systems. In this regard, Kunze and Becker propose a change in the status quo of contemporary energy systems by calling for collective, political, and public regulation of energy infrastructure based on a combination of private and State ownership under organisational forms such as cooperatives. This call responds to the high impact of energy production on humanity and the environment.[218]

Thirdly, the authors mentioned above refer to the production of surplus value and employment as part of implementing energy democracy. This aspect of energy

---

[216] Angel 2016, p. 10; Kunze and Becker (2014), p. 8.

[217] Kunze and Becker (2014), p. 9.

[218] Kunze and Becker (2014), pp. 9–10.

democracy refers to sustainability and economic viability through the exploitation of renewable sources for energy generation.[219]

In this sense, energy democracy based on renewable sources entails capital investment for developing the generation system and its maintenance. That is due to free energy carriers such as wind, sunlight, or water. For this reason, the profits derived from the commercialisation of the surplus energy generated can be reinvested in the development of the communities and the expansion of generation systems, among other purposes.[220]

In addition, the exercise of energy democracy favours the creation of jobs.[221] This employment source is because the operation, management and management of the generation systems created need a workforce to guarantee their operation. This context leads to the emergence of a source of employment that benefits the communities where these types of initiatives are developed.[222]

Finally, the fourth area of energy democracy described by Kunze and Becker is ecology and sufficiency. This area initially encompasses the rational consumption of energy by abandoning excessive consumption patterns. In addition to that, there is the obligatory ecological respect for the conservation of plant and animal species by minimising the harmful effects of using renewable energy sources. Such effects include the impact on terrestrial and aquatic ecosystems.[223]

These areas defined by Kunze and Becker have been supported by academia. An example of this is the definition of energy democracy presented by Szwed and Maciejewska and, in turn, supported by Okraszewska:

> System, in which the society is actively involved in the construction and construction of an energy model, which should be controlled by us.[224]

This conceptualisation is consistent with the second area (ownership) presented by Kunze and Becker. In this way, energy democracy is perpetuated as a manifestation of social empowerment, where society is conceived as an active entity in energy systems. This empowerment involves social participation in both the design and implementation of the energy sector and in its control. For this reason, the above context leads van Veelen and van der Horst to highlight energy democracy within the framework of democratic governance.[225]

---

[219] Kunze and Becker (2014), p. 10.

[220] Kotilainen (2020), p. 11; REScoop 20–20-20 Consortium (2020), p. 25; Heldeweg and Séverine Saintier (2020), p. 10.

[221] Kunze and Becker (2014), pp. 10–11.

[222] REScoop 20–20-20 Consortium (2020), pp. 18, 21; Ford et al. (2016), p. 13; Caramizaru and Uihlein (2020), p. 25; Leal-arcas et al. (2019), p. 44.

[223] Maradin (2021), p. 180; Sani et al. (2019), p. 550; Gómez Milian and Luis Cordova (2023), p. 4.

[224] "A system in which society actively participates in the selection and construction of the energy model, maintaining control over it". (Own translation) Szwed and Maciejewska (2014), p. 4; Okraszewska (2016), p. 40.

[225] van Veelen and van der Horst (2018), pp. 20–22.

The aforementioned social participation finds support in the field of energy justice, especially in terms of procedural justice, turning energy justice and energy democracy into analogous elements.[226] Such support evidences a coherence in the academy concerning the line of thought followed where each of the elements (energy security, energy justice, energy democracy, among others such as energy sovereignty) have been aligned in a consistent way to what this research will base as the right to energy.

In this sense, the realisation of the right to energy can be guaranteed, complementary to the State's obligation, by strengthening energy democracy through popular participation in the energy sector. That allows society to take the reins through the self-fulfilment of energy needs. In this respect, Sweeney defines:

> Energy democracy is about workers' and communities' ability to decide who owns and operates our energy systems, how energy is produced, and for what purpose.[227]

According to Sweeney, in 2015, there was a trend towards more democratic public ownership of the energy sector. This trend involved a growing proliferation of campaigns for the municipalisation and re-municipalisation of energy activity. Such campaigns aimed to create municipal utilities, picking up where the proliferation of neoliberal tendencies in the energy field had left off. In this way, there has been a relative transfer of power to communities to control the operation of public energy services.[228]

These changes in control mechanisms have meant that the scope of energy democracy has been extended. Such extension has led to a conception of energy democracy as a civic movement that links decarbonisation and social control over energy.[229] In this sense, Paddock and Greenblum have identified forms of popular control over energy decision-making regarding energy sources as a positive trend.[230]

The empowerment that energy democracy entails leads to people's self-satisfying of their energy needs as active subjects. For this reason, Morris and Jungjohann state that energy democracy enables people and energy communities to generate their energy, even though this practice may be financially costly for energy service providers.[231] Despite this, this research finds that the ability to self-serve energy needs is a matter of empowerment that seeks alternatives to secure the right to energy. In no case should such empowerment be interpreted as an exemption from the responsibilities of those liable for the right to energy vis-à-vis its holders.

The analysis developed so far regarding energy democracy leads to analysing energy prosumerism as a manifestation of empowerment in the energy sector. The term prosumer was coined in 1980 by Toffler to describe the situation in which the condition of producer and consumer becomes indistinguishable given a functional

---

[226] Weis et al. (2015), pp. 7–13.

[227] Sweeney et al. (2015), p. 23.

[228] Sweeney et al. (2015), p. 23.

[229] Strachan et al. (2015), p. 105.

[230] Paddock and Greenblum (2016), p. 157; Cumbers et al. (2013); Vansintjan (2015).

[231] Morris and Jungjohann (2016), p. vii.

fusion.[232] In this way, this theoretical creation transcended into the realm of energy democracy.

In this respect, Feldpausch-Parker et al. are of the well-founded opinion[233] that energy democracy:

> Represents an emergent social movement that re-imagines energy consumers as prosumers, or innovators, designers, and analysts who are involved in decisions at every stage, from energy production through consumption.[234]

The above definition consolidates the vision of energy democracy as an increase in citizen participation and empowerment for the benefit of citizens within the energy sector.[235] This perspective presents an evolutionary process, where people move from passive energy consumption to energy production by becoming energy prosumers.

Szulecki, going beyond this consumer-prosumer evolutionary process, refers to the energy prosumer as a typical ideal citizen of energy democracy and an emerging political subject.[236] Such an assertion leads this research to address further an emerging issue in academia that has broken with legal thinking: energy citizenship.[237]

In the ongoing analysis of energy prosumerism, it is necessary to highlight that this term brings together, on the one hand, the independent exercise of this type of practice and, on the other hand, the collective exercise under the so-called energy communities. In this respect, the European Union has been a pioneer in promoting this type of initiative.[238]

In this way, the European Union has become an example of energy democratisation at the international level by promoting decentralisation in which popular participation has been prioritised.[239] Today, the energy transition is not only associated with the responsibility of the state, but society has also taken an active role in two areas: meeting its energy demand and contributing to the transformation of energy matrices.

In this sense, it is worth highlighting the regulation of two types of energy communities: renewable energy communities and citizen energy communities contained in Directives 2018/2002 on the promotion of the use of energy from renewable sources[240] and 2019/944 on common rules for the internal electricity market.[241]

In order to gain clarity on both types of energy communities, Directive 2018/2002 regulates renewable energy communities as follows:

---

[232] Toffler (1980), p. 403; Stephens et al. (2015), p. 40.

[233] Stephens et al. (2015); Giancatarino (2013).

[234] Feldpausch-Parker et al. (2019), pp 2.

[235] Feldpausch-Parker et al. (2021), p. 172.

[236] Szulecki (2018), p. 22.

[237] Cf. infra, Sect. 5.3.2.5.

[238] Luis Cordova et al. (2023).

[239] ECRB (2020).

[240] European Parliament and European Council (2018).

[241] European Parliament and European Council (2019).

> in accordance with applicable national law, is based on open and voluntary participation, is autonomous and effectively controlled by partners or members which are located in the vicinity of the renewable energy projects owned and developed by that legal entity; whose partners or members are natural persons, SMEs or local authorities, including municipalities; whose primary purpose is to provide environmental, economic or social benefits to its partners or members or to the local areas where it operates, rather than financial gain.[242]

For its part, Directive 2019/944 defines citizen energy communities as:

> a legal entity based on voluntary and open participation and effectively controlled by partners or members who are natural persons, local authorities, including municipalities, or small enterprises, whose primary objective is to provide environmental, economic or social benefits to its members or partners or to the locality in which it operates, rather than generating a financial return, and is involved in the generation, including from renewable sources, distribution, supply, consumption, aggregation, storage of energy, provision of energy efficiency services or, provision of electric vehicle charging or other energy services to its members or partners.[243]

Both typologies share similarities and distinctions. They both possess independent legal identities and share the objective of generating environmental, social, and economic benefits for the community. Both types are overseen by their shareholders and members[244], and their primary economic activities are not energy-related. Another common element is voluntary participation in both types of energy communities.[245]

However, their notable differences include geographic scope, activities, participants, autonomy, and effective control. Renewable energy communities are linked to renewable energy projects owned by the community, whereas citizen energy communities have no such constraint. Renewable energy communities are restricted to renewable energy sources, whereas citizen energy communities can utilise both renewable and non-renewable sources. The latter can generate electricity exclusively, while the former can generate both electricity and heat.[246]

Renewable energy communities must have autonomy over their members and other stakeholders, while citizen energy communities have no autonomy requirement. However, decision-making should involve members in non-energy-related economic activities. As a result, control in renewable energy communities can be exerted by micro, small, and medium-sized enterprises, whereas large and medium-sized enterprises are excluded from citizen energy communities.[247]

Although energy prosumerism can and should be aligned with using renewable energy sources, the satisfaction of energy needs and, consequently, the right to energy, unfortunately, cannot be affected by environmental radicalism. The extreme fundamental importance of energy for the survival of the human species makes it

[242] European Parliament and European Council (2018), p. 3.

[243] European Parliament and European Council (2019).

[244] Council of European Energy Regulators (2019).

[245] Caramizaru and Uihlein (2020).

[246] Luis Cordova et al. (2023), p. 171.

[247] Luis Cordova et al. (2023), p. 171.

necessary to explore all possible alternatives, prioritising sources that are environmentally friendly. If these sources are not viable, the available sources must be used.

Following the analysis of energy democracy, the conclusion is that the creativity of academia, public decision-makers and regulatory frameworks have provided the arsenal of tools to promote the realisation of the right to energy. From an empowerment perspective, the active subjects of the right to energy, depending on the legal system in which they operate, can count on a greater or lesser degree of autonomy to meet their own energy needs in a complementary manner to the obligations of the duty-bearers of the right under study.

5.3.2.5 Energy Citizenship

For those reasons, the right to energy has also been defined as "a demand of the most vulnerable, weakest consumers against those agents with the most power, such as public administrations or energy companies".[248] Like many other rights, its constitutional recognition has resulted from the correlation of forces and the balance of power within states. For this reason, García and Mundó conceive it as an active claim by consumers against the administration and energy service providers.

In this sense, the term energy citizen has emerged as a basic concept of the right to energy in the scientific academy and is gaining momentum as an analogue concept to energy prosumerism. Energy citizenship, intricately linked to energy democracy, also introduces a change in the conception of energy consumers, empowering these subjects in the energy market.[249]

In this regard, Biresselioglu et al. argue that the conceptualisation of energy citizenship encompasses the active participation of individuals in the energy sector. This active participation involves the practice of energy prosumerism or the development of energy communities, leading to a decentralisation and democratisation of the energy system. In this way, individuals are empowered at the market level in the energy sector and the political level in energy policy.[250]

In line with the above, according to Devine-Wright's vision on energy citizenship:

> The public is conceived as active rather than passive stakeholders in energy system evolution and where the potential for action is framed by notions of equitable rights and responsibilities across society for dealing with the consequences of energy consumption, notably climate change.[251]

In this way, energy citizens are considered vital elements for the energy transition.[252] Therefore, society becomes an active agent within the energy system, and its

[248] Garcia and Mundó (2014).

[249] Ringholm (2022).

[250] Biresselioglu et al. (2022), p. 3.

[251] Devine-Wright (2007), p. 71.

[252] Beauchampet and Walsh (2021), p. 2.

members become holders of rights and obligations arising from energy consumption. The attribution of the status of energy citizens finds its brakes in the legal sphere, where citizenship is identified with belonging to a specific State that grants rights and attributes obligations. Despite this, the literature has explored alternatives beyond these traditional academic boundaries.[253]

Although energy citizenship does not correspond to the strictly legal concept of citizenship, the doctrine has adopted this description of the generated phenomenon.[254] The analysis of energy citizenship has triggered interdisciplinary assessments of this category. In this sense, Hamann et al. have recently analysed energy citizenship from an integrated perspective of psychology, law, and economics.[255] The legal perspective is particularly interesting given the traditional biases in the legal doctrine regarding citizenship as the legal link between the individual and the State.

Concerning this analysis, since 1996, O'Leary's conception has produced elements today that are used as the foundations of energy citizenship. In this respect, the author states:

> Citizenship, (...) is essentially regarded as a juridical condition which describes membership of and participation in a defined community or State. This juridical condition carries with it a number of rights and duties which are, in themselves, an expression of the political and legal link between the State and the individual. This juridical condition or status thus makes those who qualify the titleholders of a series of sometimes unpredictable rights and duties.[256]

This appreciation goes beyond the traditional legal view of citizenship. In this sense, by analysing EU citizenship, she opens the conceptual spectrum of citizenship to a new horizon. Such an opening implies loosening the connection between the nation-state and citizenship. This phenomenon is motivated by an analogy between the community and the State. For this reason, the vision of citizenship in energetic citizenship starts from considering the feeling of belonging to a political community, a region, a municipality, or other communities.[257]

To argue the above, Hamann et al. describe energy citizenship based on EU citizenship, the latter considered open and multi-layered citizenship.[258] According to the Treaty on European Union, EU citizenship is additional to and does not represent a replacement for national citizenships. Therefore, EU citizenship represents an extra layer to the citizenships of the Member States of the Union.[259] This multi-layered design of citizenship responds to the existence of an increasingly

[253] Cf. Devine-Wright (2007), p. 71.

[254] Council of European Energy Regulators (2019); Vijayan et al. (2020); Campos and Marín-González (2020).

[255] Hamann et al. (2023).

[256] O'Leary (1996), p. 13.

[257] Hamann et al. (2023), p. 6.

[258] Hamann et al. (2023), p. 7.

[259] Cf. Article 9 and article 20 respectively. European Union (2012a); European Union (2012b).

interconnected world where multilevel forms of governance are developing, making the unitary vision of citizenship centred on the nation-state a myth.[260]

For this reason, energy citizenship would constitute an extra layer to national citizenships worldwide. This view is complemented by Kostakopoulou's proposition that citizenship is a network good that:

> Implies and flows from active connections - be they vertical, that is, between the individual and the state, or horizontal, that is, between the individual and the community (the nation) which endows him/her with identity, or both.[261]

Such a statement derives the understanding of citizenship from the social networks that form between people and encourage others to join. This situation constitutes an ideal state that, applied to the energy context, contributes to broadening the networks of energy citizens from an empowerment perspective in national energy systems.

Of course, in the European Union, the legal foundations of energy citizenship can be found most strongly in primary and secondary legislation, in international legal instruments to which the European Union is a signatory and in the policy documents of this supranational body.[262] These legal foundations derive from the collective obligation around the energy transition through the establishment of objectives related to the promotion of the use of renewable energy sources in the internal energy market of the Union.[263]

Despite the normative foundation of energy citizenship in the European Union, this category is still developing and assimilating in the rest of the world. However, conceiving energy citizenship as an extra layer of national citizenship in the European Union offers a positive balance for the rest of the legal systems on a global scale. In this sense, the legal strengthening of energy citizenship would benefit the right to energy regarding the recognition of holders and their legal protection.

In addition to the above, it should be noted that the legal definition of energy citizenship has several functions that can determine the effectiveness of the legal framework of the energy transition and the realisation of the right to energy. Among these functions, the following stand out:

- Strengthen awareness of the importance of the energy transition.
- It links people and the energy transition involving duties and rights.
- It empowers communities through a set of rights linked to the energy sector.
- The concept of energy citizenship, if legally recognised, has a binding effect on state powers and allows for greater empowerment of citizens to demand the obligations derived from the law in the field of energy.[264]

---

[260] Shachar (2012), p. 1017.

[261] Kostakopoulou (2001), p. 109.

[262] Hamann et al. (2023), p. 7.

[263] Monti and Martinez Romera (2020), p. 231.

[264] Hamann et al. (2023), p. 8.

In this way, energy citizenship becomes another critical concept for delimiting the right to energy. Energy citizenship would further empower the holders of the right to energy to safeguard the realisation of the content of the right to energy.

However, there is one element that needs to be clarified. The definition and regulation of energy citizenship should not join the trend of shifting the responsibility for energy provision from the State to individuals.[265] Such responsibility is inherent to the State, and exercising energy prosumerism is only one alternative and complementary way of meeting energy needs.

In addition, the assimilation of energy citizenship excludes the possibility that only citizens, *strictu sensu*, are considered holders of the right under study. This exclusion is due to the insufficiency of the classic concept of citizenship, as it is a highly narrow concept, to support the universal nature of the right to energy and to guarantee the enforceability of this human right before the State as the leading party obliged to comply with it.

The analysis developed around energy citizenship leads to the following conclusion. From the conception of the term energy citizen, numerous forms of participation of individuals in the use and generation of energy are included so that energy consumers cease to be mere receivers to adopt an active role in the processes of elaboration of public policies focused on the energy sector, in the contribution of information to the planning and decision-making processes, among others. Similarly, from the regulatory point of view of energy citizenship, mechanisms for individual and local participation would be included to convert those who consume energy into energy producers.[266] These examples of decentralisation in energy generation contribute to realising the content of the right to energy and promote the process towards energy sovereignty, given the risk of the energy system's dependence on external variables.

5.3.2.6 Energy Sovereignty

Although sovereignty has traditionally been associated with the relationship between states regarding autonomy and self-determination, energy sovereignty assumes a different perspective.[267] As a basic concept for the right to energy configuration, energy sovereignty can be defined as the capacity to make decisions regarding the use, purpose, control, and access to energy. It is a capacity directly influenced by how society has constructed its energy needs and the social purpose assigned to it.[268] The capacity to dispose of sufficient energy resources becomes a guarantee for the materialisation of the right to energy, given that it favours the adequate functioning of the services that support it.

---

[265] Lennon et al. (2020), p. 187.

[266] Campos and Marín-González (2020); Lennon et al. (2020); Ryghaug et al. (2018).

[267] Schelly et al. (2020), pp. 109–110.

[268] Gutiérrez (2018).

According to Laldjebaev et al., energy sovereignty frames households and communities as critical arenas for eradicating energy poverty and improving energy security. In this sense, aligned with energy democracy and citizenship, the concept of energy sovereignty includes individual and collective participation in national energy security planning strategies.[269] Consequently, energy sovereignty has been another call for empowering the holders of the right to energy within energy systems.

In this regard, Thaler and Hofmann refer to two dimensions of energy sovereignty: internal and external.[270] The internal dimension involves the empowerment mentioned above of the holders of the right to energy to decide on the energy system.[271]

The external dimension of energy sovereignty offers a protectionist approach to the holders of the right to energy by regulating the energy sector.[272] This approach is in addition to protecting the holders of the right to energy from disruptions arising from the actions of various actors, including hostile political powers and influential energy market players.[273]

5.3.3 Conceptualising the Right to Energy

As analysed above, although the right to energy is being strengthened, numerous mechanisms have been created to guarantee its full realisation. Following the literature review to arrive at a conceptual delimitation of the right to energy, it is necessary to start from the assumption that it is a right that is still in the process of formation. Both legal doctrine and national legal frameworks are gradually assimilating the right to energy as an autonomous right.

Although some authors consider it a derived right, the author of this research defends the autonomy of the right, both from a legal point of view and a didactic point of view. Considering the right to energy as a derivative right would imply the disaggregation of its content. It would also subject it to the legal regimes of other rights when it must have a place in constitutional law, energy law, and the legal system recognises its fundamental nature.

This research affiliates itself with the term right to energy, as it describes in a comprehensive way the right that is the object of protection. Accordingly, it is stated that the right to energy encompasses the available, affordable and reliable access to energy services and energy sources. Availability means sufficient supply to meet energy needs. Accessibility requires the necessary infrastructure to ensure physical access to the distribution network of the energy service concerned. The prices of

[269] Laldjebaev et al. (2015), pp. 105–106.

[270] Thaler and Hofmann (2022), p. 2.

[271] Schelly et al. (2020), p. 110.

[272] Crossley (2013), p. 11.

[273] Cherp et al. (2012), p. 330.

energy services within the affordability framework must not compromise the economic capacity of energy rights holders to satisfy the rest of their vital needs. For access to be reliable, the continuity of the service, its quality, and transparent information to the consumer must be guaranteed.[274]

In the framework of the realisation of the right to energy, initiatives that promote widespread participation in energy policies and the decentralisation of energy generation must be promoted. Promoting citizen participation in energy generation as a tool of energy democracy must be built as a priority of the State to respond to the constantly increasing energy demand.

5.4 Conclusions

There is no uniform or universally recognised definition of the right to energy. The conceptual delineation of the right to energy has gone through various complexities. One of these complexities may be the conceptualisation of energy within the framework of the right to energy. This context has generated multiple approaches, given that the concept of energy is still an unresolved problem. At the same time, another complexity arises from the variety of denominations that academia has attributed to the right to energy, which has restricted or expanded its meaning and scope.

In addition to the above complex context, the doctrinal elements of the right to energy have been widely disaggregated in the academy into multiple doctrinal categories. In this sense, energy security, energy poverty, energy justice, energy democracy, energy citizenship and energy sovereignty were analysed. The emergence and evolution of each of these categories responds to economic, political, and social conditions that have arisen throughout history.

These conditions and the categories that have evolved are the foundation for the emergence of the right to energy. For this reason, the theoretical core of the right to energy has solid doctrinal foundations that allow the theoretical delimitation of the right under study in this research. Therefore, the analysis of the theoretical references allowed us to conceptually delimit the right to energy. In this sense, it is understood that the right to energy encompasses availability and affordable and reliable access to energy services and energy sources.

Nevertheless, so far, it has been found that the right to energy is a right that is in the process of being constructed so that its configurative elements are the subject of legal debate. The determination of its guiding principles, subjects, content, and status as a right will be analysed in the next chapter of this book.[275]

[274] Luis Cordova (2025), pp. 1–3.

[275] All links to the cited websites were operational as of 28 February 2025.

References

Adams J, Kenner A, Leone A, Rosenthal A, Sarao M, and Boi-Doku T (2022) What is energy literacy? Responding to vulnerability in Philadelphia's energy ecologies. Energy Res Soc Sci 91. https://doi.org/10.1016/j.erss.2022.102718. Accessed 28 February 2025

Angel J (2016) Strategies of energy democracy. Brussels. https://www.rosalux.de/fileadmin/rls_uploads/pdfs/sonst_publikationen/strategies_of_energy_democracy_Angel_engl.pdf. Accessed 28 February 2025

APERC (2007) In: Altagracia Aponte A (ed) A quest for energy security in the twenty-first century. Resources and constraints. Asia Pasific Energy Research Centre, Tokyo. https://aperc.or.jp/file/2010/9/26/APERC_2007_A_Quest_for_Energy_Security.pdf. Accessed 28 February 2025

Apergis N, Polemis M, Soursou SE (2022) Energy poverty and education: fresh evidence from a panel of developing countries. Energy Econ 106:105430. https://doi.org/10.1016/j.eneco.2021.105430. Accessed 28 February 2025

Aviles LA (2012) Electric energy access in european law: a human right? SSRN Electron J 217:1–8. http://www.ssrn.com/abstract=2008887. Accessed 28 February 2025

Azad R, Chakraborty S (2020) Green growth and the right to energy in India. Energy Policy 141:111456. https://linkinghub.elsevier.com/retrieve/pii/S030142152030207X. Accessed 28 February 2025

Baarsma BE, Hop JP (2009) Pricing power outages in the Netherlands. Energy 34(9):1378–1386. https://doi.org/10.1016/j.energy.2009.06.016. Accessed 28 February 2025

Barnett RR (1986) An economic appraisal of local energy conservation schemes. Energy Policy 14(5):425–436. https://linkinghub.elsevier.com/retrieve/pii/0301421586900406. Accessed 28 February 2025

Bazilian M, Onyeji I, Aqrawi PK, Sovacool BK, Ofori E, Kammen DM, Van de Graaf T (2013) Oil, energy poverty and resource dependence in West Africa. J Energy Nat Resourc Law 31(1):33–53. https://gspp.berkeley.edu/assets/uploads/research/pdf/Journal_of_Energy__Natural_Bazilian_et_al_%282013%29_Resources_Law_Bazilian-2013.pdf. Accessed 28 February 2025

Beauchampet I, Walsh B (2021) Energy citizenship in the Netherlands: the complexities of public engagement in a large-scale energy transition. Energy Res Soc Sci 76:102056. https://doi.org/10.1016/j.erss.2021.102056. Accessed 28 February 2025

Bertoldi P, Rezessy S, Vine E (2006) Energy service companies in European countries: current status and a strategy to foster their development. Energy Policy 34(14):1818–1832. https://www.sciencedirect.com/science/article/pii/S0301421505000303. Accessed 28 February 2025

Biresselioglu ME (2011) European energy security. Palgrave Macmillan UK, London. http://link.springer.com/10.1057/9780230306851. Accessed 28 February 2025

Biresselioglu ME, Demir MH, Solak B, Turan U (2022) Understanding the dynamics and conceptualization of environmental citizenship and energy citizenship: evidence from the existing literature. Front Energy Res 10(December):1–20. https://www.frontiersin.org/articles/10.3389/fenrg.2022.1018035/full. Accessed 28 February 2025

Boardman B (1991) Fuel poverty: from cold homes to affordable warmth. Belhaven Press. https://biblio.vub.ac.be/iguana/www.main.cls?surl=search&p=f88fe9ec-2425-11e7-a7e4-90084dd7a2c4#recordId=3.240219. Accessed 21 May 2022. Accessed 28 February 2025

Bouzarovski S (2014) Energy poverty in the European Union: landscapes of vulnerability. Wiley Interdiscipl Rev 3(3):276–289. https://onlinelibrary.wiley.com/doi/10.1002/wene.89

Bouzarovski S (2018) Energy poverty. Springer, Cham. http://link.springer.com/10.1007/978-3-319-69299-9. Accessed 28 February 2025

Bouzarovski S, Petrova (2015) A global perspective on domestic energy deprivation: overcoming the energy poverty–fuel poverty binary. Energy Res Soc Sci 10:31–40. https://doi.org/10.1016/j.erss.2015.06.007. Accessed 28 February 2025

Bradbrook AJ, Gardam JG (2006) Placing the access to energy services within a human rights framework. Hum Rights Qly 28(2):389–415. https://www.jstor.org/stable/pdf/20072742.pdf?

refreqid=excelsior%3A43476d5b7137fdcb80d186deeef37e29&ab_segments=&origin=&acceptTC=1. Accessed 28 February 2025

Brugger EC (2016) Reflections on the moral foundations of a right to energy. In: Guruswamy L, Neville E (eds) International energy and poverty. The emerging contours. Routledge, New York, pp 68–83. https://www.routledge.com/International-Energy-and-Poverty-The-emerging-contours/Guruswamy/p/book/9781138055827. Accessed 28 February 2025

Buzar S (2016) Energy poverty in Eastern Europe. Energy poverty in Eastern Europe. Routledge. https://www.taylorfrancis.com/books/9781351940252. Accessed 28 February 2025

Cabrera AT, Carrasco A, Cipriano J (2015) Impacto en la salud del uso de biocombustibles en el interior de las viviendas de la comunidad nativa de Lamas, San Martín, Perú: 2013. Revista Rebiol 35(1):6–13. https://dialnet.unirioja.es/servlet/articulo?codigo=8143154. Accessed 28 February 2025

Campbell T (2010) Justice, 3rd edn. Palgrave Macmillan, Hampshire. https://books.google.be/books?id=lo5KEAAAQBAJ&printsec=frontcover&source=gbs_ge_summary_r&cad=0#v=onepage&q&f=false. https://dialnet.unirioja.es/servlet/articulo?codigo=8143154. Accessed 28 February 2025

Campos I, Marín-González E (2020) People in transitions: energy citizenship, prosumerism and social movements in Europe. Energy Res Soc Sci 69:101718. https://doi.org/10.1016/j.erss.2020.101718. Accessed 28 February 2025

Caramizaru A, Uihlein A (2020) Energy communities: an overview of energy and social innovation. Publications Office of the European Union, Luxembourg. https://publications.jrc.ec.europa.eu/repository/bitstream/JRC119433/energy_communities_report_final.pdf. Accessed 28 February 2025

Checchi A, Behrens A, Egenhofer C (2009) Long term energy security risks for europe: a sector specific approach. Centre for European Policy Studies, Brussels. https://cdn.ceps.eu/wp-content/uploads/2009/08/1785.pdf. Accessed 28 February 2025

Cherp A, Adenikinju A, Goldthau A, Hernandez F, Hughes L, Jansen J, Bazilian M, Jewell J, Olshanskaya M, Soares de Oliveira R, Sovacool B, Vakulenko S, Fisk DJ, Pal S, Davidson O (2012) Energy and security. In: Johansson TB, Nakicenovic N, Patwardhan A, Gomez-Echeverri L (eds) Global energy assessment: toward a sustainable future. Cambridge University Press, Cambridge. https://www.cambridge.org/core/product/identifier/9780511793677/type/BOOK. Accessed 28 February 2025

Cherp A, Jewell J (2014) The concept of energy security: beyond the four as. Energy Policy 75:415–421. https://linkinghub.elsevier.com/retrieve/pii/S0301421514004960. Accessed 28 February 2025

Ciplet D (2021) From energy privilege to energy justice: a framework for embedded sustainable development. Energy Res Soc Sci 75:101996. https://doi.org/10.1016/j.erss.2021.101996. Accessed 28 February 2025

Colino Martínez A, Caro R (2010) Fuentes energéticas. La Nueva Geopolít Energía:21–34. https://dialnet.unirioja.es/servlet/articulo?codigo=4548648. Accessed 28 February 2025

Comisión Económica para América Latina y el Caribe (2016) Agenda 2030 y los Objetivos de Desarrollo Sostenible Una oportunidad para América Latina y el Caribe. Organización de Naciones Unidas. https://repositorio.cepal.org/bitstream/handle/11362/40155/24/S1801141_es.pdf. Accessed 28 February 2025

Comité de Desarrollo Campesino (2014) La Privatización del Derecho a la Energía Eléctrica. Impactos socioeconómicos y convulsión social creciente, 1st edn. Suchitepéquez, Guatemala. https://issuu.com/jubenalquispe/docs/la_privatizaci__n_del_derecho_a_la_. Accessed 28 February 2025

Couder J (2015) Energy security, including power reliability. Literature review, with a focus on the impact of energy efficiency on energy security in the EU. Antwerp. https://www.researchgate.net/profile/Johan-Couder/publication/298352053_Energy_Security_including_Power_Reliability_Literature_review_with_a_focus_on_the_impact_of_energy_efficiency_ on_energy_security_in_the_EU/links/56e85b1d08aea51e7f3b46dc/Energy-Securi. Accessed 28 February 2025

Council of European Energy Regulators (2019) Regulatory aspects of self-consumption and energy communities. Brussels. https://www.ceer.eu/wp-content/uploads/2024/04/C18-CRM9_DS7-05-03_Report-on-Regulatory-Aspects-of-Self-Consumption-and-Energy-Communities_final.pdf. Accessed 28 February 2025

Cox E (2018) Assessing long-term energy security: the case of electricity in the United Kingdom. Renew Sustain Energy Rev 82:2287–2299. https://doi.org/10.1016/j.rser.2017.08.084. Accessed 28 February 2025

Cravioto J, Yamasue E, Okumura H, Ishihara KN (2014) Energy service satisfaction in two Mexican communities: a study on demographic, household, equipment and energy related predictors. Energy Policy 73:110–126. https://doi.org/10.1016/j.enpol.2014.04.031. Accessed 28 February 2025

Crooks E (2007) Security of supply: delusional dream of independence. Financial Times. London. https://www.ft.com/content/95f4ab44-8d15-11dc-a398-0000779fd2ac. Accessed 28 February 2025

Crossley P (2013) Energy sovereignty or regulatory competition? northeast asian renewable energy regulation in the post global financial crisis era. (December 15, 2013). Oil Gas Energy Law 5. https://papers.ssrn.com/sol3/papers.cfm?abstract_id=2368087. Accessed 28 February 2025

Crossley P (2022) What is 'renewable energy'? –conceptualizing the legislative definitions of renewable energy. Renew Energy Law Policy Rev 10(3–4):39–56. https://www.elgaronline.com/view/journals/relp/10-3-4/relp.2022.03-04.06.xml. Accessed 28 February 2025

Cumbers A, Danson M, Whittam G, Morgan G, Callaghan G (2013) Repossessing the future: a common weal strategy for community and democratic ownership of Scotland's energy resources. Biggar. https://reidfoundation.scot/wp-content/uploads/2013/10/Repossessing.pdf. Accessed 28 February 2025

Dannreuther R (2010) Energy security. In: Burgess JP (ed) The Routledge handbook of new security studies. Routledge Taylor & Francis Group, Oxon. https://www.routledge.com/The-Routledge-Handbook-of-New-Security-Studies/Burgess/p/book/9780415539333. Accessed 28 February 2025

Davies AR (2006) Environmental justice as subtext or omission: examining discourses of anti-incineration campaigning in Ireland. Geoforum 37(5):708–724. https://linkinghub.elsevier.com/retrieve/pii/S001671850600008X. Accessed 28 February 2025

Dawson A (2010) Climate justice: the emerging movement against green capitalism. South Atl Q 109(2):313–338. https://read.dukeupress.edu/south-atlantic-quarterly/article/109/2/313/30137/Climate-Justice-The-Emerging-Movement-against. Accessed 28 February 2025

Day R, Walker G, Simcock N (2016) Conceptualising energy use and energy poverty using a capabilities framework. Energy Policy 93:255–264. https://linkinghub.elsevier.com/retrieve/pii/S0301421516301227. Accessed 9 January 2022. Accessed 28 February 2025

Deese DA (1979) Energy: economics, politics, and security. Int Security 4(3):140. https://www.jstor.org/stable/2626698?origin=crossref. Accessed 28 February 2025

Delgado Triana Y, Fariñas Wong EY (2016) Derecho de acceso a la energía. Protección constitucional en Cuba. Caribeña de Ciencias Sociales. https://www.eumed.net/rev/caribe/2016/04/energia.html. Accessed 28 February 2025

Deller D, Turner G, Waddams Price C (2021) Energy poverty indicators: inconsistencies, implications and where next? Energy Econ 103:105551. https://doi.org/10.1016/j.eneco.2021.105551. Accessed 28 February 2025

Department of Energy & Climate Change (2012) Energy security strategy, London. https://www.gov.uk/government/uploads/system/uploads/attachment_data/file/65643/7101-energy-security-strategy.pdf. Accessed 28 February 2025

Devine-Wright P (2007) Energy citizenship: psychological aspects of evolution in sustainable energy technologies. In: Murphy J (ed) Governing technology for sustainability. Earthscan, London. https://books.google.be/books?hl=en&lr=&id=cFsRHVKcKwsC&oi

=fnd&pg=PA63&ots=LmRfl2vzOQ&sig=oWDUzQ4IMrMTb-GM8bjiY7L7z6w&redir_esc=y#v=onepage&q&f=false. Accessed 28 February 2025
Dubois U, Meier H (2016) Energy affordability and energy inequality in Europe: implications for policymaking. Energy Res Soc Sci 18:21–35. https://doi.org/10.1016/j.erss.2016.04.015. Accessed 28 February 2025
Durán R, Condorí M (2015) El acceso a la energía desde la óptica de los derechos humanos. Su medición y relación con el acceso a otros derechos elementales en Salta, Argentina. AVERMA 19:57–67. https://sedici.unlp.edu.ar/bitstream/handle/10915/143520/Documento_completo.pdf-PDFA.pdf?sequence=1. Accessed 28 February 2025
ECRB (2020) Prosumers in the energy community legal and regulatory framework for support and treatment of small-scale generators Special focus on solar photovoltaic (PV) systems connected to the distribution network. https://energy-community.org/dam/jcr:abacd12d-283c-492a-8aa4-6da5797d044a/ECRB_prosumers_regulatory_framework_032020.pdf. Accessed 28 February 2025
Endres D (2009) From wasteland to waste site: the role of discourse in nuclear power's environmental injustices. Local Environment 14(10):917–937. http://www.tandfonline.com/doi/abs/10.1080/13549830903244409. Accessed 28 February 2025
Energy Poverty Advisory Hub (2022) What is energy poverty. https://energy.ec.europa.eu/topics/markets-and-consumers/energy-consumer-rights/energy-poverty-eu_en. Accessed 28 February 2025
Esakova N (2012) European Energy Security. VS Verlag für Sozialwissenschaften, Wiesbaden. http://link.springer.com/10.1007/978-3-531-19201-7. Accessed 28 February 2025
European Commission. 2020. Commission Recommendation (EU) 2020/1563 of 14 October 2020 on energy poverty. https://eur-lex.europa.eu/legal-content/EN/TXT/?uri=CELEX:32020H1563&qid=1606124119302. Accessed 28 February 2025
European Parliament (2008) Legislative resolution of 9 July 2008 on the proposal for a directive of the European Parliament and of the Council amending Directive 2003/55/EC concerning common rules for the internal market in natural gas (COM (2007)0529—C6–0317/2007—2007/0196(COD). Official Journal of the European Union. https://eur-lex.europa.eu/LexUriServ/LexUriServ.do?uri=OJ:C:2009:294E:0142:0180:EN:PDF. Accessed 28 February 2025
European Parliament, European Council (2018) Directive 2018/2001 on the promotion of the use of energy from renewable sources. Official Journal of the European Union. https://eur-lex.europa.eu/legal-content/EN/TXT/PDF/?uri=CELEX:32018L2001&from=EN. Accessed 28 February 2025
European Parliament, European Council (2019) Directive 2019/944 on common rules for the internal market for electricity and amending Directive 2012/27/EU. Brussels: Official Journal of the European Union. https://eur-lex.europa.eu/legal-content/EN/TXT/PDF/?uri=CELEX:32019L0944&from=EN. Accessed 28 February 2025
European Union (2012a) Consolidated Version of the Treaty on European Union. Core EU Legislation. Official Journal of the European Union. https://eur-lex.europa.eu/resource.html?uri=cellar:2bf140bf-a3f8-4ab2-b506-fd71826e6da6.0023.02/DOC_1&format=PDF. Accessed 28 February 2025
European Union (2012b) Consolidated version of the Treaty on the Functioning of the European Union. Official Journal of the European Union. https://eur-lex.europa.eu/legal-content/EN/TXT/PDF/?uri=CELEX:12012E/TXT. Accessed 28 February 2025
Feldpausch-Parker AM, Endres D, Peterson TR (2019) Editorial: a research agenda for energy democracy. Front Commun 4(October):1–8. https://www.frontiersin.org/article/10.3389/fcomm.2019.00053/full. Accessed 28 February 2025
Feldpausch-Parker AM, Endres D, Peterson TR, Gomez SL (2021) Routledge handbook of energy democracy. Routledge, London. https://www.taylorfrancis.com/books/9780429402302
Fell MJ (2017) Energy services: a conceptual review. Energy Res Soc Sci 27:129–140. https://doi.org/10.1016/j.erss.2017.02.010. Accessed 28 February 2025

Fløytrup LMS, Gabrielsson S, Mwamlima (2022) Using energy justice to contextualise existing challenges of wood charcoal against faecal sludge derived briquettes as a future cooking fuel alternative in Dar Es Salaam, Tanzania. Int J Urban Sustain Dev 14(1):91–107. https://doi.org/10.1080/19463138.2022.2067166. Accessed 28 February 2025

Ford R, Whitaker J, Stephenson J (2016) Prosumer collectives - a review. University of Otago. https://www.researchgate.net/profile/Janet-Stephenson/publication/305941797_Prosumer_Collectives_-_a_review/links/5afe4e880f7e9b98e0198285/Prosumer-Collectives-a-review.pdf?_sg%5B0%5D=Te04AMVIUSyjqQ5T_0zFlb1JfI4Zwv3tiBd69y8o9KnlG2hn7n-d1iXXBsSEfVw5vQZGyM-. Accessed 28 February 2025

Freund CL, Wallich CI (1996) The welfare effects of raising household energy prices in Poland. Energy J 17(1):53–77. https://www.jstor.org/stable/41322626. Accessed 28 February 2025

Frigo G, Baumann M, Hillerbrand R (2021) Energy and the good life: capabilities as the foundation of the right to access energy services. J Hum Dev Capab 22(2):218–248. https://www.tandfonline.com/doi/full/10.1080/19452829.2021.1887109. Accessed 28 February 2025

Fuller S, McCauley D (2016) Framing energy justice: perspectives from activism and advocacy. Energy Res Soc Sci 11:1–8. https://linkinghub.elsevier.com/retrieve/pii/S221462961530027X. Accessed 28 February 2025

Galaway B, Hudson J (1996) Restorative justice: international perspectives. Criminal Justice Press Monsey, NY, New York. https://www.rienner.com/title/Restorative_Justice_International_Perspectives. Accessed 28 February 2025

Galvin R (2020) Energy poverty research: a perspective from the poverty side. Inequal Energy: 221–248. Elsevier. https://doi.org/10.1016/B978-0-12-817674-0.00010-2. Accessed 28 February 2025

Garcia M, Mundó J (2014) La energía como derecho. Cómo afrontar la pobreza energética. Taula d'entitats del Tercer Sector Social de Catalunya, Barcelona. https://www.eapn.es/ARCHIVO/documentos/documentos/1411457073_dossier_la_energia_como_derecho._como_afrontar_la_pobreza_energetica.pdf. Accessed 28 February 2025

Gaye A (2007) Access to energy and human development. United Nations Development Programme. Brussels. https://hdr.undp.org/content/access-energy-and-human-development. Accessed 28 February 2025

Giancatarino A (2013) Energy democracy: supporting community innovation the center for social inclusion. Center for social inclusion. https://www.eesi.org/files/Giancatarino_031813.pdf. Accessed 28 February 2025

Gobierno de Navarra (2020) Introducción a los servicios energéticos y su situación en Navarra. III Plan Energético de Navarra horizonte 2020. Navarra. https://www.navarra.es/NR/rdonlyres/9F440515-BC1B-4607-888E-3DAA741E89D3/0/ServiciosEnergeticos.pdf. Accessed 28 February 2025

Goldthau A (2011) Governing global energy: existing approaches and discourses. Curr Opin Environ Sustain 3(4):213–217. https://doi.org/10.1016/j.cosust.2011.06.003. Accessed 28 February 2025

Gómez Milian JF, Luis Cordova JG (2023) Theoretical and legal perspectives on energy-smart agri-food systems: sustainability and the right to food. Glob Jurist 1–24. https://doi.org/10.1515/gj-2022-0072. Accessed 28 February 2025

Gouveia JP, Palma P, Bessa S, Mahoney K, Sequeira M (2022) Energy poverty national indicators: insights for a more effective measuring. Brussels. https://energy-poverty.ec.europa.eu/system/files/2024-05/EPAH_Energy%20Poverty%20National%20Indicators%20Report_0.pdf. Accessed 28 February 2025

Greening LA, Greene DL, Difiglio C (2000) Energy efficiency and consumption—the rebound effect—a survey. Energy Policy 28(6–7):389–401. https://linkinghub.elsevier.com/retrieve/pii/S0301421500000215. Accessed 28 February 2025

Guruswamy L (2010) Energy justice and sustainable development. J Int Env L Pol J 21(231) https://scholar.law.colorado.edu/cgi/viewcontent.cgi?article=1221&context=faculty-articles. Accessed 28 February 2025

Gutiérrez F (2018) Soberanía Energética. Propuestas y debates desde el campo popular. Ediciones Jinete Insomne, Buenos Aires. https://opsur.org.ar/wp-content/uploads/2018/12/Libro-Soberania-energetica-WEB.pdf. Accessed 28 February 2025

Haas R, Nakicenovic N, Ajanovic A, Faber T, Kranzl L, Müller A, Resch G (2008) Towards sustainability of energy systems: a primer on how to apply the concept of energy services to identify necessary trends and policies. Energy Policy 36(11):4012–4021. https://linkinghub.elsevier.com/retrieve/pii/S0301421508003017. Accessed 28 February 2025

Haghighi SS (2007) Energy security. The external legal relations of the European Union with major oil- and gas-supplying countries. Hart, Oxford. https://cadmus.eui.eu/handle/1814/7571. Accessed 28 February 2025

Hamann KRS, Bertel MP, Ryszawska B, Lurger B, Szymański P, Rozwadowska M, Goedkoop F, Jans L, Perlaviciute G, Masson T, Fritsche I, Favaro T, Hofer A, Eisenberger I, Gutschi C, Grosche C, Held J, Athenstaedt U, Corcoran K (2023) An interdisciplinary understanding of energy citizenship: integrating psychological, legal, and economic perspectives on a citizen-centred sustainable energy transition. Energy Res Soc Sci 97:102959. https://linkinghub.elsevier.com/retrieve/pii/S2214629623000191. Accessed 28 February 2025

Hancock KJ, Vivoda V (2014) International political economy: a field born of the OPEC crisis returns to its energy roots. Energy Res Soc Sci 1:206–216. https://www.sciencedirect.com/science/article/pii/S2214629614000310. Accessed 28 February 2025

Hasanuzzaman M, Kumar L (2020) Energy supply. Energy Sustain Dev: 89–104. Elsevier. https://doi.org/10.1016/B978-0-12-814645-3.00004-3. Accessed 28 February 2025

Hazrati M, Heffron RJ (2021) Conceptualising restorative justice in the energy transition: changing the perspectives of fossil fuels. Energy Res Soc Sci 78:102115. https://doi.org/10.1016/j.erss.2021.102115. Accessed 28 February 2025

Heffron RJ (2022) Applying energy justice into the energy transition. Renew Sustain Energy Rev 156:111936. https://linkinghub.elsevier.com/retrieve/pii/S1364032121012016. Accessed 28 February 2025

Heffron RJ, De Fontenelle L (2023) Implementing energy justice through a new social contract. J Energy Nat Resourc Law 41(2):141–155. https://www.tandfonline.com/doi/full/10.1080/02646811.2023.2186626. Accessed 28 February 2025

Heffron RJ, McCauley D (2017) The concept of energy justice across the disciplines. Energy Policy 105(March):658–667. https://linkinghub.elsevier.com/retrieve/pii/S0301421517301593. Accessed 28 February 2025

Heldeweg MA, Saintier S (2020) Renewable energy communities as 'socio-legal institutions': a normative frame for energy decentralization? Renew Sustain Energy Rev 119. https://linkinghub.elsevier.com/retrieve/pii/S1364032119307269. Accessed 28 February 2025

Hernandez CG (2008) Philippine energy policy: implications for human security and regional cooperation. In: Marquina A (ed) Energy security. Visions from Asia and Europe, New York. https://link.springer.com/book/10.1057/9780230595002. Accessed 28 February 2025

Hernández D (2015) Sacrifice along the energy continuum: a call for energy justice. Environ Justice 8(4):151–156. http://www.liebertpub.com/doi/10.1089/env.2015.0015. Accessed 28 February 2025

Hernández D, Yoon L, Simcock N (2022) Basing "Energy Justice" on clear terms: assessing key terminology in pursuit of energy justice. Environ Justice 15(3):127–138. https://www.liebertpub.com/doi/10.1089/env.2021.0049. Accessed 28 February 2025

Hesselman M, Tirado-Herrero S, Smith M, Antepara I, Bajomi A, Barrella R, Cao U, Chatterjee S, Cuerdo T, Dobbins A, Frigo G, Fuller S, Feenstra M, Gouveia J, Guyet R, Kizilcec V, Lennon B, González I, Robić S, Robinson C, Smilevska N, Varo A, Yoon H, Živčič L (2017) Moving forward on the right to energy in the EU. http://www.engager-energy.net/wp-content/uploads/2022/02/ENGAGER_Right-to-Energy-Toolkit_FINAL.pdf. Accessed 28 February 2025

Hesselman M, Varo A, Guyet R, Thomson H (2021) Energy poverty in the COVID-19 era: mapping global responses in light of momentum for the right to energy. Energy Res Soc Sci 81:102246. https://doi.org/10.1016/j.erss.2021.102246. Accessed 28 February 2025

Hiteva R, Sovacool B (2017) Harnessing social innovation for energy justice: a business model. Energy Policy 107:631–639. https://doi.org/10.1016/j.enpol.2017.03.056. Accessed 28 February 2025

Hughes L (2012) A generic framework for the description and analysis of energy security in an energy system. Energy Policy 42:221–231. https://doi.org/10.1016/j.enpol.2011.11.079. Accessed 28 February 2025

Hughes L, Lipscy PY (2013) The politics of energy. Annu Rev Polit Sci 16(1):449–469. https://www.annualreviews.org/doi/10.1146/annurev-polisci-072211-143240. Accessed 28 February 2025

Hughes L, Shupe D (2010) Applying the four 'A's of energy security as criteria in an energy security ranking method. In: Sovacool BK (eds) The Routledge handbook of energy security, pp 1–464. Routledge. https://www.taylorfrancis.com/books/9781136850639. Accessed 28 February 2025

Huhta K (2023) Conceptualising energy justice in the context of human rights law. Nordic J Hum Rights:1–15. https://doi.org/10.1080/18918131.2023.2210443. Accessed 28 February 2025

Illich I (2013) The social construction of energy. In: Samuel S (ed) Beyond economics and ecology: the radical thought of Ivan Illich. Marion Boyars, London. https://www.pdf-archive.com/2017/02/25/reading-3-illich-the-social-construction-of-energy/reading-3-illich-the-social-construction-of-energy.pdf. Accessed 28 February 2025

International Energy Agency, International Renewable Energy Agency, United Nations Statistics Division, The International Bank for Reconstruction and Development/The World Bank, and World Health Organization (2023) Tracking SDG 7|progress towards sustainable energy 2023. https://trackingsdg7.esmap.org/. Accessed 28 February 2025

International Institute for Applied Systems Analysis (2012) In: Johansson TB, Nakicenovic N, Patwardhan A, Gomez-Echeverri L (eds) Global energy assessment—toward a sustainable future, vol 50. Cambridge University Press, Cambridge. https://www.cambridge.org/core/books/global-energy-assessment/C3889BF364D0872AD8635D607ADC579C. Accessed 28 February 2025

Jakstas T (2020) What does energy security mean? In: Tvaronavičienė M, Beata BT (eds) Energy transformation towards sustainability. Ślusarczyk, pp 99–112. Elsevier. https://www.sciencedirect.com/science/article/pii/B9780128176887000057. Accessed 28 February 2025

Jasiūnas J, Lund PD, Mikkola J (2021) Energy system resilience—a review. Renew Sustain Energy Rev 150(2019):111476. https://linkinghub.elsevier.com/retrieve/pii/S1364032121007577. Accessed 28 February 2025

Jenkins K (2018) Setting energy justice apart from the crowd: lessons from environmental and climate justice. Energy Res Soc Sci 39:117–121. https://doi.org/10.1016/j.erss.2017.11.015. Accessed 28 February 2025

Jones O, Dodds PE (2017) Definitions of energy security. In: Steinberger-Wilckens R, Dodds PE, Kurban Z, Velazquez Abad A, Radcliffe J (eds) The role of hydrogen and fuel cells in delivering energy security for the UK. H2FC SUPERGEN, London, pp 32–45. https://discovery.ucl.ac.uk/id/eprint/10087004/6/Dodds_IMPJ5213-H2FC-Supergen-Energy-Security-032017-Chapter 2.pdf

Kessides I, Miniaci R, Scarpa C, Valbonesi P (2009) Toward defining and measuring the affordability of public utility services. World Bank Policy Research Working Paper No. 4915. Brussels. https://documents.worldbank.org/en/publication/documents-reports/documentdetail/859201468338935200/toward-defining-and-measuring-the-affordability-of-public-utility-services. Accessed 28 February 2025

Kostakopoulou D (2001) The future governance of citizenship. Cambridge University Press, Cambridge. https://www.cambridge.org/core/product/identifier/9780511619861/type/book. Accessed 28 February 2025

Kotilainen K (2020) Energy prosumers' role in the sustainable energy system. In: Leal Filho W, Marisa Azul A, Brandli L, Gökcin Özuyar P, Wall T (eds) Affordable and clean energy. Springer, Cham, pp 1–14. http://link.springer.com/10.1007/978-3-319-71057-0_11-1. Accessed 28 February 2025

Kowsari R, Zerriffi H (2011) Three-dimensional energy profile: a conceptual framework for assessing household energy use. Energy Policy 39(12):7505–7517. https://doi.org/10.1016/j.enpol.2011.06.030. Accessed 28 February 2025

Kruyt B, van Vuuren DP, de Vries HJM, Groenenberg H (2009) Indicators for energy security. Energy Policy 37(6):2166–2181. https://www.sciencedirect.com/science/article/pii/S0301421509000883. Accessed 28 February 2025

Kunze C, Becker S (2014) Energy democracy in Europe: a survey and outlook. Rosa Luxemburg Foundation (January 2014): 63. https://www.rosalux.de/fileadmin/rls_uploads/pdfs/sonst_publikationen/Energy-democracy-in-Europe.pdf. Accessed 28 February 2025

Laldjebaev M, Morreale SJ, Sovacool BK, Kassam KS (2018) Rethinking energy security and services in practice: national vulnerability and three energy pathways in Tajikistan. Energy Policy 114:39–50. https://linkinghub.elsevier.com/retrieve/pii/S0301421517308030. Accessed 28 February 2025

Laldjebaev M, Sovacool BK, Kassam KS (2015) In: Guruswamy L (ed) International energy and poverty: the emerging contours. Routledge, International energy and poverty. https://www.taylorfrancis.com/books/9781317647546. Accessed 28 February 2025

Leal-arcas R, Akondo N, Alemany Rios J (2019) Energy decentralization in the European Union. Georgetown Environ Law Rev 32(1). https://papers.ssrn.com/sol3/papers.cfm?abstract_id=3333694#:~:text=This%20article%20examines%20the%20status%20of%20energy%20decentralization,analyzes%20the%20situation%20in%20several%20EU%20member%20states. Accessed 28 February 2025

Lee J, Byrne J (2019) Expanding the conceptual and analytical basis of energy justice: beyond the three-tenet framework. Front Energy Res 7(SEP):1–10. https://www.frontiersin.org/article/10.3389/fenrg.2019.00099/full. Accessed 28 February 2025

Lehr U (2009) More baskets? Renew Energy Energy Secur 49. Osnabrück. https://papers.gws-os.com/gws-paper09-8.pdf. Accessed 28 February 2025

Lennon B, Dunphy N, Gaffney C, Revez A, Mullally G, O'Connor P (2020) Citizen or consumer? Reconsidering energy citizenship. J Environ Policy Plan 22(2):184–197. https://doi.org/10.1080/1523908X.2019.1680277. Accessed 28 February 2025

Lewis P (1982) Fuel poverty can be stopped. National Right to Fuel Campaign, Bardford

Liddell C (2012) Fuel poverty comes of age: commemorating 21 years of research and policy. Energy Policy 49:2–5. https://www.sciencedirect.com/science/article/pii/S030142151200153X?via%3Dihub. Accessed 28 February 2025

Lin B, Wang Y (2020) Does energy poverty really exist in China? From the perspective of residential electricity consumption. Energy Policy 143:111557. https://doi.org/10.1016/j.enpol.2020.111557. Accessed 28 February 2025

Löfquist L (2020) Is there a universal human right to electricity? Int J Hum Rights 24(6):711–723. https://www.tandfonline.com/doi/full/10.1080/13642987.2019.1671355. Accessed 28 February 2025

Lubell H (1961) Security of supply and energy policy in Western Europe. World Polit 13(3):400–422. https://www.cambridge.org/core/journals/world-politics/article/abs/security-of-supply-and-energy-policy-in-western-europe/E3A94F450D9D5BBB8AB677887957A44F#. Accessed 28 February 2025

Luis Cordova JG (2025) The right to energy and the data protection and privacy rights: towards a coherent enforcement under EU law within the energy transition. Eur J Risk Regul 1–15. https://doi.org/10.1017/err.202530. Accessed 28 February 2025

Luis Cordova J G (2026) Energy justice in the twin transitions: assessing EU law and policy. Eur J Risk Regulat: 1–15. https://doi.org/10.1017/err.2026.10101. Accessed 24 April 2026

Luis Cordova JG, Byttebier K, Delgado Triana Y (2023) Decentralized energy generation for sustainable energy development in EU. Eur Energy Environ Law Rev 32(4):164–176. https://kluwerlawonline.com/journalarticle/European+Energy+and+Environmental+Law+Review/32.4/EELR2023010. Accessed 28 February 2025

Luis Cordova JG, and Milian Gómez JF (2025) Energy and food poverty in Latin America, towards a rights perspective in energy poverty, justice and gender in Latin America, Springer Nature, Cham. pp 205–224. https://link.springer.com/10.1007/978-3-031-80068-9. Accessed 28 February 2025

Maradin D (2021) Advantages and disadvantages of renewable energy sources utilization. Int J Energy Econ Policy 11(3):176–183. https://econjournals.com/index.php/ijeep/article/view/11027. Accessed 28 February 2025

Masud J, Sharan D, Lohani BN (2007) Addressing energy, environment and policy nexus in India. Asian Development Bank, Philippines. https://www.adb.org/sites/default/files/publication/29137/energy-all.pdf. Accessed 28 February 2025

McCauley D, Heffron RJ, Stephan H, Jenkins K (2013) Advancing energy justice: the triumvirate of tenets. Int Energy Law Rev 32(3):107–110. https://www.researchgate.net/profile/Kirsten-Jenkins/publication/259459020_Advancing_Energy_Justice_The_triumvirate_of_tenets/links/5583e35f08ae89172b86158a/Advancing-Energy-Justice-The-triumvirate-of-tenets.pdf. Accessed 28 February 2025

McHarg A (2020) Energy justice. Energy Justice Energy Law 35:15–30. Oxford University Press. https://www.taylorfrancis.com/books/9781315312569/chapters/10.4324/9781315312576-17. Accessed 28 February 2025

Milne G, Boardman B (2000) Making cold homes warmer: the effect of energy efficiency improvements in low-income homes a report to the energy action grants agency charitable trust. Energy Policy 28(6–7):411–424. https://linkinghub.elsevier.com/retrieve/pii/S0301421500000197. Accessed 28 February 2025

Ministerio de Energía y Minas (2018) Resolución No. 152: 'Manual de Inspección a los Portadores Energéticos'. Gaceta Oficial de la República de Cuba, Cuba. https://www.gacetaoficial.gob.cu/sites/default/files/goc-2018-ex61.pdf. Accessed 28 February 2025

Mitchell C, Watson J (2013) New challenges in energy security: the UK in a multipolar world — conclusions and recommendations. In: New challenges in energy security. Palgrave Macmillan UK, London, pp 238–257. http://link.springer.com/10.1057/9781137298850_11. Accessed 28 February 2025

Modi V, McDade S, Lallement D (2005) Energy services for the millennium development goals, New York. https://lutw.org/wp-content/uploads/Energy-services-for-the-millennium-development-goals.pdf. Accessed 28 February 2025

Monti A, Martinez Romera B (2020) Fifty shades of binding: appraising the enforcement toolkit for the EU's 2030 renewable energy targets. Rev Eur Comp Int Environ Law 29 (2): 221–231. https://onlinelibrary.wiley.com/doi/10.1111/reel.12330. Accessed 28 February 2025

Morris C, Jungjohann A (2016) Energy democracy. Energy democracy: Germany's energiewende to renewables. Springer, Cham. http://link.springer.com/10.1007/978-3-319-31891-2. Accessed 28 February 2025

Nussbaum MC (2001) Women and human development: the capabilities approach. Cambridge University Press, Cambridge. https://www.cambridge.org/core/books/women-and-human-development/58D8D2FBFC1C9E902D648200C4B7009E. Accessed 28 February 2025

Nussbaum M, Sen A (1993) The quality of life. Oxford University Press, Oxford. https://global.oup.com/academic/product/the-quality-of-life-9780198287971?cc=gb&lang=en&. Accessed 28 February 2025

Nussbaumer P, Bazilian M, Modi V (2012) Measuring energy poverty: focusing on what matters. Renew Sustain Energy Rev 16(1):231–243. https://doi.org/10.1016/j.rser.2011.07.150. Accessed 28 February 2025

O'Leary S (1996) The evolving concept of Community citizenship: from the free movement of persons to Union citizenship. Kluwer Law International, The Hague, Boston. https://

law-store.wolterskluwer.com/s/product/evolving-concept-community-citizenship-from-the-free/01t0f00000J3aQzAAJ. Accessed 28 February 2025

Okraszewska E (2016) Demokracja energetyczna - społeczeństwo jako prosument energii elektrycznej. Gospodarka w Praktyce i Teorii 43(2) https://czasopisma.uni.lodz.pl/gospodarka/article/view/1181. Accessed 28 February 2025

Organización Mundial de la Salud (2014) Quema de Combustibles en los Hogares. Ginebra. https://www.paho.org/hq/dmdocuments/2016/HAP-ExecSumm-Sp.pdf. Accessed 28 February 2025

Osbaldeston J (1984) Fuel poverty in UK cities. Cities 1(4):366–373. https://www.sciencedirect.com/science/article/pii/026427518490009X. Accessed 28 February 2025

Paddock LC, Greenblum M (2016) Community benefit agreements for wind farm siting in context. In: Sharing the costs and benefits of energy and resource activity. Oxford University Press, Oxford, pp 155–172. https://academic.oup.com/book/5621/chapter/148628670. Accessed 28 February 2025

Pan K (2020) Energy security and 'Big Stick' legislation. SSRN Electron J 37(5):607–625. https://www.ssrn.com/abstract=3671131. Accessed 28 February 2025

Paškevičius J (2020) The conceptualization of energy justice: the EU sphere. Baltic J Law Polit 13(1):163–190. https://www.sciendo.com/article/10.2478/bjlp-2020-0007. Accessed 28 February 2025

Peña Pupo L, Fariña Wong EY, Luis Cordova JG, Delgado Triana Y (2020) Quality of energy, energy access and law within the cuban hydropower context. Glob Jurist 20(3) https://www.degruyter.com/document/doi/10.1515/gj-2020-0012/html. Accessed 28 February 2025

Pereira G, González A, Ríos R (2021) Capturing multidimensional energy poverty in south america: a comparative study of Argentina, Brazil, Uruguay, and Paraguay. Front Sustain Cities 3(July) https://www.frontiersin.org/articles/10.3389/frsc.2021.632009/full. Accessed 28 February 2025

Pirstner-Ebner R (2019) Energierecht. Institut für Öffentliches Recht und Politikwissenschaft, Graz. https://www.facultas.at/item/Energierecht/Renate_Pirstner-Ebner/46348447. Accessed 28 February 2025

Prieto Valdés M (2016) Las garantías constitucionales de los derechos fundamentales y la Constitución de 1976. In La Constitución cubana de 1976: cuarenta años de vigencia, edited by Andry Matilla Correa, 17. La Habana: Unión Nacional de Juristas de Cuba. https://cuba.vlex.com/vid/garantias-constitucionales-derechos-fundamentales-647584885. Accessed 28 February 2025

Przybojewska I (2017) Right to energy? The protection of vulnerable recipients on national and international level. Law Admin Post-Soviet Eur 4(1):31–41. https://www.sciendo.com/article/10.1515/lape-2017-0003. Accessed 28 February 2025

Ramírez FA (2020) Aproximación a la Teoría del Derecho. Editorial Universidad de Almería, Almería. https://editorial.ual.es/libro/aproximacion-a-la-teoria-del-derecho_144246/. Accessed 28 February 2025

Reddy AKN (2000) Energy and social issues. In: World energy assessment: enerrgy and the challenge of sustainability. United Nations Development Programme, New York. https://sustainabledevelopment.un.org/content/documents/2423World_Energy_Assessment_2000.pdf. Accessed 28 February 2025

Redgwell C, Rajamani L (2020) And justice for all? Energy justice in international law. Energy Justice Energy Law 2:48–64. https://academic.oup.com/book/33728/chapter/288354610. Accessed 28 February 2025

Ren J, Sovacool BK (2014) Quantifying, measuring, and strategizing energy security: determining the most meaningful dimensions and metrics. Energy 76:838–849. https://doi.org/10.1016/j.energy.2014.08.083. Accessed 28 February 2025

REScoop 20–20-20 Consortium (2020) Best practices report II. https://www.rescoop.eu/uploads/rescoop/downloads/REScoop-Best-Practices-Report-2.pdf. Accessed 28 February 2025

Right to Energy Coalition | Take Action to End Energy Poverty in Europe (2022). https://righttoenergy.org/. Accessed 28 February 2025

Ringholm T (2022) Energy citizens—conveyors of changing democratic institutions? Cities 126. Elsevier Ltd. https://doi.org/10.1016/j.cities.2022.103678. Accessed 28 February 2025
Romero JC, Linares P, López X (2018) The policy implications of energy poverty indicators. Energy Policy 115:98–108. https://doi.org/10.1016/j.enpol.2017.12.054. Accessed 28 February 2025
Rudge J (2012) Coal fires, fresh air and the hardy British: a historical view of domestic energy efficiency and thermal comfort in Britain. Energy Policy 49:6–11. https://doi.org/10.1016/j.enpol.2011.11.064. Accessed 28 February 2025
Ryghaug M, Skjølsvold TM, Heidenreich S (2018) Creating energy citizenship through material participation. Soc Stud Sci 48(2):283–303. http://journals.sagepub.com/doi/10.1177/0306312718770286. Accessed 28 February 2025
Salter R, Gonzalez CG, Kronk Warne EA (2018) Energy justice: frameworks for energy law and policy. Edward Elgar, Massachusetts. https://www.amazon.com/Energy-Justice-International-Perspectives-Environmental/dp/1786431750. Accessed 28 February 2025
Sani GD, Sahabi S, Ibrahim A, Lailaba BB (2019) Renewable energy: environmental impacts and economic benefits for sustainable development. Int J Eng Res 8(8):547–555. https://www.ijert.org/renewable-energy-environmental-impacts-and-economic-benefits-for-sustainable-development. Accessed 28 February 2025
Schelly C, Bessette D, Brosemer K, Gagnon V, Arola KL, Fiss A, Pearce JM, Halvorsen KE (2020) Energy policy for energy sovereignty: can policy tools enhance energy sovereignty? Solar Energy 205 (May). Elsevier:109–112. https://doi.org/10.1016/j.solener.2020.05.056. Accessed 28 February 2025
Schlosberg D (2007) Defining environmental justice. Oxford University PressOxford, Oxford. https://academic.oup.com/book/4798. Accessed 28 February 2025
Sen A (1992) Inequality reexamined. Harvard University Press, Cambridge. https://www.hup.harvard.edu/catalog.php?isbn=9780674452565. Accessed 28 February 2025
Sen A (1999) Development as freedom. Oxford University Press, Oxford. https://scholar.harvard.edu/sen/publications/development-freedom. Accessed 28 February 2025
Shachar A (2012) Citizenship. In: Rosenfeld M, Sajó A (eds) The Oxford handbook of comparative constitutional law. Oxford University Press. https://academic.oup.com/edited-volume/43728/chapter-abstract/367620340?redirectedFrom=fulltext. Accessed 28 February 2025
Sharifuddin S (2014) Methodology for quantitatively assessing the energy security of malaysia and other southeast asian countries. Energy Policy 65:574–582. https://doi.org/10.1016/j.enpol.2013.09.065. Accessed 28 February 2025
Shove E, Walker G (2014) What is energy for? Social practice and energy demand. Cult Soc 31(5):41–58. https://journals.sagepub.com/doi/10.1177/0263276414536746. Accessed 28 February 2025
Shyu CW (2021) A framework for 'right to energy' to meet UN SDG7: policy implications to meet basic human energy needs, eradicate energy poverty, enhance energy justice, and uphold energy democracy. Energy Res Soc Sci 79:102199. https://linkinghub.elsevier.com/retrieve/pii/S2214629621002929. Accessed 28 February 2025
Simcock N (2016) Procedural justice and the implementation of community wind energy projects: a case study from South Yorkshire, UK. Land Use Policy 59:467–477. https://doi.org/10.1016/j.landusepol.2016.08.034. Accessed 28 February 2025
Simcock N, Walker G, Day R (2016) Fuel poverty in the UK: beyond heating? People place and policy online, vol 10. Centre for Regional and Economic Development, Sheffield Hallam University. https://research.birmingham.ac.uk/en/publications/fuel-poverty-in-the-uk-beyond-heating. Accessed 28 February 2025
Sin-Hang Ngai J (2012) Energy as a human right in armed conflict: a question of universal need, survival, and human dignity. Brook J Int Law 37(2):579–622. https://core.ac.uk/download/pdf/228597477.pdf. Accessed 28 February 2025
Sokołowski J, Lewandowski P, Kiełczewska A, Bouzarovski S (2020) A multidimensional index to measure energy poverty: the Polish case. Energy Sources B 15(2):92–112. https://doi.org/10.1080/15567249.2020.1742817. Accessed 28 February 2025

Solis MPS (2014) From right to light: a human rights- based approach to universal access to modern energy services. Adelaide University. https://digital.library.adelaide.edu.au/dspace/bitstream/2440/92548/3/02whole.pdf. Accessed 28 February 2025

Sovacool BK (2011a) Conceptualizing urban household energy use: climbing the "Energy Services Ladder". Energy Policy 39(3):1659–1668. https://doi.org/10.1016/j.enpol.2010.12.041. Accessed 28 February 2025

Sovacool BK (2011b) Security of energy services and uses within urban households. Curr Opin Environ Sustain 3(4):218–224. https://doi.org/10.1016/j.cosust.2011.06.004. Accessed 28 February 2025

Sovacool BK (2012) The political economy of energy poverty: a review of key challenges. Energy Sustain Dev 16(3):272–282. https://doi.org/10.1016/j.esd.2012.05.006. Accessed 28 February 2025

Sovacool BK (2016) The political ecology and justice of energy. In: Van de Graaf T, Sovacool BK, Ghosh A, Kern F, Klare MT (eds) The palgrave handbook of the international political economy of energy. Palgrave Macmillan UK, London, pp 529–558. http://link.springer.com/10.1057/978-1-137-55631-8. Accessed 28 February 2025

Sovacool BK, Cooper C, Bazilian M, Johnson K, Zoppo D, Clarke S, Eidsness J, Crafton M, Velumail T, Raza HA (2012b) What moves and works: broadening the consideration of energy poverty. Energy Policy 42:715–719. https://linkinghub.elsevier.com/retrieve/pii/S0301421511009992. Accessed 28 February 2025

Sovacool BK, Dworkin M (2012) Overcoming the global injustices of energy poverty. Environment 54(5):14–28. http://www.tandfonline.com/doi/abs/10.1080/00139157.2012.711669. Accessed 28 February 2025

Sovacool BK, Dworkin MH (2014) Global energy justice. problems, principles, and practices. Cambridge University Press, Reino Unido. https://www.cambridge.org/core/books/global-energy-justice/A3607C67A4798DC19AD73A4B11AFC28C. Accessed 28 February 2025

Sovacool BK, Dworkin MH (2015) Energy justice: conceptual insights and practical applications. Appl Energy 142:435–444. https://doi.org/10.1016/j.apenergy.2015.01.002. Accessed 28 February 2025.

Sovacool BK, Heffron RJ, McCauley D, Goldthau A (2016) Energy decisions reframed as justice and ethical concerns. Nat Energy 1(5):16024. https://www.nature.com/articles/nenergy201624. Accessed 28 February 2025

Sovacool BK, Linnér BO (2016) Introduction to the political economy of climate change adaptation. In: The political economy of climate change adaptation. Palgrave Macmillan UK, London, pp 1–32. http://link.springer.com/10.1057/9781137496737_1. Accessed 28 February 2025

Sovacool BK, Mukherjee I (2011) Conceptualizing and measuring energy security: a synthesized approach. Energy 36(8):5343–5355. https://doi.org/10.1016/j.energy.2011.06.043. Accessed 28 February 2025

Sovacool BK, Saunders H (2014) Competing policy packages and the complexity of energy security. Energy 67:641–651. https://doi.org/10.1016/j.energy.2014.01.039. Accessed 28 February 2025

Sovacool BK, Valentine SV, Jain Bambawale M, Brown MA, Cardoso TF, Nurbek S, Suleimenova G, Li J, Xu Y, Jain A, Alhajji AF, Zubiri A (2012a) Exploring propositions about perceptions of energy security: an international survey. Environ Sci Policy 16:44–64. https://linkinghub.elsevier.com/retrieve/pii/S1462901111001699. Accessed 28 February 2025

Spreng D, Pachauri S (2003) Energy use and energy access in relation to poverty. Econ Polit Wkly 39(3):271–278. JSTOR. http://www.jstor.org/stable/4414526. Accessed 28 February 2025

Stephens JC, Wilson EJ, Peterson TR (2015) Smart grid (r)evolution. Electric power struggles. Cambridge University Press. https://www.cambridge.org/core/product/identifier/9781107239029%23c04728-9-0/type/book_part. Accessed 28 February 2025

Strachan PA, Cowell R, Ellis G, Sherry-Brennan F, Toke D (2015) Promoting community renewable energy in a corporate energy world. Sustain Dev 23(2):96–109. https://onlinelibrary.wiley.com/doi/10.1002/sd.1576. Accessed 28 February 2025

Sustainable Energy for All (2013) Renewable energy. https://www.seforall.org/sites/default/files/l/2013/09/9-gtf_ch4.pdf. Accessed 28 February 2025

Sweeney JL (2001) Energy economics. In: International encyclopedia of the social & behavioral sciences. Elsevier, pp 4513–4520. https://linkinghub.elsevier.com/retrieve/pii/B0080430767041747. Accessed 28 February 2025

Sweeney S, Benton-Connell K, Skinner L (2015) Power to the people: toward democratic control of electricity generation. Ithaca. https://www.rosalux.de/fileadmin/rls_uploads/pdfs/engl/tued-workingpaper4powertothepeople.pdf. Accessed 28 February 2025

Szulecki K (2018) Conceptualizing energy democracy. Environ Polit 27(1):21–41. https://doi.org/10.1080/09644016.2017.1387294. Accessed 28 February 2025.

Szwed D, Maciejewska B (2014) Demokracja Energetyczna. Warszawa. http://zielonyinstytut.pl/wp-content/uploads/2016/10/demokracja_energetyczna_publikacja.pdf. Accessed 28 February 2025

Thaler P, Hofmann B (2022) The impossible energy trinity: energy security, sustainability, and sovereignty in cross-border electricity systems. Polit Geogr 94:102579. https://doi.org/10.1016/j.polgeo.2021.102579. Accessed 28 February 2025

The Secretary-General's Advisory Group on Energy and Climate Change (2010) Energy for a sustainable future. United Nations, New York. https://www.undp.org/sites/g/files/zskgke326/files/publications/AGECCsummaryreport.pdf. Accessed 28 February 2025

Thomson H, Bouzarovski S, Snell C (2017) Rethinking the measurement of energy poverty in Europe: a critical analysis of indicators and data. Indoor Built Environ 26(7):879–901. http://journals.sagepub.com/doi/10.1177/1420326X17699260. Accessed 28 February 2025

Thomson H, Snell C, Liddell C (2016) Fuel poverty in the European Union: a concept in need of definition? People Place Policy Online 10(1):5–24. http://extra.shu.ac.uk/ppp-online/fuel-poverty-in-the-european-union-a-concept-in-need-of-definition/. Accessed 28 February 2025

Timilsina GR (2019) Energy demand. In: Soytaş U, Sarı R (eds) Routledge handbook of energy economics. Routledge. https://www.taylorfrancis.com/books/9781315459646. Accessed 28 February 2025

Toffler A (1980) The third wave: the classic study of tomorrow, New York. https://books.google.be/books/about/The_Third_Wave.html?id=ViRmAAAAIAAJ&redir_esc=y. Accessed 28 February 2025

Tully SR (2006) The contribution of human rights to universal energy access. Northw J Int Hum Rights 4(3) http://scholarlycommons.law.northwestern.edu/njihr/vol4/iss3/3. Accessed 28 February 2025

Tully S (2009) The human right to access clean energy. J Green Build 2(1):140–148. https://www.scienceopen.com/document_file/c3efa42a-b169-4440-bf3b-42335b42ee2f/API/i1943-4618-3-2-140.pdf

U.S. Energy Information Administration (2020.) What is energy? https://www.eia.gov/energyexplained/what-is-energy/. Accessed 28 February 2025

Vågerö O, Zeyringer M (2023) Can we optimise for justice? Reviewing the inclusion of energy justice in energy system optimisation models. Energy Res Soc Sci 95:102913. https://doi.org/10.1016/j.erss.2022.102913. Accessed 28 February 2025

van Veelen B, van der Horst D (2018) What is energy democracy? Connecting social science energy research and political theory. Energy Res Soc Sci 46: 19–28. https://doi.org/10.1016/j.erss.2018.06.010. Accessed 28 February 2025

Vanderheiden S (2008) Atmospheric justice. Atmospheric justice. Oxford University Press. https://academic.oup.com/book/11169. Accessed 28 February 2025

Vansintjan D (2015) Power to the people. The energy transition to energy democracy. Final results oriented report of the REScoop 20–20-20 Intelligent Energy Europe project. Antwerp. https://www.rescoop.eu/uploads/rescoop/downloads/REScoop-Energy-Transition-to-Energy-Democracy-English.pdf. Accessed 28 February 2025

Vijayan M, Patil A, Kapse V (2020) Assessing the evolution of human settlements with 'energy' as a determinant. In: Sanap SB, Bhojwani VK, Mathew VK (eds) E3S web of conferences

170:01010. https://www.e3s-conferences.org/10.1051/e3sconf/202017001010. Accessed 28 February 2025
Vine M (2012) Energy security, oil and the transport sector - is Australia's policy adequate, reliable and affordable? Environ Plan Law J 29(5):401–414. https://www.academia.edu/16522810/Energy_security_oil_and_the_transport_sector_is_Australia_s_policy_adequate_reliable_and_affordable. Accessed 28 February 2025
Walker G (2009) Beyond distribution and proximity: exploring the multiple spatialities of environmental justice. Antipode 41(4):614–636. https://onlinelibrary.wiley.com/doi/10.1111/j.1467-8330.2009.00691.x. Accessed 28 February 2025
Walker G (2016a) The right to energy: meaning, specification and the politics of definition. L'Europe Form 378 (4):26–38. https://www.cairn.info/revue-l-europe-en-formation-2015-4-page-26.htm?ref=doi. Accessed 28 February 2025
Walker G (2016b) The right to energy: meaning, specification and the politics of definition. L'Europe en Form 378 (4):26–38. https://www.cairn.info/revue-l-europe-en-formation-2015-4-page-26.htm?ref=doi. Accessed 28 February 2025
Walker G, Day R (2012) Fuel poverty as injustice: integrating distribution, recognition and procedure in the struggle for affordable warmth. Energy Policy 49: 69–75. https://doi.org/10.1016/j.enpol.2012.01.044. Accessed 28 February 2025
Walker G, Day R, Simcock N (2015) The right to energy: an analysis of meaning and implications. https://www.sciencespo.fr/ceri/sites/sciencespo.fr.ceri/files/G.%20Walker%20Right%20to%20Energy%20CERI%20EDF%20Oct15.pdf. Accessed 28 February 2025
Weis L, Becker S, Naumann M (2015) Energiedemokratie - Grundlage und Perspektiven einer kritischen Energieforschung, Berlin. https://www.rosalux.de/fileadmin/rls_uploads/pdfs/Studien/Studien_01-15_Energiedemokratie.pdf. Accessed 28 February 2025
Willrich M (1976) International Energy Issues and Options. Annual Review of Energy 1(1):743–772. https://www.annualreviews.org/doi/10.1146/annurev.eg.01.110176.003523. Accessed 28 February 2025
Wood N, Roelich K (2020) Substantiating energy justice: creating a space to understand energy dilemmas. Sustainability 12(5):1917. https://doi.org/10.1016/j.eist.2018.12.001. Accessed 28 February 2025.
Yepes Stork R (2018) El origen de la «energeia» en Aristóteles. Anuario Filosófico 22(1): 93–109. https://dadun.unav.edu/bitstream/10171/716/3/5. EL ORIGEN DE LA ENERGIA EN ARISTÓTELES%2C RICARDO YEPES STORK.pdf. Accessed 28 February 2025
Yergin D (1991) The prize: the epic quest for oil, money and power. Simon & Schuster, New York. https://books.google.be/books?hl=en&lr=&id=WiUTwBTux2oC&oi=fnd&pg=PR3&ots=_4EXs7865-&sig=_YDlhhhX7tSt5tBjx4lmUZUHvzA&redir_esc=y#v=onepage&q&f=false. Accessed 28 February 2025
Yergin D (2006) Ensuring energy security. Foreign Affairs 85(2):69. https://www.jstor.org/stable/20031912. Accessed 28 February 2025

Chapter 6
The Right to Energy as a Right Under Construction

6.1 The Right to Energy from the Perspective of Human and Fundamental Rights Theory

The international legal order, regional normative frameworks and national legal systems currently face the challenge of assimilating, recognising, and protecting the right to energy in their legal instruments. The study has revealed multiple approaches, trends in recognition, and avenues for protecting the right in question. In this sense, the doctrine shapes the theoretical foundations of the right to energy to lay the foundations for its recognition and protection in legal systems.

Following the analysis developed above, there are common elements in the doctrine that allow the theoretical structuring of the right to energy, but, at the same time, there are points of divergence in terms of its configuring elements. The first element to be determined by the present research would be the nature of the right to energy and the subsequent determination of its configuring elements.

Although the construction of the right to energy is still in development, identifiable characteristics frame it as a new human and fundamental right. It is necessary to start with analysing and understanding human rights[1] and fundamental rights and the interrelation between them to determine the legal nature of the right to energy.

The attribution of the category of human rights to the right to energy is not isolated from the debate that has revolved around them. This affirmation is because, concerning human rights, they have generated a broad discussion on which there has not been a total consensus in the doctrine. The origin and evolution of human rights have a varied spectrum of positions, ranging from iusnaturalism, considering

[1] Valadés and Gutiérrez Rivas (2001), Donnelly (2011), Instituto Interamericano de Derechos Humanos (1996), Nikken (1987), Instituto Interamericano de Derechos Humanos (1997), Comisión Nacional de los Derechos Humanos (2016), Pizarro Sotomayor and Méndez Powell (2006), Carpizo (2011), Galvis Sánchez (2007) and Selayaram (2009).

J. G. Luis Cordova, *Theoretical and Legal Dimensions of the Right to Energy*, Economic and Financial Law & Policy – Shifting Insights & Values 9,
https://doi.org/10.1007/978-3-032-33252-3_6

human rights as the product of an order deduced from human nature itself,[2] to positivism, where if the law is not positivised, it does not exist.[3]

The present research does not take part in any of the extreme positions. Although it starts from the assumption that the full existence of human rights is achieved through their legal positivisation, the law does not assume a role in creating human rights but rather in protecting and regulating them. As the Universal Declaration of Human Rights rightly states, the role of law is to protect human rights[4] and not to create them. According to the Office of the United Nations High Commissioner for Human Rights, human rights are legal rights inherent to the human condition. They are protected and not created by law.[5]

If one were to follow a strictly positivist criterion, taking into consideration the list of human rights in the Universal Declaration and subsequent treaties would deny the right to energy as a human right. Although such legal instruments guarantee the defence of human rights, Nickel states that: "there is no reason to consider the list of human rights as sacrosanct"[6] since it primarily reflects contemporary human rights ideals. While Nickel takes a historicist position, he recognises that human rights do not have a strictly normative origin.

The question arises: What is their source if human rights do not originate in the norm? The creation of human rights from divine or natural laws would be ruled out based on a materialist-dialectical criterion. Human rights are considered to have their origin before their positivisation in international legal instruments. They originate in "an axiological or value-based ethical foundation, based on demands considered essential as unavoidable conditions for a dignified life, i.e., demands derived from the idea of human dignity."[7] However, the role of the norm is undeniable in the full existence of human rights, which, although a political and philosophical category, is also legal.

As a basic human need, energy impacts life's development in dignity conditions. In turn, if this need is affected, it would violate the rest of the human rights that depend on this condition. The protection of the rest of human rights without the recognition and protection of the right to energy would be, itself, incomplete and insufficient, given that without energy, the realisation of many human rights such as the right to health, education, work, adequate housing, among many others, would not be complete and in some cases impossible.

Borowski, for his part, takes sides in the debate by defining human rights as moral rights whose fundamental nature is oriented towards the protection and satisfaction of fundamental interests and needs and considers them to be the core of

---

[2] Fernández García (1982).

[3] Benavides Ordóñez (2012), p. 36.

[4] "Considering it essential that human rights be protected by the rule of law (…)". Organización de Naciones Unidas (1948).

[5] Office of the United Nations High Commissioner for Human Rights (2007), pp. 2–3.

[6] Nickel (1987), p. 186.

[7] Fernández García (1982), p. 98.

theories of justice. He sees human rights as prioritising positive law since they legitimise it.[8] In this way, Borowski appreciates the validity of human rights independently of their positivisation. Such an explanation supports human rights at a time, ex-ante to the norm. Among such rights is the right to energy, the full positivisation of which is still in the development process in the international legal framework.

Also, from this theoretical approach, Aparicio Wilhelmi and Pisarello Prados place human rights in the spheres of moral, political, and religious reflection. In turn, they consider them to be well-founded or just claims, according to a particular conception of values, which is why they express a moral or political duty.[9] A clear example is the Right to Energy Coalition. This initiative brings together trade unions, NGOs, environmentalists, health organisations and energy cooperatives to fight against energy poverty in the European Union at national and local levels.[10]

As a human right, the right to energy originates in moral rights, like many other rights of the exact nature. A broad sector of the doctrine supports this position,[11] which considers human rights as ethical-moral demands and rights inherent to the human condition itself, sufficiently relevant to be recognised, protected, and guaranteed by political power and the law. In this sense, those moral rights intricately linked to human dignity will be considered human rights.

In this framework, Brugger, in analysing the moral foundations of the right to energy as a human right, declares energy to be a common good over which no group or individual can claim absolute possession. Considering energy as a common good qualifies it as a condition for complete personality fulfilment. Brugger links the right to energy with distributive justice within and between nations concerning the obligations of states in the fair distribution of available energy resources. Another moral foundation of the human right to energy is considering energy as an instrumental human good, which makes well-being possible and enables the existence of the most basic conditions for life in dignity.[12]

Despite the moral origin of human rights, such as the right to energy, they reach their full maturity through their positivisation in international instruments. The role of international human rights law is undeniable, as it guarantees the binding nature of human rights for national states. This binding character is based on the essential characteristics of human rights. The Office of the United Nations High Commissioner for Human Rights (OHCHR) has stated that the essential characteristics of human rights are based on respect for human dignity and the value of everyone. It declares human rights universal, inalienable, indivisible, interrelated and interdependent. Because of these characteristics, states should not selectively develop respect for

---

[8] Borowski (2003), pp. 30–31.

[9] Aparicio Wilhelmi and Pisarello Prados (2008).

[10] Right to Energy Coalition | Take Action to End Energy Poverty in Europe (2022).

[11] Dávila (2022), Stolerman and Lagnado (2020), Schilling (2020), Carchidi (2020), Goodale (2020), Zysset (2019), Fellmeth (2016) and Solanes Corella (2018).

[12] Brugger (2016).

human rights and their protection since violating one human right can negatively impact the rest.[13]

The Universal Declaration of Human Rights and the other international legal instruments that make up international human rights law are based on these pillars. In this context, as already analysed, the international framework has been projected, throughout history, towards recognising and protecting the right to energy as a human right per se.[14]

Based on the above, this research considers the right to energy as a new human right.[15] The formation of the human right to energy has been one of its main normative milestones, the Convention on the Elimination of All Forms of Discrimination against Women, based on the provision of the right to electricity as a part of the right to energy. The evolution of the doctrine itself has refined this restrictive approach, the political aspirations of pressure groups, and legal instruments at national and international levels. Thus, Recommendation 34 of the Committee on the Elimination of All Forms of Discrimination against Women[16] extends the scope of the right to energy described in the Convention to access energy sources and energy services beyond electricity as the energy service par excellence.

Although the right to energy is a human right, this does not guarantee its complete protection. According to Aparicio Wilhelmi and Pisarello Prados, human rights manifest a political commitment, but this commitment must be reflected in legal systems, where human rights can be protected by substantive law in the form of fundamental rights.

For his part, Navarro Cuipal echoes the previous statement when he says: "Fundamental rights are those human rights positivised at the internal level, while the formula of human rights is the most usual one in the level of international declarations and conventions".[17] An example of this has occurred in States such as Nicaragua and Bolivia, where the political commitment of the international community to the recognition and protection of the right to energy has led to its constitutionally expressed assimilation as a human right and as a fundamental right, given the very fundamental nature of its essence.

---

[13] Office of the United Nations High Commissioner for Human Rights (2007).

[14] Cf. already supra, Chap. 3.

[15] New human rights are those that are not recognised by any human rights treaty but are candidates for legal recognition under international public law. To reach this stage, they must pass through three main phases. The first of these is the pretence in which activists, intellectuals, and politicians, as well as part of the doctrine, take part in discussions on how the law can best protect human interests. From this there is a growing awareness that exerts pressure on decision-making mechanisms. The second phase is an emergence in which new human rights become relevant in new norms of international public law. This second phase involves new actors such as states, international organisations, human rights courts, among others. The third phase is the full recognition of the new human rights in binding international legal instruments. von der Decken and Koch (2020); Finnemore and Sikkink (1998), pp. 894–905; Nickel (1987), p. 29.

[16] UN CEDAW (2016).

[17] Navarro Cuipal (2010).

Borowski states that international fundamental rights are enshrined in international legal instruments to protect human rights. He also recognises supranational fundamental rights contained in regional legal instruments. Finally, he recognises national fundamental rights as those rights with a positive provision in the legal-constitutional framework. Borowski thus defines fundamental rights as transforming human rights into positive law.[18]

This view is also shared by Peces Barba, de Asís Roig and Llamas Cascón, who, although they consider the denomination of human rights as an ambiguous category, consider fundamental rights as a transposition of human rights within the legal system, through their concrete recognition and protection under the constitutional articles. These authors define fundamental rights as an expression of basic morality and legality.[19]

What has been described by Peces Barba, de Asís Roig, and Llamas Cascón is evident in some legal-constitutional systems analysed above.[20] Although several international legal instruments call for a right to energy, its true essence is legally developed by the legal systems that have provided recognition based on solid principles and mechanisms that guarantee its protection. Conversely, in States that have not taken sides in the recognition and protection of the right to energy, the international political commitment in this sense has remained only in diplomatic dialogue with limited impact on the legal sphere of individuals.

The fundamental nature of the right to energy is given by two factors: a fundamental need and the constitutional recognition of this need in the fundamental right norm. In this sense, the need for energy becomes basic and is established as the foundation of the fundamental right to energy.[21] Energy is framed as a radical need that, if unsatisfied, the primary conditions for a dignified human life would not exist.[22] This radical need would imply the existence of survival situations or a progressive deterioration that could lead to the disappearance of the human being.[23] In turn, the right to energy must have a legal-constitutional backing within States to guarantee that its content is safeguarded within the legal sphere of individuals.

Considering the above, the declaration of the right to energy as a fundamental right would result in the constitutional recognition of a basic need that is, per se, fundamental. In turn, recognising the right to energy as a fundamental right would contribute to the legitimacy of the state and the law since it would give way to the demand for accountability in the maintenance of the right in question and would set a limit for the state and the law. Consequently, a new legal subsystem would be

[18] Borowski (2003).

[19] Peces-Barba et al. (1995).

[20] Cf. already supra, Sect. 4.5.

[21] Peña Luño (1993), Peces-Barba et al. (1995), Fernández (1993) and Castillo Córdova (2010).

[22] Cf. supra, Sect. 2.2.

[23] Peces-Barba et al. (1995).

created[24] based on values such as freedom, equality, and solidarity from a material perspective and on security from a formal approach.[25] Constitutional recognition of the fundamental nature of the right to energy would provide security for its holders by extending the legal sphere of rights, protecting a need on which many other fundamental rights depend. The opposability also influences this before third parties, which would entail recognising the fundamental right to energy.[26] Such recognition also implies, according to Ferrajoli, the creation of a system of primary and secondary guarantees to ensure the realisation of the right to energy.[27] Among these guarantees is establishing the necessary channel for creating justiciability mechanisms[28] as a secondary guarantee. In turn, the recognition and regulation of the right to energy as a fundamental right would allow the determination of its meaning and scope in the legal system. Despite these elements, in many cases, States have not taken an active role in the field of energy law, leaving many legal gaps in its normative regulation.

This research considers the right to energy in its dual capacity as a human right within the formation process and as a fundamental right in specific national legal systems.[29] Once the nature of the right to energy has been analysed, the next step is to determine its constituent elements. To this end, a doctrinal and legal analysis of the principles that underpin it, its subjects, content, and guarantees will be carried out.[30]

6.2 Essential Principles of the Right to Energy

While some States have ventured to offer a system of principles[31] to underpin the right to energy, this is a subject that is still in the process of being refined. For this reason, this research will analyse the diversity of criteria offered to underpin the essential principles of the right to energy.

---

[24] The establishment of a legal subsystem of the right to energy would place it in a higher hierarchical context in the legal system as it is contained in the Constitution, developed from implementing regulations and jurisprudence. Such a hierarchical positioning would allow the determination of interpretation criteria in case of conflicts of rights. In turn, the establishment of a legal subsystem of the right to energy would imply the existence of subjects, content and its system of guarantees and principles. Peces-Barba et al. (1995), pp. 379–380; Garrido Gómez (2020), p. 314.

[25] Garrido Gómez (2020), pp. 315–316.

[26] Borowski (2020).

[27] Ferrajoli (2006).

[28] Carbonell (2002), Hesse (2001), Restrepo-pimienta and Cotrina-gulfo (2020) and Parra Cortés (2018).

[29] Cf. already supra, Chap. 4.

[30] Peces-Barba et al. (1995).

[31] According to the Theory of Fundamental Rights, Alexy defines the principles of fundamental rights as optimisation mandates without binding force with respect to legal and factual possibilities, and therefore they belong to the deontological plane. In turn, Alexy establishes the link between principles and values by claiming that the identification of a principle implies the recognition of a value, so that a collision between the former can be expressed as a collision between the

The international legal system considers the right to energy a new human right. Hence, this right must be underpinned by general principles such as universality and inalienability, indivisibility, interdependence and interrelatedness, equity and non-discrimination, participation and inclusion, accountability, and the rule of law.[32] Integrating these principles into national legal frameworks and energy policies would ensure that the right to energy is protected from a human rights-based approach.

Implementing these principles contributes to protecting the right to the energy of all, promoting the realisation of the rest of human rights equitably and without any distinction. Mechanisms for popular participation in energy policies and the diversification of energy generation are created. Similarly, under the principle of responsibility and the rule of law, a political and regulatory framework is needed to guarantee the full realisation of the right to energy.

Despite the importance of these principles, there are principles of energy law which must be considered to support the realisation of the right to energy. In this sense, Del Guayo Castiella establishes the security of supply as the first principle to be considered. Although it is explained from the perspective of consumer rights, it is essential to highlight that it guarantees the satisfaction of energy needs at any time.[33] It also includes the protection of the holders of the right to energy and their property.

Security of supply is intricately linked to the state's responsibility to ensure energy security through its four basic pillars and energy sovereignty through diversification of supply, where renewable energy sources play a significant role. From this, the accessibility and affordability of modern energy services are a principle. This principle emerges directly from SDG #7 of the 2030 Agenda so that the right to energy goes beyond the limits of accessibility to modern energy services such as air conditioning and transportation, among many others, based on clean energy.

The content of the security of supply principle is also related to two of the principles outlined by Heffron et al.: energy security and reliability and resilience. The former refers to the continuity of supply and affordability of energy service prices, while the latter refers to the ability of the energy system to withstand unfavourable events.[34] In the case of energy-importing countries, this poses many challenges, such as the diversification of suppliers. In turn, the creation of incentives to achieve energy sovereignty must be a priority for the state to guarantee supply. The European Union and other states, because of the 2022 energy crisis, are today facing the consequences of not developing sufficient alternatives to guarantee energy sovereignty.[35]

---

latter and/or vice versa. A clear example of this is dignity, as a principle-value that stands as the foundation of human rights and, therefore, of the right to energy. Alexy (1993), pp. 112, 138, 141; Velasco Gutiérrez (2013), p. 11.

[32] United Nations Population Fund (2005).

[33] Cf. Del Guayo Castiella (2020), p. 326.

[34] Heffron et al. (2018).

[35] International Renewable Energy Agency (2022).

Another principle underpinning the right to energy is explained by Sovacool et al.: energy justice. These authors define it as a global energy system that distributes both the benefits and costs of energy services equitably, where representative and impartial energy decision-making is promoted. The implementation of this principle is materialised through three elements: the distribution of costs (how the risks and externalities of the energy system are distributed in society), the distribution of benefits (how access to modern energy systems and services is distributed throughout society) and the procedures for ensuring respect for due process and representation in decision-making related to the energy sector.[36]

Economic efficiency is considered another principle underpinning the right to energy. It aims to reduce the costs of energy services.[37] It is important not to confuse this principle with energy efficiency, which, although it has a marked impact on the right to energy, seeks to reduce energy loss and consumption. In this sense, it should be noted that energy loss is understood as transforming energy into other energy that is useless for satisfying energy needs.

Given the call for sustainable development, environmental sustainability is another of the principles that should underpin the right to energy. To this end, energy policies must be oriented towards reducing the environmental impact of energy services. According to Del Guayo Castiella, the content of this principle is embodied in the reduction of the decarbonisation of the energy sector, the prudent, rational, and sustainable use of natural resources, and decentralisation and empowerment.[38] Such empowerment is materialised through participation mechanisms and effective protection of the holders of the right to energy.

Several principles should underpin the right to energy in the legal system, among which the following can be mentioned: general human rights principles, energy security, energy justice, economic efficiency, and environmental sustainability. Many of these general principles are closely related to the meaning and scope of the right under study in this research. It is, therefore, necessary to delimit the subjects of the right to energy.

6.3 Subjects of the Right to Energy

Following the diversity of trends in the legal treatment of the right to energy, different approaches have been taken regarding its subjects. Once issued, legal rights norms are addressed to specific subjects that emerge as their addressees. Bastida et al. divide the addressees of these norms into two main groups: on the one hand, the beneficiaries of the area of freedom protected by law and, on the other hand,

---

36 Sovacool et al. (2016).

37 Del Guayo Castiella (2020).

38 Del Guayo Castiella (2020).

those obliged to guarantee it.[39] The subjects obliged to guarantee the right to energy are the State and energy service providers, which can be both public and private.

Beneficiaries, on the other hand, are also referred to as right-holders. This status can be defined as "a normative status or legal condition by which a subject of law is constituted who benefits from the protection of the right, equality or freedom that a legal system considers to be a fundamental right".[40] Based on this conception, the rights holders are those active subjects endowed by the legal system with the protection of an enforceable specific power. This power contains the obligation of the duty-bearers to guarantee its content.

Determining who can hold such status is an essential element to highlight in this context. Without entering into doctrinal disquisitions on the conceptualisation of the subjects of fundamental rights, it is crucial to highlight Adulante Lizana, who states that the subjects of rights can be natural persons, legal persons, and collectives without legal personality, also known as moral persons. This view is shared by Varsi Rospigliosi, who defines collectives without legal personality as non-personified entities. This entity type is: "a group of persons who have come together to satisfy their needs and fulfil their desires collectively, who may have been subject to a form established by law, but who have not complied with the registration requirement in the corresponding register. The legal relations are assumed by its members jointly and severally. It could be said that the unincorporated entity is a dual legal entity since its members are individually liable but act collectively".[41]

The elements described so far apply to the right to energy as a right of a human and fundamental nature. Based on the analysis developed in the preceding sections,[42] two main approaches can be identified for determining the active subjects of the right to energy, which, in turn, are inextricably linked.

The first approach identifies all human beings as subjects of the right to energy. This approach can be seen in SDG #7, which advocates for access to energy for all.[43] Similarly, in the constitutional orders analysed, the Constitution of Ecuador stands out when it mentions in Article 52 the right of all people to receive quality services.[44] This article opens the framework for the second approach, identifying energy consumers as the active subjects of the right to energy. An example of this position is the European Union Directive 2019/944, where energy consumers are empowered to demand the realisation of the right to energy. Similarly, this position is

[39] Bastida et al. (2004).

[40] Contreras Vásquez (2017), p. 120.

[41] Varsi Rospigliosi (2017).

[42] Cf. already supra, Sects. 6.1 and 6.2.

[43] Comisión Económica para América Latina y el Caribe (2016).

[44] Cf. Article 52. Asamblea Constituyente de Ecuador (2008).

ratified in the states that have taken up the trend of protecting the right to energy within the consumer rights framework.[45]

While both approaches may have a broader or narrower meaning, they both seek respect for universality as a principle of fundamental rights and thus, the principle of universality is highlighted as a pillar of the right to energy. Nevertheless, the approach associated with identifying energy consumers may be far-reaching. The notion of the energy consumer is a legal construct that is still in the process of development.

The theoretical approach to the figure of the energy consumer is based on the conceptualisation of the consumer as a general category. In the conceptual analysis of this category, two tendencies have been presented: an abstract and a concrete notion. The abstract notion of consumer considers in this status all citizens, in general, who purchase or use goods and services. In this sense, the consumer is equated with the citizen. According to Acedo Penco, this notion is beneficial for the collective exercise of rights but is limited to the individual exercise of rights. As a counterpart to the abstract notion of consumer, the concrete notion emerges, which provides the framework for exercising consumer rights individually.[46]

Two types of consumers derive from the concrete notion of consumer: the customer consumer and the final consumer. The category of client-consumer deals with consumption per se without considering the final destination of the object of consumption. The notion of the end consumer safeguards this issue.[47] In the context of the consumption of energy services, the notion of consumer customer would become apparent in those legal systems in which the right to energy can only be exercised by the customer under a contractual-legal relationship. The notion of the end consumer would protect people who consume energy services such as electricity and gas services, among others, whether they are customers or not.

Following this description, it is essential to highlight that determining the active subjects of the right to energy as a fundamental right within national legal systems results from the State's regulatory action. Therefore, to the extent that the approach adopted by the legal system favours the universality of the right to energy, there will be a more inclusive protective framework. The normative determination of the active subject status of the right to energy in national norms does not exclude the universal nature of the right. Its very nature as a human right implies that all members of the human family, acting individually or collectively, are active subjects as established in the Universal Declaration of Human Rights preamble,[48] which would make the mechanisms for protecting human rights available.[49]

---

[45] Cf. already supra, Chap. 4.

[46] Acedo Penco (2000).

[47] Castañeda (2002).

[48] Organización de Naciones Unidas (1948).

[49] Langford (2009) and Nolan et al. (2017).

6.4 Content of the Right to Energy

The delimitation of the content of the right to energy has gone through the prism of determining the content of the rest of the rights of a fundamental nature. The content of fundamental rights, as a configuring element, has been the subject of analysis in legal doctrine. According to Castillo Córdova, there are three criteria for determining the content of a fundamental right. The first of these criteria is the literal interpretation criterion, under which the constitutional provision recognising the fundamental right in question would be considered. This criterion lacks precision because of the general approach taken by the rules of constitutional law. A second criterion is a systemic interpretation, under which the content of the fundamental right is determined by all related provisions, starting with the provision recognising the right in question. The third criterion is the international clause, based on the binding supranational instruments that regulate a specific right.[50]

Although these criteria respond to a legal dogmatic character, in those cases where the normative order does not expressly recognise the right to energy, it would be difficult to apply them. In this context, the criterion of teleological interpretation arises. This criterion seeks to delimit the right to energy and aligns with the protected human good: energy as a radical need. In this way, the satisfaction of the legally protected interest is pursued.[51]

Parejo Alfonso considers the essential content of fundamental rights an indeterminate legal concept that can be used technically. He considers that the essential content of fundamental rights comprises two elements: internal and external. The first of these is made up of the elements essential for the right's legal recognisability, and the second is the protection it receives from the legal system.[52] This position takes part in the different theories on the limits and content of fundamental rights, taking up the theory of the essential content of rights. This research will determine the delimitation of the content of the right to energy by deconstructing its conceptualisation,[53] considering the broad theoretical debate on the content of fundamental rights.[54]

The author's conceptual delimitation of the right to energy sheds light on the elements that make up its content. Nevertheless, it is relevant to emphasise that the theoretical elements presented below are not immutable. They may vary from one legal system to another, so their legal protection will be determined by the meaning and scope that the legal system grants to the right to energy and the content of the needs that it safeguards.

Energy availability is the first element of the right to energy content, starting from the conceptual assumption of energy from a double dimension: energy

[50] Castillo Córdova (2010).

[51] Castillo Córdova (2010).

[52] Parejo Alfonso (1981).

[53] Cf. already supra, Sect. 5.3.2.

[54] Cf. Maldonado Muñoz (2020).

services and energy sources.[55] Availability, in the framework of the right to energy, requires, in the case of energy services, the generation of sufficient energy to meet the energy needs of the holders of the right under study. Therefore, duty-bearers must be able to meet these needs. Although in this context, using renewable energy sources is the ideal way forward, this element should not be a limit for the realisation of the right.

Another element of the content of the right to energy is accessibility.[56] The right to energy requires the necessary infrastructure to ensure two elements. Firstly, the transmission of energy or its carriers from where it is generated to where it is consumed. While this is highly oriented towards energy services, accessibility to energy sources depends on the availability and affordability of the technological equipment necessary for energy generation. Accessibility does not include the exploitation of all available energy sources in each territorial context, as such exploitation depends on administrative concessions, considering the state's sovereignty over natural wealth and resources.[57]

The accessibility described above will be highly determined by the affordability of energy services and the technology needed to exploit energy sources. The understanding of affordability,[58] as another integral element of the content of the right to energy, is a multifactorial-dependent phenomenon. This integral element of the content of the right to energy depends on social, economic, political, cultural, and other aspects. For this reason, in the framework of energy policies and through the legal system, indicators must be established to measure, from a multidisciplinary approach, the impact of energy prices on the economic capacity of the holders of the right to energy.

The fourth element of the content of the right to energy is reliability.[59] This element is divided into three elements that contribute to its existence. The first of these is the continuity of energy supply, which is an insurmountable characteristic to guarantee the functioning of energy-dependent processes. The second element that integrates reliability is the quality of energy services, for which energy quality standards must be adopted to guarantee the safety of people and their goods. The third element is access to information. This element guarantees that the holders of the

[55] Organización de Naciones Unidas (1987), Soytas and Sari (2019), Ibrahim Marei (2015), Ostojic et al. (2011) and Salter et al. (2018).

[56] Gutiérrez (2018), Caldeira Brant (2016), Velo García (2005), Rivera Staff (2014), Pellicer-sifres (2017), Sovacool and Dworkin (2014), Acheampong et al. (2021), Refaat and Ismail (2017) and Hostettler and Gadgil (2015).

[57] Organización de Naciones Unidas (1962).

[58] Eisman (2016), Organismo Internacional de Energía Atómica, Departamento de Asuntos Económicos y Sociales de Las Naciones Unidas, and Agencia Internacional de la Energía (2008), Moncayo Vives (2017), Carvajal et al. (2020), Castro Soto (2009), Jiménez Guanipa and Tous Chimá (2017), Hesselman et al. (2021) and Sovacool et al. (2016).

[59] Costa (2009), Moncayo Vives (2017), Jiménez Guanipa and Tous Chimá (2017), Vergara Blanco (2004), Del Guayo Castiella (2020), Decker (2020), Bhatia and Angelou (2015), Tully (2006), Sovacool et al. (2014) and Olivares Gallardo (2012).

right to energy obtain timely and necessary information regarding the energy services they consume.

In this way, availability, affordability, accessibility, and reliability are considered the essential elements of the content of the right to energy. Despite having so far developed the delimitation of the subjects and content of the right to energy, this is not enough to guarantee its full realisation. That is why the guarantees for its materialisation must be defined.

6.5 Basic Guarantees of the Right to Energy

As an element that shapes the right to energy, guarantees share common aspects with the rest of the fundamental rights. Even though guarantees, as a legal institution, originated in Roman Law from a civil law perspective, they are nowadays constituted as a means of realisation par excellence of fundamental rights. In this sense, guarantees are "any obligation corresponding to a subjective right."[60]

The right to energy, like other rights of a socio-economic nature, according to Hesse, does not become effective by the mere fact that they are respected and protected, but instead, they require actions on the part of the State for their content to be fully realised. Therefore, legislative action alone does not fully guarantee the right to energy. However, the recognition and legal configuration of the right in question are necessary for the administration to act to realise the right to energy.[61]

In addition to the above, Ferrajoli's theory of guaranteeing rights, in which two types of constitutional guarantees are made explicit: positive and negative. Positive guarantees are defined as obligations to provide services, while negative guarantees are conceived as prohibitions on harming the expectations contained in subjective economic and fundamental rights. Ferrajoli further explains, as guarantees, the obligations concerning the expectations of reparation by sanctioning or annulling acts that violate subjective rights. On this basis, Ferrajoli's theory of guaranteeing rights makes a distinction between primary or substantive guarantees and secondary or jurisdictional guarantees.[62]

However, Escobar Roca calls only the secondary guarantees described by Ferrajoli guarantees, while he considers primary guarantees to fulfil fundamental rights.[63] Despite the different denominations, Escobar Roca shares the essence of

[60] Ferrajoli (2010), p. 61.

[61] Hesse (2001), p. 98.

[62] The primary or substantial guarantees are "the guarantees consisting of the obligations or prohibitions corresponding to the guaranteed subjective rights (…)" and the secondary or jurisdictional guarantees are the "obligations, on the part of the jurisdictional bodies, to apply sanctions or declare the nullity (…) of illicit acts and invalid acts that violate the subjective rights and, with them, their respective primary guarantees". (Own translation) Ferrajoli (2010), p. 64; Ferrajoli (2006).

[63] Escobar Roca (2018), p. 147.

Ferrajoli's guarantees. Brewer-Carías, for his part, considers secondary guarantees as the fundamental guarantee of rights.[64] While it is true that the mechanisms of effective jurisdictional protection guarantee the restoration or sanctioning of violations of fundamental rights, primary guarantees play a crucial role in the realisation of these rights.

Therefore, the present research is affiliated with Ferrajoli's guarantee theory by considering the constitutional guarantees of rights in its two typologies: primary guarantees (positive and negative) and secondary guarantees. Without establishing a hierarchy between the two typologies, primary and secondary guarantees form a system that ensures the realisation of fundamental rights and, consequently, of the right to energy.

Structuring the system of guarantees of the right to energy has a constitutional origin to protect its binding nature and observance. Based on the legal framework, from the constitutional level down to the lower hierarchy, the normative bases of the right under study must be developed to regulate four essential guarantees: constitutional recognition, security of energy supply, the prohibition of disconnection and justiciability.

In this sense, the first and most immediate guarantee that a fundamental right must have been constitutional recognition. This guarantee converts the right to energy into a constitutional norm and places it in a higher hierarchical rank, given the principle of the supremacy of the Constitution within the legal system.[65] In this way, the binding nature of fundamental rights vis-à-vis the public authorities is ensured. Thus, rights and obligations are formed and declared immediately applicable in jurisdictional or administrative jurisdiction without the extreme need for other bodies of law intermediation.[66]

In addition, other positive and negative guarantees are needed as primary guarantees of the right to energy. As a positive primary guarantee of the right to energy, the security of the energy supply is presented as an obligation of the state.[67] This primary guarantee compels the State to ensure the availability of reliable energy services to the holders of the right to energy and is, therefore, a duty of the State. Within this framework, the state is responsible for structuring the energy supply based on its energy policy and regulation and for choosing the energy sources to use.

As part of guaranteeing the security of the energy supply,[68] the state must create the conditions for energy democracy based on the empowerment of the holders of the right to energy. Such empowerment involves popular participation in energy

[64] Brewer-Carías (2017), p. 335.

[65] Paredes Paredes (2015), pp. 247, 249.

[66] Cotino Hueso (2018), p. 502.

[67] Wilson and Dobreva (2019).

[68] The security of supply as a constitutional guarantee constitutes the obligation of those liable for the right to energy to quantitatively satisfy the energy needs of the holders of the right in question in accordance with normatively determined quality parameters in an affordable and reliable manner where environmental protection is promoted. Cf. Szalbierz and Ropuszyńska-Surma (2010), p. 1.

policies and developing energy generation initiatives using renewable sources. In this sense, strategies must be consolidated to encourage self-consumption initiatives[69] so that the holders of the right to energy can generate part or all the energy they need and, if they exist, can market the surplus energy generated.

Another of the primary guarantees is the prohibition of disconnection,[70] which is a negative primary guarantee.[71] That guarantee, par excellence, safeguards the accessibility of energy services for energy rights holders. It is the responsibility of states to adopt measures aimed at preventing self-disconnection, which is linked to the prohibition of disconnection.[72]

While the need for access to energy services is a fundamental necessity, excessive tariffs can lead to a hierarchy of needs on the part of energy rights holders.[73] Affordability of energy is a priority element to guarantee the effective exercise of the right to energy, and the protection of energy rights holders from abusive tariffs and practices should be a matter of special attention by States.

As a fundamental right, the justiciability of the right to energy is a secondary guarantee. Justiciability guarantees redress in the event of violations of its content, following the normative framework that determines its recognition, regulation, and protection.[74] For this reason, as part of the system of guarantees of the right to energy, the appropriate procedural channels must be devised to promote "jurisdictional interventions aimed at repairing or sanctioning violations of the primary guarantees".[75]

Once the primary guarantees of the right to energy have been violated, effective judicial protection becomes the safeguard and reparation mechanism par excellence.[76] In this sense, the holders of the right to energy must have jurisdictional defence mechanisms at their disposal in the face of violating the primary guarantees of the right to which they are entitled. Such mechanisms for the defence of the right to energy must be based on three basic principles set out by Paredes Paredes: coherence, universality, and participation. The first principle obliges the courts to make decisions deliberately in the cases submitted to them; the second principle aims to

---

[69] Cf. Interreg Europe (2020); ECRB (2020); Jyotsna Melanchthon (2018), pp. 49–66; Kotilainen (2020), pp. 1–14; Palm (2021); Heldeweg and Saintier (2020); Sokołowski (2020), pp. 289–304; Milčiuvienė et al. (2019), p. 5286; Fleming et al. (2021); Council of European Energy Regulators (2019).

[70] This guarantee refers to the constitutional mandate of a prohibitive nature regarding the interruption of access to energy services in case of non-payment by energy right holders. For this reason, preventive measures for the support of low-income households should be promoted. The disconnection ban directly protects the accessibility of energy and, indirectly, protects affordability by obliging those liable for the right to energy to establish energy tariffs that allow for the universal satisfaction of energy needs. See Benito Sanchez (2022), pp. 12–13.

[71] Ferrajoli (2014), p. 56.

[72] Benito Sanchez (2022), pp. 12–13.

[73] Right to Energy Coalition (2021).

[74] Gentile (2022).

[75] Ferrajoli (2016), p. 14.

[76] Carrasco Durán (2020).

reduce the casuist character in the interest of a vocation to produce general effects based on the guarantees of the right to energy; and the third principle is oriented towards guaranteeing citizen participation as a manifestation of democracy.[77] These principles jointly seek to complement, in the case of the right to energy, its content to prevent arbitrariness in the exercise of effective protection as a secondary guarantee.

Like any other right, the right to energy requires guarantees to ensure its enjoyment and protection. For this reason, creating a system of guarantees that integrates constitutional recognition, security of supply, protection from disconnection, and justiciability would provide the basic guarantees for its realisation.

6.6 Conclusions

The doctrinal dispersion of the elements that make up the right to energy at the international level has made its theoretical understanding and even its legal regulation difficult. Based on this research, it is considered that the right to energy has a dual status, as a (new) human right in a formation process and as a fundamental right in some legal systems.

Based on the dual legal nature of the right to energy, this research bases its configurative elements. Firstly, the principles that should underpin the right to energy were identified and substantiated, starting from the principles derived from its status as a human right and those specific principles that should underpin the recognition and configuration of the aforementioned right. The specific principles that should underpin the right to energy are the security of energy supply, energy justice, economic and energy efficiency, and environmental sustainability.

Considering this, the subjective element of the right to energy is composed of the holders of the right to energy as a universal right and the subjects of the obligations. The duty-bearers are the state and the energy service providers. In addition to this, the content of the right to energy comprises the following elements: availability, accessibility, affordability, and reliability of energy.[78] These obligations cannot be contained in mere legal formulas as part of the legal system. For this reason, the basic guarantees that must ensure the full realisation of the right to energy were identified. In that sense, the four basic guarantees with a normative basis are express constitutional recognition, security of energy supply, prohibition of disconnection and justiciability.

[77] Paredes Paredes (2015), pp. 261–263.

[78] Luis Cordova (2025), pp. 2–4.

References[79]

Acedo Penco A (2000) La nocion de consumidor y su tratamiento en el derecho comunitario, estatal y autonómico. Breve referencia al concepto de consumidor en el derecho extremeño. Anuario de la Facultad de Derecho. Universidad de Extremadura 18:297–340. https://dialnet.unirioja.es/descarga/articulo/831211.pdf. Accessed 3 Mar 2025

Acheampong AO, Dzator J, Shahbaz M (2021) Empowering the powerless: does access to energy improve income inequality? Energy Econ 99:105288. https://linkinghub.elsevier.com/retrieve/pii/S0140988321001936. Accessed 3 Mar 2025

Alexy R (1993) Teoría de los Derechos Fundamentales. Centro de Estudios Constitucionales, Madrid. http://arquimedes.adv.br/livros100/TeoriadelosDerechosFundamentales-RobertAlexy.pdf. Accessed 3 Mar 2025

Aparicio Wilhelmi M, Pisarello Prados G (2008) Los derechos humanos y sus garantías: nociones básicas. Catalunya. https://openaccess.uoc.edu/bitstream/10609/139190/2/Concepto%20y%20fundamentos%20de%20los%20derechos%20humanos_M%C3%B3dulo%204_Los%20derechos%20humanos%20y%20sus%20garant%C3%ADas,%20nociones%20b%C3%A1sicas.pdf. Accessed 3 Mar 2025

Bastida FJ, Villaverde I, Requejo P, Aláez B, Sarasola IF (2004) Teoría General de los Derechos Fundamentales en la Constitución Española de 1978. Editorial Tecnos, Madrid. https://digibuo.uniovi.es/dspace/handle/10651/37481. Accessed 3 Mar 2025

Benavides Ordóñez J (2012) Los derechos humanos como norma y decisión: una lectura desde la filosofía política. In: Crítica y Derecho, p 136. Corte Constitucional, Quito. https://repositorio-interculturalidad.ec/xmlui/handle/123456789/36870. Accessed 3 Mar 2025

Benito Sanchez JC (2022) Right to affordable clean energy for all Europeans! https://www.epsu.org/sites/default/files/article/files/Right%20to%20Energy_EPSU%20%20EAPN_EN.pdf. Accessed 3 Mar 2025

Bhatia M, Angelou N (2015) Beyond connections: energy access redefined. Washington DC. https://openknowledge.worldbank.org/bitstream/handle/10986/24368/Beyond0connect0d000technical0report.pdf?sequence=1&isAllowed=y. Accessed 3 Mar 2025

Borowski M (2003) La estructura de los derechos fundamentales. In: Serie, de Teoría Jurídica y Filosofía del Derecho. 25. Universidad Externado de Colombia, Colombia. https://www.marcialpons.es/libros/la-estructura-de-los-derechos-fundamentales/9789586166898/. Accessed 3 Mar 2025

Borowski M (2020) La Drittwirkung ante el trasfondo de la transformación de los derechos morales en derechos fundamentales. Revista Derecho del Estado (45). Universidad Externado de Colombia: 3–27. https://revistas.uexternado.edu.co/index.php/derest/article/view/6327/8881. Accessed 3 Mar 2025

Brewer-Carías AR (2017) Derecho y Garantías Constitucionales y La Acción de Amparo. Editorial Jurídica Venezolana, Caracas. https://allanbrewercarias.com/wp-content/uploads/2021/02/A.R.-BREWER-CARIAS.-DERECHO-Y-ACCION-DE-AMPARO-CONSTITUCIONAL.-con-Portada-2-2021.pdf. Accessed 3 Mar 2025

Brugger EC (2016) Reflections on the moral foundations of a right to energy. In: Guruswamy L, Neville E (eds) International energy and poverty. The emerging contours. Routledge, New York, pp 68–83. https://www.routledge.com/International-Energy-and-Poverty-The-emerging-contours/Guruswamy/p/book/9781138055827. Accessed 3 Mar 2025

Caldeira Brant LN (2016) Desarrollo Sostenible y Matriz Energética en América Latina. La universalización del acceso a la energía limpia. Konrad-Adenauer-Stiftung, Belo Horizonte. https://www.kas.de/c/document_library/get_file?uuid=7953d15d-8f4f-4dea-5ced-6c8e6930eaff&groupId=252038. Accessed 3 Mar 2025

[79] All links to the cited websites were operational as of 3 March 2025.

Carbonell M (2002) Derechos fundamentales, Estado democrático y justicia constitucional, 1ra ed. Instituto de Investigaciones Jurídicas, México, D.F. https://archivos.juridicas.unam.mx/www/bjv/libros/1/209/2.pdf. Accessed 3 Mar 2025

Carchidi VJ (2020) The nature of morals: how universal moral grammar provides the conceptual basis for the universal declaration of human rights. Hum Rights Rev 21(1):65–92. http://link.springer.com/10.1007/s12142-019-00576-8. Accessed 3 Mar 2025

Carpizo J (2011) Los derechos humanos: naturaleza, denominación y características. Revista Mexicana de Derecho Constitucional (25). https://scielo.org.mx/pdf/cconst/n25/n25a1.pdf. Accessed 3 Mar 2025

Carrasco Durán M (2020) La definición constitucional del derecho a la tutela judicial efectiva. Revista de Derecho Político (107):13–40. http://revistas.uned.es/index.php/derechopolitico/article/view/27182. Accessed 3 Mar 2025

Carvajal F, López-Soto D, Sanin ME, Mejdalani A, Ravillard P, Chueca-Montuenga JE, García-Ochoa R, Hallack M (2020) Más allá de la electricidad: Cómo la energía provee servicios en el hogar. Inter-American Development Bank. https://publications.iadb.org/publications/spanish/document/Mas-alla-de-la-electricidad-Como-la-energia-provee-servicios-en-el-hogar.pdf. Accessed 3 Mar 2025

Castañeda JE (2002) Nota breve sobre el concepto de consumidor. Cuadernos de Estudios Empresariales 12:315–321. https://revistas.ucm.es/index.php/CESE/article/viewFile/CESE0202110315A/9898. Accessed 3 Mar 2025

Castillo Córdova L (2010) El contenido constitucional de los derechos fundamentales como objeto de protección del amparo. Anuario Iberoamericano de Justicia Constitucional (14):89–118. https://dialnet.unirioja.es/descarga/articulo/3331524.pdf. Accessed 3 Mar 2025

Castro Soto G (2009) El agua y la luz como derechos humanos. Derecho y Realidad (13):7–22. https://1library.co/document/z3epjeeq-el-agua-y-la-luz-como-derechos-humanos.html. Accessed 3 Mar 2025

Comisión Económica para América Latina y el Caribe (2016) Agenda 2030 y los Objetivos de Desarrollo Sostenible Una oportunidad para América Latina y el Caribe. Organización de Naciones Unidas. https://repositorio.cepal.org/bitstream/handle/11362/40155/24/S1801141_es.pdf. Accessed 3 Mar 2025

Comisión Nacional de los Derechos Humanos (2016) Los principios de Universalidad, interdependencia, indivisibilidad y progresividad de los derechos humanos. Ciudad de México. https://www.cndh.org.mx/sites/all/doc/cartillas/2015-2016/34-Principios-universalidad.pdf. Accessed 3 Mar 2025

Constitución del Ecuador (2008) Ecuador. https://www.cancilleria.gob.ec/wp-content/uploads/downloads/2013/02/constitucion_mreci.pdf. Accessed 3 Mar 2025

Contreras Vásquez P (ed) (2017) Manual sobre derechos fundamentales. Teoría general. LOM ediciones, Santiago de Chile. https://www.pcontreras.net/uploads/9/6/2/1/9621245/contreras___salgado_2017_manual_sobre_derechos_fundamentales_introducci%C3%B3n.pdf. Accessed 3 Mar 2025

Costa MD (2009) O Direito De Acesso À Energia Meio E Pré-Condição Para O Exercício Do Direito Ao Desenvolvimento E Dos Direitos Humanos. Universidade de São Paulo. https://www.teses.usp.br/teses/disponiveis/86/86131/tde-11082011-112846/publico/MariaDAssuncao.pdf. Accessed 3 Mar 2025

Cotino Hueso L (2018) Garantías de los derechos fundamentales. In: Andreu JMC (ed) Derecho Constitucional Básico, 4ta ed. Huygens Editorial, pp 501–526. https://tinyurl.com/43cskz58. Accessed 3 Mar 2025

Council of European Energy Regulators (2019) Regulatory aspects of self-consumption and energy communities. Brussels. https://www.ceer.eu/wp-content/uploads/2024/04/C18-CRM9_DS7-05-03_Report-on-Regulatory-Aspects-of-Self-Consumption-and-Energy-Communities_final.pdf#:~:text=This%20document%20seeks%20to%20analyse%20the%20regulatory%20implications,to%20analyse%20these%20developments%20in%20the%20energy%20market. Accessed 3 Mar 2025

Dávila JA (2022) The problematic of conceiving human rights as legal demand-rights. Age Hum Rights J (18):377–395. https://revistaselectronicas.ujaen.es/index.php/TAHRJ/article/view/6735. Accessed 3 Mar 2025

Decker C (2020) Consumer protection frameworks for new energy products and services and the traditional sale of energy in Australia. https://www.aemc.gov.au/sites/default/files/documents/consultant_final_report_-_consumer_protection_frameworks.pdf. Accessed 3 Mar 2025

Del Guayo Castiella I (2020) Concepto, contenidos y principios del Derecho de la Energía. Revista de Administración Pública (212):309–345. https://dialnet.unirioja.es/servlet/articulo?codigo=7516099. Accessed 3 Mar 2025

Donnelly J (2011) La construcción social de los derechos humanos. Relaciones Internacionales (17):153–184. https://repositorio.uam.es/bitstream/handle/10486/677599/RI_17_7.pdf?sequence=1. Accessed 3 Mar 2025

ECRB (2020) Prosumers in the energy community legal and regulatory framework for support and treatment of small-scale generators Special focus on solar photovoltaic (PV) systems connected to the distribution network. https://energy-community.org/dam/jcr:abacd12d-283c-492a-8aa4-6da5797d044a/ECRB_prosumers_regulatory_framework_032020.pdf. Accessed 3 Mar 2025

Eisman J (2016) Acceso Universal a la Energía y Energías Renovables. Consorcio de Investigación Económica y Social, Lima. https://www.researchgate.net/profile/Julio-Eisman/publication/303947040_Acceso_Universal_a_la_Energia_y_Energias_Renovables/links/575ff04308aec91374b6262f/Acceso-Universal-a-la-Energia-y-Energias-Renovables.pdf. Accessed 3 Mar 2025

Escobar Roca G (2018) Nuevos derechos y garantías de los derechos. Editorial Macial Pons. https://www.marcialpons.es/libros/nuevos-derechos-y-garantias-de-los-derechos/9788491235958/. Accessed 3 Mar 2025

Fellmeth, AX (2016) Paradigms of International Human Rights Law. Oxford University Press. https://doi.org/10.1093/acprof:oso/9780190611279.001.0001

Fernández E (1993) Concepto de derechos humanos y problemas actuales 1(1):45–49. https://dialnet.unirioja.es/servlet/articulo?codigo=174987. Accessed 3 Mar 2025

Fernández García E (1982) El problema del fundamento de los derechos humanos. Anuario de Derechos Humanos, vol 1. Universidad Complutense: Facultad de Derecho. https://e-archivo.uc3m.es/handle/10016/8227. Accessed 3 Mar 2025

Ferrajoli L (2006) Las garantías constitucionales de los derechos fundamentales. Doxa. Cuadernos de Filosofía del Derecho (29):16–31. https://doxa.ua.es/article/view/2006-n29-las-garantias-constitucionales-de-los-derechos-fundamentales. Accessed 3 Mar 2025

Ferrajoli L (2010) In: Carbonell M (ed) Democracia y garantismo. Editorial Trotta, Madrid. https://www.marcialpons.es/libros/democracia-y-garantismo/9788498790054/. Accessed 3 Mar 2025

Ferrajoli L (2014) In: Ibáñez PA (ed) La democracia a través de los derechos. El constitucionalismo garantista como modelo teórico y como proyecto político. Editorial Trotta, Madrid. https://www.trotta.es/libros/la-democracia-a-traves-de-los-derechos/9788498795363/. Accessed 3 Mar 2025

Ferrajoli L (2016) Los derechos y sus garantías. Conversando con Mauro Barberis. Editorial Trotta, Madrid. https://www.casadellibro.com/libro-los-derechos-y-sus-garantias-conversacion-con-mauro-barberis/9788498796209/2913324. Accessed 3 Mar 2025

Finnemore M, Sikkink K (1998) International norm dynamics and political change. Int Organ 52(4):887–917. https://www.jstor.org/stable/pdf/2601361.pdf?refreqid=excelsior%3A0bd696a7c927e42ece50e06010d9c386&ab_segments=&origin=. Accessed 3 Mar 2025

Fleming R, Huhta K, Reins L (2021) Sustainable energy democracy and the law. In: Fleming R, Huhta K, Reins L (eds) Legal aspects of sustainable development, vol 26. Brill | Nijhoff. https://brill.com/view/title/60361. Accessed 3 Mar 2025

Galvis Sánchez C (2007) La construcción histórica de los Derechos Humanos. Revista Latinoamericana de Bioética 8(13) http://www.redalyc.org/articulo.oa?id=127012923005. Accessed 3 Mar 2025

Garrido Gómez MI (2020) El subsistema de los derechos fundamentales. Estudios de Deusto 68(1):307–334. http://revista-estudios.revistas.deusto.es/article/view/1826. Accessed 3 Mar 2025

Gentile G (2022) Effective judicial protection: enforcement, judicial federalism and the politics of EU law. Eur Law Open 12:1–16. https://www.cambridge.org/core/journals/european-law-open/article/effective-judicial-protection-enforcement-judicial-federalism-and-the-politics-of-eu-law/5B5E39FFB0AC3D4D6BC7E293E64CA04C. Accessed 3 Mar 2025

Goodale M (2020) The UN at 75: human rights and global pandemic. Netherlands Q Hum Rights 38(3):163–168. http://journals.sagepub.com/doi/10.1177/0924051920943492. Accessed 3 Mar 2025

Gutiérrez F (2018) Soberanía Energética. Propuestas y debates desde el campo popular. Ediciones Jinete Insomne, Buenos Aires. https://opsur.org.ar/wp-content/uploads/2018/12/Libro-Soberania-energetica-WEB.pdf. Accessed 3 Mar 2025

Heffron RJ, Rønne A, Tomain JP, Bradbrook A, Talus K (2018) A treatise for energy law. J World Energy Law Bus 11(1):34–48. https://academic.oup.com/jwelb/article/11/1/34/4792991. Accessed 3 Mar 2025

Heldeweg MA, Saintier S (2020) Renewable energy communities as 'socio-legal institutions': a normative frame for energy decentralization? Renew Sustain Energy Rev 119. https://linkinghub.elsevier.com/retrieve/pii/S1364032119307269. Accessed 3 Mar 2025

Hesse K (2001) Significado de los derechos fundamentales. In: Benda E et al (eds) Manual de Derecho Constitucional, 2da ed. Editorial Macial Pons, Madrid, pp 83–115. https://www.leo-bw.de/en/detail/-/Detail/details/DOKUMENT/bsz_swb/1330199995/Significado%20de%20los%20derechos%20fundamentales%20Conrado%20Hesse. Accessed 3 Mar 2025

Hesselman M, Varo A, Guyet R, Thomson H (2021) Energy poverty in the COVID-19 era: mapping global responses in light of momentum for the right to energy. Energy Res Soc Sci 81:102246. https://doi.org/10.1016/j.erss.2021.102246. Accessed 3 Mar 2025

Hostettler S, Gadgil A (2015) Sustainable access to energy in the global south. Springer International Publishing, Cham. https://link.springer.com/book/10.1007/978-3-319-20209-9. Accessed 3 Mar 2025

Ibrahim Marei IF (2015) The law and policy for electricity generated by renewable energy: greening the power in three middle eastern jurisdictions. Queensland University of Technology. https://www.researchgate.net/profile/Ibrahim-Marei/publication/314518793_The_Law_and_Policy_for_Electricity_Generated_by_Renewable_Energy_Greening_the_Power_in_Three_Middle_Eastern_Jurisdictions/links/58dddba0aca27206a8a1c3b9/The-Law-and-Policy-for-Electr. Accessed 3 Mar 2025

Instituto Interamericano de Derechos Humanos (1996) Estudios Básicos de Derechos Humanos. In: IIDH Serie Estudios de Derechos Humanos, 1ra ed. San José

Instituto Interamericano de Derechos Humanos (1997) Seminario sobre Derechos Humanos. La Habana, Cuba

International Renewable Energy Agency (2022) Energy transition holds key to tackle global energy and climate crisis. https://www.irena.org/News/pressreleases/2022/Mar/Energy-Transition-Holds-Key-to-Tackle-Global-Energy-and-Climate-Crisis. Accessed 3 Mar 2025

Interreg Europe (2020) Renewable energy self-consumption: a policy brief from the policy learning platform on low-carbon economy. https://www.interregeurope.eu/sites/default/files/2021-12/Policy%20brief%20on%20renewable%20energy%20self-consumption.pdf. Accessed 3 Mar 2025

Jiménez Guanipa H, Tous Chimá J (2017) Cambio climático, energía y derechos humanos. Desafíos y perspectivas. Universidad del Norte & Fundación Heinrich Böll, Oficina Bogotá, Barranquilla. https://uft.cl/images/noticias/2018/abril/publicacion-cambio-climatico/capitulo-interrelacion-comercio-cc-andrea-lucas-garin.pdf. Accessed 3 Mar 2025

Kotilainen K (2020) Energy prosumers' role in the sustainable energy system. In: Filho WL, Azul AM, Brandli L, Özuyar PG, Wall T (eds) Affordable and clean energy. Springer International

Publishing, Cham, pp 1–14. http://link.springer.com/10.1007/978-3-319-71057-0_11-1. Accessed 3 Mar 2025
Langford M (2009) The justiciability of social rights: from practice to theory. In: Social rights jurisprudence, pp 3–45. Cambridge University Press. https://www.cambridge.org/core/books/abs/social-rights-jurisprudence/justiciability-of-social-rights-from-practice-to-theory/923E57BD27B623A5C1FC09F3DE595FE8. Accessed 3 Mar 2025
Luis Cordova JG (2025) The right to energy and the data protection and privacy rights: towards a coherent enforcement under EU law within the energy transition. Eur J Risk Regul: 1–15. https://doi.org/10.1017/err.2025.30. Accessed 3 Mar 2025
Maldonado Muñoz M (2020) Límites y contenido esencial de los derechos (un marco conceptual problemático). Revista Derecho del Estado (47):79–112. https://doi.org/10.18601/01229893.n47.03. Accessed 3 Mar 2025
Melanchthon MJ (2018) Unleashing the power of community renewable energy. In: The future of the biblical past. Society of Biblical Literature, pp 49–66. https://www.jstor.org/stable/10.2307/j.ctt32c046.8. Accessed 3 Mar 2025
Milčiuvienė S, Kiršienė J, Doheijo E, Urbonas R, Milčius D (2019) The role of renewable energy prosumers in implementing energy justice theory. Sustainability 11(19):5286. https://www.mdpi.com/2071-1050/11/19/5286. Accessed 3 Mar 2025
Moncayo Vives GA (2017) Soporte teórico de derechos de las personas usuarias de servicios públicos domiciliarios en Ecuador. Defensoría del Pueblo, Ecuador, Quito. https://www.academia.edu/42974580/SOPORTE_TE%C3%93RICO_DE_DERECHOS_DE_LAS_PERSONAS_USUARIAS_DE_SERVICIOS_P%C3%9ABLICOS_DOMICILIARIOS_EN_ECUADOR. Accessed 3 Mar 2025
Navarro Cuipal MG (2010) Los derechos fundamentales de la persona. Derecho y Cambio Social (21). https://dialnet.unirioja.es/descarga/articulo/5500999.pdf. Accessed 3 Mar 2025
Nickel JW (1987) Making sense of human rights: philosophical reflections on the universal declaration of human rights. University of California Press, Berkeley
Nikken P (1987) In: Editorial Civitas S.A. (ed) La protección internacional de los derechos humanos: su desarrollo progresivo, 1ra ed. Instituto Interamericano de Derechos Humanos, Madrid
Nolan A, Porter B, Langford M (2017) The justiciability of social and economic rights: an updated appraisal. In: Kamminga MT (ed) Challenges in international human rights law, vol 3. Routledge. https://www.taylorfrancis.com/books/9781351572507. Accessed 3 Mar 2025
Office of the United Nations High Commissioner for Human Rights (2007) Human rights: a basic handbook for UN Staff. United Nations, Ginebra. https://www.ohchr.org/sites/default/files/Documents/Publications/HRhandbooken.pdf. Accessed 3 Mar 2025
Olivares Gallardo A (2012) Servicio público y sector eléctrico: Evolución en Europa desde la experiencia española. Revista de Derecho de la Pontificia Universidad Católica de Valparaíso (39). Pontificia Universidad Católica de Valparaíso. Escuela de Derecho: 437–471. http://www.scielo.cl/scielo.php?script=sci_arttext&pid=S0718-68512012000200016&lng=es&nrm=iso&tlng=es. Accessed 3 Mar 2025
Organismo Internacional de Energía Atómica, Departamento de Asuntos Económicos y Sociales de Las Naciones Unidas, and Agencia Internacional de la Energía (2008) Indicadores energéticos del desarrollo sostenible: directrices y metodologías. OIEA, Viena. https://www-pub.iaea.org/MTCD/publications/PDF/Pub1222s_web.pdf. Accessed 3 Mar 2025
Organización de Naciones Unidas (1948) Declaración Universal de los Derechos Humanos. https://www.ohchr.org/sites/default/files/UDHR/Documents/UDHR_Translations/spn.pdf. Accessed 3 Mar 2025
Organización de Naciones Unidas (1962) Resolución 1803 (XVII) de la Asamblea General, 'Soberanía permanente sobre los recursos naturales'. https://www.ohchr.org/es/instruments-mechanisms/instruments/general-assembly-resolution-1803-xvii-14-december-1962-permanent. Accessed 3 Mar 2025
Organización de Naciones Unidas (1987) Report of the World Commission on Environment and Development. New York. http://digitallibrary.un.org/record/139811. Accessed 3 Mar 2025

Ostojic D, Jammi R, Barnes D, Sanghvi A, Mathur S, Zhang Y, Durix L (2011) One goal, two paths. Achieving universal access to modern energy in East Asia and the Pacific. The International Bank for Reconstruction and Development/The World Bank, Washington DC. https://documents.worldbank.org/en/publication/documents-reports/documentdetail/281841468245390286/one-goal-two-paths-achieving-universal-access-to-modern-energy-in-east-asia-and-the-pacific. Accessed 3 Mar 2025

Palm J (2021) Energy communities in different national settings – barriers, enablers and best practices. https://lucris.lub.lu.se/ws/portalfiles/portal/193525419/NEWCOMERS_Deliverable_3.3._version_2.0_final.pdf. Accessed 3 Mar 2025

Paredes Paredes FI (2015) La Tutela Jurisdiccional de los Derechos Fundamentales: Una Propuesta Clave Democrática. Revista Chilena de Derecho 42(1):245–265. http://www.scielo.cl/scielo.php?script=sci_arttext&pid=S0718-34372015000100010&lng=en&nrm=iso&tlng=en. Accessed 3 Mar 2025

Parejo Alfonso LJ (1981) El contenido esencial de los derechos fundamentales en la jurisprudencia constitucional: a propósito de la sentencia del Tribunal Constitucional de 8 de abril de 1981 - Dialnet. Revista española de derecho constitucional 1(3):169–190. https://dialnet.unirioja.es/servlet/articulo?codigo=249648. Accessed 3 Mar 2025

Parra Cortés LV (2018) Exigibilidad política y jurisdiccional de los derechos sociales. Universidad Carlos III de Madrid. https://e-archivo.uc3m.es/handle/10016/27848#preview. Accessed 3 Mar 2025

Peces-Barba G, de Asís Roig R, Llamas Cascón A (1995) Cursos de derechos fundamentales. Teoría general. Editorial Universidad Carlos III, Madrid. https://www.corteidh.or.cr/tablas/17289.pdf. Accessed 3 Mar 2025

Pellicer-sifres V (2017) Reconceptualizando la pobreza energética desde el Desarrollo: hacia una definición más inclusiva y transformadora. Universitat Politècnica de València, Valencia. https://www.researchgate.net/profile/Victoria-Pellicer-Sifres/publication/313846905_Reconceptualizando_la_pobreza_energetica_desde_el_Desarrollo_Humano_hacia_una_definicion_mas_inclusiva_y_transformadora/links/58aad9b492851cf0e3c75cfb/Reconceptualizando-l. Accessed 3 Mar 2025

Peña Luño AE (1993) El concepto de los derechos humanos y su problemática actual. Derechos y libertades: revista del Instituto Bartolomé de las Casas I (1):179–195. https://e-archivo.uc3m.es/handle/10016/1416. Accessed 3 Mar 2025

Pizarro Sotomayor A, Méndez Powell F (2006) Manual de Derecho Internacional de Derechos Humanos. Aspectos Sustantivos, 1ra ed. Universal Books, Panamá

Refaat AA, Ismail IM (2017) Water food and energy sustainability nexus. In: International conference on sustainable futures, Bahrain. https://www.researchgate.net/profile/Ibrahim-Ismail-13/publication/321579870_Water_Food_and_Energy_Sustainability_Nexus/links/5a3a8393458515889d2de6f2/Water-Food-and-Energy-Sustainability-Nexus.pdf. Accessed 3 Mar 2025

Restrepo-pimienta J, Cotrina-gulfo Y (2020) Obligaciones de los Estados en materia de derechos económicos, sociales y culturales en el sistema universal de derechos humanos. Encuentros 18(2):164–173. https://dialnet.unirioja.es/descarga/articulo/7772905.pdf. Accessed 3 Mar 2025

Right to Energy Coalition (2021) Shield energy poor from rising energy bills, say NGOs and trade unions. https://righttoenergy.org/shield-energy-poor-from-rising-energy-bills-say-ngos-and-trade-unions/. Accessed 3 Mar 2025

Right to Energy Coalition | Take Action to End Energy Poverty in Europe (2022). https://righttoenergy.org/. Accessed 3 Mar 2025

Rivera Staff J (2014) Análisis jurídico del sector eléctrico en Panamá para su evolución hacia las energías renovables: una aproximación desde el Derecho español. Universidad Complutense de Madrid. https://eprints.ucm.es/id/eprint/28143/1/T35659.pdf. Accessed 3 Mar 2025

Salter R, Gonzalez CG, Kronk Warne EA (2018) Energy justice: frameworks for energy law and policy. Edward Elgar Publishing, Inc., Massachusetts. https://www.amazon.com/Energy-Justice-International-Perspectives-Environmental/dp/1786431750. Accessed 3 Mar 2025

Schilling T (2020) The recognition of human rights: a threefold myth. Hum Rights Law Rev 20(2):210–235. https://academic.oup.com/hrlr/article/20/2/210/5854039. Accessed 3 Mar 2025
Selayaram R (2009) La construcción de los derechos humanos. Anuario de Derecho Constitucional Latinoamericano. https://biblioteca.corteidh.or.cr/tablas/r23558.pdf. Accessed 3 Mar 2025
Sokołowski MM (2020) Renewable and citizen energy communities in the European Union: how (not) to regulate community energy in national laws and policies. J Energy Nat Resour Law 38(3):289–304. https://www.tandfonline.com/doi/full/10.1080/02646811.2020.1759247. Accessed 3 Mar 2025
Solanes Corella A (2018) The political, legal and moral scope of the universal declaration of human rights: pending issues. Age Hum Rights J (11):1–23. https://revistaselectronicas.ujaen.es/index.php/TAHRJ/article/view/4523. Accessed 3 Mar 2025
Sovacool BK, Dworkin MH (2014) Global energy justice. Problems, principles, and practices. Cambridge University Press, Reino Unido. https://www.cambridge.org/core/books/global-energy-justice/A3607C67A4798DC19AD73A4B11AFC28C. Accessed 3 Mar 2025
Sovacool BK, Sidortsov RV, Jones BR (2014) Energy security, equality, and justice. Routledge, New York. https://www.routledge.com/Energy-Security-Equality-and-Justice/Sovacool-Sidortsov-Jones/p/book/9780415815208. Accessed 3 Mar 2025
Sovacool BK, Heffron RJ, McCauley D, Goldthau A (2016) Energy decisions reframed as justice and ethical concerns. Nat Energy 1(5):16024. https://www.nature.com/articles/nenergy201624. Accessed 3 Mar 2025
Soytas U, Sari R (2019) In: Soytaş U, Sarı R (eds) Routledge handbook of energy economics. Routledge. https://www.taylorfrancis.com/books/9781315459646
Stolerman D, Lagnado D (2020) The moral foundations of human rights attitudes. Polit Psychol 41(3):439–459. https://onlinelibrary.wiley.com/doi/10.1111/pops.12539. Accessed 3 Mar 2025
Szalbierz Z, Ropuszyńska-Surma E (2010) The security of energy supply and regulatory procedures. In Proceedings - international symposium: modern electric power systems, MEPS'10, pp 1–5. Institute of Electrical and Electronic Engineers. https://ieeexplore.ieee.org/stamp/stamp.jsp?tp=&arnumber=6007166. Accessed 3 Mar 2025
Tully SR (2006) The contribution of human rights to universal energy access. Northwest J Int Hum Rights 4(3). http://scholarlycommons.law.northwestern.edu/njihr/vol4/iss3/3. Accessed 3 Mar 2025
UN CEDAW (2016) General recommendation no. 34 on the rights of rural women. https://digitallibrary.un.org/record/835897?ln=en&v=pdf. Accessed 3 Mar 2025
United Nations Population Fund (2005) Human rights principles. https://www.unfpa.org/resources/human-rights-principles#:~:text=Human. Accessed 3 Mar 2025
Valadés D, Gutiérrez Rivas R (2001) Derechos humanos. Instituto de Investigaciones Jurídicas, México, D.F.
Varsi Rospigliosi E (2017) Clasificación del sujeto de Derecho frente al avance de la geoómica y la procreática. Acta Bioethica 23(2):213–225. https://scielo.conicyt.cl/pdf/abioeth/v23n2/1726-569X-abioeth-23-02-00213.pdf. Accessed 3 Mar 2025
Velasco Gutiérrez Y (2013) La dignidad humana como valor, principio y derecho en la jurisprudencia constitucional colombiana. Criterios 6(2):81–130. https://revistas.usb.edu.co/index.php/criterios/article/view/2006. Accessed 3 Mar 2025
Velo García E (2005) Desafíos del sector de la energía como impulsor del desarrollo humano Enrique Velo García cuadernos internacionales de tecnología para el desarrollo humano 01_ Desafíos del sector de la energía como impulsor del desarrollo humano. Cuadernos Internacionales de Tecnología para el Desarrollo Humano. Barcelona. https://core.ac.uk/download/pdf/41777398.pdf. Accessed 3 Mar 2025
Vergara Blanco A (2004) Derecho Eléctrico. Editorial Jurídica de Chile, Santiago de Chile. https://www.academia.edu/5386911/_2004_Derecho_El%C3%A9ctrico_Santiago_2004_. Accessed 3 Mar 2025
von der Decken K, Koch N (2020) Recognition of new human rights. Phases, techniques and the approach of 'differentiated traditionalism'. In: von Arnauld A, von der Decken K, Susi M (eds)

The Cambridge handbook of new human rights. Cambridge University Press, pp 7–15. https://www.cambridge.org/core/product/identifier/9781108676106/type/book. Accessed 3 Mar 2025

Wilson B, Dobreva A (2019) Approvisionnement et sécurité énergétiques. Brusels. https://www.europarl.europa.eu/RegData/etudes/BRIE/2018/630275/EPRS_BRI(2018)630275_FR.pdf. Accessed 3 Mar 2025

Zysset A (2019) Human rights: moral or political? Jurisprudence 10(2):281–288. https://www.tandfonline.com/doi/full/10.1080/20403313.2019.1575617. Accessed 3 Mar 2025

Chapter 7
Historical, Political, and Legal Background to the Construction of the Right to Energy in Cuba

7.1 Cuba Before 1959: Conditioning Premises for a Right to Energy

The evolution of the right to energy and the realisation of its content has been inextricably linked to the history of dependence, progress, and setbacks in the energy sector at national and international levels. The realisation of the right to energy has been, is and will be a determining element of social and economic development, the improvement of living conditions and human dignity.

Undoubtedly, the Cuban context does not escape the situation described above. From the Indigenous communities, the colonial and neo-colonial stages, and the reality since the Triumph of the Cuban Revolution, each stage has faced dissimilar challenges in satisfying the elements that make up the content of the right to energy.

This chapter will analyse the historical, political, and legal background that conditioned the realisation of what, in this research, is defined as the right to energy. In this sense, the availability, accessibility, affordability, and reliability of energy will be crucial in determining the background of the right to energy.

Dependence on available energy sources has marked Cuba's development from the earliest stages. The existence of the first settlers of the Cuban archipelago depended on the use of the surrounding biomass, given that the generation of heat energy at the time depended on the exploitation of the available wood resources. In this way, energy availability was linked to the availability of traditional biomass as an energy resource during this period. In turn, using fire contributed to the survival and expansion of the Indigenous communities settled in the archipelago. In this context, changes were introduced in the cooking of food, and clay tools were created.[1]

[1] Gonzáles Herrera (2015).

J. G. Luis Cordova, *Theoretical and Legal Dimensions of the Right to Energy*, Economic and Financial Law & Policy – Shifting Insights & Values 9,
https://doi.org/10.1007/978-3-032-33252-3_7

However, the processes for the ignition of wood, still rudimentary, transcended into social dynamics through the creation of practices for the maintenance of embers by members of the communities. In this way, the marked importance of the traditional energy generation from biomass influenced the development of social relations in Cuban Indigenous communities, primarily through groupings around the fire.[2]

After the beginning of Spanish colonisation, profound changes were introduced in the sources used to guarantee energy availability. Establishing new productive relations in Cuba's economic structure and population growth affected availability as a part of the right to energy content. All this implied an increase in the demand for energy in all sectors.

With Spanish colonisation, from the end of the eighteenth century onwards, Cuba's economic growth was pursued following the interests of the Havana-based producing oligarchy. For these reasons, the growing demand for sugar and other agricultural products led Cuba to enter the international market. This context subsequently led to a liberalisation of trade on the island. At the same time, however, these expectations also implied an increase in the demand for energy to guarantee the functioning of production processes.[3]

An example was the beginning of sugar production, which imposed an exponentially higher energy demand than the primitive stages. The response to such an increase was not long in coming. Therefore, animal traction[4] and slave labour[5] began to satisfy the energy demand of the main production processes.

The growing development of the sugar industry at the time led to increased consumption of available energy carriers, causing large areas of wood resources to be exploited.[6] In addition, sugar cane bagasse was used as an alternative energy carrier in the sugar mills. However, the overexploitation of forest resources led to a decrease in forest areas and thus affected the availability of timber. This scenario even meant that sugar mills were demolished and relocated to areas with sufficient timber resources.[7]

The profound reduction of the forest population was highlighted by many prominent voices of the time. Among them were the Count of Jaruco and Mompox and José Ricardo O'Farril. From the allegations of these figures, the excessive impact on the availability of timber resources as one of the primary energy sources can be seen. Such a decrease implied a limitation in the satisfaction of energy needs, which depended on wood as an energy carrier.[8]

---

[2] Ríos Hernández (2018).

[3] García (2021), p. 377.

[4] Rubio González (2016); Funes Monzote (2009), p. 38.

[5] Altshuler (1998); García Molina (2005), p. 8.

[6] "In 1670, Governor Francisco Rodríguez Ledesma complained that, because he was misinformed or for other reasons, other Governors had allowed two sugar mills in the area to consume more than 30,000 loads of firewood (…)". (Own translation) Funez Monzote (2002), p. 73.

[7] Funez Monzote (2002), p. 76.

[8] Núñez Jiménez (1998), p. 422.

Because of that reason, José Pizarro spoke out in favour of reforesting forests for energy purposes to replenish the resources affected by extractive practices. Pizarro proposed the cultivation of royal palms because of their energy potential and the number of specimens that can be cultivated without covering large areas of land.[9]

However, energy availability was also affected by another significant factor. The destruction of the primary energy source of the time was dazzled later in history, around 1859, with the felling of Cuban forests to expand the railways. All of the above meant that the protection of the forests became an extremely prominent issue for Ramón de la Sagra, another of the public figures of the time. De la Sagra was responsible for drawing attention to the importance of forests in the life of the Cuban population, and his written works were reproduced in the Diario de la Marina. However, these concerns were not widely supported.[10]

The reduction in the primary energy source at the time not only harmed the sugar sector. The reduced availability of timber led to conflicts with the Spanish Navy, given the versatility of uses of timber, especially for shipbuilding. This situation led to the creation of the Junta de Maderas in 1776, whose function was to manage available timber resources.[11] This deficit of energy resources jointly affected the population, which was affected by energy availability for domestic purposes, such as cooking and lighting, among other needs.

Despite the distribution of lands from the Cáceres Ordinances, the mountains were considered communal property, given the resources they provided, including timber.[12] The attribution of this status is one of the most remote regulatory antecedents in the normative guarantee of energy accessibility by the population to the energy source par excellence of this period. Although there was no right to energy, promoting the fair distribution of natural resources positively impacted energy access.

Another of the measures related to the right to energy was establishing the urban lighting network in 1786 because of the first private decree of the then Captain General of Havana. This measure aimed to improve the quality of habitability of the cities and was conceived as progress, given its positive impact on security and order. To this end, structures were created to guarantee the functioning of public lighting and to place Havana on par with the leading European and American cities.[13]

In the legal-constitutional sphere, with the entry into force of the Cadiz Constitution, despite its focus on civil liberties, Article 13 declared the happiness of the nation as the object of government. Such a declaration is constitutionally based on welfare as the end of all political society.[14] From this point of view, leaving aside the fact that a right to energy was still unthinkable at the time, the satisfaction of the population's energy needs was directly related to welfare.

---

[9] Núñez Jiménez (1998), p. 422.

[10] Núñez Jiménez (1998), p. 422.

[11] Jordan Reyes (2006), p. 86.

[12] Funez Monzote (2002), pp. 69–70.

[13] Cf. Azorín García (2021), pp. 178–185.

[14] Cf. Article 13. Constitución Política de la Monarquía Española (1812).

As Cuba's history progressed in the mid-nineteenth century, the increase in the number of sugar mills brought about another increase in energy demand, especially with the introduction of internal combustion engines in sectors such as rail and maritime transport. Thus, the Cuban economy and society required the exploitation of other energy sources to meet their needs.

As a result, in 1847, the Junta de Fomento was urged to open the free importation of stone coal as it had more significant energy potential than other energy carriers such as charcoal, firewood or bagasse. Stone coal importation was the solution used at the time for the benefit of energy availability to deal with the energy crisis in which the country was immersed.[15]

At the constitutional level, during the nineteenth and early twentieth centuries, there were still no advances in constitutional matters regarding socio-economic rights. This phenomenon resulted from the Constitution of Guáimaro,[16] the Constitution of Baraguá,[17] the Constitution of Jimaguayú,[18] the Constitution of La Yaya,[19] and the 1901 Constitution,[20] which focused on civil liberties and what is now known as civil and political rights and the organic functioning of the government.

Despite the above, an important element to highlight in the Mambí Constitutions is Article 28 of the Guáimaro Constitution. This article focuses on the protection of the freedoms of worship, printing, peaceful assembly, teaching, and petition. However, Article 28 leaves the framework open to protect the so-called "inalienable rights of the people". Although the right to energy has not been recognised, the protection of all inalienable rights of the people offers room for the interpretation and inclusion of all such rights.[21]

Another relevant element for this research, regarding the Mambi Constitutions, is presented in the Constitution of La Yaya. This body of law, focusing on civil and political liberties, in Article 13 allows for assembly and association for lawful purposes. This right could be interpreted in such a way as to allow citizens to act collectively to defend and claim their rights, which could have included some of the artists of the right to energy.[22]

This was retained in Article 28 of the 1901 Constitution, but this body of law added new elements that can be associated with the right to energy. These elements include justice and the general welfare as ends of the state recognised in the preamble, as well as the right to petition in Article 27. This article expressly recognises the catalogue of rights recognised by the 1901 Constitution as non-exclusive. For this reason, the recognition of such rights did not exclude others deriving from the

[15] Funes Monzote (2009), p. 39.

[16] Constitución de Guáimaro (1869).

[17] Constitución de Baraguá (1878).

[18] Constitución de Jimaguayú (1895).

[19] Constitución de La Yaya (1897).

[20] Constitución de 1901 (1901).

[21] Cf. Article 28. Constitución de Guáimaro (1869).

[22] Cf. Article 13. Constitución de La Yaya (1897).

sovereignty of the people and the republican form of government, where the right to energy could have been included.[23]

However, it is vital to highlight one of the measures aimed at promoting the availability and accessibility of energy in the middle of the twentieth century. This measure consisted of granting the Havana City Council a concession on 24 April 1844 to James Robb and Manuel Silva. This concession covered the supply of purified gas to the population and equipment for gas lighting in Havana, Matanzas, and Santiago de Cuba. This concession was ceded on 13 May 1844 to the Compañía Española de Alumbrado de Gas, a limited company based in Havana.[24]

Years later, in 1877, another similar concession was granted to Juan Domingo Stable, who ventured into the distribution and commercialisation of gas.[25] With this step forward, the gas service, one of the energy services par excellence, was introduced in Cuba. Although this service contributed significantly to the realisation of what is defined in this research as the right to energy, the accessibility of gas was one of the elements that did not have a universal character. This restriction was because, ab initio, this service was not made available across the entire national territory.

Years later, another relevant event regarding the right to energy was the session of the rights granted to Domingo Stable in favour of the American company Havana Light Co. In this way, some competition was generated in the Cuban energy market, which was eradicated over the years with foreign capital's domination of this sector. The eradication of competition in the energy market can be seen in the constitution of Spanish American Light and Power as the sole supplier of gas in Havana. In turn, after requesting authorisation to install the electric lighting service, this company received authorisation in November 1888 and began to provide this service in 1889.[26]

Thus, the first public electricity companies were established between 1889 and 1895.[27] A portion of the population witnessed a diversification of the energy services provided in Cuba with the commencement of operations of this particular facility, leading to an enhanced realization of the right to energy. Despite this, it should be noted that Cuban and foreign businesspeople initially owned these electricity supply companies.[28] That situation resulted in a mix of foreign and national control over electricity services.

This reality changed at the beginning of the twentieth century[29] when the Compañía Cubana de Electricidad, a subsidiary of American Foreign Power and

[23] Cf. Articles 27, 28 y 36. Constitución de 1901 (1901).

[24] Reglamento Constitutivo de La Compañía Española del Alumbrado de Gas de Matanzas (1855).

[25] De las Cuevas Toraya and Rey (2015), pp. 119–120.

[26] De las Cuevas Toraya and Rey (2015), pp. 119–120.

[27] Luis Cordova (2024).

[28] Altshuler (1998).

[29] The monopoly control of electricity service by the US capital was strengthened during the government of Gerardo Machado. By 1925, the island's ruler pushed through Congress a law that empowered the US companies that controlled electricity service and transportation to expropriate

Light Inc., monopolised the electricity sector.[30] For this reason, by 1928, this company developed and priced national electricity generation.[31]

The high electricity tariffs brought about a response at the time, with the entry of the Hundred Days Government and the actions of Antonio Guiteras, which promoted measures such as a 45% reduction in electricity tariffs. At the same time, the new government intervened in the Cuban Electricity Company.[32] However, these measures did not have the desired effect because of Fulgencio Batista's coup d'état.

For these reasons, the monopolistic practice of the Cuban Electricity Company was perpetuated over time. Such monopolistic practices were compounded by the lack of "an effective and fair legal regime that, through adequate regulation and control, would prevent abuses or deficiencies and safeguard the nation's legitimate interests".[33] Such were the allegations of Martínez Fraga, senator for Las Villas and leading president of the Democratic Party's Parliamentary Committee in the Senate, in his investigative motion against the electric power and light monopoly at the time.

For these reasons, the nationalisation of public utilities was included in Chapter III of Title IV of the Democratic Party's programme. Given this situation, Martínez Fraga set out in the motion presented, with manifest clarity, the involvement of energy services in the economic life of the country and their essential nature for reasons of national interest.

The Unión de Asociaciones de Consumidores de Electricidad (Union of Electricity Consumers' Associations) joined this initiative. This body constituted one of the most remote institutional antecedents for defending the holders of what this investigation calls the right to energy. Although the motion presented by the Democratic Party to create an investigative commission did not succeed, Carlos Prío Socarrás, the country's president at the time, was able to enact a decree lowering electricity rates as an emergency measure.[34] In this way, the political pressure exerted by the strong support for the motion presented by Martínez Fraga to the Senate forced the government to take measures to improve energy affordability services at the time, which benefited the Cuban population.

In the constitutional sphere, a benchmark that cannot be ignored in this period is the 1940 Constitution. This body of law enacted social justice and welfare as the ends of the State. These ends require the satisfaction of energy needs to be fulfilled. Although this Constitution did not express the right to energy, it left the plexus of fundamental rights open to others of an analogous nature or deriving from the sovereignty of the people.[35]

---

land, property and other rights if they deemed it convenient for the expansion of their services. Aguiar (1933), p. 64.

[30] Dominguez (1978), p. 114.

[31] García Molina (2005), p. 28.

[32] Le Riverend et al. (1978), p. 127.

[33] Martínez Fraga (1949), p. 9.

[34] Martínez Fraga (1949), p. 9.

[35] Cf. Articles 1 and 40. Constitución de 1940 (1940).

However, considering the importance of public energy services for the right to energy, it is vital to highlight the constitutional protection of such services.[36] However, such constitutional pronouncements were not enough to guarantee the universality of energy services, as they remained a dead letter.[37]

Following the elements described in this section, it is essential to highlight that although the diversification of energy services placed Cuba at the forefront globally, unfortunately, these services were not universal. According to official statistics, only 58% of the Cuban population had access to public electricity services.[38]

The other 44% meant that almost three million people were deprived of electricity services, even though this was one of the most widespread energy services at the time.[39] This situation undermined accessibility as an integral element of the content of the right to energy. This result was also related to electricity affordability,[40] so almost half of the Cuban population did not have the necessary income to cover their energy needs.[41] Accessibility and affordability were significantly affected, as they are two elements theoretically defined as components of the content of the right to energy.

7.2 The Impact of the Triumph of the Cuban Revolution on the Realisation of the Right to Energy

7.2.1 The Scenario from January 1959 Onwards

The realisation of the right to energy in Cuba underwent a dramatic turnaround after the Triumph of the Revolution. The satisfaction of energy needs in Cuba underwent a complete turnaround after the triumph of the Revolution. From the

[36] In turn, constitutional article 116 creates the Tribunal de Oficios Públicos as an autonomous body to settle issues related to public services. To this is added the attribution of responsibility to municipal and provincial governments for the provision of public services depending on their scope. To this end, Article 213 empowers municipal governments to purchase, build and operate companies that provide services of this nature, and Article 242 regulates the responsibility of the Provincial Council for public services of this scope. In Article 227, the Constitution of 1940 makes the councillor's remuneration dependent on the proper functioning of public services. Another element denoting the constitutional interest in the protection of public utilities is found in Article 277, where they are declared to be of social interest. Constitución de 1940 (1940).

[37] Miranda Bravo (2000), p. 27.

[38] Oficina Nacional de Estadística e Información de la República de Cuba (2020).

[39] Moregón Ramos (2023), p. 298.

[40] The disproportionate enrichment of electricity service providers drastically affected the affordability of this service. This was related to the wide commercial margins applied at the time. Although the cost of generating 1 kW around 1925 was 1.5 cents, the tariffs imposed amounted to 7 cents per kW. Subsequently, with the coming to power of Ramón Grau, the affordability of electricity service benefited with the reduction of electricity tariffs by 40%. Aguiar (1933), pp. 65 and 174.

[41] IAEA (2008).

beginning, one of the first steps of the new government was to re-establish constitutional order, starting with the Fundamental Law of 1959, which was one of the most advanced constitutions in Cuban constitutional history. In this way, the revolutionary government restored the constitutional order violated by the dictator Fulgencio Batista, adopting the Fundamental Law of 1959 on February 7, 1959.[42] This Constitution took up the central elements of the 1940 Constitution.[43] As a consequence, the postulates of the 1940 Constitution legally reinforced the right to energy.

In this context, it is worth noting that the Fundamental Law of 1959 reinstated social justice and welfare as ends of the State in its Article 1. Furthermore, like the 1940 Constitution, the 1959 Fundamental Law left the plexus of fundamental rights open to others of an analogous nature or derived from the sovereignty of the people.[44]

In line with the above, through Article 88, social welfare became the purpose of any public utility. This includes energy service providers. At the same time, Article 116 takes up the postulates of the 1940 Constitution by creating the Tribunal de Oficios Públicos as the body in charge of resolving issues related to public utilities.[45]

At the same time, Article 191 a) gives municipal governments the obligation to provide all local public services. This responsibility is reinforced by the following powers: "to purchase, construct and operate public utility companies, or to provide such services by concession or contract with all the guarantees established by law; and to acquire, by expropriation or by purchase, for the purposes indicated, the necessary properties. They may also operate companies of an economic nature." (Own translation) Undoubtedly, the fulfilment of this responsibility results in the availability and accessibility of energy.[46]

Another element linked to the right to energy emerges from Article 228. This article considers public utilities as a matter of social interest and empowers the State and governmental bodies at the provincial and municipal levels to supervise these utilities.[47]

The Triumph of the Revolution implied multiple benefits for the realisation of the right to energy in Cuba. An example of this was the reduction, by the revolutionary government, of the prices of electricity services to guarantee the satisfaction of energy needs.[48] In turn, to a large extent, the profound changes in the national energy sector determined the material guarantees that underpinned the elements that make up the content of the right under study. However, the imposition of measures by the US government against Cuba drastically attacked the energy sector.

---

42 Bell et al. (2006), pp. 39–40.

43 Miranda Bravo (2000), p. 27.

44 Cf. Articles 1 and 40 de la Ley Fundamental de 1959 in Bell et al. (2006).

45 Cf. Articles 88 and 116, Ley Fundamental de 1959 in Bell et al. (2006).

46 Cf. Article 191, Ley Fundamental de 1959 in Bell et al. (2006).

47 Cf. Article 228, Ley Fundamental de 1959 in Bell et al. (2006).

48 Le Riverend et al. (1978), p. 148; Dominguez (1978), p. 184.

An example of this was the elimination of all oil imports from the United States in 1960.[49] In this context, the Cuban government took action to guarantee stability in energy generation. For this reason, it began importing oil from the Union of Soviet Socialist Republics (USSR). Faced with this scenario, and in retaliation, US companies based in Cuba refused to refine Soviet oil.[50]

The situation described above, therefore, forced the Cuban government to adopt contingency measures to guarantee the availability of the energy necessary for the economy's functioning and the Cuban population's subsistence. Thus, the intervention and nationalisation process of the US refineries established in Cuba began.[51]

In the mentioned process of forced expropriation, energy availability, a vital necessity for the Cuban nation, was imposed as a reason for public utility. This process is a political and legal measure supporting access to energy in Cuba, converting these foreign capital companies into the socialist property of all the people[52] as a safeguard of the content of the right to energy.

The legal basis for the process of forced expropriation was contained in laws 851,[53] 890 and 891.[54] With this normative backing, the Hernández y Hno. Electricity Company and oil refineries were nationalised to transform the national economy, as declared in these laws.[55]

This nationalisation process resulted in safeguarding the content of the right to energy. It allowed, together with the support of the USSR, the level of energy accessibility in Cuba to increase dramatically until the 1990s. This increase can be seen in the fact that the 58% electrification rate reached up to 1959 was transformed into 94.2% by 1990, according to official statistics shown in Fig. 7.1.[56]

Within the context experienced in its first years, the new Cuban government focused on guaranteeing energy availability. Therefore, even though oil activity in Cuba dates back to 1881, it was not until 1960 that a systematic and detailed programme of exploration began in the nation through geological and geophysical studies for the future of oil drilling.[57] According to Mateo Rodríguez in 2018, following studies of oil availability in Cuba, the reserves of this fossil energy resource are only sufficient to satisfy 30% of the national energy demand.[58]

Another of the energy carriers on which the government emphasized to guarantee energy availability in the country was sugarcane bagasse. This waste from the

---

[49] Luis Cordova (2024).

[50] Cf. Miranda Bravo (2007).

[51] Carriazo Moreno (2011), p. 484.

[52] Constitución de la República de Cuba (2019).

[53] Poder Ejecutivo del Consejo de Ministros (1960a).

[54] Poder Ejecutivo del Consejo de Ministros (1960b).

[55] Prieto Valdés and Pérez Hernández (2000), p. 32.

[56] Oficina Nacional de Estadística e Información de la República de Cuba (2020).

[57] Fernández Márquez and Pérez de los Reyes (2009), p. 24.

[58] Mateo Rodríguez (2018), p. 22.

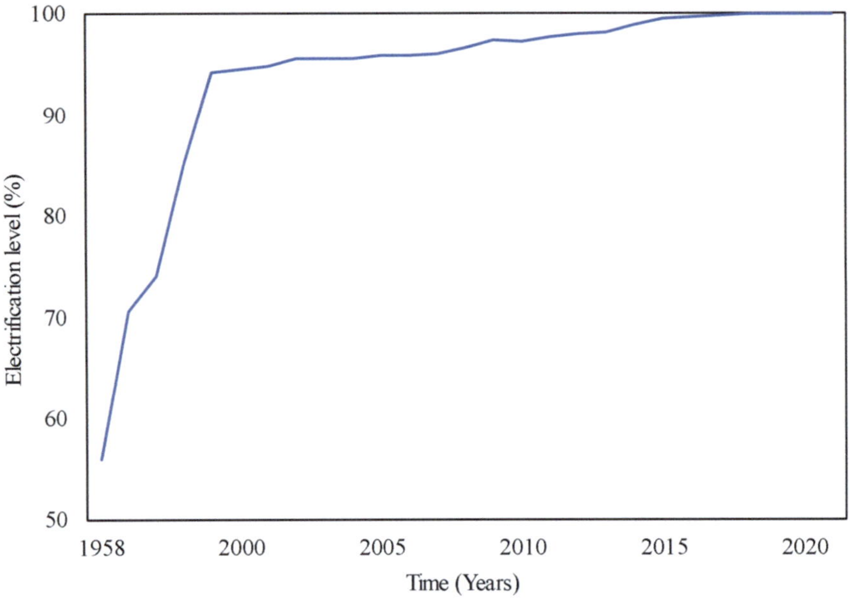

Fig. 7.1 Evolution of electrification level in Cuba. Own elaboration

sugar refining process is not new in the country's history, but it continued to be exploited for energy purposes.[59] In addition, other energy carriers, such as peat, were also exploited. Although peat does not have a high energy potential, this was another of the alternatives implemented by the government to satisfy Cuba's energy needs. To this end, the Ensenada de la Broa Cove was closed for subsequent dewatering.[60]

However, at the normative level, there was still no express recognition of the right to energy with the entry into force of the 1976 Constitution.[61] It only recognised fundamental rights, the realisation of which depends on the right in question. Nevertheless, the right to energy has been legally linked to Article 27 on the environment and natural resources.[62]

In the same year, Cuba implemented the Research Programme on the use of solar energy. This program originated with the establishment of the Energy Group, which had been actively engaged in research and development related to energy efficiency and renewable energies since 1968.[63]

On the factual level, other advances related to the right to energy existed. Among them, it is worth highlighting those related to availability, the first premise

---

[59] Urkidi et al. (2015), p. 43.

[60] Mateo Rodríguez (2018), p. 11.

[61] Constitución de la República de Cuba (1976).

[62] Cf. Delgado Triana and Fariñas Wong (2016), p. 7.

[63] Moregón Ramos (2023), p. 300.

for the realisation of the right to energy, which was palpably increasing during this stage.

In this context, it is crucial to recognise Cuba's progress in diversifying energy sources to meet energy needs. An example of this is the use of biogas as an energy carrier. Although the use of anaerobic digestion technology in sewage treatment plants dates back to 1920 and the use of biodigesters for biogas collection to 1940, it was only around 1970 that its use for energy purposes began. As an alternative to fuel shortages, this energy source represented a step forward, especially in empowering people to meet their energy needs. In the 1980s, energy prosumerism practices began to be identified in Cuba by exploiting biogas. This practice was accompanied by the subsequent creation of the Biogas Users' Movement in 1983, which promoted capacity building for exercising energy prosumerism by combining scientific-technical knowledge and popular wisdom.[64]

At the same time, Cuba's energy development continued to increase. This increase can be seen in Fig. 7.2,[65] which reflects the growth of the national energy sector's gross energy generation capacity per capita until the subsequent collapse of the USSR.

Moreover, to guarantee energy availability, around 1980, with the support of the USSR, Cuba began developing the nuclear sector by constructing the first-generation plant in the national territory.[66] With the start of the nuclear programme in Cuba, the first nuclear reactor designed in the USSR with automatic control systems from the Siemens company was imported into the country.

The start of the nuclear energy industry in Cuba was motivated by several elements. Among them was the fact that nuclear generation was a clean method of generating electricity. In experts' opinion, this represented an energy source to boost the nation's economic development without atmospheric pollution. Although this argument is highly questionable, and history has shown the danger that nuclear generation poses to humanity and nature, the acceptance of this type of energy source at the global level markedly influenced the Caribbean nation.[67]

Despite the actions taken by the Cuban government to strengthen the national energy matrix at the time, the construction of the nuclear plant was halted in 1992 when it had reached 70%. This stoppage was the result of the collapse of the USSR and, consequently, of the Cuban state's financial limitations for this purpose.[68]

Undoubtedly, the USSR played a significant role in the development of the energy sector in Cuba. Considering that the functioning of the energy sector determines the availability, accessibility, affordability and reliability of energy services, the realisation of the right to energy fundamentally depends on this economic

[64] Guardado-Chacón and Arencibia (2021), p. 242.

[65] Oficina Nacional de Estadística e Información de la República de Cuba (2020).

[66] Castro Diaz-Balart (1991).

[67] Castro Díaz-Balart (1999), p. 16.

[68] IAEA (2008), pp. 100–101.

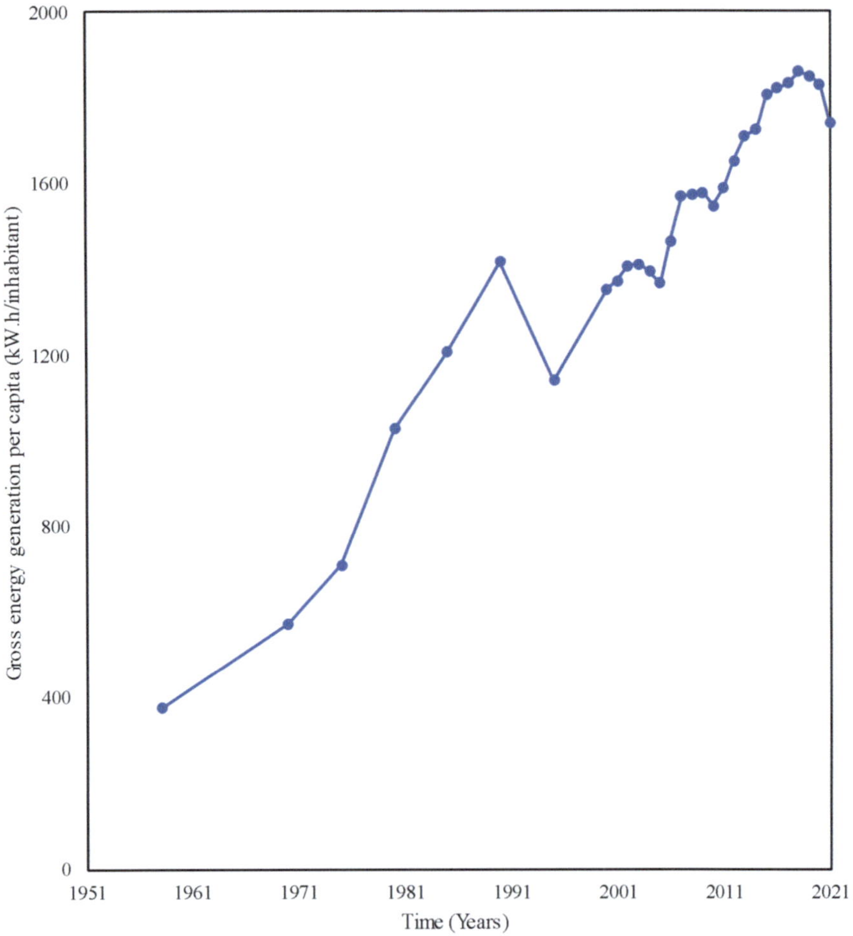

Fig. 7.2 Gross energy generation per capita (kWh/inhabitant). Own elaboration

sector. In this sense, it is essential to highlight that the support of the USSR for Cuba's energy development allowed a notable increase in energy availability, from 377.7 kWh to 1476.7 kWh from 1959 to 1990.[69]

Despite this, the central national energy development was focused on fossil fuel technologies, which is why, in the 1990s, the collapse of the USSR drastically affected the energy sector. Such an effect can be perfectly contrasted with the fact that between 1967 and 1976, Cuba was 98% dependent on oil imported from the USSR.[70]

[69] Cf. Fig. 7.2.

[70] Mesa-Lago (1982), p. 68.

The USSR's collapse profoundly affected the agricultural sector. This essential sector for food production, given the Soviet influence, was based on an extensive system with prominent levels of mechanisation. This situation meant that it was an energy-intensive sector. As a result, the functioning of the processes from production to commercialisation of agricultural products was deeply affected by the energy crisis due to the USSR's collapse.[71]

Among the effects of the above was the accelerated agricultural transition to a more sustainable model. In this way, the satisfaction of the energy demand imposed by the agricultural sector was built on agroecological bases such as animal traction due to the sudden halt of energy imports in Cuba.[72]

Despite the stance taken by the Cuban government to deal with the energy availability deficit in this period, only some of the effects were minimised. However, the energy crisis caused 50% of the land to cease to be exploited. The impact on access to energy for productive purposes in the agricultural sector led to a profound decrease in yields due to the reduction of more than 70% of the fuel arriving in the country.[73]

Extreme energy dependence on the USSR brought with it a contraction that affected every aspect of Cuban reality, especially the realisation of the right to energy. Cuba's extreme energy dependence on the USSR grew stronger over the years. The advantages of the Council for Mutual Economic Assistance steadily boosted the Cuban economy. Fuel imports from the Soviet Bloc amounted to 12 million tons in 1989. As a result, there was no urgent incentive to develop domestic energy sources. The non-development of national energy sources meant that the Fall of the Berlin Wall brought an immediate energy crisis in Cuba that affected the satisfaction of energy availability.[74]

Cuba's energy dependence after the collapse of the USSR posed a severe threat to energy accessibility. Examples include access to energy to satisfy basic needs such as cooking and lighting, among many others. To provide a more straightforward illustration of the previous points, the usage of kerosene as the primary energy carrier for cooking food in Cuban households during that period was analysed. The average kerosene consumption in 1989 was 60 kgep/inhabitant,[75] and after the fall of the USSR in 1993, this consumption decreased drastically to 20 kgep/inhabitant. The consumption of this energy carrier continued to decrease to 19 kgep/inhabitant in 1998.[76]

Such a decline in access to energy meant a forced decline of the Cuban population towards other traditional energy carriers, which involved a detriment of life in dignity. Such detriment of life in dignity is expressed in the fact that traditionally

[71] Fernández Márquez and Pérez de los Reyes (2009), p. 33.

[72] Vázquez et al. (2017), p. 108.

[73] Mateo Rodríguez (2018), p. 13.

[74] Moreno Figueredo and Montesinos Larrosa (2010), p. 266.

[75] Kilogram oil equivalent.

[76] Urkidi et al. (2015), pp. 41–42.

responsible for cooking food, women were forced to spend more hours in this process. This situation was associated with using firewood, charcoal, and diesel to meet household energy needs. Although gas and electricity were still used, both were extremely limited.[77]

Especially the public electricity service was interrupted for 8–10 h a day. The transport sector compounded this situation. As energy availability was affected by the sharp reduction in oil imports, the transport sector suffered a marked detriment. Comparing figures between 1989 and 2000, the number of passengers in public bus transport fell from 2,693 thousand to 461.2 thousand. All of the above meant that the satisfaction of two elements (energy availability and energy accessibility) that this research defines as part of the content of the right to energy was reduced.[78]

As a consequence of Cuban energy dependence, the government's concern to guarantee the proper functioning of the Cuban energy sector to satisfy the national energy demand became evident again in 1993. This year, the National Environment and Development Programme was approved. In this national programme, the energy issue was closely related to sustainable social, environmental, and economic development. In this way, sustainability was integrated into the national energy programme.[79]

This perspective assumed by the Cuban Energy Policy was shaped in a complex context where concerns about the looming energy crisis and climate change were latent. For this reason, the State directed its efforts towards increasing energy efficiency in producing and using national energy sources. To this end, emphasis was placed on renewable sources based on the recognition of the need for technological reconversion on a national scale and the financial requirements involved.[80]

In turn, the National Environment and Development Programme reflected the government's interest in guaranteeing energy accessibility in Cuba. This interest can be seen in the fact that this instrument emphasises using renewable energy sources in rural communities to guarantee the basic needs of the rural population and improve productivity. As a result, wind energy, hydropower, and biogas were promoted for domestic and agricultural use.[81]

The exploitation of those renewable energy sources was complemented by implementing solar photovoltaic systems for electricity generation and solar dryers. Another of the national programme lines related to meeting energy needs was associated with the transport sector. This line of action led to the formulation of proposals for a more sustainable and less polluting transport system, including the massive use of bicycles and animal traction in rural and suburban areas.[82]

---

[77] Urkidi et al. (2015), pp. 41–42.

[78] Urkidi et al. (2015), pp. 41–42.

[79] Morejón Ramos et al. (2019), pp. 110–111.

[80] Morejón Ramos et al. (2019), pp. 110–111.

[81] Morejón Ramos et al. (2019), p. 111.

[82] Morejón Ramos et al. (2019), p. 111.

Accordingly, the National Programme for the Development of National Energy Sources was established in 1993. It included among its measures the substitution of imported oil, the increased exploitation of national oil resources, and accompanying gas with sources for electricity generation. Other measures in the national programme included improving energy efficiency in using bagasse and other waste from the sugar industry. Those measures aimed to provide the sugar industry with energy self-sufficiency, significantly reducing the energy demand the national energy system had to meet.[83]

That reduction in energy demand would lead to an increase in energy availability at the national level. This availability would also benefit from the third measure to be implemented, which involved the expansion of renewable sources such as solar-thermal, solar-photovoltaic, hydropower, wind energy and biogas. However, the implementation of the national plan was severely threatened by the country's complex economic situation at the time. For this reason, there was no exact planning for its implementation.[84]

It was not until 1995 that the first impacts of the emerging measures implemented by the Cuban government were seen. Among them was the promotion of foreign investment, especially in the exploitation of non-renewable energy resources. This measure was a consequence of the structure of the energy matrix at the time, where most energy generation depended on the availability of fossil fuels. To this were added new agreements with the new Russian government for the purchase of fuels as well as the granting of loans amounting to 350 million dollars to finance energy projects that the now-extinct USSR had sponsored.[85]

The Cuban government's heightened concern about the country's energy crisis at the time resulted in changes in national energy policy. These changes were aimed at promoting energy savings and efficiency and exploiting national energy resources.[86] For this reason, between 1990 and 1998, there was an 80% increase in the exploitation of national crude oil, which can be seen in the variation in energy dependence between 1989 and 1998, according to Fig. 7.3.[87]

Moreover, financial resources were mobilised to guarantee energy accessibility and reduce energy losses. To this end, part of the Cuban state budget was addressed towards rehabilitating transmission and distribution grids. This investment process included rehabilitating electricity generation units throughout the national territory.

Another of the contingency measures aimed at guaranteeing energy availability in Cuba was the oil industry's expansion. With an energy matrix dependent on fossil fuels and scarce financial resources, the Cuban state relied on foreign investment for oil exploration. As a result, from 1991 onwards, exploration activities developed by

[83] Moreno Figueredo and Montesinos Larrosa (2010), p. 268.

[84] Moreno Figueredo and Montesinos Larrosa (2010), p. 268.

[85] Suárez et al. (2012), p. 2727.

[86] Suárez et al. (2012), p. 2730.

[87] Rodríguez Castellón (2002), p. 94.

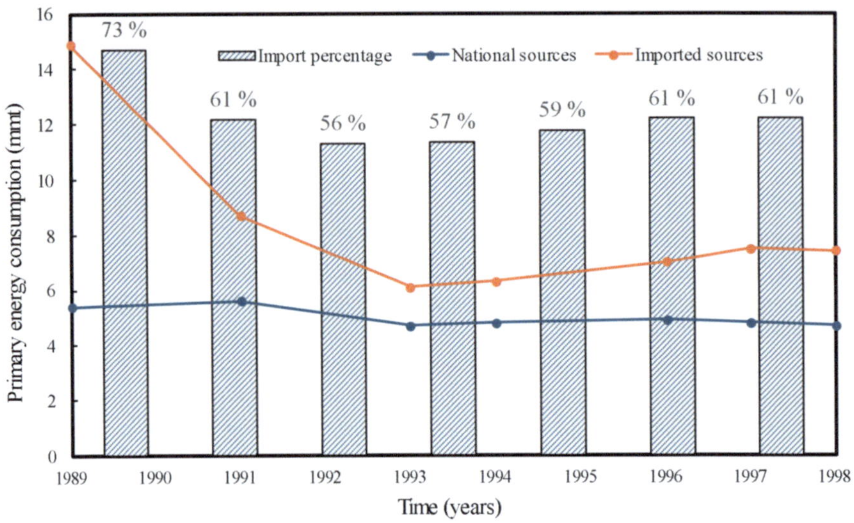

Fig. 7.3 Energy dependence in Cuba [million tonnes (mmt) of oil equivalent] (Rodríguez Castellón 2002, p. 94). Own elaboration

foreign companies began, which led to the delineation of 45 exploration blocks for interested foreign companies.[88]

The increase in oil and natural gas extraction was remarkable from this moment on. This increase is illustrated by comparing national oil extraction between 1991 and 2004, where 526.8 Mt and 3253.0 Mt, respectively, were extracted, an increase of 2726.2 Mt. Meanwhile, natural gas extraction in the same period comprised 29.6 MMm^3 and 704.2 MMm^3 for an increase of 674 MMm^3. This context is shown in Fig. 7.4.[89]

At the same time, natural gas, which had hitherto been flared unproductively, was used to generate electricity[90] in combined cycle gas turbine plants. This practice led to re-evaluating this product towards its use to ensure energy availability. This re-evaluation led to the founding of ENERGAS in 1998 as a joint venture, the

[88] Fernández Márquez and Pérez de los Reyes (2009), p. 24.

[89] Oficina Nacional de Estadística e Información de la República de Cuba (2020).

[90] In this sense, according to the speech of Commander-in-Chief Fidel Castro in 1997: "There are productions that have risen. In oil, from around half a million in recent times, this year we will produce around one and a half million. It is a heavy oil, one heavier than the other, but it is used in the production of cement, for example, mixed in some thermoelectric plants; certain productions of oil derivatives that solve problems. It has gas, and we are going to use the gas to generate electricity, also for domestic use; but with the gas from the oil produced in the central zone we can sustain a 100,000 kilowatt thermoelectric plant, and the gas that comes out of the deposits does not go into the atmosphere". Castro Ruz (1997).

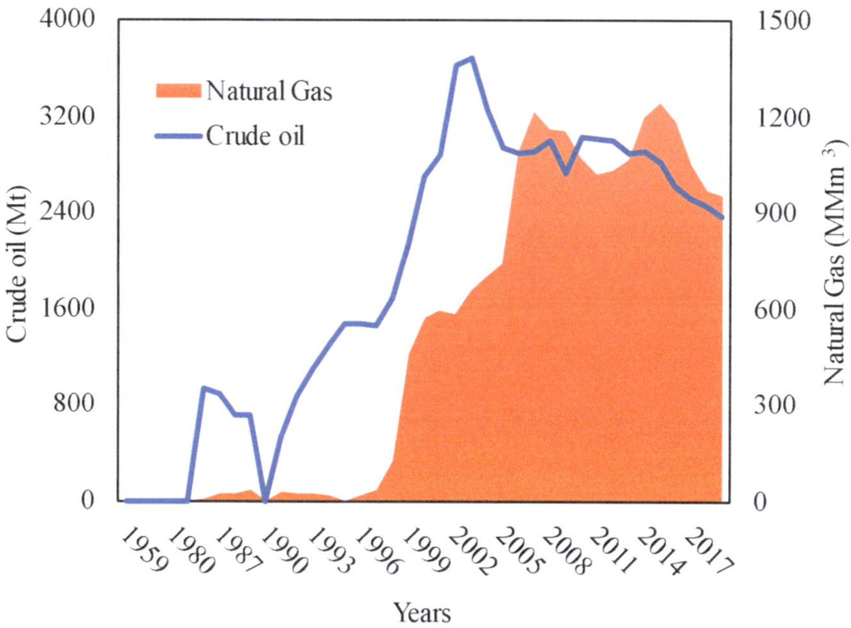

Fig. 7.4 Fossil primary energy production. Own elaboration

purpose of which includes the productive use of natural gas, especially in fields where this valuable energy carrier was used only occasionally.[91]

In addition, after Hugo Chávez became president, Venezuela became one of Cuba's main trading partners, especially in the energy sector, in 1998. Although Cuba had opted to exploit national energy sources, most of the oil used for energy generation was of Venezuelan origin.[92] Thus, Venezuela became one of the leading exporters of oil to Cuba, which undoubtedly had a positive impact on the Cuban energy sector and the realisation of the right to energy, but at the same time, reaffirmed the country's energy dependence on imports.[93]

Among the measures that emerged at this time was the implementation of the National Electricity Saving Programme in 1997. Through this energy policy instrument at that time, the aim was to control demand to benefit energy availability. Among the measures included in the national programme were the following:

- Install refrigerators in a cool place away from the wall, with good sealing and tightness of doors.
- To turn off unused lights.
- Use fluorescent lamps and reduce incandescent bulbs as much as possible.

[91] Fernández Márquez and Pérez de los Reyes (2009), p. 24.

[92] Urkidi et al. (2015), pp. 40–41 and 44–45.

[93] Saunders Vázquez et al. (2022a), p. 43.

- To paint walls in light colours, thus requiring less artificial lighting.
- To use translucent tiles in storerooms, corridors, and stairwells.
- Systematically clean dust from fan blades to adjust fan speed according to ambient temperature.
- Gather as much laundry as possible to iron once a week.
- Place the TV set in a cool place out of direct sunlight; unplug it when unused.
- To use the washing machine once a week during off-peak hours.
- To avoid pumping water in social buildings during peak hours.[94] (Own translation)

The energy policy of this period relied on every possible measure to counteract a context of extreme scarcity, including energy. However, the promotion of energy savings contributed to opting for an energy solidarity model that guaranteed equitable access to energy, regardless of its type. Nevertheless, without a doubt, the profound energy crisis that hit Cuba at the time severely restricted the satisfaction of the Cuban population's energy needs.

The measures described above boosted the energy sector until 2004, when a new national energy crisis again affected the satisfaction of the population's energy needs.[95] The origins of this crisis can be traced back to several factors. Despite the reduction of national energy consumption due to the implemented energy-saving measures, this new energy crisis was aggravated by the increasing electrification of the population, which put the national energy system to the test.

While increased electrification was a decisive process in guaranteeing access to energy, it was also a challenge for the energy sector. The consequences of the use of domestic oil with high density and high sulphur content in Cuban thermoelectric plants compounded this.[96] Using domestic oil led to a reduction in the maintenance periods of generation plants and, consequently, to an increase in the number of power outages, which affected the satisfaction of energy needs in Cuba.

In addition, energy availability was also affected by the reduction of power generation in the sugar mills due to the decline of the sugar sector.[97] This reduction can be contrasted with the 50% reduction in bagasse production around 2002 compared to the pre-1990 period, which led to the lower availability of this type of energy carrier.[98]

This energy crisis was, in turn, aggravated by the low resilience of the national energy system in the face of climatic phenomena, which, at this time, caused significant damage to the transmission and distribution networks in Cuba.[99] This whole context affected the availability, accessibility and reliability as integral elements of the content of the right to energy, the realisation of which was marked by long-term

[94] Urkidi et al. (2015), pp. 44–45.

[95] Luis Cordova (2024), p. 145.

[96] Evenson (1998), p. 493.

[97] Comisión Económica para América Latina y el Caribe (2005), pp. 9–10.

[98] Rodríguez Castellón (2002), p. 93.

[99] Comisión Económica para América Latina y el Caribe (2005), pp. 9–10.

power outages.[100] To alleviate this situation and reduce its effects, the Cuban government took measures to reorganise productive economic activities at peak demand. These actions were aimed at reducing energy demand, which benefited energy availability.[101]

In this context, the so-called Energy Revolution was launched at the energy policy level, which included aspects such as the rational use of energy, energy efficiency and distributed generation systems as an energy reserve.[102] At the same time, through what is known today as energy diplomacy,[103] Cuba managed to reaffirm and strengthen ties with Venezuela, to guarantee a supplier for oil imports, and with Russia for acquiring credits, part of which were oriented towards developing the national energy sector.[104]

With the arrival of 2005 and the implementation of the Energy Revolution, Cuba assumed a very advanced position by placing energy efficiency and clean cooking[105] at the core of the national programme.

The implementation of the Energy Revolution consisted of five programmes. The first of these was addressed energy saving and efficient use of energy. The second aimed to increase the availability of electricity by developing a distributed generation system based on small-scale power plants and rehabilitating electricity grids. Moreover, the third programme was addressed to promote the participation of renewable sources (wind, hydro, biomass, and solar energy) in the Cuban energy matrix. The fourth programme targeted oil and gas exploration and production. Finally, the fifth programme aimed to promote international collaboration in the energy field. By 2007, investments in the Energy Revolution amounted to $2 billion.[106]

The impacts pursued with the implementation of the energy revolution cover three main areas: economic, social, and environmental:

- In the economic sphere, the aim was to reduce the impact of the high imported energy prices on the national economy. This goal was pursued through energy savings and the efficient use of energy carriers.
- In the social sphere, the Energy Revolution sought to improve the quality of life through:
  - Reduction of power outages

[100] Benjamin-Alvarado (2010), p. 51.

[101] Comisión Económica para América Latina y el Caribe (2005), pp. 9–10.

[102] Saunders Vázquez et al. (2022b).

[103] Energy diplomacy is a growing diplomatic field in international relations that aims to provide energy security. Energy issues have therefore been included in foreign policy through national security and/or the economy of states as the main channels. Bovan et al. (2020), p. 5.

[104] Suárez et al. (2012), p. 2727.

[105] Access to clean cooking methods is included in SDG#7 of the 2030 Agenda adopted just over 10 years after the implementation of the Energy Revolution in Cuba. United Nations Development Programme (2023).

[106] Pichs Madruga (2008), p. 107.

  - Distribution of modern, energy-efficient household appliances under flexible payment systems.
  - Electrification of food cooking as a substitute for traditional energy carriers.
- In the environmental sphere, the Energy Revolution aimed to reduce greenhouse gas emissions into the atmosphere.[107]

The Energy Revolution initiated a process of replacing household equipment with more modern and energy-efficient ones. This process involved implementing a system of bank credits with flexible payment systems and, in some cases, the distribution of the mentioned equipment free of charge.[108]

In this way, incandescent light bulbs, fans, cooking equipment and, among others, refrigeration equipment were replaced free of charge. In the latter case, 50% of the value of this equipment was covered by the state budget. Such actions covered the entire national territory, reforming life in Cuban homes regarding efficient energy use and modern technologies. In this sense, it is essential to highlight that these changes towards modern cooking methods led to a reduction in the consumption of kerosene in Cuban households, the use of which was increased in the country due to the financial benefits of its importation during the support of the USSR.[109]

The electrification of Cuban homes was a significant step forward in terms of the right to energy, guaranteed by modern technologies that replaced others with a high negative impact on people's health.

The use of kerosene as a domestic fuel has been identified by the World Health Organisation as a source of indoor air pollution with several adverse effects. The combustion of this energy carrier generates multiple carcinogenic compounds that are easily absorbed through the digestive and respiratory tract. This leads to an increased risk of oesophageal cancer. In this respect, Maiyoh et al. point to kerosene as a generator of toxicity with harmful effects on the pulmonary, neuro-endocrine, cardiovascular, dermal, auditory, ocular, hepatic, renal, immunological, haematological, gastrointestinal, reproductive, and other systems. Similarly, these negative effects are recognised by Arku et al. and Qazi.[110]

In this way, electricity became the primary energy used in the residential sector while other traditional energy carriers like firewood, kerosene and charcoal were reduced.

Figure 7.5 shows the energy consumption mix in Cuban households in 2020.[111]

This process brought with it the implementation of a new system of energy-saving tariffs and a process of energy literacy[112] from the early stages of

---

[107] Pichs Madruga (2008), pp. 173–174.

[108] Saunders Vázquez et al. (2022a), p. 46.

[109] Saunders Vázquez et al. (2022a), p. 46.

[110] International Agency for Research on Cancer (2020), Maiyoh et al. (2015), Arku et al. (2020) and Qazi (2017).

[111] Oficina Nacional de Estadística e Información de la República de Cuba (2020).

[112] Energy literacy has been situated in academia as a category with a multiplicity of interpretations according to different approaches. However, in this research, energy literacy is understood as the

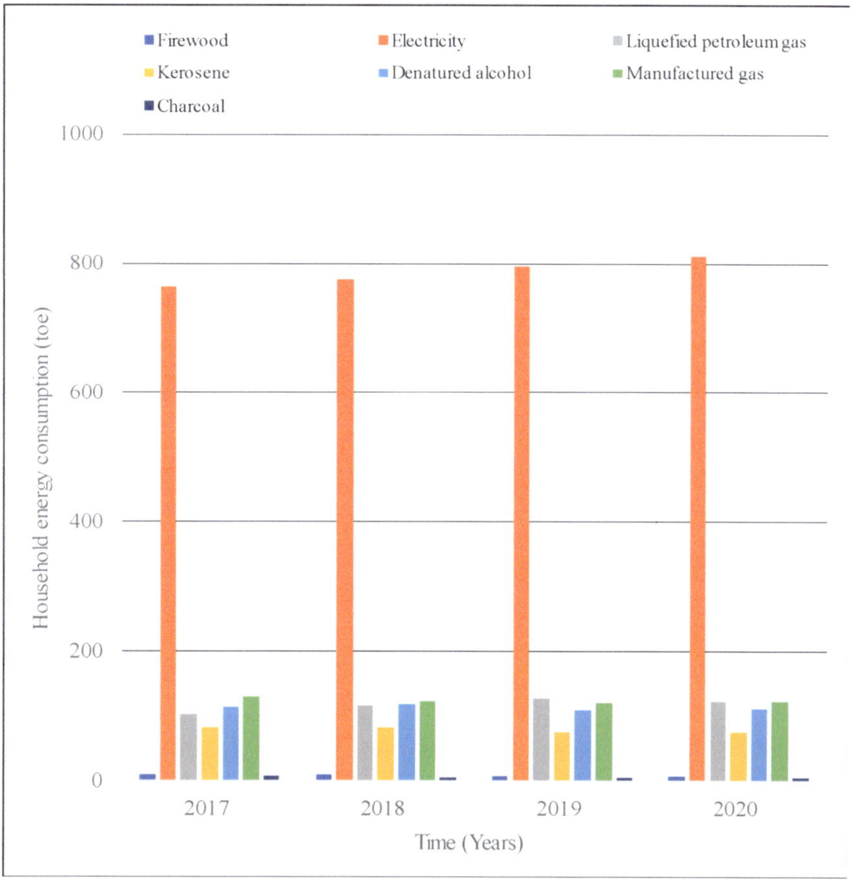

Fig. 7.5 Energy consumption of Cuban households 2020. Toe (Tonne of oil equivalent). Own elaboration

education.[113] Within this context, one of the aims of the Energy Saving Programme in the Ministry of Education was to promote the rational and efficient use of energy.[114]

In terms of electricity generation by type of energy source, the Energy Revolution also introduced significant changes. Domestically produced crude oil in 2003

process of raising awareness of individual energy consumption, energy saving and efficiency and access to information about the functioning of the energy sector. Energy literacy involves the process of energy price formation, energy finance, sector structuring and other relevant information that empowers the holders of the right to energy as part of the energy sector. Trotta et al. (2017) and Martins et al. (2020).

[113] Cf. Saunders Vázquez et al. (2022a).

[114] Ministerio de Energía y Minas and Oficina Nacional de Estadística e Información de la República de Cuba (2015), p. 20.

accounted for 70% of the fuel used for electricity generation, while this percentage was reduced to 49% in 2006. In turn, the use of other energy carriers in 2003, such as fuel oil (29%), diesel (8%) and natural gas (14%), was reduced to 17%, 0.8% and 12% by 2006 in the same order.[115]

An extensive process of implementing distributed generation systems took place as part of the Energy Revolution to guarantee the satisfaction of the growing demand, especially that of the Cuban population, and to reduce energy losses. The expansion of distributed generation systems throughout the country led to a greater decentralisation of the national energy generation system and increased its resilience in the face of natural disasters.[116] In turn, the development of such systems further contributed to the country's electrification. This deployment process resulted in 25.6% of the country's energy demand being met by the installed distributed generation systems.[117]

This distributed generation system was installed using small-scale power plants, diesel engines and fuel oil engines with autonomous starting systems. This type of system resulted in lower fuel consumption through reduced energy losses in the grids. At the same time, they contributed to the resilience of the national energy system in the face of climatic phenomena. In addition, these types of systems involve lower emissions of polluting gases into the atmosphere. Priority areas were identified for the installation of small-scale power plants, such as food preservation, the public health sector, and others. As a result, by 2007, the number of small-scale power plants installed amounted to 6841.[118]

Although this measure contributed to the realisation of the right to energy in Cuba, it also negatively impacted the national economy. These negative impacts were caused by distributed generation systems involving excessive costs related to their operation and maintenance. In addition, it affected the stability of the energy supply, another disadvantage of this type of technology.[119] At the same time, it generated a dependence on this type of generation, becoming, by 2021, the second largest generation source. In this regard, Fig. 7.6 shows gross electricity generation by source till 2021.[120]

Despite the mistakes in implementing the Energy Revolution at the energy policy level, it was proof of the importance the Cuban government gave to developing the national energy system. The recognition of the need to make progress in terms of energy availability, accessibility, affordability, and reliability is evident in the analysis of an unprecedented instrument in Cuban energy policy. Basing the implementation of the Energy Revolution on pillars such as the development of renewable

[115] Fernández Márquez and Pérez de los Reyes (2009), p. 45.

[116] Riverón Mena and Machín Armas (2017), p. 3.

[117] Arrastía-Avila and Glidden (2017).

[118] Pichs Madruga (2008), pp. 174–175.

[119] Benjamin-Alvarado (2010), p. 54.

[120] Oficina Nacional de Estadística e Información de la República de Cuba (2020).

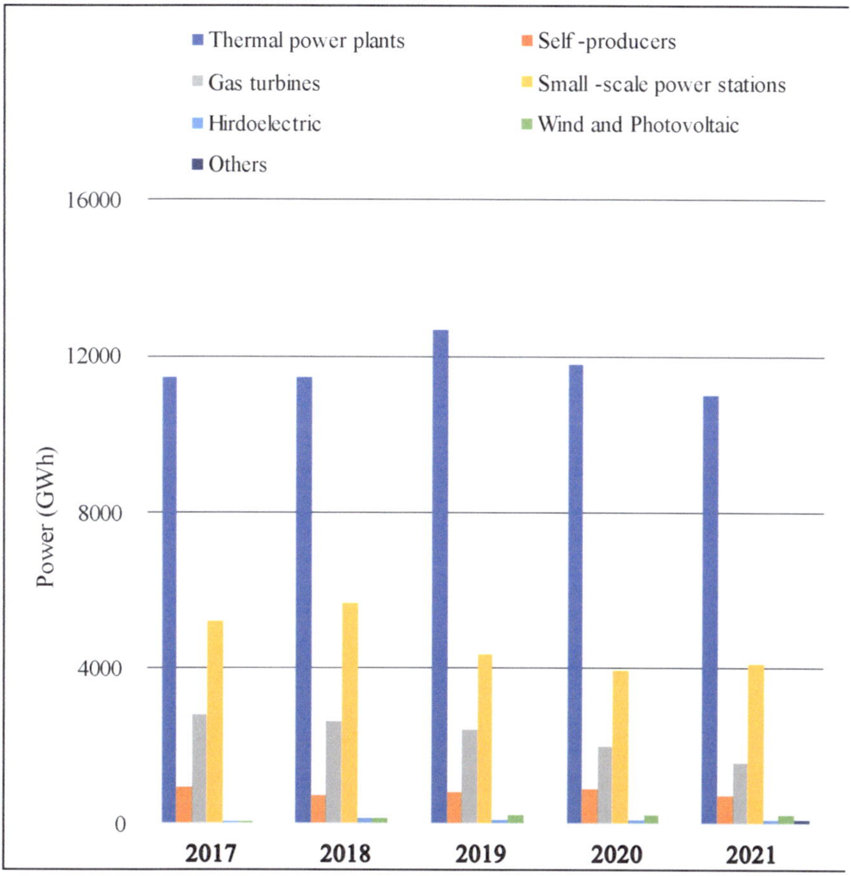

Fig. 7.6 Gross electricity generation by source. Own elaboration

sources, energy efficiency, and energy savings placed Cuba in a very advanced position compared to previous historical stages.

Furthermore, the Energy Revolution represented a step forward in terms of human dignity through the realisation of what this research defines as the right to energy. In this sense, it is crucial to highlight multiple positive elements that resulted in achievements in the realisation of the right under study, including the increase in the level of electrification, the resilience of the energy system, and energy literacy, among others.

Regarding the multiplicity of benefits from the Energy Revolution implementation, Fernández Márquez and Pérez de los Reyes analyse each from economic, social, and environmental perspectives. These include:

- In the economic sphere:

- Increased efficiency in the use of energy carriers and, therefore, a reduction in their consumption.
- Modernisation of energy technologies in two contexts, within households and in the productive sector, resulting in the rational use of raw materials.
- Reduction of electricity interruptions by 90%.
- Flexibilisation and strengthening of the electro-energy system with positive impacts on the productive sector and the dignified life of the Cuban population.
- Increase in the extraction of natural gas and its exploitation in electricity generation, as well as in the production of liquefied petroleum gas.
- Increase the participation of renewable sources in energy generation, especially wind energy.
- Introduction of technologies for power generation from different renewable energy carriers (water, wind, sunlight, and biomass).
- Introduction of cogeneration of energy.

• In the social sphere:

- Increased satisfaction of basic energy needs through modern energy services (Replacing traditional energy carriers with electricity).
- Increased energy literacy emphasises raising environmental awareness among the Cuban population.

• In the environmental sphere:

- Profound changes in energy management and use by saving energy and increasing the quality of energy services.
- The transition from polluting and health-hazardous energy carriers in food cooking and water heating.
- Significant reduction of pollutant gas emissions into the atmosphere.
- Increase in the share of renewable energy sources in the national energy matrix.
- Better management and rational use of natural resources
- Implementation of measures to prevent oil spills in vulnerable ecosystems.[121]

7.2.2 The Right to Energy in the Post-Energy Revolution Scenario

Despite the Cuban government's constant efforts to guarantee what this research defines as the right to energy, its full realisation faces multiple challenges. For this reason, Cuban energy policy and its regulatory framework seek solutions to guarantee national energy sovereignty.

In that sense, with the 2011 Guidelines of the Economic and Social Policy of the Party and the Revolution, the development of renewable energy sources was

[121] Fernández Márquez and Pérez de los Reyes (2009), p. 43.

declared a priority for foreign investment and scientific development in this field. These guidelines included the use of biogas, hydropower, wind energy, solar energy, and the use of biomass.[122]

One of the first consequences of the Guidelines of the Economic and Social Policy of the Party and the Revolution came at the end of 2011. In this period, research was begun into using marabú (Dichrostachys mutans) for energy to strengthen the participation of renewable sources in energy generation. This initiative was conceived to reduce Cuba's energy dependence on imported fossil fuels and reduce the harmful impacts of such dependence on energy availability.[123]

As another result of the Guidelines of the Economic and Social Policy of the Party and the Revolution, the Prospective Policy for the Development of Renewable Sources and the Efficient Use of Energy for 2014–2030 was developed. The Energy Policy 2015 initially declared a target of 24% of electricity generation from renewable energy sources by 2030.[124] In this way, Cuba conceived the energy transition as a path to follow, which undoubtedly resulted in the realisation of the right to energy.

Despite this, this right faces various challenges, such as high energy dependence on imported fossil fuels, the high average cost of generation, high environmental pollution, the low energy efficiency of thermal generation and high energy losses in distribution networks.[125]

This approach was in line with the political priorities of the Cuban nation. Therefore, given this scenario, it is essential to highlight the priority given at the political level to raising the standard of living and quality of life as a priority issue in the guidelines of the VII Party Congress in 2017 as the leading political force of society and the State.[126] To this end, the country's leading political guidelines emphasise energy security as a fundamental premise.[127]

For this reason, the Economic and Social Policy of the Party and the Revolution Programme recognises the country's capacity to exploit renewable energy sources. Therefore, the transformation and accelerated and efficient development of the national energy matrix for sustainable energy development are proposed, considering Cuba's potential.[128]

In this way, the national energy policy was aligned with sustainable development goal 7. This alignment has a particular implication regarding the strategic axis on infrastructure, which establishes the general objective of guaranteeing energy supply under specific requirements, which impacts the realisation of the right to energy in Cuba.

---

[122] Partido Comunista de Cuba (2011).

[123] Urkidi et al. (2015), p. 49.

[124] Ministerio de Energía y Minas and Oficina Nacional de Estadística e Información de la República de Cuba (2015).

[125] Ministerio de Energía y Minas and Oficina Nacional de Estadística e Información de la República de Cuba (2015).

[126] Cf. Article 5. Constitución de la República de Cuba (2019).

[127] Partido Comunista de Cuba (2017).

[128] Partido Comunista de Cuba (2017).

Subsequently, the Guidelines of the Economic and Social Policy of the Party and the Revolution for the Period 2021–2026 were approved at the 8th Congress of the Communist Party of Cuba. This new programmatic guide continued to be aligned with the guidelines adopted in 2017 by endorsing the raising of the standard of living and quality of life as a permanent priority objective. Following this affirmation, the guidelines for the period 2021–2026 emphasise energy security.[129]

Consequently, other pronouncements in these guidelines seek to guarantee the availability of energy. In this respect, Guideline 124 promotes the development of energy forests for the supply of bioelectric power plants. In addition, Guideline 144, concerning Energy Policy, aims to progressively increase national oil and gas production, recover existing oil fields, and accelerate the exploration of new fields in order to increase national production.[130]

While these measures aim to increase the availability of energy in the national context, they maintain dependence on fossil fuel generation. This is not an unfounded measure but rather a response to the growing need to satisfy the national energy demand in the medium term in an energy system based mainly on non-renewable energy sources. For this reason, the construction, assembly, and commissioning of new thermal generation capacity is also being promoted.[131]

Another of the elements to be highlighted within the guidelines for the period 2021–2026 is the promotion of energy accessibility and reliability through the Programme for the Rehabilitation and Modernisation of Electricity Networks and Substations. This promotes the elimination of low-voltage areas and the reduction of energy losses in the transmission and distribution process. In addition, the approved Programme for Electrification in Isolated Areas of the National Electro-energy System will have a positive impact on access to energy.[132] However, in this respect, guideline number 148 refers to the use of more economical energy sources. Would this imply a backward step to traditional sources such as the use of kerosene or wood charcoal?

In addition, another relevant element of the guidelines for the period 2021–2026 for this research is the allusion to aspects associated with energy literacy, among which the aim is to "Consolidate the educational system, intersectoral and social communication, encouraging the population, especially children and young people, the culture of saving, efficient use and sustainability of energy, using the communication media and digital social networks".[133]

The above context is complemented by guideline 149 on accelerating compliance with the Programme for the Development of Renewable Sources and Efficient

[129] Partido Comunista de Cuba (2021), p. 50.
[130] Partido Comunista de Cuba (2021), p. 77.
[131] Partido Comunista de Cuba (2021), p. 78.
[132] Partido Comunista de Cuba (2021), p. 78.
[133] Partido Comunista de Cuba (2021), p. 78.

Energy Use, approved until 2030. In this way, the Cuban Energy Policy is once again aligned with SDG #7.[134]

According to Cuba's National Voluntary Report on the fulfilment of the 2030 Agenda by 2021, the Policy for the Prospective Development of Renewable Sources and the Efficient Use of Energy (2014–2030) focuses on increasing energy efficiency and developing renewable energy sources.

A second element to understand Cuba's progress in the realisation of the right has been the country's efforts to increase energy availability. This indispensable premise for the satisfaction of energy needs prioritises the increase in the penetration of renewable sources, where photovoltaic solar energy has been the fastest growing.

The energy policy foresees an increase of 3506 MW in new electricity capacity based on renewable sources. In this sense, Cuba has set the goal of satisfying the increase in electricity demand by generating electricity from renewable sources. In addition, the planned increase of 800 MW in thermoelectric generation for greater security and flexibility of the national electro-energy system.[135]

At the same time, the report notes the increase in electrification from 94% in 2000 to 99.5% in 2015. This electrification process has multiple benefits regarding energy accessibility, given the political will to guarantee access in at least one way. To this end, the rural population has benefited from installing 15,924 solar photovoltaic modules. The report also reflects the projected increase in the quality of electricity service by 2030 for "customers" with an inadequate electricity connection and those who do not yet have this service. Considering quality as an element of energy reliability, meeting this objective would contribute to the realisation of the right to energy.[136]

Another element that benefits the realisation of the right to energy, according to Sustainable Development Goal 7, is access to clean technologies for cooking and lighting. In this sense, the volunteering report recognises that in 2019, this indicator reached a remarkable increase of 44.1% compared to 2015, when only 27.9% of the population had this type of technology.[137]

Even though environmental sustainability is a condition for energy supply,[138] the exploration and refining of oil and gas resources remain part of the National Economic and Social Development Plan. This situation is evidenced by the interest in maintaining an energy model with a predominance of fossil fuels as the primary energy source, for which actions have been directed towards the exploration and extraction of crude oil. Such projections extend to 2030, intending to exploit such

[134] Partido Comunista de Cuba (2021), p. 78.

[135] Ministerio de Economía y Planificación (2021), pp. 113–114.

[136] Ministerio de Economía y Planificación (2021), p. 113.

[137] Ministerio de Economía y Planificación (2021), p. 113.

[138] "To guarantee, under environmentally sustainable conditions, an adequate, reliable, diversified and modern energy supply that substantially increases the percentage of renewable energy sources in the national energy matrix, essentially biomass, wind and photovoltaic." (Own translation) Partido Comunista de Cuba (2017).

energy resources in the sea and land.[139] For this reason, the satisfaction of the right to energy remained dependent on non-renewable energy sources as the first guideline of national energy policy.

In this context, it is worth noting that the government's energy projection prioritises the recovery of oil fields in the national territory. To this end, the country has provided for the introduction of modern technologies for enhanced recovery. As of April 2019, 24 blocks located in the exclusive economic exploitation zone of the Gulf of Mexico out of the 79 blocks available in this area were opened to bidding for oil recovery and exploitation. In addition, there were nine other blocks for exploitation under contracts distributed on land.[140]

Nevertheless, in terms of energy planning, a new target of 37% of electricity generation from renewable energy sources was set for 2022. The projections of the Ministry of Energy and Mines of Cuba conceive the programme for the development of renewable energy sources in Cuba. This programme aims to expand electricity generation from renewable energy sources according to the following distribution percentages: 15% from bioelectricity, 9% from wind farms, 12% from solar photovoltaic energy, and 1% from small hydroelectric plants.[141]

However, in 2021, only 4.8% of electricity was generated from renewable energy sources,[142] while this percentage fell to 4.1% in 2022,[143] which is a step backward on the path to the 2030 target. Among the renewable energy sources, the most widespread is photovoltaic solar energy, which is 98% advanced. This progress is due to the installation of 67 photovoltaic parks. In second place is the exploitation of biomass from the Sugar Cane Biomass Programme using energy carriers such as marabú and bagasse.[144]

In addition to the above, there are two significant challenges to the full realisation of the right to energy in Cuba. One of these is the inability of the national energy system to meet energy demand. An example of this is the energy crisis that the country faced at the end of 2022, which extends until 2025. This energy crisis can be contrasted by the fact that the reported average energy deficit in the first 19 days of October 2022 represented 33% of the country's reported average demand, as shown in Fig. 7.7.[145] This situation has worsened over the years. An example is the relation between the average demand and average deficit in April 2025, when the reported average energy deficit represented 45.33% of the reported average demand in the first 19 days of that month (Fig. 7.8).[146]

[139] Moregón Ramos (2023), p. 315.

[140] Moregón Ramos (2023), p. 308.

[141] Delgado Triana et al. (2023).

[142] Oficina Nacional de Estadística e Información (2022), p. 13.

[143] Oficina Nacional de Estadística e Información (2023), p. 13.

[144] Moregón Ramos (2023), p. 315.

[145] Cf. Redacción Digital (2022).

[146] Cf. Redacción Digital (2025).

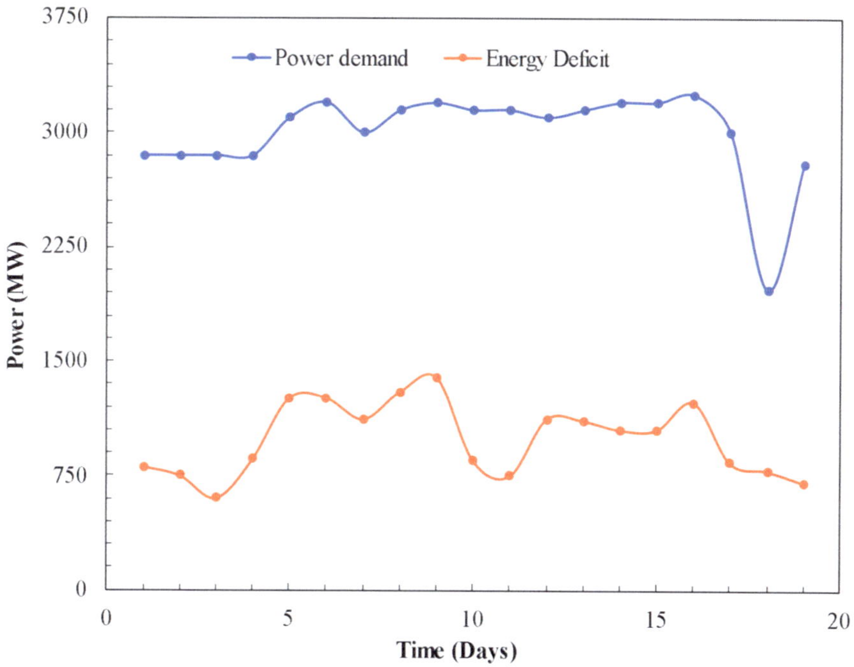

Fig. 7.7 Energy demand-energy deficit ratio (October 2022). Own elaboration

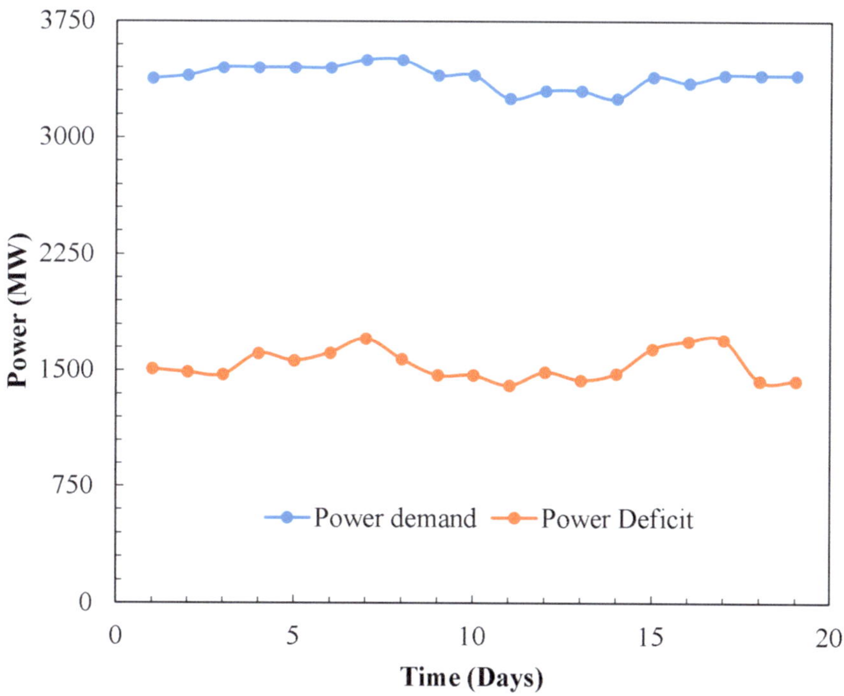

Fig. 7.8 Energy demand-energy deficit ratio (April 2025). Own elaboration

This situation is not an isolated or eventual phenomenon but is due to multiple causes. Among them are the increase in energy demand during the isolation imposed by the COVID-19 pandemic, the impact of the global economic crisis and the incidence of climatological phenomena on the distribution network.[147] These events have hurt national electricity generation and, therefore, energy availability as an indispensable premise for the realisation of the right to energy.

The consequences of the previous context were aggravated by the collapse of several of the central generation systems due to financing limitations to conducting planned maintenance actions. In addition, there has been a decrease in electricity generation due to the scarcity of fuels for the operation of distributed generation systems, which, in the past, represented a viable way to overcome previous energy crises and to increase the levels of electrification on a national scale.[148] These are, without a doubt, consequences that reaffirm Cuba's energy dependence and a reason to move towards energy sovereignty to guarantee the realisation of the right to energy.

Despite the above, it is essential to highlight that the limitations in terms of financing and resources to achieve and maintain the stability of the national energy system are, to a substantial extent, a consequence of the US blockade in Cuba. Significantly, during Donald Trump's administration, the sanctions system against the Caribbean nation was strengthened, and its impact on the energy sector was not long in coming.

For this reason, the quantified impact on the mining-energy sector in 2022 amounted to 136,063,043 dollars that could have been invested in the sustainable energy development of the country. Other effects on the import of energy resources such as oil and liquefied gas must be added to this due to the persecution of the leading suppliers of this type of product.[149]

This persecution also affected the realisation of the right to energy in Cuba, regarding the satisfaction of energy needs that depend on this type of resource. To give an example of the impact that sanctions have had on the import of energy resources, Unión Cuba-Petróleo, after its inclusion by the Office of Foreign Assets Control - Sanctions Programs and Information (OFAC) on the list of Specially Designated Entities since 2019, has been affected to the tune of 17 million 391,640 dollars.[150]

Despite the complex situation facing the realisation of the right to energy in practice, the government has taken emergency measures to reduce the impact. Thus, despite the high cost to the national economy, productive activities have been reorganised to reduce energy demand and power outages.[151] Although not new in Cuba's

[147] Cf. Redacción Digital (2022).

[148] Alonso Falcón et al. (2022).

[149] Ministerio de Relaciones Internacionales de Cuba (2022).

[150] Ministerio de Relaciones Internacionales de Cuba (2022).

[151] Herrera Reyes (2022).

history in the face of this type of energy contingency, this measure highlights the government's interest in protecting the population to satisfy its energy needs.

However, the precariousness of the functioning of the national energy system puts the components of the right to energy at risk. An example of this is the low availability of energy, which affects not only the functioning of the public electricity service but also the processes of fuel supply within Cuba. This context is drastically manifested in the national transport sector. This situation is because, since the beginning of 2023, Cuba has faced an unstable situation with the fuel supply,[152] which could be framed as transport poverty.[153]

This situation is due to Cuba's limitations in importing refined crude oil, diesel, and gasoline derivatives, which has meant that national refineries have not been able to satisfy domestic demand for fuel. This scenario responds again to the national dependence on imported fuels, given that suppliers have not been able to fulfil the contracts contracted with the Caribbean nation. The complexity of this context is due to the fact that there is not enough crude oil in the national territory that can be refined to meet the national energy demand.[154]

The tense energy situation in Cuba between 2022 and 2025 has determined the degree of realisation of the content of the right to energy in the country. This realisation has been in line with the Caribbean nation's energy history. Although the history of the Cuban energy sector has not been far removed from humanity's energy problems, the consequences of energy dependence have been reiterated over time.

Despite the above, progress in the realisation of the right to energy in Cuba has been palpable since the triumph of the Cuban Revolution. If one considers that before 1959, the country's energy development contributed to the partial realisation of the right to energy, the triumph of the Cuban Revolution set a standard in the development of the energy sector as an insurmountable premise to guarantee the right to energy.

Among the main positive results regarding the realisation of the right to energy, the increase in installed capacity and the country's electrification, which reached 99.98% in 2021, can be highlighted.[155] In turn, the energy transition for sustainable energy development has been promoted in the national energy policy since 2011. Despite this, the goals set have been affected by numerous challenges that consequently affect the right to energy in Cuba.

Those challenges include:

- Dependence on fossil fuels and foreign suppliers

---

[152] Sardiñas (2023), p. 1.

[153] Transport poverty can be defined as a situation where: "No transport option available that suits their needs; they do not reach their destinations to satisfy their daily activities, such as education, health and employment; the weekly amount spent on transport is above the official poverty line; travel times are long; or travel conditions are unsafe, dangerous or unhealthy."

Pérez-Peña et al. (2021), p. 1; Thitheridge et al. (2014).

[154] Figueredo Reinaldo (2023).

[155] Oficina Nacional de Estadística e Información de la República de Cuba (2022), p. 270.

- The impact of the sanctions regime imposed by the US government over Cuba.
- The growth of energy demand
- The financial limitations for investment in the energy sector and its technological obsolescence.

These conditions have plunged the country into one of the most notable energy crises the country has ever faced and, therefore, determine the realisation of the right to energy.

7.3 Conclusions

Cuba's history has revealed important antecedents related to the right to energy. The historical, political, social, and legal analysis developed in this chapter revealed the main conditions that have determined the realisation of the right to energy. Since the colonial period in Cuba, numerous advances have been made in the energy field. As in the rest of the world, Cuba's economic development brought an increase in energy demand, which resulted in energy crises that, in turn, jeopardised the realisation of the right to energy.

Despite the advances in the energy sector during the colonial period, not all of them benefited the entire Cuban population. Only some of the country's inhabitants experienced the benefits of new energy services such as electricity and gas, while high prices or their geographical location marginalised others. Then, energy services were reserved for those for whom they were affordable, excluding half of the Cuban population.

After the triumph of the Cuban Revolution, this situation was reversed by the measures of the new government in power through multiple initiatives based on strategic alliances with commercial partners such as the Soviet Union. The new legal and political measures were prioritised to guarantee availability, accessibility, affordability, and reliability for the entire Cuban population as elements of the right to energy.

Despite the strength of such an alliance, after the collapse of the Soviet Union, the realisation of the right to energy was severely affected by the energy sector's extreme dependence on energy supplies obtained from the Council for Mutual Economic Assistance. This critical point prompted a series of measures that revived the Cuban energy sector, which, since then, has had other energy crises due to multiple causes, including endogenous and exogenous conditions threatening the realisation of the right to energy.

Despite the public policies designed by the Cuban government, the Cuban energy sector has enjoyed temporary stability. Still, the electricity generation systems are characterised by an obsolescence that prevents them from responding to the national energy demand. This obsolescence is due to multiple causes, including the Caribbean nation's scarce financial resources and the economic-financial siege imposed by the

US government. In this context, over the last 3 years, Cuba has experienced a new energy crisis threatening the realisation of the right to energy.

References[156]

Aguiar LE (1933) Cuba 1933. Prologue to revolution. Cornell University Press, London. https://read.dukeupress.edu/hahr/article/53/1/135/151614/Cuba-1933-Prologue-to-Revolution. Accessed 3 Mar 2025

Alonso Falcón R, Figueredo Reinaldo O, Fuentes Puebla T, Jorge Blanco A, Rodríguez Martínez C, Fonseca Sosa K (2022) Cuba: Actualización sobre la situación del sistema electroenergético. Cubadebate, La Habana. http://www.cubadebate.cu/noticias/2022/05/26/cuba-actualizacion-sobre-la-situacion-del-sistema-electroenergetico/. Accessed 3 Mar 2025

Altshuler J (1998) Impacto Social y Espacial de las Redes Eléctricas en Cuba. Scripta Nova. Revista Electrónica de Geografía y Ciencias Sociales (17):1–13. http://www.ub.edu/geocrit/sn-18.htm. Accessed 3 Mar 2025

Arku RE, Brauer M, Duong M, Wei L, Hu B, Tse LA, Mony PK, Lakshmi PVM, Pillai RK, Mohan V, Yeates K, Kruger L, Rangarajan S, Koon T, Yusuf S, Hystad P (2020) Adverse health impacts of cooking with kerosene: a multi-country analysis within the Prospective Urban and Rural Epidemiology Study. Environ Res 188:109851. https://linkinghub.elsevier.com/retrieve/pii/S0013935120307465. Accessed 3 Mar 2025

Arrastía-Avila MA, Glidden LM (2017) Cuba's energy revolution and 2030 policy goals: more penetration of renewable energy in electricity generation. Int J Cuban Stud 9(1):73–90. https://scienceopen.com/hosted-document?doi=10.13169/intejcubastud.9.1.0073. Accessed 3 Mar 2025

Azorín García E (2021) Alumbrado, limpieza y recogida de basuras en La Habana de Ezpeleta: bandos y reglamento (1786-1787). Revista de Humanidades (43). https://dialnet.unirioja.es/servlet/articulo?codigo=8062258&info=resumen. Accessed 3 Mar 2025

Bell J, López DL, Caram T (2006) Documentos de la Revolución cubana, 1959. Editorial de Ciencias Sociales, La Habana. http://www.fidelcastro.cu/sites/default/files/fichero_libros/Documentos%2D%2DRevolucion%2D%2Dcubana.pdf. Accessed 3 Mar 2025

Benjamin-Alvarado J (2010) Cuba's energy future: strategic approaches to cooperation. The Brookings Institution Press, Washington, D.C.. https://www.jstor.org/stable/10.7864/j.ctt127wfv. Accessed 3 Mar 2025

Bovan A, Vučenović T, Peric N (2020) Negotiating energy diplomacy and its relationship with foreign policy and national security. Int J Energy Econ Policy 10(2):1–6. https://www.econjournals.com/index.php/ijeep/article/view/8754. Accessed 3 Mar 2025

Carriazo Moreno G (2011) Las relaciones económicas Cuba-Estados: una mirada al futuro. Estudios Internacionales 26(103) http://www.revistaei.uchile.cl/index.php/REI/article/view/15387. Accessed 3 Mar 2025

Castro Diaz-Balart F (1991) Energía Nuclear y Desarrollo. Realidades y Desarfíos en los Umbrales del Siglo XXI. Ediciones Colihue, Buenos Aires

Castro Díaz-Balart F (1999) Energía nuclear ¿Peligro ambiental o solución para el siglo XX? Editorial Grijalbo, Barcelona

Castro Ruz F (1997) Informe Central al V Congreso del Partido Comunista de Cuba, presentado por el Comandante en Jefe Fidel Castro Ruz, Primer Secretario del Comité Central del Partido Comunista de Cuba y Presidente de los Consejos de Estado y de Ministros, en el Palacio de. Fidel, Soldado de las Ideas, La Habana. http://www.fidelcastro.cu/es/discursos/informe-

[156] All links to the cited websites were operational as of 3 March 2025.

central-al-v-congreso-del-partido-comunista-de-cuba-presentado-en-el-palacio-de. Accessed 3 Mar 2025

Comisión Económica para América Latina y el Caribe (2005) Evolución Económica durante 2004 y Perspectivas para 2005, Cuba. https://repositorio.cepal.org/bitstream/handle/11362/25716/LCmexL664_es.pdf?sequence=1&isAllowed=y. Accessed 3 Mar 2025

Constitución de 1901 (1901) Cuba: Asamblea Nacional del Poder Popular. https://www.parlamentocubano.gob.cu/index.php/constitucion-de-1901. Accessed 3 Mar 2025

Constitución de 1940 (1940) Cuba: Asamblea Nacional del Poder Popular. https://www.parlamentocubano.gob.cu/index.php/constitucion-de-1940. Accessed 3 Mar 2025

Constitución de Baraguá (1878) Cuba: Asamblea Nacional del Poder Popular. https://www.parlamentocubano.gob.cu/index.php/constitucion-de-baragua. Accessed 3 Mar 2025

Constitución de Guáimaro (1869) Cuba: Asamblea Nacional del Poder Popular. https://www.parlamentocubano.gob.cu/index.php/constitucion-de-guaimaro. Accessed 3 Mar 2025

Constitución de Jimaguayú (1895) Cuba: Asamblea Nacional del Poder Popular. https://www.parlamentocubano.gob.cu/sites/default/files/documento/2022-06/Constituci%C3%B3n-de-Jimaguay%C3%BA-de-1895_0.pdf. Accessed 3 Mar 2025

Constitución de la República de Cuba (1976) Cuba: Asamblea Nacional del Poder Popular. https://www.parlamentocubano.gob.cu/sites/default/files/documento/2022-06/Constituci%C3%B3n-de-la-Rep%C3%BAblica-de-Cuba-1976.pdf. Accessed 3 Mar 2025

Constitución de la República de Cuba (2019) Gaceta Oficial No. 5 Extraordinaria de 10 de abril de 2019. Gaceta Oficial de la República de Cuba, La Habana. https://www.gacetaoficial.gob.cu/sites/default/files/goc-2019-ex5.pdf. Accessed 3 Mar 2025

Constitución de La Yaya (1897) Cuba: Asamblea Nacional del Poder Popular. https://www.parlamentocubano.gob.cu/sites/default/files/documento/2022-06/Constituci%C3%B3n-de-La-Yaya-de-1897.pdf. Accessed 3 Mar 2025

Constitución Política de la Monarquía Española (1812) España: Congreso de los Diputados. https://www.congreso.es/constitucion/ficheros/historicas/cons_1812.pdf. Accessed 3 Mar 2025

De las Cuevas Toraya J, Rey G (2015) Las Construcciones Cuentan su Historia. Ciudades, Pueblos y Caseríos de Cuba. Ediciones Bologna, La Habana. https://sedhc.es/biblioteca/actas/138-Rey.pdf. Accessed 3 Mar 2025

Delgado Triana Y, Fariñas Wong EY (2016) Derecho de acceso a la energía. Protección constitucional en Cuba, Caribeña de Ciencias Sociales. https://www.eumed.net/rev/caribe/2016/04/energia.html. Accessed 3 Mar 2025

Delgado Triana Y, Luis Cordova JG, Milian Gómez JF, Fariña Wong EY (2023) The use of GIS and the right to energy in Cuba. In: Aragão A (ed) Transforming spatial data into public policies for social justice and environmental sustainability. Cambridge Scholars Publishing, Newcastle upon Tyne, pp 143–169. https://www.cambridgescholars.com/product/978-1-5275-0925-2. Accessed 3 Mar 2025

Dominguez JI (1978) Cuba: order and revolution. The Belknap Press, Massachusetts. https://hdl.handle.net/2027/heb.03476. Accessed 3 Mar 2025

Evenson F (1998) No A deeper shade of green: the evolution of Cuban environmental law and policy. Golden Gate Univ Law Rev 28(3). https://digitalcommons.law.ggu.edu/cgi/viewcontent.cgi?article=1733&context=ggulrev. Accessed 3 Mar 2025

Fernández Márquez A, Pérez de los Reyes R (eds) (2009) Evaluacion del Medio Ambiente Cubano - GEO Cuba. Programa de las Naciones Unidas para el Medio Ambiente (PNUMA) para Ministerio de Ciencia, Tecnología y Medio Ambiente (CITMA), La Habana. https://wedocs.unep.org/20.500.11822/9354. Accessed 3 Mar 2025

Figueredo Reinaldo O (2023) Cupet confirma limitaciones en la importación de combustibles y niega que Cuba exporta gasolina. Cubadebate, La Habana. http://www.cubadebate.cu/especiales/2023/04/23/cupet-confirma-limitaciones-en-la-importacion-de-combustibles-y-niega-que-cuba-exporta-gasolina/. Accessed 3 Mar 2025

Funes Monzote R (2009) Plantaciones esclavistas azucareras y Transformación ecológica en Cuba. Revista Historia (59–60):35–54. https://dialnet.unirioja.es/servlet/articulo?codigo=6820124. Accessed 3 Mar 2025

Funez Monzote R (2002) Propiedad y Uso de los Bosques Habaneros. Sobre un 'Bien Común' en el Contexto Colonial Cubano hasta Finales del XVIII. In: Piqueras Arenas JA (ed) Bienes comunales: propiedad, arraigo y apropiación. Ministerio de Agricultura, Alimentación y Medio Ambiente/Secretaría General Técnica, Madrid, pp 63–94. https://www.mapa.gob.es/ministerio/pags/biblioteca/fondo/pdf/33579_4.pdf. Accessed 3 Mar 2025

García AS (2021) La colonia económica. Cuba en el siglo XIX. In: Campos Álvarez XR (ed) Cando caen as follas. Homenaxe ao profesor Carlos Sixirey. Ir Indo Editions, Vigo, pp 377–397. https://digital.csic.es/bitstream/10261/253240/1/Carlos%20Sixirei_Libro%20Homenaje%20art%c3%adculo.pdf. Accessed 3 Mar 2025

García Molina JM (2005) La economía cubana desde el siglo XVI al XX: del colonialismo al socialismo con mercado. In: Serie: Estudios y Persepectivas, vol 28. Unidad de Desarrollo Económico, México, D.F. https://repositorio.cepal.org/entities/publication/8e033c5c-23cf-4e84-8f47-274c54e1767e. Accessed 3 Mar 2025

Gonzáles Herrera U (2015) Las cronicas generales de Indias en la Arqueologia de Cuba. Límites y perspectivas en la reconstrucción etnohistóricas de las sociedades aborígenes. Cuba Arqueologica (4). https://www.researchgate.net/publication/328130589_Las_cronicas_generales_de_Indias_en_la_Arqueologia_de_Cuba_Limites_y_perspectivas_en_la_reconstruccion_etnohistorica_de_las_sociedades_aborigenes. Accessed 3 Mar 2025

Guardado-Chacón JA, Arencibia A (2021) Una mirada desde el Movimiento de Usuarios del Biogás (MUB) a la transición energética en Cuba. Gestión y Ambiente 24(Supl2):238–251. https://revistas.unal.edu.co/index.php/gestion/article/view/92940. Accessed 3 Mar 2025

Herrera Reyes A (2022) Detallan medidas para recuperación del Sistema Eléctrico Nacional. Agencia Cubana de Noticias, La Habana. https://www.acn.cu/cuba/detallan-medidas-para-recuperacion-del-sistema-electrico-nacional. Accessed 3 Mar 2025

IAEA (2008) Cuba: a country profile on sustainable energy development. International Atomic Energy Agency, Vienna. https://www-pub.iaea.org/MTCD/Publications/PDF/Pub1328_web.pdf. Accessed 3 Mar 2025

International Agency for Research on Cancer (2020) Indoor burning of biomass and kerosene fuels is associated with higher risk of developing several types of digestive cancers. Lyon. https://www.iarc.who.int/wp-content/uploads/2020/06/pr285_E.pdf. Accessed 3 Mar 2025

Jordan Reyes M (2006) La deforestación de la isla de Cuba durante la dominación española. (1492-1898). Universidad Politécnica de Madrid. https://oa.upm.es/436/1/MIGUEL_JORDAN_REYES.pdf. Accessed 3 Mar 2025

Le Riverend J, Bervil D, Dumpierre E, Aruca A (1978) Historia de Cuba. Editorial Pueblo y Educación, La Habana

Luis Cordova J G (2024) Past, present and future of the Cuban energy sector: between challenges and perspectives in energia progresiva. Springer Nature, Cham, pp 137–161. https://link.springer.com/10.1007/978-3-031-68846-1_6. Accessed 3 Mar 2025

Maiyoh GK, Njoroge RW, Tuei VC (2015) Effects and mechanisms of kerosene use-related toxicity. Environ Toxicol Pharmacol 40 (1):57–70. https://doi.org/10.1016/j.etap.2015.05.010. Accessed 3 Mar 2025

Martínez Fraga A (1949) Moción: Monopolio de Luz y Fuerza Eléctrica. Partido Demócrata, La Habana

Martins A, Madaleno M, Ferreira Dias M (2020) Energy literacy: what is out there to know? Energy Rep 6:454–459. https://doi.org/10.1016/j.egyr.2019.09.007. Accessed 3 Mar 2025

Mateo Rodríguez JM (2018) Cuba: los retos de un país en revolución para enfrentar la crisis ambiental. In Feria de La Habana 2019, Ministerio de Cultura de Cuba Instituto, Instituto Cubano del Libro Red, Red en Defensa de la Humanidad, Editorial Nuevo Milenio, La Habana, pp 1–36. https://dialnet.unirioja.es/servlet/articulo?codigo=9545310. Accessed 3 Mar 2025

Mesa-Lago C (1982) La dependencia económica externa de Cuba y su repercusión sobre su política exterior. Estudios Internacionales (57):60–87. https://www.jstor.org/stable/pdf/41391042.pdf. Accessed 3 Mar 2025

Ministerio de Economía y Planificación (2021) ODS 7: Garantizar el acceso a una energía asequible, fiable, sostenible y moderna para todos. Informe Nacional Voluntario. Cuba 2021. La Habana. https://www.presidencia.gob.cu/media/filer/public/2022/05/07/inv_cuba_agenda_2030_nnuu_2021.pdf

Ministerio de Energía y Minas, Oficina Nacional de Estadística e Información de la República de Cuba (2015) Taller: Desarrollo de Capacidades para la Integración de Objetivos de Desarrollo Sostenible de Energía, Metas e Indicadores en los Programas Nacionales de Estadísticas en Países de América Latina. La Habana. https://sustainabledevelopment.un.org/content/documents/280872021_VNR_Report_Cuba.pdf. Accessed 3 Mar 2025

Ministerio de Relaciones Internacionales de Cuba (2022) Informe de Cuba en virtud de la resolución 75/289 de la Asamblea General de las Naciones Unidas, titulada "Necesidad de poner fin al bloqueo económico, comercial y financiero impuesto por los Estados Unidos de América contra Cuba". La Habana. https://cubaminrex.cu/es/informe-de-cuba-en-virtud-de-la-resolucion-75289-de-la-asamblea-general-de-las-naciones-unidas. Accessed 3 Mar 2025

Miranda Bravo O (2000) Las nacionalizaciones cubanas. In: Valdés MP, Hernández LP (eds) Temas de Derecho Constitucional Cubano. Editorial Félix Varela, La Habana, pp 25–33

Miranda Bravo O (2007) El bloqueo y las nacionalizaciones. Revista Cubana de Derecho (29):50–64. https://cuba.vlex.com/vid/bloqueo-nacionalizaciones-50068079. Accessed 3 Mar 2025

Moregón Ramos A (2023) Soberanía energética, agricultura sostenible y cambio climático en Cuba: entre políticas públicas y proyectos de la sociedad civil desde 1959 hasta la etapa pandémica. Collectivus. Revista de Ciencias Sociales 10(1):289–320. https://tinyurl.com/8erfjuw7. Accessed 3 Mar 2025

Morejón Ramos A, Bayón Martínez P, Rodríguez Alomar YE (2019) In: Morejón Ramos A (ed) Cambio ambiental global: desafíos para la sostenibilidad de la vida. Editorial filosofi@.cu, Rosa Luxemburg Stiftung, Ediciones Uache, La Habana, pp 107–125. https://www.researchgate.net/publication/371635769_Cambio_ambiental_global_Desafios_y_alternativas_en_las_apuestas_por_la_sostenibilidad_de_la_vida. Accessed 3 Mar 2025

Moreno Figueredo C, Montesinos Larrosa A (2010) The role of renewable energy sources in de development of Cuban society. In: Abramsky K (ed) Sparking in a worldwide energy revolution. Social struggles in the transition to a post-petrol world. AK Press, Oakland, pp 264–276. https://www.amazon.com/Sparking-Worldwide-Energy-Revolution-Post-Petrol/dp/1849350051. Accessed 3 Mar 2025

Núñez Jiménez A (1998) Hacia una cultura de la naturaleza. Editorial Letras Cubanas, La Habana. https://www.abebooks.co.uk/9789592300156/Hacia-cultura-Naturaleza-Antonio-N%C3%BA%C3%B1ez-9592300151/plp. Accessed 3 Mar 2025

Oficina Nacional de Estadística e Información (2022) Electricidad en Cuba. Indicadores seleccionados 2021. https://onei.gob.cu/electricidad-en-cuba-indicadores-seleccionados-enero-diciembre-2021. Accessed 3 Mar 2025

Oficina Nacional de Estadística e Información (2023) Electricidad en Cuba. Indicadores seleccionados 2022. La Habana. http://www.onei.gob.cu/sites/default/files/electricidad_en_cuba._2022_edic_2023.pdf. Accessed 3 Mar 2025

Oficina Nacional de Estadística e Información de la República de Cuba (2020) Series Estadísticas de Minería y Energía. http://www.onei.gob.cu/node/15786. Accessed 3 Mar 2025

Oficina Nacional de Estadística e Información de la República de Cuba (2022) Anuario Estadístico de Cuba 2021. Medio Ambiente. La Habana. http://www.onei.gob.cu/sites/default/files/02_medio_ambiente_2021-.pdf. Accessed 3 Mar 2025

Partido Comunista de Cuba (2011) Lineamientos de la Política Económica y Social del Partido y Las Revolución. La Habana. https://www.tsp.gob.cu/sites/default/files/documentos/1%20lineamientos-politica-partido-cuba.pdf. Accessed 3 Mar 2025

Partido Comunista de Cuba (2017) Documentos del 7mo. Congreso del Partido aprobados por el III Pleno del Comité Central Documentos del 7mo. Congreso del Partido del PCC el 18 de mayo de 2017 y respaldados por la Asamblea Nacional del Poder Popular el 1 de junio de 2017. Periódico Granma, La Habana. https://www.granma.cu/file/pdf/gaceta/%C3%BAltimo%20PDF%2032.pdf. Accessed 3 Mar 2025

Partido Comunista de Cuba (2021) Conceptualización del modelo económico y social de desarrollo socialista. Lineamientos de la Política Económica y Social del Partido y la Revolución para el Período 2021-2026. Partido Comunista de Cuba, La Habana. http://media.cubadebate.cu/wp-content/uploads/2021/06/documentos-partido-cuba.pdf. Accessed 3 Mar 2025

Pérez-Peña MC, Jiménez-García M, Ruiz-Chico J, Peña-Sánchez AR (2021) Transport poverty with special reference to sustainability: a systematic review of the literature. Sustainability 13(3):1451. https://www.mdpi.com/2071-1050/13/3/1451. Accessed 3 Mar 2025

Pichs Madruga R (2008) Cambio climático, globalización y subdesarrollo. Editorial Científico-Técnica, La Habana. https://www.academia.edu/40724225/Cambio_climatico_globalizacion_y_subdesarrollo_Ramon_Pichs_Madruga. Accessed 3 Mar 2025

Poder Ejecutivo del Consejo de Ministros (1960a) Ley 851. Gaceta Oficial de la República de Cuba, La Habana

Poder Ejecutivo del Consejo de Ministros (1960b) Ley 890 y 891. Gaceta Oficial de la República de Cuba, La Habana

Prieto Valdés M, Pérez Hernández L (2000) Temas de Derecho Constitucional cubano. Editorial Félix Varela, La Habana

Qazi S (2017) Portable standalone PV systems for disaster relief and remote areas. In: Standalone photovoltaic (PV) systems for disaster relief and remote areas. Elsevier, pp 113–138. https://linkinghub.elsevier.com/retrieve/pii/B9780128030226000046. Accessed 3 Mar 2025

Redacción Digital (2022) Unión Eléctrica. Cubadebate, La Habana. http://www.cubadebate.cu/etiqueta/union-electrica-une/. Accessed 3 Mar 2025

Redacción Digital (2025) Unión Eléctrica. Cubadebate, La Habana. http://www.cubadebate.cu/etiqueta/apagones/. Accessed 19 Apr 2025

Reglamento Constitutivo de La Compañía Española del Alumbrado de Gas de Matanzas (1855) Imprenta y papelería de J. M. Barcina

Ríos Hernández A (2018) Medios y tecnologías de los aborígenes cubanos para su subsistencia. Revista Ingeniería Agrícola 8(3):67–72. https://rcta.unah.edu.cu/index.php/IAgric/article/view/979/1496

Riverón Mena AN, Machín Armas FO (2017) Derecho Ambiental Cubano y Revolución Energética. In: 8va Conferencia Científica Internacional de la Universidad de Holgín, Universidad de Holguín, Guardalavaca, pp 1–8. https://www.researchgate.net/profile/Francisco-Octavio-Machin-Armas/publication/383623184_Derecho_Ambiental_Cubano_y_Revolucion_Energetica_Cuban_Environmental_Right_and_Energetic_Revolution_8va_Conferencia_Cientifica_Internacional_de_la_Universidad_de_Holguin_Abril_de_2017/links/66db0fdcfa5e11512ca3798f/Derecho-Ambiental-Cubano-y-Revolucion-Energetica-Cuban-Environmental-Right-and-Energetic-Revolution-8va-Conferencia-Cientifica-Internacional-de-la-Universidad-de-Holguin-Abril-de-2017.pdf. Accessed 3 Mar 2025

Rodríguez Castellón S (2002) Sector Energético. In: Montero AC (ed) Estructura Económica de Cuba. Editorial 'Félix Varela', La Habana, pp 88–121

Rubio González A (2016) La energía en Cuba. Historia, actualidad y perspectivas. In: Conferencia de Ingeniería Mecanica de la UCLV. Santa Clara. https://www.researchgate.net/profile/Angel-Rubio-Gonzalez/publication/333759634_LA_ENERGIA_EN_CUBA_Historia_actualidad_y_perspectivas_2016/links/5d02af5c4585157d15a941b1/LA-ENERGIA-EN-CUBA-Historia-actualidad-y-perspectivas-2016?origin=publication_detail. Accessed 3 Mar 2025

Sardiñas EM (2023) Cuban energy law and green energy transition. SSRN Electr J (04). https://www.ssrn.com/abstract=4372069. Accessed 3 Mar 2025

Saunders Vázquez A, Luukkanen J, Laitinen J, Auffermann B (2022a) Futuro energético en Cuba. La transición hacia un Sistema Renovable de Energía – Factores Políticos, Económicos, Sociales y Medioambientales. Writers & Finland Futures Research Centre, University of Turku, Turku. https://www.utupub.fi/bitstream/handle/10024/154403/FFRC_eBook_4-2022.pdf?sequence=1&isAllowed=y. Accessed 3 Mar 2025

Saunders Vázquez A, Luukkanen J, Santos Fuentefría A, Majanne Y, Filgueiras Sainz de Rozas ML, Laitinen J (2022b) Desarrollo del sistema energético cubano - desafíos y posibilidades tecnológicas. Writers & Finland Futures Research Centre, University of Turku, Turku. https://www.researchgate.net/publication/361942520_DESARROLLO_DEL_SISTEMA_ENERGETICO_CUBANO_-Desafios_y_Posibilidades_Tecnologicas. Accessed 3 Mar 2025

Suárez JA, Beatón PA, Faxas Escalona R, Pérez Montero O (2012) Energy, environment and development in Cuba. Renew Sustain Energy Rev 16(5):2724–2731. https://doi.org/10.1016/j.rser.2012.02.023. Accessed 3 Mar 2025

Thitheridge H, Oviedo Hernandez R, Ye R, Chritie N, Mackett R (2014) Transport poverty: concepts, measurement and policy perspectives. The Association of American Geographers' Annual Meeting, Tampa, Florida, 8th–12th April 2014. https://www.researchgate.net/publication/270887255_Transport_Poverty_Concepts_Measurement_and_Policy_Perspectives. Accessed 3 Mar 2025

Trotta G, Kalmi P, Kazukauskas A (2017) The role of energy literacy as a component of financial literacy: survey – based evidence from Finland. In: 15th IAEE European conference, September, 21pp. https://www.researchgate.net/publication/325467432_The_Role_of_Energy_Literacy_as_a_Component_of_Financial_Literacy_Survey_-_based_evidence_from_Finland. Accessed 3 Mar 2025

United Nations Development Programme (2023) Access to clean cooking solutions. https://www.undp.org/energy/our-work-areas/energy-access/access-clean-cooking-solutions. Accessed 3 Mar 2025

Urkidi L, Lago R, Basurko I, Mantxo M, Barcena I, Akizu O (2015) Transiciones energéticas: sostenibilidad y democracia energética. Servicio Editorial de la Universidad del País Vasco, Leioa. https://issuu.com/ekologistakmartxanboletina/docs/tradebu. Accessed 3 Mar 2025

Vázquez LL, Marzin J, Gonzále N (2017) Políticas públicas y transición hacia la agricultura sostenible sobre bases agroecológicas en Cuba. In: Schmitt C, Niederle P, Ávila M, Sabourin E, Petersen P, Silveira L, Assis W, Palm J (eds) Políticas a favor de la Agroecología en América Latina y El Caribe. Red Políticas Publicas en América Latina y el Caribe, Brasilia, pp 108–131. https://www.pp-al.org/content/download/4658/34602/version/1/file/PP_Agroecologia_VF-17-05-2017.pdf. Accessed 3 Mar 2025

Chapter 8
Constitutional Premises of the Right to Energy in Cuba

8.1 The Right to Energy Under Fundamental Principles of the Cuban Constitution

Despite the Cuban government's constant efforts to guarantee what this research defines as the right to energy, there are no express references to the right in question at the regulatory level. An example is the Constitution of the Republic of Cuba of 2019, which does not recognise the right to energy as a fundamental right. However, throughout the constitutional text, numerous constitutional norms constitute the basis and foundation of the need to include the right to energy in the catalogue of fundamental rights.

The Cuban Constitution reflects its time and the result of the popular will expressed through a constitutional referendum. However, even the National Assembly of People's Power, as the supreme organ of state power and representative of the will of all the people,[1] has not (constitutionally) considered the fundamental nature of the right to energy. Despite this, the constitutional postulates put into effect in 2019 enshrine the importance of the right to energy as a fundamental right for constitutional effectiveness in the national legal system.

For the constitutional analysis of this section, this research, to establish a didactic order, will analyse the constituent parts of the Constitution of the Republic of Cuba of 2019 under the light of the right to energy. To do so, it will start from the constitutional preamble, where socialism and communism are declared as the only systems where human beings achieve their full dignity. From this proclamation, human

[1] Cf. Article 102. "The National Assembly of People's Power is the supreme organ of state power. It represents the whole people and expresses their sovereign will." (Own translation) Constitución de la República de Cuba (2019).

J. G. Luis Cordova, *Theoretical and Legal Dimensions of the Right to Energy*, Economic and Financial Law & Policy – Shifting Insights & Values 9, https://doi.org/10.1007/978-3-032-33252-3_8

dignity as the supreme constitutional value is imposed on the legal system, which is reinforced in Article 1.

> **Article 1**
> "Cuba is a socialist state of law and social justice, democratic, independent and sovereign, organised with all and for the good of all as a unitary and indivisible republic, founded on the work, dignity, humanism and ethics of its citizens for the enjoyment of freedom, equity, equality, solidarity, well-being and individual and collective prosperity." (Own translation)[2]

This position is reaffirmed by the "enhanced protection clause"[3] contained in the formula of article 13 (f) as one of the purposes of the State and that, in article 40, dignity is conceived as "the supreme value that underpins the recognition and exercise of the rights and duties enshrined in the Constitution, treaties and laws."[4]

To guarantee the effectiveness of dignity as a constitutional value, access to energy is an indispensable need for all human beings.[5] Therefore, the fundamental right to energy must be recognised, respected, protected, and fulfilled unconditionally by the State to guarantee human dignity.[6]

Human dignity as a fundamental value is intrinsically related to the unity of human rights as a whole. In this sense, Barak conceives of this phenomenon through three ways of manifestation that have implications for the conception of human dignity as an essential principle that should inform the right to energy in Cuba. In this regard, Barak defines the implications of human dignity as the normative basis of constitutional rights, as a principle of interpretation of constitutional rights, and as a determining element of proportionality in the legal limits of constitutional rights.[7]

Therefore, the conception of human dignity as the supreme constitutional value of the Constitution of the Republic of Cuba of 2019 implies that it becomes an argument for the existence of the right to energy as a human right. In turn, this constitutional value becomes a principle of interpretation of the fundamental norms that make up the Cuban Constitution, opening the framework for recognising the right to energy as a fundamental right.

In addition, given the constitutional supremacy principle, human dignity becomes a principle of interpretation of the infra-constitutional norms that make up the Cuban legal system. This effect impacts the protection of the right to energy, given that an affectation to the satisfaction of energy needs implies a detriment to human dignity. Thus, the competent body must determine the meaning and scope of the

---

[2] Cf. Article 1. Constitución de la República de Cuba (2019).

[3] Attard Bellido (2021), p. 67.

[4] Cf. Article 40. Constitución de la República de Cuba (2019).

[5] Costa (2009), p. 132.

[6] Sin-Hang Ngai (2012), p. 605.

[7] Barak (2015), pp. 103–104; Chaskalson (2011); Kroeze (2001); Henk (2009); Woolman (2012).

legal norms related to the abovementioned violation to protect the elements that this research defines as part of the right to energy.

The third implication of the recognition of human dignity as a fundamental value in the Constitution of the Republic of Cuba of 2019 concerns the limits of fundamental rights established in Article 45.

Article 45

"The exercise of the rights of individuals is limited only by the rights of others, collective security, general welfare, respect for public order, the Constitution and the law." (Own translation)[8]

In this sense, human dignity is a limit to the limits imposed on exercising fundamental rights in Cuba. For this reason, any limit applied to the exercise of fundamental rights must consider the relationship between the harm it will cause to human dignity and the benefits that will result from it. Based on the above, it is considered that the declaration of human dignity as a supreme value obliges a cost-benefit assessment in establishing limits to the exercise of fundamental rights. In particular, this obligation must be respected concerning socio-economic rights because of the determining function of existence in conditions of dignity.

The Constitution of the Republic of Cuba of 2019 enshrines humanism as another constitutional value in conjunction with the above.[9] This value has an inescapable relationship with the right to energy due to several factors. One is the status of the right to energy as a human right in the process of formation. If the constitutional text frames human beings as central, the recognition and protection of the right to energy is enshrined as a premise for the protection of human beings. In this sense, the enshrinement of humanism is closely related to energy justice since it emphasises the protection of human beings regarding the satisfaction of their energy needs.[10]

Linked to the humanist character of the Cuban state, another of the elements that can be deduced from Article 1 of the Cuban Constitution is the condition of a Socialist State based on the rule of law and social justice. During the constitutional referendum process, the first definition of this notion declared that the structure and functioning of the Cuban state are governed by the Constitution and the rest of the normative provisions that make up the Cuban legal system.

However, according to Villabella Armengol, understanding the notion of the Socialist State of Law and Social Justice is still developing. Villabella Armengol defends a series of postulates that involve, among others, the rule of the constitution and the direct efficacy of its norms, the recognition and guarantee of all fundamental rights, human dignity and non-discrimination as essential values, and the development of public policies oriented towards equity and social justice. All these

[8] Cf. Article 45. Constitución de la República de Cuba (2019).

[9] Cf. Article 1. Constitución de la República de Cuba (2019).

[10] Bombaerts et al. (2020), p. 249.

premises are closely related to the need for constitutional recognition of the right to energy.[11]

From this context, the ideal of social justice on which the Cuban state is constituted has particular implications for a future fundamental right to energy in Cuba. Once again, energy manifests itself as a factor interconnected with social justice, giving rise to energy justice as an emerging concept.[12] In this way, the constitutional configuration of social justice as a pillar of the Socialist State of Law in Cuba implies a commitment to energy justice and the right to energy. Thus, this commitment implies providing energy to all regarding availability, accessibility, affordability, and reliability.[13]

Another of the pillars of the Cuban state is its democratic, independent, and sovereign character. For the materialisation of these three categories, the energy sphere cannot be ignored, and this would benefit what this research understands as the right to energy. The dependence of Cuban society, like any other society in the world, on the energy system makes it vulnerable.

This vulnerability increases as energy dependence increases, so control over the efficient functioning of the national energy system strengthens Cuba's independence and sovereignty. The consumption of energy for the functioning of society cannot be avoided, but how energy is produced and consumed becomes a goal and a challenge[14] for the Cuban energy system for the observance of Article 1 of the Constitution. Therefore, for the Cuban state to preserve its democratic, independent, and sovereign character, these three characteristics must also be transferred to the energy sector of the Caribbean nation. In this way, the future constitutional recognition of the right to energy would have several ways of being realised.

Added to this is the link between the right to energy and other constitutional postulates, such as those encapsulated in Article 1 of the Cuban Constitution. This article enshrines "freedom, equity, equality, solidarity, well-being and individual and collective prosperity"[15] as objectives of the Socialist State of Law and social justice.

Such affirmations support the need for the right to energy as a fundamental right with profound implications for fulfilling the objectives constitutionally enshrined in Article 1. These implications have globally placed issues related to energy security and access to energy as central issues of justice today. For this reason, according to Sovacool and Dworkin, a decent and stable society must be free of energy injustices.[16]

The enforceability of Article 1 of the Constitution in all its magnitude and of the rest of the constitutional mandates is safeguarded by constitutional supremacy as

[11] Villabella Armengol (2023), p. 4.

[12] Bombaerts et al. (2020), p. 5.

[13] McCauley (2018), p. 11.

[14] Timmermann and Noboa (2022), p. 54.

[15] Cf. Article 1. Constitución de la República de Cuba (2019).

[16] Sovacool and Dworkin (2014), p. 436; Sovacool and Dworkin (2015), p. 5; Pachauri et al. (2013), p. 1.

the guiding principle of the Cuban Constitution. Accordingly, Article 7 is formulated, declaring the Constitution the supreme norm.

> **Article 7**
> "The Constitution is the supreme legal norm of the State. Everyone is obliged to comply with it. The provisions and acts of the organs of the State, its managers, officials, and employees, as well as of organisations, entities, and individuals, shall follow its provisions." (Own translation)[17]

The configuration of this constitutional article ensures the observance of the fundamental norm of the Cuban legal system. The above is a consequence of the principle of constitutional supremacy, which reflects the quality of the Cuban Constitution as the norm that gives origin and validity to the national legal system.[18]

Therefore, according to Kelsen, every norm's validity depends on the norm's validity that gave rise to it.[19] This affirmation means that the norms developed by the Cuban Constitution obey its mandates and, therefore, contribute to the realisation of its content. This undeniable reality has an impact on the support of the right to energy as a future fundamental right.

Obeying constitutional supremacy obliges legislative bodies to ensure the coherence of the legal system by revoking, suspending, or repealing legal norms that contradict the Constitution of the Republic of Cuba of 2019. The enactment of all provisions at the constitutional level that safeguard the elements that make up the right to energy is safeguarded in the effectiveness of the principle of constitutional supremacy. This context also concerns the justiciability of fundamental rights through effective protection mechanisms configured by the legal system.[20] Therefore, constitutional supremacy encompasses the indirect protection of the right to energy, as will be analysed later in this research.

Another essential constitutional premise of the right to energy is Article 8, which declares international treaties in force for Cuba as part of the Cuban legal system or integrated into it.

---

[17] Cf. Article 8. Constitución de la República de Cuba (2019).

[18] Ferrer Mac-Gregor Poisot et al. (2006), p. 17.

[19] Kelsen (1982), p. 202.

[20] Prieto Valdés (2022), p. 97.

Article 8

"The provisions of international treaties in force for the Republic of Cuba form part of or are integrated, as appropriate, into the national legal system. The Constitution of the Republic of Cuba takes precedence over these international treaties." (Own translation)[21]

This constitutional norm substantially impacts the recognition of human rights contained in international legal instruments to which Cuba is a signatory.[22] This impact is reinforced by the principle of constitutional supremacy, making international legal treaties part of the Cuban Constitution, as it happens in similar cases.[23] The reinforcement is also made by Article 16, paragraph g), through which the defence and protection of human rights become a basis for the international relations of the Caribbean state.[24]

Article 9

"Strict compliance with socialist legality is an obligation of all. The organs of the state, its managers, officials, and employees ensure that it is respected in the life of society as a whole and act within the limits of their respective competencies." (Own translation)[25]

Another relevant constitutional premise not only for the right to energy but also for the observance of the law in Cuba is the principle of socialist legality. This principle, in continuity with the 1976 Constitution, is rooted in Article 9 of the Constitution of the Republic of Cuba of 2019.

In the opinion of Justafré García and León Rodríguez, the principle of socialist legality breaks with the tradition of the principle of bourgeois legality since, according to these authors, for the first time, laws do not arise from class contradictions. Thus, socialist legality in Cuba governs the state and society. The socialist legality principle implies that the constitutional pronouncements that have been and will be analysed and their implications have a strict application reinforced by the principle of constitutional supremacy. Socialist legality is a guiding principle of public power, administration, and Cuban society, which obliges the strict observance of the Constitution and the laws.[26]

This principle affects the realisation of the normative provisions supporting the right to energy. The promulgation of the constitutional principles and values, the

[21] Cf. Article 8. Constitución de la República de Cuba (2019).

[22] The incorporation of international human rights treaties into the Cuban legal system demonstrates the importance that the Cuban government attaches to the full exercise of these rights. However, this entails the subsequent promulgation of infra-constitutional norms that develop the precepts of the Constitution of the Republic of Cuba of 2019 relating to the aforementioned international treaties. Diéguez La O and Fraga Acosta (2022), p. 46.

[23] Cf. de Luna Ávila et al. (2005), p. 17; Uribe Benítez (2009), p. 36.

[24] Cf. Article 16 g). Constitución de la República de Cuba (2019).

[25] Cf. Article 8. Constitución de la República de Cuba (2019).

[26] Justafré García and León Rodríguez (2014), pp. 4–5.

fundamental rights, and other provisions of the Constitution of the Republic of Cuba of 2019, as well as the rest of the legal system norms, have become applicable. Thus, the principle of socialist legality reinforces the protection of the right to energy and calls on the legal system to recognise it as a means of realising its norms.

Following the analysis of socialist legality as a constitutional principle and its impact on the observance of Cuba's fundamental norm, the constitutional system leads this investigation to Article 10.[27] This article establishes popular control as a mechanism for state and government oversight through the following formula.

The analysis of this article is based on the urgency of satisfying everyone's energy needs, which is a fundamental necessity for everyone. In this context, the following question arises: How would the state and the government be subject to popular control in cases where decisions of any kind are taken that result in a detriment to the satisfaction of energy needs?

Given that the Cuban Constitution does not expressly recognise the right to energy, the context described above would be affected by a relative absence of constitutional foundations for exercising popular control in the energy sphere. Article 10, although it suffers from shortcomings due to the limited scope of the Cuban Constitution in protecting the right to energy, becomes a call for reflection on the part of the legislative function in Cuba. In this sense, recognising this right is imperative for popular and other types of control over the right to energy.

> **Article 10**
> "The organs of the State, their managers, officials and employees are obliged to respect, attend to and respond to the people, maintain close ties with them and submit to their control, in the forms established in the Constitution and the laws."[28]

Continuing with the constitutional analysis, article 11, without constituting a reference for the recognition of the right to energy, in paragraphs b) and c) establishes the sovereignty and jurisdiction of the State over natural resources, which include energy resources.[29] This constitutional provision allows the State to dispose of the energy resources available in the national territory to guarantee the satisfaction of energy availability as an element of the content of the right under study.

In this way, it contributes to guaranteeing the enjoyment and exercise of the rest of the rights enshrined in the Constitution as another of the essential purposes of the State according to Article 13.

[27] Cf. Article 101. "The organs of the state are constituted and carry out their activities on the basis of the principles of socialist democracy, which are expressed in the following rules: (…) b) the popular control the activity of state bodies, their managers and officials, deputies, and delegates, in accordance with the provisions of the law." (Own translation) Constitución de la República de Cuba (2019).

[28] Cf. Article 10. Constitución de la República de Cuba (2019).

[29] Cf. Article 11 (b) and (c). Constitución de la República de Cuba (2019).

Article 13

"The essential aims of the state are:

a) to channel the efforts of the nation into the construction of socialism and to strengthen national unity,

b) to maintain and defend the independence, integrity, and sovereignty of the homeland,

c) to preserve national security,

d) to guarantee effective equality in the enjoyment and exercise of rights and the fulfilment of the duties enshrined in the Constitution and the laws,

e) to promote sustainable development that ensures individual and collective prosperity, and to obtain greater levels of equity and social justice, as well as to preserve and multiply the achievements of the Revolution,

f) to guarantee the full dignity of the people and their full development,

g) to strengthen the ideology and ethics inherent to our socialist society,

h) to protect the natural, historical, and cultural heritage of the nation and

i) to ensure the educational, scientific, technical, and cultural development of the country." (Own translation)[30]

In addition, according to subparagraph (c), the realisation of the right to energy even becomes a matter of national security, another of the essential purposes of the State. This relationship is because the impact on energy services has consequences on other essential services of various kinds, such as transport, communications, water supply and other systems that have come to be defined as critical infrastructures.[31]

Since Article 1 and reaffirmed by Article 13 d) and e) of the Constitution, equity and equality have been constitutional paradigms extended to the rest of this legal body. That is why equity and equality are reinforced by the wording of Article 42, which states:

[30] Cf. Article 13. Constitución de la República de Cuba (2019).

[31] Cornell (2009), p. 69.

Article 42

"All persons are equal before the law, receive equal protection and treatment from the authorities and enjoy the same rights, freedoms and opportunities, without any discrimination based on sex, gender, sexual orientation, gender identity, age, ethnic origin, skin colour, religious belief, disability, national or territorial origin, or any other personal condition or circumstance that implies a distinction detrimental to human dignity." (Own translation)[32]

Equity and equality, as constitutional principles, have notable implications for the right to energy. Such principles have been incorporated into the energy justice framework. In this area, the two constitutional principles oblige maintaining a balanced relationship between those considered active and passive subjects of the right to energy. These principles presuppose the fair participation of both subjects in energy decision-making processes.[33]

In addition to equity and equality among the subjects of the right to energy, there is an equal balance among all population sectors for universal and fair access to energy. This balance within the Cuban population implies the disparity that may occur between the different sectors of Cuban society, whether due to geographic location (urban or rural contexts), differences in economic income, or any other condition that causes similar effects.

Related to the promotion of equity and equality concerning the right to energy, one element that cannot be left out of the analysis is the gender issue. For this reason, Article 43 is aligned with gender equality as follows:

Article 43

"Women and men have equal rights and responsibilities in the economic, political, cultural, labour, social, family, and other fields. The state guarantees that both are offered the same opportunities and possibilities.

The state promotes the integral development of women and their full social participation. (…)" (Own translation)[34]

This article has broad implications, given the link between energy and gender, which has generated much international debate. Despite the variety of genders in today's society, it is undeniable that access to energy has been considered an empowering factor in the fight against discrimination and the social inclusion of women and girls. This reality led to the appearance of the first antecedent of the right to energy in the Convention on the Elimination of All Forms of Discrimination Against Women.

In this way, the Cuban Constitution echoes gender equality and implies adopting policies and regulations that make this aspiration a reality. Especially in the case of women and girls as the gender most affected by energy poverty at the global level,[35]

---

[32] Cf. Article 42. Constitución de la República de Cuba (2019).

[33] Sovacool et al. (2014), p. 13.

[34] Cf. Article 43. Constitución de la República de Cuba (2019).

[35] Winther et al. (2017) and Rewald (2017).

the Cuban legal system is obliged by constitutional mandate to fight against this phenomenon. Access to energy facilitates the full social participation of women and girls, leaving behind the harmful effects of the lack of this essential resource.[36]

In addition to the above, there is another aspect of equity. This condition transcends generations, which is why intergenerational equity is prioritised regarding energy justice.[37] Therefore, the declaration of the constitutional principle of equity obliges energy policy and energy law in Cuba to ensure the satisfaction of the energy needs of present generations without putting at risk the satisfaction of the energy needs of future generations.[38] This obligation to ensure the satisfaction of energy needs also implies the rational use of natural resources, especially non-renewable ones, due to their limited lifespan and polluting nature.[39]

Among other essential purposes of the Cuban State, where the right to energy has a determining character, are those defined in article 13, which are contained in paragraphs e), f) and i).

The first refers to sustainable development, individual and collective prosperity, equity, and social justice. These last three elements have already been analysed above as part of Article 1 of the Constitution. That is why the analysis will focus on sustainable development and prosperity.

Without entering doctrinal disquisitions regarding the conceptualisation of sustainable development and prosperity, it is necessary to consider several relevant factors. Without implying an order of priority, the first element is the 2030 Agenda. This roadmap outlines the main guidelines for sustainable development based on the combination of economic, social, and environmental aspects.

Sustainable Development Goal 7, closely related to the right to energy, aims to achieve universal access to affordable, reliable, sustainable, and modern energy services.[40] Given the spirit of this sustainable development goal, it is impossible to promote sustainable development and prosperity as an essential goal of the Cuban state without guaranteeing the realisation of the right to energy.

In this sense, States have taken advantage of this undeniable reality, and as a result, sustainable development goal 7 has become the most influential within the 2030 Agenda in public policies.[41] The aforementioned sustainable development goal has a determining nature in other goals of the 2030 Agenda, such as the eradication of poverty and hunger, health and well-being, quality education, gender equality and the empowerment of women and girls, access to water, economic growth, reduction of inequalities, climate action, sustainable cities and communities, among others.

In this context, it is impossible not to mention the role of renewable energy sources, which have undeniably proven to be a practical and realistic alternative for

[36] Pueyo and Maestre (2019), Pueyo (2020), Wilhite (2017) and Clancy et al. (2017).

[37] Sovacool (2013), pp. 164–193.

[38] Opal and Nathwani (2023), p. 301.

[39] Caney (2011).

[40] Department of Economic and Social Affairs (2015).

[41] Heffron (2021), p. 13.

sustainable development.[42] Renewable energy sources have been considered in Article 16 f) of the Constitution of the Republic of Cuba of 2019, which promotes the protection and conservation of the environment and the fight against climate change,[43] whereby the energy transition to renewable energy sources is the only way forward.

Another of the purposes of the State contained in Article 13, paragraphs f) and i) are those aimed at guaranteeing and ensuring the full dignity of persons and their full development within the educational, scientific, technical, and cultural development of persons. This aim is accompanied by Article 47, which recognises the fundamental right to the free development of the personality.

Article 47

"People have the right to the free development of their personality and must behave towards each other in a spirit of respect, fraternity and solidarity."[44]

The interrelation between a dignified life and the integral development of people is undeniable, and in this area, the right to energy is a basic premise for the materialisation of both conditions. This interrelation is evident in the psychological, affective, social, and cultural development, which, according to Martínez Miguélez, has as one of its central nuclei the variety of opportunities for interaction provided by the surrounding environment.[45] In this sense, full development will be determined by the variety of resources available to the individual, including access to energy as one of the most important.

Following the analysis of the essential ends of the Cuban state, one element worth highlighting is that the recognition and protection of the right to energy transcend its obvious necessity as a fundamental right. The right to energy becomes a matter of national interest, given that the satisfaction of most of the essential ends of the Cuban State, contained in Article 13, depends on the realisation of the right to energy. The electrification of Cuban households marked a significant advancement in fulfilling the right to energy, facilitated by modern technologies that replaced previous ones known for their detrimental effects on people's health.

8.2 Constitutional Economic Foundations and the Right to Energy

The right to energy also finds part of its constitutional basis in the interrelationship between Article 18 and Article 23. From this interrelationship, elements aligned with the Cuban social project can be deduced that positively impact the right to energy. Article 18 establishes:

---

[42] Singh et al. (2021), p. 3.

[43] Cf. Article 16 f). Constitución de la República de Cuba (2019).

[44] Cf. Article 47. Constitución de la República de Cuba (2019).

[45] Martínez Miguélez (2009), p. 126.

Article 18
"The Republic of Cuba is governed by a system of socialist economy based on the ownership by all the people of the basic means of production as the principal form of property, and the planned management of the economy, which takes into consideration, regulates and controls the market in the interests of society." (Own translation)[46]

While article 23 declares:

Article 23
"Belongs to the socialist property of the whole people: the lands that do not belong to private individuals or cooperatives formed by them, the subsoil, mineral deposits, mines, forests, waters, beaches, communication routes and natural resources, both living and non-living, within the exclusive economic zone of the Republic." (Own translation)[47]

Two essential elements emerge from the two previous articles that impact the protection of what this research defines as the right to energy. The first of these is the ownership by all the people of the principal means of production, and the second is economic regulation following the interests of society.

The first of these elements has been rooted in the Cuban constitutional tradition since the 1976 Constitution and is maintained in the current constitution. Although the type of socialist ownership by all the people of the principal means of production still suffers from certain inaccuracies,[48] it has a deep political background.

Nevertheless, technically and legally, the Cuban Constitution recognises the ownership of all the people over the national energy resources. These include mineral deposits, mines, forests, water, and other natural resources. Although this type of ownership is exercised by the Cuban state, constitutionally, the Cuban state reflects the people's power;[49] therefore, the use of energy resources will always be in the interests of Cuban society.

The people's power is reinforced by the declaration in Article 18, which states that the Cuban state considers, regulates, and controls the economy in the best interests of Cuban society. This context places the satisfaction of the energy needs of Cuban society as a priority at the level of constitutional technique.

This scenario is echoed in Article 24 when it states:

---

[46] Cf. Article 18. Constitución de la República de Cuba (2019).

[47] Cf. Article 23. Constitución de la República de Cuba (2019).

[48] Cutié Mustelier and Méndez López (2008), p. 63; Fernández Martínez (2020), p. 80.

[49] Cf. Article 22. "The following forms of property are recognised: a) socialist property of the whole people: in which the State acts on behalf of and for the benefit of the people as owner (…)" (Own translation) Constitución de la República de Cuba (2019).

Article 24

"The socialist property of the whole people includes other assets such as infrastructures of general interest, major industries and economic and social facilities, as well as others of a strategic nature for the economic and social development of the country." (Own translation)[50]

This constitutional pronouncement declares infrastructures of general interest and large industries to be the socialist property of the whole people. This pronouncement implies that, under this type of ownership, the energy industry is part of the energy sector that guarantees the availability, accessibility, and reliability of energy. According to Article 24, this type of industry is focused on economic and social development and, therefore, positively impacts the satisfaction of Cuban society's energy needs.

Continuing with this thread, the satisfaction of energy needs thus becomes a state responsibility exercised through the socialist state enterprise. This economic actor is designated as the main subject of the national economy in Article 27 of the Constitution.

Article 27

"The socialist state enterprise is the main subject of the national economy. It has autonomy in its administration and management; it mainly produces goods and services and fulfils its social responsibilities." (Own translation)

Thus, under the formula of "social responsibility", this research elucidates the protection of availability, accessibility, affordability, and reliability as elements that make up the content of the right to energy. However, energy production is a social necessity on which the materialisation of constitutional postulates depends, despite being an economic necessity for the country, especially those related to fundamental rights.

Another constitutional premise, which relates to affordability as an element of the right to energy, is interpreted in the third paragraph of Article 31 of the Constitution of the Republic of Cuba of 2019. This postulate declares that "remuneration by the work contributed is supplemented by the equal and free provision of universal social services and other allowances and benefits."[51]

Although the direct reference of such a precept is to public services such as health and education, in the view of the author of this research, it also concerns, to some extent, public energy services. This consideration is based on how the tariffs for energy services work in Cuba. Without sufficient quantitative references regarding the system of energy subsidies in Cuba, including electricity,[52] gas, and fuels

[50] Cf. Article 24. Constitución de la República de Cuba (2019).

[51] Cf. Article 31. Constitución de la República de Cuba (2019).

[52] According to Dacal Díaz, subsidies related to social spending, including electricity tariffs, amounted to 36.554 billion pesos in 2017. Dacal Díaz (2020), p. 50.

such as gasoline and diesel, this reality today has multiple implications for the national economy.

Although the practice in neoliberal economies in the face of energy crises is to deregulate price increases, in Cuba, the reality is entirely different. Energy tariffs and prices may seem immutable over time, with one of the most recent exceptions being the monetary reunification process that the country faced in 2021.[53]

At the end of 2019, with the approval of the monetary unification process, a tariff reform of the prices of energy services was developed in Cuba. This reform was aimed at eliminating undue energy subsidies. After the dissemination of the new tariffs within the broad publicity campaign surrounding the process of monetary reordering, a broad wave of debate was generated, given that the new tariffs were not coherent with the salaries received by the Cuban population.[54]

The increase in electricity prices rose from 4 CUP to 7.5 CUP for households with consumption between 301–350 KWh/month. In cases where consumption was above 351 KWh/month, the price of energy was no longer subsidised, which would have a negative impact on the affordability of energy. Following the unfavourable public opinion on this measure, the tariffs were reduced based on the reduction of costs, and the subsidised consumption was extended to 500 KWh per month, among other measures.[55]

Considering the country's difficulty in developing normal commercial relations with suppliers, the Cuban government has maintained a protective umbrella over the Cuban population in the face of the volatility of the world energy market. Such subsidies, while they may be ignored by many of the Caribbean nation's inhabitants, serve to supplement their economic income. Such income could be insufficient to cover people's energy needs if they were fully exposed to energy shocks as much of the world's population is.

8.3 Framing the Right to Energy Within the Interconnectedness of Fundamental Rights

Following the logic of constitutional systematics, by analysing the dogmatic part of the Cuban Constitution, new elements appear that serve as a basis for the right to energy. To begin the analysis, we start with the interdependence of human rights as indicated in article 41.

[53] Ministerio de Economía y Planificación de Cuba (2021).

[54] Cf. Ministerio de Economía y Planificación de Cuba (2021) and Alonso Falcón et al. (2020).

[55] Cf. Ministerio de Economía y Planificación de Cuba (2021) and Alonso Falcón et al. (2020).

Article 41

"The Cuban State recognises and guarantees the unrenounceable, imprescriptible, indivisible, universal and interdependent enjoyment, and exercise of human rights, following the principles of progressiveness, equality, and non-discrimination. Respect for and guarantee of these rights is obligatory for all." (Own translation)[56]

This article establishes the obligation of the Cuban state to recognise and guarantee human rights and obliges everyone to respect them. This article points out several elements inherent to exercising human rights, including their inalienable, imprescriptible, indivisible, universal and interdependent nature.

These postulates have a remarkable impact on the right to energy as a human right. In this sense, interdependence is highlighted as an aspect of significant importance for studying the constitutional bases of the right to energy in Cuba. Interdependence means that the infringement of the right to energy "inexorably implies the infringement of other rights that form a coherent and harmonious whole".[57]

The constitutional provisions of Article 41 regarding human rights support the right to energy in the Convention on the Elimination of All Forms of Discrimination against Women (CEDAW).[58] In this context, it is essential to point out that Cuba was the first country to sign and the second to ratify the Convention. As a result, according to the Committee on the Elimination of Discrimination against Women in 1999, Cuba was recognised as a country entirely consistent with the principles and legislation to protect women's rights in all areas of society.[59] By signing and ratifying the Convention, Cuba committed to the realisation of its postulates and, as part of them, to the right to energy.[60]

Moreover, article 41 is a solid basis for analysing the right to energy and its interdependence with the plexus of fundamental rights in the Constitution of the Republic of Cuba of 2019. The implications of the right to energy on fundamental rights in Cuba are highly relevant to assessing the importance of its recognition as a fundamental right.

Despite the multiple interconnections of the right to energy with the rest of the fundamental rights, this analysis will focus on those rights where the right under study has a more significant impact. This situation is most pronounced in the case of fundamental rights of a socio-economic nature. This result is because the internal relationship between socio-economic rights is characterised by reinforcing connections between them.[61]

---

[56] Cf. Article 41. Constitución de la República de Cuba (2019).

[57] Rafael Urquilla (1995), p. 262.

[58] Organización de Naciones Unidas (1979).

[59] Committee on the Elimination of Discrimination Against Women (1999), p. 2.

[60] Cf. already supra, pp. 56–57.

[61] Farese (2020), p. 105.

Such reinforcement implies that, while interdependence is an intrinsic characteristic of human rights,[62] it manifests itself most strongly in the relationships between socio-economic rights. Considering that such a typology of rights aims to achieve "an adequate standard of living for people within a concept of human dignity,"[63] the right to energy is recognized and integrated as a socio-economic right and, thus, an indispensable right.

From the context described above, the analysis of the dogmatic part of the Constitution of the Republic of Cuba of 2019 begins with Article 46.

> **Article 46**
> "All persons have the right to life, physical and moral integrity, liberty, justice, security, peace, health, education, culture, recreation, sport and to their full development." (Own translation)[64]

This article is loaded with meaning with a multiplicity of fundamental rights subsequently developed constitutionally, including the right to life, health, education, recreation, sport and, as already analysed, the right to complete development.

Recognizing and protecting those fundamental rights and the right to energy have a clear interdependent relationship. In this regard, in 2010, the United Nations Secretary-General's Advisory Group on Energy and Climate Change established an incremental system of access levels in defining access to energy.

This system is based on three levels according to the type of needs that energy access satisfies at each level. The first level of energy access declares basic needs intricately linked to the fundamental rights recognised by Article 46, including health, education, communication, and community services.[65]

The second level of access is the productive uses of energy, which includes agricultural production related to water pumping, irrigation, fertilisers, and mechanised land use. Commercial energy use and energy use in the transport sector are also included. In this way, the Consultative Group highlights the importance of these two levels of energy access to satisfy basic and productive needs for improving life and economic development in developing countries.[66]

In this way, without the realisation of the right to energy, fundamental rights such as life, health, education, and even physical education, sports, and recreation would only be partially realised.

---

[62] Neves-Silva et al. (2019).

[63] González Monguí (2009), p. 5.

[64] Cf. Article 46. Constitución de la República de Cuba (2019).

[65] The Secretary-General's Advisory Group on Energy and Climate Change (2010), p. 13.

[66] The Secretary-General's Advisory Group on Energy and Climate Change (2010), p. 13.

Article 72
Public health is a right of all people, and it is the responsibility of the State to guarantee access to free and quality care, protection, and recovery services.

To make this right effective, the State institutes a health system at all levels accessible to the population and develops prevention and education programmes to which society and families contribute.

The law defines how health services are provided.

Article 73
Education is the right of all persons and the responsibility of the State, which guarantees free, affordable, and quality education services for comprehensive training from early childhood to postgraduate university education.

The state establishes a broad system of educational institutions at all types and levels of education to make this right effective, which provides the possibility of studying at any stage of life following aptitudes, social demands, and the needs of the country's economic and social development.

Society and families are responsible for education. The law defines the scope of compulsory education, the basic general education that, as a minimum, must be acquired, the education of adults and those postgraduate or other complementary studies that, exceptionally, may be remunerated.

Article 74
"People have the right to physical education, sports, and recreation as essential elements of their quality of life.

The national education system guarantees the inclusion of physical education and sports teaching and practice as part of the comprehensive education of children, adolescents, and young people.

The State creates the conditions to guarantee the necessary resources dedicated to the promotion and practice of sport and recreation for the people and for the preparation, care, and development of sporting talent." (Own translation)[67]

To better understand the above, the implications of the right to energy on the above-mentioned fundamental rights will be analysed in detail.

The fundamental right to life, as the first right outlined in article 46 of the Cuban Constitution, according to the Inter-American Court of Human Rights, not only involves the right not to be arbitrarily deprived of life. Its content extends to the right of human beings not to be prevented from accessing the conditions that determine a dignified existence. Hence, the state's obligation to guarantee and protect

[67] Cf. Articles 72, 73, 74. Constitución de la República de Cuba (2019).

access to energy services and conditions arises as a basic premise for the realisation of the right to life in Cuba.[68]

Regarding the right to health, the level of realisation of the right to energy primarily impacts two scenarios. According to the World Health Organisation, the first scenario arises at the household level, where the lack of clean fuels and cooking technologies leads to prominent levels of air pollution, causing 3.2 million deaths per year. Such cases arise especially for women and children, who are usually responsible for collecting firewood and cooking food. The second scenario is in health care facilities. Here, energy access is vital to ensure the quality, accessibility, and reliability of health services.[69]

Regarding the right to education, energy is an indispensable commodity and the right to energy guarantees diverse benefits in the education sector. In this regard, the United Nations Department of Economic and Social Affairs points out that among the most important are lighting and the extension of study hours.[70]

Those conditions facilitate the improvement of the quantity and quality of learning and, therefore, directly impact literacy. Facilities for using information and communication technologies are also noted, leading to improved student performance and schooling, among many other benefits. In turn, the availability of and access to energy contributes to teacher retention and training. All the benefits of energy availability and access, in turn, result in improved school performance and can have a measurable impact on communities regarding reduced migration and women's empowerment, among others.[71]

Regarding the right to physical education, sport and recreation, Article 74 recognises that it is the responsibility of the State to create the necessary conditions for the realisation of this fundamental right.[72] The creation of such conditions involves the development of the necessary energy infrastructure and the supply of energy to meet the energy demand of these types of activities. Given the importance of energy for developing sporting activities, their energy consumption is a determining factor. For this reason, sporting activities have even been intended as a context for combating climate change by exploiting renewable energy sources.[73]

---

[68] Para. 144. "The right to life is a fundamental human right, the enjoyment of which is a prerequisite for the enjoyment of all other human rights. prerequisite for the enjoyment of all other human rights. If it is not respected, all rights are meaningless. Because of the fundamental nature of the right to life, restrictive approaches to it are not admissible. In essence, the fundamental right to life comprises not only the right of every human being not to be arbitrarily deprived of life, but also the right not to be denied access to conditions that guarantee a dignified existence. States have the obligation to ensure the creation of the conditions required to prevent violations of this basic right and, in particular, the duty to prevent their agents from violating it." (Own translation) Corte Interamericana de Derechos Humanos (1999); Galán Melo (2019), p. 130.

[69] World Health Organization (2023).

[70] Cf. Department of Economic and Social Affairs (2014).

[71] Cf. Department of Economic and Social Affairs (2014).

[72] Cf. Article 74. Constitución de la República de Cuba (2019).

[73] Bas and Zohouri Haghian (2022).

An extremely relevant right is recognised by Article 77, which considers basic and productive needs as the first two incremental levels of access to energy.

Article 77
"Everyone has the right to healthy and adequate food. The state creates the conditions to strengthen the food security of the entire population." (Own translation)[74]

From this constitutional postulate, the right to food is recognised as a fundamental right, which depends to a substantial extent on agricultural production for its realisation. In this way, it is essential to highlight that agricultural production depends on the existence of the second incremental level of access to energy. Considering the importance of this type of food production, agriculture constitutes the basis of food security.[75] Consequently, due to the energy-food nexus,[76] the realisation of the right to energy depends on agricultural production and, therefore, on the right to food in Cuba.

In conjunction with the incremental levels of energy access, the UN Secretary General's Advisory Group on Energy and Climate Change highlights a third level: modern societal needs. This level encompasses modern household appliances, space and water cooling and heating needs, and private transport. While all these elements relate to the fundamental rights described so far, the right to adequate housing and a safe and healthy habitat has a particular implication.

Article 71
"The right to adequate housing and safe and healthy habitat is recognised for all persons.

The State makes this right effective through housing construction, rehabilitation, and conservation programmes, with the participation of entities and the population, following public policies, land and urban planning regulations and laws." (Own translation)[77]

The realisation of the right to housing, constitutionally recognised as a fundamental right in Cuba, with its normative origin in the Universal Declaration of Human Rights[78] and the International Covenant on Economic, Social and Cultural Rights,[79] depends on the right to energy. Without the latter's realisation, the satisfaction of basic human needs and others considered inherent to modern societies would be only partial. Energy is the basis for such needs within the home, such as lighting,

[74] Cf. Article 77. Constitución de la República de Cuba (2019).

[75] García et al. (2006), p. 1.

[76] Refaat and Ismail (2017), Allan et al. (2015), Abdi et al. (2020), Yadav et al. (2021), Huntington et al. (2021) and van Gevelt (2020).

[77] Cf. Article 71. Constitución de la República de Cuba (2019).

[78] Cf. Article 25. Organización de Naciones Unidas (1948).

[79] Cf. Article 11. Organización de Naciones Unidas (1976).

cooking and refrigeration, learning, communication and entertainment, and air conditioning, among many others.[80]

For these reasons, the Office of the High Commissioner for Human Rights stresses that it is a progressive obligation of states to take measures to ensure universal and non-discriminatory access to energy services as essential services.[81] In this way, the realisation of the right to energy determines the satisfaction of the standards for the right to adequate housing.[82]

Energy affordability, for the complete satisfaction of the basic needs of all, plays a vital role in this objective, especially in vulnerable sectors with low incomes. As a measure of economic support, the Constitution of the Republic of Cuba of 2019 states:

> **Article 70**
> "The State, through social assistance, protects persons without resources or protection, unfit to work, who do not have family members in a position to help them, and families who, due to the insufficiency of their income, require it, following the law." (Own translation)[83]

The creation of a social assistance system, while not a mechanism to ensure universal energy affordability, provides support of an economic nature. This governmental support helps cover, among other basic needs, the energy costs of those vulnerable sectors of the population that cannot work. In this sense, the social assistance system derived from Article 70 covers those persons who do not have other economic support from family members for the reasons described in this article. Although policies and regulations for energy affordability must be promoted, whenever there is a situation of energy vulnerability, the intervention of the Cuban state will be required in coherence with the premises of the Constitution for the sake of human dignity.

Another fundamental right in the Constitution of the Republic of Cuba of 2019, where the right to energy has implications, is the right to information.

> **Article 53**
> "All persons have the right to request and receive truthful, objective and timely information from the State, and to access information generated by State bodies and entities, following established regulations." (Own translation)[84]

The interdependence between the two rights is appreciable. On the one hand, access to information depends on technological infrastructures that need energy to function. On the other hand, the realisation of the right to information greatly impacts the right to energy, especially reliability as part of its content.[85]

---

[80] Carvajal et al. (2020), pp. 19–32; Tirado-herrero (2023), p. 2.

[81] Oficina del Alto Comisionado para los Derechos Humanos (2010), p. 36.

[82] World Health Organization Regional Office for Europe (2007).

[83] Cf. Article 70. Constitución de la República de Cuba (2019).

[84] Cf. Article 53. Constitución de la República de Cuba (2019).

[85] Cf. already supra, Sect. 6.4.

Constitutional Article 61 establishes the channel for processing complaints and petitions before the competent authorities.

Article 61

"Individuals have the right to address complaints and petitions to the authorities, who are obliged to process them and provide timely, relevant and substantiated responses within the timeframe and according to the procedure established by law." (Own translation)[86]

This provision becomes a defence mechanism for holders in the event of violations of the right to energy. The right to complain or petition plays a significant role in Cuban reality, considering the structure and functioning of the energy sector. In this sense, the provision of energy services such as electricity and gas are qualified under the condition of public services in the framework of which the right of complaint or petition becomes a tool for the empowerment of the holders of the right to energy. Such empowerment is essential for situations of violation of the right to energy.

In this sense, providing energy services becomes an obligatory activity given that it satisfies a general interest of the State and, therefore, the object of public energy services. This situation is also because the organisation and operation of the energy sector in Cuba is the responsibility of the public administration.[87] This obligation to provide this type of public service is also protected by Article 98.

Article 98

"Any person who suffers damage or harm caused unduly by directors, officials and employees of the State because of the exercise of the functions proper to their positions has the right to claim and obtain the corresponding reparation or compensation in the manner established by law." (Own translation)[88]

This article constitutionally guarantees the right to claim and compensate the holders, in the case of the right to energy, for damages and losses caused unduly by directors, officials and employees of the State due to the exercise of their functions.

Another fundamental right intricately connected to the right to energy, and therefore deserving of analysis, is the right to work. Within the framework of this fundamental right, which is enshrined in Article 64 of the Constitution, in conjunction with Article 69 on the right to occupational safety and health, the right to energy is particularly important regarding adequate working conditions.

---

[86] Cf. Article 61. Constitución de la República de Cuba (2019).

[87] Cf. Matilla Correa (2008), pp. 421 and 431.

[88] Cf. Article 98. Constitución de la República de Cuba (2019).

Article 64
"The right to work is recognised. The person in a position to work has the right to obtain decent employment, following his or her choice, qualifications, aptitude and the demands of the economy and society. The state organises institutions and services to help working families carry out their responsibilities."

Article 69
"The State guarantees the right to safety and health at work by adopting appropriate measures to prevent occupational accidents and diseases. A person who suffers an accident at work or contracts an occupational disease is entitled to medical care, benefit, or retirement in temporary or permanent incapacity for work or other forms of social security protection." (Own translation)[89]

The fundamental right to work, with its normative origin in Article 23 of the Universal Declaration of Human Rights, requires satisfactory working conditions.[90] The interconnectivity of the right to energy and the right to work is an element worth highlighting. In this sense, the affectation of the right to energy will have repercussions on the existence of adequate working conditions and, consequently, will have marked impacts on workers' health and productivity.

Among the other fundamental rights enshrined in the constitutional text, in which the right to energy plays a significant role, is the right to water, recognised in Article 76.

Article 76
"Everyone has the right to water. The State creates the conditions to guarantee access to drinking water and sanitation, with due remuneration and rational use." (Own translation)[91]

Due to the energy-water nexus,[92] the two rights involved are interdependent. In this sense, the Cuban constitution makes the state responsible for creating the conditions to guarantee access to drinking water and sanitation. Because of the multiple energy uses, the realisation of the right to energy determines access to drinking water.

This condition can be seen in the set of activities that require energy for their proper functioning, among which can be mentioned pumping water, not only for distribution but also for lifting it to storage systems in the home, purification before use, collection and purification after use, and its transfer to different destinations depending on its purpose. In this context, it is essential to note that 5% of global energy use goes to water treatment and distribution. The right to energy is so

[89] Cf. Articles 64 and 69. Constitución de la República de Cuba (2019).

[90] Cf. Article 23. Organización de Naciones Unidas (1948).

[91] Cf. Article 76. Constitución de la República de Cuba (2019).

[92] Sklarew and Sklarew (2018), pp. 12–13; Fayiah et al. (2020); OECD and IEA (2016); Komendantova et al. (2020); Macharia et al. (2020).

necessary for the right to water that the increase in energy consumption in a country can be directly proportional to improving access to safe drinking water.[93]

So far, it has been explained how the non-realisation or partial realisation of the right to energy seriously threatens a large part of Cuba's constitutional dogma. In addition, Article 78 provides for the fundamental right to consume goods and services following requirements such as quality, equitable access, the safeguarding of health, and dignified and equitable treatment.

Article 78

"All persons have the right to consume quality goods and services that do not harm their health, and to have access to accurate and truthful information about them, as well as to be treated fairly and with dignity following the law." (Own translation)[94]

Such a constitutional provision is one of the most important foundations of the right to energy and one of the constitutional guarantees of its realisation. Although the approach to the right to energy from a consumer law perspective is incomplete for protecting the right to energy,[95] this constitutional reference is of utmost relevance.

The formula of Article 78 allows the inclusion of the Cuban Constitution in the trend of protecting the right to energy within the framework of the rights of users or consumers.[96] In this case, the Constitution of the Republic of Cuba of 2019 has followed this trend that has spread throughout the regulatory frameworks of Latin American and European continents. Although such an approach is unfinished, it can normatively offer a set of rights to the holders of the right to energy that promotes its protection.

However, in Cuba, energy services, like others of a public nature, face numerous challenges that jeopardise the realisation of the right to energy. In this sense, the lack of legal determination of essential public services under the state monopoly regime challenges public administration. This challenge harms the right to energy given the lack of regulation of the guarantees for providing public energy services.[97] Given this situation, the constitutional recognition and protection of the right to energy as a fundamental right in Cuba would legally guarantee its realisation by binding it on the state.

---

[93] Cf. Lloyd (2017), p. 57; Sovacool (2006).

[94] Cf. Article 78. Constitución de la República de Cuba (2019).

[95] Cf. already supra, pp. 181–182 and infra 332–333.

[96] Cf. already supra, Sect. 4.3.

[97] Gutiérrez Castillo et al. (2019), p. 72.

8.4 Effectiveness of Family Constitutional Provisions: A Call for a Right to Energy?

The analysis of the constitutional basis of the right to energy in Cuba continues with Chapter III of Title V: Families. The constitutional advances in family matters were palpable after their approval by referendum. In addition, the implications of the realisation of the right to energy in the family sphere are related to the arguments already analysed in this section. In this sense, Articles 86, 87, 88 and 89 aim to protect children, youth, older adults, and persons with disabilities.

> **Article 86**
> "The state, society, and families provide special protection to children and adolescents and guarantee their harmonious and comprehensive development by considering their best interests when making decisions and actions concerning them.
>
> Children and adolescents are considered full subjects of rights and enjoy those recognised in this Constitution and those inherent to their particular condition as developing persons. They are protected against all types of violence."
>
> **Article 87**
> "The state, society and families recognise young people as active participants in society and create the conditions for the full exercise of their rights and their full development."
>
> **Article 88**
> "The state, society, and families, as far as they are concerned, must protect, assist, and facilitate the conditions to satisfy the needs and raise the quality of life of older adults. Similarly, they must respect their self-determination, guarantee the full exercise of their rights, and promote their integration and social participation."
>
> **Article 89**
> "The state, society, and families must protect, promote, and ensure the full exercise of the rights of persons with disabilities. The state creates the conditions required for their rehabilitation or the improvement of their quality of life, personal autonomy, inclusion, and social participation." (Own translation)[98]

These constitutional norms establish a regime of co-responsibility between the State, society, and the family, with the creation of conditions that guarantee the protection and full development of children, the full exercise of rights and the full

[98] Cf. Articles 86, 87, 88 and 89. Constitución de la República de Cuba (2019).

development of youth, the satisfaction of the needs of the older adults and the improvement of their quality of life, as well as the full exercise of the rights of persons with disabilities. In all these areas, the realisation of the right to energy is a determining factor. The creation and maintenance of the necessary conditions that guarantee the satisfaction of the energy needs of each of these sectors is, therefore, a reality on which the full implementation of these constitutional postulates depends.

The right to energy in the stages of childhood and youth determines full development. In this sense, the United Nations Children's Fund (UNICEF) recognises that access to energy, especially from renewable sources, is critical to the quality, accessibility and reliability of essential services related to education, universal health, and access to water, among others. Despite this, children and youth are the most affected in contexts of inaccessibility to reliable energy services, which undermines their ability to survive, grow and thrive.[99]

In the case of older adults, the realisation of the right to energy is not only a question of quality of life but also a question of survival. It is common for people in these states to have condition-specific needs that require energy for the normal development of their lives. Such needs are linked to the operation of assistive technologies to support the independent living of older adults and people with disabilities. In addition, older adults and people with disabilities tend to spend more time at home, which can expose them to indoor pollution due to using traditional energy sources for lighting or cooking. This sector is also more vulnerable to variations in energy affordability due to price fluctuations.[100]

Following this analysis, the constitutional advances in family matters would not be fully realised if the necessary conditions for the realisation of the right to energy were not created. It would have profound negative consequences for vulnerable sectors such as children, youth, older people, and people with disabilities. The satisfaction of energy needs in these cases of energy vulnerability must be consolidated as a priority for the Cuban state.

8.5 Sufficiency of Fundamental Rights' Justiciability for the Right to Energy. What Needs to be Done?

Based on the assessment of the constitutional foundations of the right to energy in Cuba, the analysis of Chapter VI on the guarantees of rights follows. Although this subject will be dealt with in depth later,[101] it is essential to highlight that the Cuban legislator not only limited himself to the recognition of fundamental rights but also included effective protection as a mechanism of protection.

---

[99] Fondo de las Naciones Unidas para la Infancia (2022).

[100] United Nations Department of Economic and Social Affairs (2019), p. 134.

[101] Cf. infra, Sect. 10.6.

Article 99

"Any person whose rights enshrined in this Constitution are violated and who, as a consequence, suffers damage or harm by State bodies, their directors, officials or employees, because of the improper action or omission of their functions, as well as by private individuals or non-State entities, has the right to claim before the courts for the restitution of the rights and to obtain, following the law, the corresponding reparation or compensation. The law establishes those rights protected by this guarantee and the preferential, expeditious and concentrated procedure for their enforcement." (Own translation)[102]

However, the formula of Article 99 leaves the justiciability of the right to energy as an autonomous fundamental right partially unprotected. This lack of protection responds to the dogmatic approach of the Constitution of the Republic of Cuba of 2019 by making justiciable only the rights enshrined in the Fundamental Law of the national legal system.

However, based on the interconnectivity that initiated the analysis of the implications of the right to energy on the rest of the fundamental rights of the Cuban Constitution, the right under study is not entirely exempt from legal protection. The content of the right to energy can be indirectly protected based on the protective channel of the rest of the fundamental rights. Although this "solution" may not be the most appropriate, this is the reality of the legal protection of the right to energy in Cuba.

Based on the above, to conclude the analysis of the Constitution of the Republic of Cuba of 2019, it is crucial to determine how the right to energy can obtain recognition as a fundamental right. In this sense, the path to follow is the exercise of constitutional reform as established in Title XI. The regulations contained in this title declare the National Assembly of People's Power as the only body competent to reform the Constitution. In this regard, Article 227 provides for the exercise of the legislative initiative to promote constitutional reforms to:

(a) The President of the Republic
(b) The Council of State
(c) The Council of Ministers
(d) The deputies to the National Assembly of People's Power, through a proposal signed by no less than one-third of its members.
(e) The National Council of the Central de Trabajadores de Cuba and the national directions of other mass and social organisations; and
(f) Through a petition addressed to the National Assembly of People's Power, the citizens signed before the National Electoral Council by at least fifty thousand voters. (Own translation)[103]

It is essential to highlight the variety of entities competent to exercise a legislative initiative to advocate for the constitutional recognition of the right to energy. In this

[102] Cf. Articles 99. Constitución de la República de Cuba (2019).

[103] Cf. Article 227. Constitución de la República de Cuba (2019).

sense, the right to energy is recognised by state and government bodies. To these is added the possibility of the leaderships of political and mass organisations. In turn, section f) includes the exercise of the popular legislative initiative, which has not enjoyed the same acceptance as the referendum in the Latin American region[104] and has been recognised by the Cuban Constitution.

However, such recognition, like the others, is subject to further regulation of the procedure, requirements and guarantees for its application. Article 228 of the Constitution should be noted in this context. This article is particularly relevant for the future recognition of the right to energy. Article 228 establishes that when the reform's content is oriented towards constitutional rights, duties and guarantees, ratification is required through the favourable vote of the majority of the electors through a referendum.

Despite considering the non-express recognition, the national legal system offers other alternatives that promote and support the realisation of the right to energy. Based on the fundamental importance of energy as a premise for a dignified life and human survival, the Cuban legal framework has its strengths and weaknesses concerning the right to energy, which will be analysed below.

8.6 Conclusion

Despite being a relatively recent constitutional body, the Cuban Constitution of 2019 does not offer express recognition of the right to energy. However, this right can be grounded in Cuba's constitutional system. In this sense, the relevance of constitutional principles stands out. Article 1 of the Constitution begins to lay the foundations for advocating a right to energy. Principles such as human dignity, humanism, the rule of law, welfare, social justice, and many other guiding principles of the Constitution of the Republic of Cuba of 2019 lay the first foundations for the future constitutional recognition of the right to energy in Cuba.

In turn, the economic constitutional foundations of the aforementioned legal body lay many normative foundations to ensure the realisation of the right to energy. This issue is essential for the constitutional effectiveness itself. The relevance of the realisation of the right to energy is also evident in the constitutional effectiveness of fundamental rights in Cuba, especially those of a socio-economic nature. Such rights would become a mere legal formula without the realisation of what this research defines as the right to energy.

A similar situation occurs in the effectiveness of constitutional provisions relating to the family, taking the importance of the right to energy for human dignity and the full development of the personality as a prelude to constitutional norms concerning the protection of children and older people. Constitutional protection would remain a dead letter without the realisation of the right to energy.

[104] Guzman Hernández (2019), p. 36.

In turn, this chapter concludes that the lack of constitutional recognition of the right to energy has a negative impact on its justiciability. Despite the new constitutional article 99, the courts remain tied to a catalogue of fundamental rights where the right to energy only obtains indirect protection under the protective umbrella of other rights that depend on it. Article 78, which subjects the right to energy to the legal regime of Consumer Law in Cuba, can be mentioned in this case.

In this context, it is necessary to establish the theoretical-legal elements that should underpin the recognition and configuration of the right to energy. Such a foundation will contribute to laying the basis for the future exercise of the constitutional legislative initiative based on the process regulated by the Cuban constitution of 2019.

References[105]

Abdi H, Shahbazitabar M, Mohammadi-Ivatloo B (2020) Food, energy and water nexus: a brief review of definitions, research, and challenges. Inventions 5(4):56. https://www.mdpi.com/2411-5134/5/4/56. Accessed 3 Mar 2025

Allan T, Keulertz M, Woertz E (2015) The water–food–energy nexus: an introduction to nexus concepts and some conceptual and operational problems. Int J Water Resour Dev 31(3):301–311. https://www.tandfonline.com/doi/full/10.1080/07900627.2015.1029118. Accessed 3 Mar 2025

Alonso Falcón R, Figueredo Reinaldo O, García Acosta D, Carmona Tamayo E, Rodríguez Martínez K, Carmenate R (2020) Modifican tarifas eléctricas para el sector residencial y precios del gas licuado de petróleo. Cubadebate, La Habana. http://www.cubadebate.cu/noticias/2020/12/28/modifican-tarifas-electricas-para-el-sector-residencial-y-precios-del-gas-licuado-de-petroleo/. Accessed 3 Mar 2025

Attard Bellido ME (2021) La Constitución de Cuba de 2019: la interpretación de derechos con enfoque de género decolonial. In: Villabella Armengol CM, Pérez Gallardo LB (eds) Claves para la interpretación de la Constitución cubana de 2019. Ediciones Jurídicas Olejnik, Santiago de Chile. https://marcialpons.es/libros/claves-para-la-interpretacion-de-la-constitucion-cubana-de-2019/9789564070926/. Accessed 3 Mar 2025

Barak A (2015) The role of human dignity as a constitutional value. Hum Dignity 4:103–113. https://www.cambridge.org/core/books/abs/human-dignity/role-of-human-dignity-as-a-constitutional-value/66223CDACA7314775101208D7A310677#:~:text=The%20constitutional%20value%20of%20human%20dignity%20has%20a,It%20ensures%20the%20normative%20unity%20of%20human%20rights. Accessed 3 Mar 2025

Bas D, Zohouri Haghian P (2022) Addressing climate change through sport. Future of the world. https://www.un.org/development/desa/dpad/wp-content/uploads/sites/45/PB_128.pdf. Accessed 3 Mar 2025

Bombaerts G, Jenkins K, Sanusi YA, Guoyu W (2020) Energy justice across borders. In: Bombaerts G, Jenkins K, Sanusi YA, Guoyu W (eds) Energy justice across borders. Springer International Publishing, Cham. https://link.springer.com/10.1007/978-3-030-24021-9. Accessed 3 Mar 2025

Caney S (2011) Climate change, energy rights, and equality. In: Arnold DG (ed) The ethics of global climate change. Cambridge University Press, Cambridge, pp 77–103. https://www.cambridge.org/core/books/abs/ethics-of-global-climate-change/climate-change-energy-rights-and-equality/946875A79CC31A9723B93AF1075167D4. Accessed 3 Mar 2025

[105] All links to the cited websites were operational as of 3 March 2025.

Carvajal F, López-Soto D, Sanin ME, Mejdalani A, Ravillard P, Chueca-Montuenga JE, García-Ochoa R, Hallack M (2020) Más allá de la electricidad: Cómo la energía provee servicios en el hogar. Inter-American Development Bank. https://publications.iadb.org/es/mas-alla-de-la-electricidad-como-la-energia-provee-servicios-en-el-hogar#:~:text=Esta%20publicaci%C3%B3n%20analiza%20el%20acceso%20de%20los%20servicios,Caribe%20%28ALC%29%20desde%20la%20perspectiva%20sus%20usos%20finales. Accessed 3 Mar 2025

Chaskalson CJA (2011) Dignity as a constitutional value: a South African perspective. Am Univ Int Law Rev 26(5):1377. https://digitalcommons.wcl.american.edu/cgi/viewcontent.cgi?article=2030&context=auilr. Accessed 3 Mar 2025

Clancy J, Daskalova V, Feenstra M, Franceschelli N, Sanz M (2017) Gender perspective on access to energy in the EU. Brussels. https://www.europarl.europa.eu/RegData/etudes/STUD/2017/596816/IPOL_STU(2017)596816_EN.pdf. Accessed 3 Mar 2025

Committee on the Elimination of Discrimination Against Women (1999) Fourth periodic report of Cuba on. https://documents-dds-ny.un.org/doc/UNDOC/GEN/N00/224/70/IMG/N0022470.pdf?OpenElement. Accessed 3 Mar 2025

Constitución de la República de Cuba (2019) Gaceta Oficial No. 5 Extraordinaria de 10 de abril de 2019. Gaceta Oficial de la República de Cuba, La Habana. https://www.gacetaoficial.gob.cu/sites/default/files/goc-2019-ex5.pdf. Accessed 3 Mar 2025

Cornell PE (2009) Energy and the three levels of national security: differentiating energy concerns within a national security context. Connections 8(4):63–80. https://www.jstor.org/stable/pdf/26326186.pdf?refreqid=excelsior%3A536c7382d72771. Accessed 3 Mar 2025

Corte Interamericana de Derechos Humanos (1999) Sentencia de 19 de noviembre: Caso de los Niños de la Calle (Villagrán Morales y otro) Vs Guatemala. http://www.corteidh.or.cr/docs/casos/articulos/Seriec_63_esp.pdf. Accessed 3 Mar 2025

Costa MD (2009) O Direito De Acesso À Energia Meio E Pré-Condição Para O Exercício Do Direito Ao Desenvolvimento E Dos Direitos Humanos. Universidade de São Paulo. https://www.teses.usp.br/teses/disponiveis/86/86131/tde-11082011-112846/publico/MariaDAssuncao.pdf. Accessed 3 Mar 2025

Cutié Mustelier D, Méndez López J (2008) La Propiedad en Cuba. Una visión desde la Constitución. Foro Constitucional Iberoamericano (13):45–71. https://core.ac.uk/download/pdf/30047175.pdf. Accessed 3 Mar 2025

Dacal Díaz A (2020) Constitución y economía. Ajustes y tensiones del pacto social. In: Burgos Matamoros M, Del Pozo Martínez E (eds) Constitución de la República de Cuba 2019. Sistema político, derechos, género y medio ambiente. Heinrich Böll Stiftung, Ciudad de México. https://mx.boell.org/sites/default/files/2021-02/Constituci%C3%B3n%20de%20la%20Rep%C3%BAblica%20de%20Cuba%202019.pdf. Accessed 3 Mar 2025

de Luna Ávila A, Ferrer Mac-Gregor Poisot E, Bolívar Galindo C, Camacho Squivias LV, Cabrera Acevedo L (eds) (2005) Supremacía constitucional. In: ¿Qué es el Poder Judicial de la Federación? Colección SCJN, 19, 4th edn. Suprema Corte de Justicia de la Nación, Mexico, D.F. https://archivos.juridicas.unam.mx/www/bjv/libros/11/5357/15.pdf. Accessed 3 Mar 2025

Department of Economic and Social Affairs (2014) Electricity and education: the benefits, barriers, and recommendations for achieving the electrification of primary and secondary schools. Energy and Education. https://sustainabledevelopment.un.org/content/documents/1608Electricity%20and%20Education.pdf. Accessed 3 Mar 2025

Department of Economic and Social Affairs (2015) Transforming our world: the 2030 Agenda for Sustainable Development | Department of Economic and Social Affairs. https://sdgs.un.org/2030agenda. Accessed 3 Mar 2025

Diéguez La OT, Fraga Acosta MA (2022) La Constitución cubana de 2019 y la incorporación de los tratados del Derecho Internacional de los Derechos Humanos. Hacia la unidad sistémica del ordenamiento jurídico nacional. Política Internacional 4(1):44–55. http://portal.amelica.org/ameli/journal/332/3322913005/. Accessed 3 Mar 2025

Farese G (2020) Socio-economic rights. In: McCann G, O hAdhmaill F (eds) International human rights, social policy and global development. Bristol University Press, pp 105–116. https://

www.cambridge.org/core/books/abs/international-human-rights-social-policy-and-global-development/socioeconomic-rights/453681D0F0A182860F844EAA58217BA4. Accessed 3 Mar 2025

Fayiah M, Dong S, Singh S, Kwaku EA (2020) A review of water–energy nexus trend, methods, challenges and future prospects. Int J Energy Water Resour 4(1):91–107. https://doi.org/10.1007/s42108-020-00057-6. Accessed 3 Mar 2025

Fernández Martínez M (2020) Comentario a las formas de propiedad como estatuto jurídico regulado en el artículo 22 constitucional. UH (289):71–86. http://scielo.sld.cu/scielo.php?script=sci_arttext&pid=S0253-92762020000100071. Accessed 3 Mar 2025

Ferrer Mac-Gregor Poisot E, Bolívar Galindo C, Camacho Squivias LV, Molina Suárez CJ, Cárdenas Gutiérrez S (eds) (2006) Los tribunales constitucionales y la Suprema Corte de Justicia de la Nación. Suprema Corte de Justicia de la Nación, Mexico, D.F.. https://sistemabibliotecario.scjn.gob.mx/sisbib/CST/57179/57179.pdf. Accessed 3 Mar 2025

Fondo de las Naciones Unidas para la Infancia (2022) Key asks. SDG7: Affordable and Clean Energy. https://www.unicef.org/media/138096/file/SDG%207%202023%20rev.pdf. Accessed 3 Mar 2025

Galán Melo GS (2019) La justiciabilidad de los derechos económicos, sociales y culturales. Evolución de su aplicación en la Corte Interamericana de Derechos Humanos. Iuris Tantum 33(30):115–142. http://revistas.anahuac.mx/iuristantum/article/view/516. Accessed 3 Mar 2025

García Z, Nyberg J, Owaise Saadat S (2006) Agricultura, expansión del comercio y equidad de género. Organización de las Naciones Unidas para la Agricultura y la Alimentación, Roma. https://www.fao.org/3/a0493s/a0493s00.htm#Contents. Accessed 3 Mar 2025

González Monguí PE (2009) Derechos económicos, sociales y culturales. Cátedra Gerardo Molina de la Universidad Libre de Colombia, Bogotá. https://www.corteidh.or.cr/tablas/26759.pdf. Accessed 3 Mar 2025

Gutiérrez Castillo O, Tabares Neyra L, Pérez Hernández L (2019) Retos de la Administración Pública en Cuba. UH (287):64–74. http://scielo.sld.cu/pdf/uh/n287/0253-9276-uh-287-64.pdf. Accessed 3 Mar 2025

Guzman Hernández TY (2019) La iniciativa legislativa popular en América Latina – Un análisis comparado en clave axiológico-procedimental. Revista de Investigações Constitucionais 6(1):35. https://revistas.ufpr.br/rinc/article/view/58984. Accessed 3 Mar 2025

Heffron RJ (2021) Inclusive energy transition. Commonwealth Secretariat. https://www.thecommonwealth-ilibrary.org/index.php/comsec/catalog/book/343#:~:text=This%20paper%20identifies%20how%20to%20deliver%20an%20inclusive,change%20accelerates%20in%20the%20next%20decade%20and%20beyond. Accessed 3 Mar 2025

Henk B (2009) Human dignity in comparative perspective. Stellenbosch Law Rev 20(2):171–220. https://journals.co.za/doi/epdf/10.10520/EJC54707. Accessed 3 Mar 2025

Huntington HP, Schmidt JI, Loring PA, Whitney E, Aggarwal S, Byrd AG, Dev S, Dotson AD, Huang D, Johnson B, Karenzi J, Penn HJF, Salmon AA, Sambor DJ, Schnabel WE, Wies RW, Wilber M (2021) Applying the food–energy–water nexus concept at the local scale. Nat Sustain 4(8):672–679. https://doi.org/10.1038/s41893-021-00719-1. Accessed 3 Mar 2025

Justafré García Y, León Rodríguez A (2014) La legalidad socialista. Su fundamento constitucional. Revista Caribeña de Ciencias Sociales (10):1–10. https://www.eumed.net/rev/caribe/2014/10/legalidad-socialista.pdf. Accessed 3 Mar 2025

Kelsen H (1982) In: Vernengo RJ (ed) Teoría pura del Derecho. Universidad Nacional Autónoma de México, Mexico, D.F.. https://www.academia.edu/38391947/Teor%C3%ADa_Pura_del_Derecho_Hans_Kelsen. Accessed 3 Mar 2025

Komendantova N, Marashdeh L, Ekenberg L, Danielson M, Dettner F, Hilpert S, Wingenbach C, Hassouneh K, Al-Salaymeh A (2020) Water–energy nexus: addressing stakeholder preferences in Jordan. Sustainability 12(15):6168. https://www.mdpi.com/2071-1050/12/15/6168. Accessed 3 Mar 2025

Kroeze IJ (2001) Doing things with: the role of constitutional values in constitutional interpretation. Stellenbosch Law Rev 12(2):265–276. https://heinonline.org/HOL/

PDFsearchable?handle=hein.journals/stelblr12&collection=journals&section=26&id=&print=section&sectioncount=1&ext=.pdf&nocover=&display=0. Accessed 3 Mar 2025

Lloyd PJ (2017) The role of energy in development. J Energy South Afr 28(1):54–62. https://journals.assaf.org.za/jesa/article/view/1498. Accessed 3 Mar 2025

Macharia P, Kreuzinger N, Kitaka N (2020) Applying the water-energy nexus for water supply - a diagnostic review on energy use for water provision in Africa. Water (Switzerland) 12(9). https://www.mdpi.com/2073-4441/12/9/2560#:~:text=This%20work%20explores%20the%20application%20of%20the%20Water-Energy,and%20their%20influence%20on%20energy%20use%20are%20examined. Accessed 3 Mar 2025

Martínez Miguélez M (2009) Dimensiones Básicas de un Desarrollo Humano Integral. Polis (Santiago) 8(23):119–138. https://www.scielo.cl/scielo.php?script=sci_arttext&pid=S0718-65682009000200006. Accessed 3 Mar 2025

Matilla Correa A (2008) Derecho Administrativo Y Servicio Público. Trazos Inconclusos Desde Una Perspectiva Histórica. Actualidad de los servicios públicos en Iberoamérica, pp 383–449. https://archivos.juridicas.unam.mx/www/bjv/libros/6/2544/18.pdf. Accessed 3 Mar 2025

McCauley D (2018) Energy justice. Springer International Publishing, Cham. https://link.springer.com/10.1007/978-3-319-62494-5. Accessed 3 Mar 2025

Ministerio de Economía y Planificación de Cuba (2021) Ordenamiento monetario. Tarea Ordenamiento. https://www.mep.gob.cu/es/taxonomy/term/210. Accessed 3 Mar 2025

Neves-Silva P, Martins G, Heller L (2019) Human rights' interdependence and indivisibility: a glance over the human rights to water and sanitation. BMC Int Health Hum Rights 19(1):14. https://bmcinthealthhumrights.biomedcentral.com/articles/10.1186/s12914-019-0197-3. Accessed 3 Mar 2025

OECD, IEA (2016) Water energy nexus - excerpt from the World Energy Outlook 2016. Paris. https://iea.blob.core.windows.net/assets/e4a7e1a5-b6ed-4f36-911f-b0111e49aab9/WorldEnergyOutlook2016ExcerptWaterEnergyNexus.pdf. Accessed 3 Mar 2025

Oficina del Alto Comisionado para los Derechos Humanos (2010) El derecho a una vivienda adecuada. Organización de Naciones Unidas, Ginebra. https://www.ohchr.org/sites/default/files/Documents/Publications/FS21_rev_1_Housing_sp.pdf. Accessed 3 Mar 2025

Opal A, Nathwani J (2023) Global energy transition risks: evaluating the intergenerational equity of energy transition costs. In: Energy democracies for sustainable futures, pp 301–310. https://doi.org/10.1016/B978-0-12-822796-1.00032-2. Accessed 3 Mar 2025

Organización de Naciones Unidas (1948) Declaración Universal de los Derechos Humanos. https://www.ohchr.org/sites/default/files/UDHR/Documents/UDHR_Translations/spn.pdf. Accessed 3 Mar 2025

Organización de Naciones Unidas (1976) Pacto Internacional de Derechos Económicos, Sociales y Culturales. https://www.ohchr.org/es/instruments-mechanisms/instruments/international-covenant-economic-social-and-cultural-rights. Accessed 3 Mar 2025

Organización de Naciones Unidas (1979) Convention on the elimination of all forms of discrimination against women. Oficina del Alto Comicionado para los Derechos Humanos. https://www.ohchr.org/en/instruments-mechanisms/instruments/convention-elimination-all-forms-discrimination-against-women. Accessed 3 Mar 2025

Pachauri S, van Ruijven BJ, Nagai Y, Riahi K, van Vuuren DP, Brew-Hammond A, Nakicenovic N (2013) Pathways to achieve universal household access to modern energy by 2030. Environ Res Lett 8(2):024015. https://iopscience.iop.org/article/10.1088/1748-9326/8/2/024015. Accessed 3 Mar 2025

Prieto Valdés AL (2022) La defensa de los derechos constitucionales: presupuestos jurídicos para el perfeccionamiento del proceso de amparo en Cuba. Universidad de La Habana, La Habana. https://accesoabierto.uh.cu/files/original/2139036/TDAmanda_Laura_Prieto_Valdes_[9-1-23].pdf. Accessed 3 Mar 2025

Pueyo A (2020) Introduction: gender and energy – opportunities for all. IDS Bull 51(1):1–6. https://bulletin.ids.ac.uk/index.php/idsbo/article/view/3071. Accessed 3 Mar 2025

Pueyo A, Maestre M (2019) Linking energy access, gender and poverty: a review of the literature on productive uses of energy. Energy Res Soc Sci 53:170–181. https://doi.org/10.1016/j.erss.2019.02.019. Accessed 3 Mar 2025

Rafael Urquilla C (1995) Los derechos económicos, sociales y culturales en el contexto de la reforma al sistema interamericano de protección de los derechos humanos. Revista IIDH (1):259–281. https://biblioteca.corteidh.or.cr/tablas/R06837-11.pdf. Accessed 3 Mar 2025

Refaat AA, Ismail IM (2017) Water food and energy sustainability nexus. In: International conference on sustainable futures. Bahrain. https://www.researchgate.net/profile/Ibrahim-Ismail-13/publication/321579870_Water_Food_and_Energy_Sustainability_Nexus/links/5a3a8393458515889d2de6f2/Water-Food-and-Energy-Sustainability-Nexus.pdf. Accessed 3 Mar 2025

Rewald R (2017) Energy and women and girls: analyzing the needs, uses and impacts of energy on women and girls in the developing world. https://www.researchgate.net/publication/321224995_Energy_and_Women_and_Girls_Analyzing_the_needs_uses_and_impacts_of_energy_on_women_and_girls_in_the_developing_world. Accessed 3 Mar 2025

Singh P, Singh S, Kumar G, Baweja P (2021) Energy: crises, challenges and solutions. Wiley. https://www.powells.com/book/energy-9781119741442. Accessed 3 Mar 2025

Sin-Hang Ngai J (2012) Energy as a human right in armed conflict: a question of universal need, survival, and human dignity. Brooklyn J Int Law 37(2):579–622. https://core.ac.uk/download/pdf/228597477.pdf. Accessed 3 Mar 2025

Sklarew D, Sklarew J (2018) Integrated water-energy policy for sustainable development. Foresight STI Gov 12(4):10–19. https://www.researchgate.net/publication/330884707_Integrated_Water-Energy_Policy_for_Sustainable_Development. Accessed 3 Mar 2025

Sovacool B (2006) Using distributed generation and renewable energy systems to empower developing countries. Int J Environ Cult Econ Soc Sustain 2(3):77–86. https://cgscholar.com/bookstore/works/using-distributed-generation-and-renewable-energy-systems-to-empower-developing-countries. Accessed 3 Mar 2025

Sovacool BK (2013) Energy and ethics. Justice and the global energy challenge. Palgrave Macmillan UK, London. http://link.springer.com/10.1057/9781137298669. Accessed 3 Mar 2025

Sovacool BK, Dworkin MH (2014) Global energy justice. Problems, principles, and practices. Cambridge University Press, Reino Unido. https://www.cambridge.org/core/books/global-energy-justice/A3607C67A4798DC19AD73A4B11AFC28C. Accessed 3 Mar 2025

Sovacool BK, Dworkin MH (2015) Energy justice: conceptual insights and practical applications. Appl Energy 142:435–444. https://doi.org/10.1016/j.apenergy.2015.01.002. Accessed 3 Mar 2025

Sovacool BK, Sidortsov RV, Jones BR (2014) Energy security, equality, and justice. Routledge, New York. https://www.routledge.com/Energy-Security-Equality-and-Justice/Sovacool-Sidortsov-Jones/p/book/9780415815208. Accessed 3 Mar 2025

The Secretary-General's Advisory Group on Energy and Climate Change (2010) Energy for a sustainable future. United Nations, New York. https://www.undp.org/sites/g/files/zskgke326/files/publications/AGECCsummaryreport.pdf. Accessed 3 Mar 2025

Timmermann C, Noboa E (2022) Energy sovereignty: a values-based conceptual analysis. Sci Eng Ethics 28(6):54. https://doi.org/10.1007/s11948-022-00409-x. Accessed 3 Mar 2025

Tirado-herrero S (2023) Pobreza energética y vivienda: una perspectiva social. Arbor 199(807) https://arbor.revistas.csic.es/index.php/arbor/article/view/2678/3919. Accessed 3 Mar 2025

United Nations Department of Economic and Social Affairs (2019) Ensuring access to energy for persons with disabilities (Goal 7). In: Disability and Development Report 2018, pp 134–149. United Nations. https://www.un-ilibrary.org/content/books/9789210479035s006-c007/read. Accessed 3 Mar 2025

Uribe Benítez O (2009) Supremacia constitucional. Cámara de Diputados, Mexico, D.F.. http://koha.uan.mx/cgi-bin/koha/opac-detail.pl?biblionumber=286290. Accessed 3 Mar 2025

van Gevelt T (2020) The water–energy–food nexus: bridging the science–policy divide. Curr Opin Environ Sci Health 13:6–10. https://doi.org/10.1016/j.coesh.2019.09.008. Accessed 3 Mar 2025

Villabella Armengol CM (2023) El Estado socialista de derecho y justicia social en Cuba. Cubadebate, La Habana. http://www.cubadebate.cu/especiales/2023/06/12/el-estado-socialista-de-derecho-y-justicia-social-en-cuba/. Accessed 3 Mar 2025

Wilhite H (2017) Gender implications of energy use and energy access. Energy and Economic Growth (EEG) State of Knowledge Paper Series. https://assets.publishing.service.gov.uk/media/5a265db9e5274a75088c42ae/Line_17_-Gender_Wilhite.pdf. Accessed 3 Mar 2025

Winther T, Matinga MN, Ulsrud K, Standal K (2017) Women's empowerment through electricity access: scoping study and proposal for a framework of analysis. J Dev Effectiveness 9 (3):389–417. https://doi.org/10.1080/19439342.2017.1343368. Accessed 3 Mar 2025

Woolman S (2012) Dignity. In: Woolman S, Bishop M, Brickhill J (eds) Constitutional law of South Africa. Juta and Company (Pty) Ltd, Cape Town, pp 1–40. https://constitutionallawofsouthafrica.co.za/wp-content/uploads/2018/10/Chap36.pdf. Accessed 3 Mar 2025

World Health Organization (2023) Energy and health. Health topics. https://www.who.int/health-topics/energy-and-health#tab=tab_2. Accessed 3 Mar 2025

World Health Organization Regional Office for Europe (2007) Housing, energy and thermal comfort: a review of 10 countries within the WHO European Region. World Health Organization, Copenhagen. https://apps.who.int/iris/bitstream/handle/10665/107815/E89887.pdf. Accessed 3 Mar 2025

Yadav K, Geli HME, Cibils AF, Hayes M, Fernald A, Peach J, Sawalhah MN, Tidwell VC, Johnson LE, Zaied AJ, Gedefaw MG (2021) An Integrated Food, Energy, and Water Nexus, Human Well-Being, and Resilience (FEW-WISE) Framework: New Mexico. Front Environ Sci 9(June):1–20. https://www.frontiersin.org/articles/10.3389/fenvs.2021.667018/full. Accessed 3 Mar 2025

Chapter 9
Scope of the Cuban Legal Framework for the Recognition and Configuration of the Right to Energy

9.1 Introductory Idea

To analyse the Cuban infra-constitutional legal system in the "light" of the right to energy, one must start with the complexity of the energy regulatory framework. In Cuba, the analysis of this sector of the legal system is highly complex due to "obsolescence, dispersion and legislative inadequacies, further accentuated by the limited scope of the norms, legal gaps and contradictions between these provisions."[1] For this reason, this research will follow a chronological criterion according to the entry into force of the infra-constitutional normative provisions with implications on the components, according to this research, of the right to energy.

9.2 Law on Combustible Minerals

In this sense, the analysis will begin with the still-valid 1938 Law on Combustible Minerals.[2] This body of law regulates everything related to the exploration and exploitation of oil deposits and other hydrocarbon substances.

---

[1] Luis Cordova (2022), p. 180.

[2] The Law on Combustible Minerals was one of the most important regulatory initiatives of its time. Its enactment responded to the need for a regulatory framework appropriate to the historical context, the needs of the time and the development of the national economy. These motives were aligned with the growing development of the exploitation of mineral fuel resources at that time and to renew the obsolete regulatory framework that was a legacy of Cuba's colonial era. Le Riverend (1974), p. 640.

J. G. Luis Cordova, *Theoretical and Legal Dimensions of the Right to Energy*, Economic and Financial Law & Policy – Shifting Insights & Values 9,
https://doi.org/10.1007/978-3-032-33252-3_9

Article 2

"The following are declared to be of public utility and social interest and shall be governed by the provisions of this law:

- The exploration and exploitation of deposits of petroleum and other hydrocarbon substances found on the surface or in the interior of the earth, whether solid, liquid, or gaseous
- all matters relating to the manufacture and refining of the minerals exploited and their transport by all means requiring specific routes, and
- all matters relating to the exploration of fossil coal deposits, their mechanical preparation, and the transport of their ores." (Own translation)[3]

Given the heading of Article 2, the question arises: What are the implications of the declaration of public utility and social interest for the so-called combustible minerals on the right to energy? The first part of the answer to this question is as follows. Applying such indeterminate legal concepts to these non-renewable energy carriers subjects them to the discretionary powers of the public administration.[4]

On this basis, the public administration is empowered to exploit or grant administrative concessions to interested third parties to satisfy the national energy demand as a matter of public or general interest. This energy demand includes the non-inconsiderable energy needs of the Cuban population. For these reasons, since the Law on Combustible Minerals, the public administration in Cuba has been vested with powers to ensure the realisation of the right to energy.[5]

The Law on Combustible Minerals, according to Article 2, regulates the exploration and exploitation of petroleum deposits and other hydrocarbon substances located on the surface or in the earth's interior. It also regulates the manufacture and refining of exploited minerals and their transport. This regulation also includes fossil coal deposits. Article 3 defines the mineral substances protected and regulated by the law. For this purpose, it classifies them into three groups. The first group includes petroleum and its natural liquid or gaseous associates. The second group includes asphalt, whatever its state. The third group includes fossil fuels such as anthracite, hard coal, and lignite, among many others.[6]

---

[3] Cf. Article 2. Poder Ejecutivo (1938).

[4] Article 3. "The granting of the concessions referred to in this law is the responsibility of the Executive Branch (...)" (Own translation) Poder Ejecutivo (1938).

[5] García de Enterría (1975); De Cores and Cal (2007), p. 132; Mexico Suprema Corte de Justicia and Universidad Nacional Autónoma de México Instituto de Investigaciones (2009), p. 72.

[6] Cf. Article 3. "The mineral substances whose exploitation and exploitation are protected and regulated by this law are: First: Petroleum and its natural, liquid, or gaseous associates, such as naphtha, natural kerosene, hydrocarbon gases and helium. Second: Asphalt, in whatever state it could be found, bitumen, pitch, elaterite, ozokerite and other similar minerals, as well as wax and fossil resins. Third: Fossil coals, including anthracite, coal, lignite, and other combustible minerals with the exception of peat."

Article 4

"The Nation has inalienable and imprescriptible dominion over all natural mineral fuels and all mixtures of hydrocarbons of hydrogen found in its deposits, whatever their physical state.

The State may grant to private individuals, as concessions, the right to exploit or explore the deposits of these minerals, following the provisions of this law." (Own translation)[7]

This law has many implications for the realisation of the right to energy in Cuba. These implications are determined by the availability of fossil fuels, given the energy sector's dependence on this type of resource. In turn, the Law on Combustible Minerals regulates, starting with Article 4, the mechanisms for granting concessions for the exploitation of oil deposits without the state losing its inalienable and imprescriptible domain over all natural combustible minerals and all hydrogen hydrocarbon mixtures.

In addition, Article 44 obliges refineries located in Cuba to refine state oil when the government so defines it.

Article 44

"Existent Petroleum refineries or to be established in the Republic shall comply with the following requirements: (…)

3. Their plants shall be obliged to refine the State's oil when the Government so agrees, establishing the corresponding share between them if the quantities to be refined so require or impose it so that it is possible to refine all the oil necessary and at a price that does not exceed the cost of the operation, plus a reasonable industrial profit." (Own translation)[8]

As stated in the article, the oil refining price does not exceed the cost of operation plus a reasonable industrial profit. This condition positively affects the affordability of the energy produced by making oil refining cheap.

Another of the elements regulated by the Law on Combustible Minerals that safeguard energy availability is contained in Chapter V. This chapter regulates the Cuban state's combustible mineral reserves. In this respect, it establishes the functioning of this type of reserve system, backing the availability of these fossil energy carriers. These regulations constitute a normative guarantee to protect the

---

Concessions granted expressly for the substances belonging to the first group authorise exploration or exploitation also for the other two groups, if the conditions imposed by this law are met. Concessions granted for substances included in the second and third groups shall give the right to explore or exploit those included in both groups, if the conditions imposed by this Act are fulfilled, but shall not cover the exploration or exploitation of substances included in the first group. Poder Ejecutivo (1938).

[7] Cf. Article 4. Poder Ejecutivo (1938).

[8] Cf. Article 44. Poder Ejecutivo (1938).

satisfaction of energy needs regardless of the administrative concessions that have been or are issued in favour of natural or legal persons.[9]

9.3 Law 1287/1975 "Electricity Law"

Another normative instrument with extraordinary implications for the right to energy is Law 1287, "Electricity Law".[10] Despite its entry into force on 2 January 1975, this body of law is still in force as part of the regulatory framework of the energy sector in Cuba.

Since it entered into force, this body of law has had wide-ranging implications for the energy sector and the right to energy. In this sense, Law 1287 recognises the importance of the generation, transmission, and distribution of electricity for the economic and social development of the country. However, this law has no provisions relating to the recognition or protection of the right to energy or the rights of so-called energy users or consumers. This has a negative impact on their protection.

However, from Law 1287's legislative declaration on the importance of the electricity service onwards, the Cuban government's awareness of the essential nature of the electricity service as a public energy service par excellence is evident. This essential character transcends not only the nation's economic reality but also the Cuban population's dignified life and the effective realisation of the fundamental rights recognised by the Constitution. In this sense, Law 1287 considers electricity supply a vital economic and social development service.

This motive is why the Electricity Law recognises the government's efforts at the time to guarantee energy availability by constructing thermal power stations. The background to this statement is the leading role that fossil energy generation played in the Cuban economy in 1975. This reality was undoubtedly a consequence of the economic and trade links under the Council for Mutual Economic Assistance.

This legal body also recognizes the efforts to achieve energy accessibility by developing electricity transmission and distribution networks in urban and rural areas. The spirit of Law 1287 sought to unify and update the Cuban legal system in the mid-1970s, thus reducing the dispersion of regulations existing at that time.

Even though the mentioned legal norm contributed to the organisation of the national energy sector through its coherent regulation, it is currently considered obsolete. This condition undermines the realisation of the right to energy, especially regarding identifying those who could be identified as subjects.

The obsolescence of the Electricity Law extends to the conclusion of the adhesion contract used by UNE for the public electricity service. In this adhesion contract, the now-defunct Ministry of Electricity Industry is still declared one of the

[9] Cf. Chapter 5. Poder Ejecutivo (1938).

[10] Poder Ejecutivo del Consejo de Ministros (1975).

parties. This declaration is a clear error in identifying one of the parties to the contract that has gone unnoticed in the Cuban legal system over the years.

Even though, in practice, the entity responsible for providing the service is the UNE, the electricity service contract has remained unchanged over time despite the changes that the Cuban energy legal framework has undergone. Another of the shortcomings of this adhesion contract is the non-recognition of the rights that should be granted to the so-called service users, except for compensation for damages and claims for undue payments or debts. This omission is also a consequence of the non-recognition and non-regulation of users' rights in the Electricity Law, whose will be constrained to accept or not the contract used by UNE as the only wholesale electricity trader in Cuba.

Specifically, given the structural changes in the energy sector that have been oversold, identifying the subjects obliged to guarantee the right to energy is an unresolved issue in the Electricity Act. In this sense, this body of law made the now-extinct Ministry of the Electricity Industry responsible for electricity supply.[11]

> **Article 1**
> "The Ministry of Electricity Industry shall provide electricity service, following the priorities established by the Government for the development of the country's economic and social plans."[12]

In turn, regarding identifying the holders of the right to energy, Law 1287 does not provide clarity. In this sense, this legal norm only refers, within its scope of competence, to the users of the electricity service, which cannot be identified with the holders of the right to energy, considering the regulatory approach adopted. The legal provisions of articles 2, 3, 4 and 5 recognise diverse types of users. In this context, private and state users are differentiated. Depending on the characteristics of the energy service use, a distinction is made between residential, commercial, social service, industrial and agricultural users.[13]

---

[11] Cf. Article 1: "The Ministry of the Electricity Industry will generate and provide to its users, electrical energy (...)" Ministro de la Industria Eléctrica (1975).

[12] Cf. Article 1. Poder Ejecutivo del Consejo de Ministros (1975).

[13] Cf. Article 2. "For the purposes of supplying and contracting electricity, users shall be classified in belonging to the -private area- or to the -state area-. Likewise, and according to the characteristics of their use, the services will be identified as: • residential; • commercial and social service; • industrial; • agricultural.

Article 3. Residential service shall mean the supply of electricity to buildings used primarily as dwellings, where it is used for lighting and the operation of electrical appliances in general.

Article 4. Commercial and social service' shall mean the supply of electricity to clothing or grocery shops, butchers' shops, goods warehouses, warehouses in general, garages, offices, hotels, hospitals or clinics, schools, universities, properties dedicated to holiday plans or other services with similar characteristics.

Article 5. Industrial service shall mean the supply of electricity to any manufacturing or processing activity, which modifies the material used. supply of electrical energy to any manufacturing or processing activity, which modifies the material used.

Article 6. Agricultural service shall mean the supply of electricity to activities, such as dairies, irrigation, and workshops, which are directly or indirectly related to this sector." (Own translation) Poder Ejecutivo del Consejo de Ministros (1975).

Although the Electricity Law assumes a user or energy consumer approach, some shortcomings undermine the clarity of regulating such status. This situation is due to the legislative suppression of the requirements for acquiring user status, the need for user registration and the need for a bank account, among others.[14] The regulation of these requirements was at the discretion of the Ministry of Electricity Industry.[15]

Another of the regulatory elements of Law 1287 that undermines the protection of the right to energy is the possibility of complaint. This body of law only provides for the possibility of complaint in the case of undue payments and debts, for which 12 months have been established since the payment was made or the debt was incurred.

> **Article 11**
> "The action to reclaim from each other by the Ministry of Electricity Industry and the user, for undue payments and outstanding debts, shall be barred by the expiry of twelve months after the payment has been made or the debt has been incurred."[16]

As these are the only grounds for claims established in the Electricity Law, violations of the content of the right to energy are not claimable, especially considering the absence of express recognition of this right.

It is essential to highlight that since the Electricity Law, regulating the energy sector has included mechanisms to control energy demand. The control of the economy, exercised by the state over the socialist state enterprise as the leading economic actor, has become a tool that benefits energy availability. In this sense, Article 16 states:

> **Article 16**
> "It is forbidden for state-owned facilities to install new equipment or alter their work regime if this increases the demand foreseen for this service, without prior authorisation from the Ministry of the Electricity Industry, and the administration of these facilities must comply with the above, and they will be held responsible in the event of non-compliance." (Own translation)[17]

Through this regulation and others that result in the same outcome, which will be analysed later in this research, any increase in demand in state-owned facilities is regulated. This regulation implies a centralised management mechanism that results in the stability of the energy system and, therefore, in availability and reliability as elements of the right to energy.

Thus, the satisfaction of energy needs is not affected by the actions of the state-owned company, even though this may affect the functioning of productive activities. Such an effect would be caused by the need to follow the authorisation procedure for increased demand that has not been foreseen.

---

[14] Luis Cordova et al. (2022), p. 15.

[15] Cf. Article 7. "The Ministry of the Electricity Industry, through the competent bodies, shall establish the requirements that must be compulsorily complied with by both state and private users, for the purposes of requesting, contracting and using the electricity service." (Own translation) Poder Ejecutivo del Consejo de Ministros (1975).

[16] Cf. Article 11. Poder Ejecutivo del Consejo de Ministros (1975).

[17] Article 16. Poder Ejecutivo del Consejo de Ministros (1975).

Some reliability protection, as part of the right to energy, can be seen in Article 18. In this postulate, the now-extinct Ministry of the Electricity Industry is once again held responsible for the stability of the electricity service.[18] In this sense, it is declared legally responsible for any damage or harm that could be caused by anomalies in the electricity supply to the equipment that depends on it for its operation. Although this prohibition is intended to protect users' assets, it creates a civil legal liability regime for the electricity service provider.

This liability regime was reinforced by Resolution 64 of 2009, which was issued by the Ministry of Basic Industry. This resolution establishes the following as grounds for the claim: the electrical service affectations reported to the Electricity Company, the electrical service affectations due to manipulations of opening and closing of the circuit without more than 3 min between them, the disconnection or faulty connection (false contact) of the neutral of the network and the wear or lack of maintenance of the materials and equipment of the distribution installations.[19] All these causes for determining the civil liability of the electricity service provider are directly linked to the reliability of these services, even though it is not expressly recognised.

Another article of the Electricity Law with a direct implication on the realisation of the right to energy is Article 19, which refers to the disconnection of electricity[20] concerning Articles 33 and 34 of the Electricity Service Regulations.[21]

---

[18] Article 18. "Abnormalities in the supply of electrical energy which cause damage and/or harm to the electrical equipment of the users shall oblige the Ministry of Electricity Industry o arrange with the corresponding bodies or companies for their appropriate repair at the Ministry's expense, if such abnormalities have not been caused by compliance with the provisions or orders of civil or military authorities, or by a fortuitous event or force majeure." (Own translation) Poder Ejecutivo del Consejo de Ministros (1975).

[19] Article 6. "Causes for a claim for damage to property to be accepted for processing and evaluation are considered to be those attributable to the activity of the Unión Eléctrica and which come exclusively from: a) Affectations of the electricity service reported to the Unión Eléctrica. b) Power service disruptions due to manipulation of the opening and closing of the circuit without a period of more than three minutes between them. c) Disconnection or defective connection (false contact) of the network's "neutral". d) Wear and tear or lack of maintenance of the materials and equipment of the distribution installations." (Own translation) Ministerio de la Industria Básica (2009).

[20] Cf. Article 19. "The Ministry of the Electricity Industry may withdraw the service and terminate the contract from those users who fail to comply with any of the following conditions of the obligations incumbent upon them in accordance with this Law and the Regulations." (Own translation) Poder Ejecutivo del Consejo de Ministros (1975).

[21] Cf. Article 33. "All users of the private area shall be obliged to pay their account within ten working days of notification."

Article 34. "Failure of the user to comply with the provisions of the previous article will be cause for termination of the service. It which will be re-established once the pending debt has been paid, plus the sum of three pesos ($3.00) for the expenses incurred due to reconnection within the following 48 hours. The user's disagreement with the billed amount shall not be considered a pretext for non-payment, which shall be credited subject to the outcome of the complaint." (Own translation) Ministro de la Industria Eléctrica (1975).

These regulations authorise the disconnection of users in the event of non-payment of electricity bills. In this way, both legal norms fail to consider the existence of users or consumers, as they are also legally called,[22] in situations of energy poverty. In this sense, the definition of vulnerability and energy poverty are still pending issues for the Cuban legal system.[23]

An element related to the above, with a particular implication for the sectors of the Cuban population concerning the realisation of the right to energy, arises in the interaction between Administrative Sanctioning Law and Criminal Law. To analyse this interaction, we analyse Article 29 of the Electricity Law regulations, which establishes some of the requirements for contracting electricity services.[24]

One of the essential requirements for the application for electricity service is the presentation of a suitable document that accredits the applicant with the legality of the possession or ownership of the property. This essential requirement means that persons living in illegally constructed dwellings are not eligible to contract electricity service.

This situation is a problem to which the Cuban legal system offers no response. For this reason, a complex situation arises in the national territory[25] about settlements where the inhabitants have no way of accrediting the legality of their properties and, therefore, are excluded from the possibility of contracting the electricity service.

Despite this situation, the right to energy seeks to satisfy a fundamental need, which is why protecting these population sectors is one of the challenges presented by the national legal system. Even though, at the political level, the disconnection of

[22] Despite the denomination of user assumed by the Electricity Law and its regulation, in subsequent regulations such as Decree 260 of 2009, such status is recognised under the denomination of consumer. The Article 2 states: "When the violation is committed by a consumer in the exercise of private non-residential activities, regardless of the application of the provisions of Article 1, the accessory measure of withdrawal of the corresponding licence shall be applied for a period of not less than six months, which may be extended to its definitive withdrawal." (Own translation) Comité Ejecutivo del Consejo de Ministros (1998).

[23] Cf. Thomson et al. (2022).

[24] Cf. Article 29. "In addition to the requirements set out in the preceding articles, the residential service user shall be required to meet the following requirements the following requirements shall be required of the residential service user: a) The application for the supply of electricity shall be submitted to the regional or local office of the relevant Provincial Enterprise of the Ministry of Electricity Industry (…); b) Such an application shall also include: (…) 4. Submission of the appropriate document proving that the applicant is in a position and/or ownership of the property in question. (…)" (Own translation) Ministro de la Industria Eléctrica (1975).

[25] Figueredo Reinaldo et al. (2021) and Redacción Digital (2020).

these dwellings has not been promoted, the subtraction of electricity is conceived as an administrative contravention[26] and as a crime.[27]

9.4 Resolution 1034/2015 of the Ministry of Finance and Prices

After analysing Law 1287 and its interaction with its regulation and other norms of the legal system, another normative body of marked importance in the development of the national energy sector is Resolution 1034 of the Ministry of Finance and Prices, which came into force in January 2016.[28] Considering that the degree of realisation of the right to energy depends to a large extent on the capacity of the energy sector to sustain itself, Resolution 1034 reformed the taxation regime imposed on Unión Eléctrica.

The motivation for this resolution was determined by the need to increase the profits of Unión Eléctrica. According to Resolution 1034, this decision responded to the need to favour the development of Unión Eléctrica as the sole entity in charge of the transmission and distribution of electricity. This measure aimed to increase the investment capital for the development of the electricity-energy sector, which would positively impact the guarantee of the material conditions necessary for the realisation of the right to energy.

---

[26] Article 1. "The following are contraventions of the electricity service regulations and are therefore liable to a fine and the other measures indicated in each case: a) Whoever manipulates, changes, or alters the metering equipment and the service connection, preventing the correct operation of the aforementioned equipment and the free passage of all the energy consumed through it, 500 pesos and the withdrawal of the service for 72 hours. b) In the event of a repeat offence of the previous paragraph, both the commission of fraud and the reconnection of the offender, the fine to be imposed will be 1000 pesos and the withdrawal of the service for 15 days. c) Whoever hinders the reading of the metering equipment, intentionally damages said equipment or its cabinet, or changes its location together or not with the service connection, 500 pesos: d) Whoever illegally connects to someone else's installation (clotheslines) or allows it to be connected to his own, 300 pesos and the obligation to remove the illegal installation. e) Whoever provides electricity to a dwelling that has incurred in electricity fraud, 500 pesos and the obligation to withdraw the service. f) Whoever re-establishes in any way the electrical service that has been previously disconnected due to non-payment of the same, 100 pesos and the withdrawal of the service until the debt is paid." (Own translation) Comité Ejecutivo del Consejo de Ministros (1998).

[27] Cf. Article 413. "Whoever steals electricity, gas, water or power, from personal or collective installations, is punished with imprisonment from six months to one year or a fine of one hundred to three hundred quotas, or both." (Own translation) Asamblea Nacional del Poder Popular (2022c).

[28] Ministerio de Finazas y Precios (2015).

9.5 Regulation for Liquefied Petroleum Gas Service to the Population

Another of the legal norms with a marked influence on the realisation of the right to energy is the Regulation of the service of liquefied petroleum gas to the population. The gas service becomes a necessary guarantee for the satisfaction of energy needs, considering the breadth of the conceptualisation of energy in the framework of the right under study.

This regulation, put into effect through Resolution 92 of 2017, issued by the Ministry of Energy and Mines, aims to regulate aspects related to the provision of gas, especially the contracting of this type of service, among other elements. This regulatory body came to promote the right to energy from the perspective of the consumer-customer relationship between the consumer-customer and the service provider.[29]

In this regard, Article 2 of Resolution 92 defines the customer as:

> A person in whose name a liquefied petroleum gas service contract is held and is supplied individually either at home in ten (10) or forty-five (45) kg cylinders, or at points of sale in ten (10) kg cylinders, as appropriate for the residence area. (Own translation)[30]

This definition restricts the scope of protection only to persons having such status. This restriction is initially endorsed by Article 3 when it refers to the legal-contractual relationship contracted by the liquefied petroleum gas service contract. This legal relationship, regulated by Resolution 92, as *pacta sunt servanda*, establishes the covenants, terms and conditions between the customer and the service provider.[31]

This reality, in turn, is reinforced in Article 51 of Resolution 92. This article is a limitation that leaves unprotected those persons who benefit from the liquefied petroleum gas service without being parties to the contract to satisfy part of their energy needs. Although this reality is ordinary in consumer legal relations, in this area, it is a limitation that threatens the satisfaction of a fundamental need.[32]

Article 53 seems to shed some light on this issue in this context. This article allows third parties to participate in disputes over the best right to liquefied petroleum gas service. In this type of litigation, interested third parties can participate by submitting their pleadings and evidentiary material.[33]

---

[29] Cf. Article 1. "The purpose of the Regulation is to regulate the service of liquefied petroleum gas to the population with regard to applications, transfers, registrations, cancellations, changes of name, transfers, exchanges, rights in the event of divorce, deaths, new installations from the sale released and other aspects related to said service". (Own translation) Ministerio de Energía y Minas (2017).

[30] Cf. Article 2. Ministerio de Energía y Minas (2017).

[31] Cf. Article 3. Ministerio de Energía y Minas (2017).

[32] Cf. Article 51. Ministerio de Energía y Minas (2017).

[33] Cf. Article 53. "In the case of a dispute over a better right to liquefied gas service involving one or more other interested persons, the other party is given notice of the claim before it is settled, in order that it may express its views and submit any evidence it deems relevant". (Own translation) Ministerio de Energía y Minas (2017).

An essential element from Resolution 92 is the structure of the liquefied petroleum gas service contract. In contrast to the public electricity service contract, the liquefied petroleum gas service contract establishes in its structure the rights and obligations of the parties, which the public electricity service contract lacks concerning the rights of the users.[34]

Even though the right to energy in both contexts is based on a legal relationship of consumption, recognising the users' rights, customers, or consumers provides legal certainty. As both contracts are laws between the parties, they must be aware of their rights and obligations, and the conditions and terms agreed upon must be clear.

The design of energy service contracts should be precise and avoid ambiguities. If the parties' rights and obligations are unclear, they are left to the free interpretation of the court or arbitrator, which could make consumers vulnerable vis-à-vis service providers. This possibility is further reinforced by the adhesion contracts used in Cuba to contract energy services and the limited options regarding suppliers.

An example of the above is the obligation to report price changes. Article 8 of Resolution 92 states:

> **Article 8**
> " (…) If these prices are modified during the term of the contract, the entity is obliged to inform the customer within the period established by the relevant body. (...)" (Own translation)[35]

In turn, such regulation is included as a right for the customer in the liquefied petroleum gas service contract and thus becomes an obligation for the supplier. This reality is not the case for public electricity service contracts since the Electricity Law and its regulations are omitted in this respect. This situation applies to the public electricity service contract, which has remained unchanged for almost 50 years.

9.6 Resolution 152/2018 of the Ministry of Energy and Mines

Subsequently, Resolution 152 of the Ministry of Energy and Mines came into force in 2018. This legal instrument has implications for the realisation of the right to energy. Such implications directly impact energy availability as a basic premise for the realisation of the right under study. In this sense, the purpose of Resolution 152 is to establish the "Manual for the Inspection of Energy Carriers, whose objective is to contribute to the rational use and control of energy carriers in the national territory".[36]

Through Resolution 152 of the Ministry of Energy and Mines, among other purposes, it pursued the control of energy demand in "national entities, state enterprises, superior business management organisations, budgeted units, organs and bodies of the Central State Administration, administration councils, organisations

---

[34] Ministerio de Energía y Minas (2017).

[35] Cf. Article 8. Ministerio de Energía y Minas (2017).

[36] Cf. Article 1. Ministerio de Energía y Minas (2018).

and associations, trading companies with 100 per cent Cuban capital, international economic associations, agricultural and non-agricultural cooperatives and other forms of non-state management".[37]

The regulations of that legal instrument establish measures to control energy demand in the regulated entities, representing an essential part of the national energy demand. Such control allows energy availability to guarantee the satisfaction of the energy needs of the residential sector and, thus, the satisfaction of part of the content of the right to energy. In this context, controlling the entities' energy demand is vital, especially at peak times of energy consumption. In this sense, the peak hour is defined as:

> Period when the maximum electricity demand of the National Electricity System occurs, which the Ministry of Energy and Mines defines. (Own translation)[38]

To this end, Article 11 of Resolution 152 establishes special provisions in the consumption plan of the entities during peak hours, which are subject to measurement.[39] The National Office will supervise measures for the Control of the Rational Use of Energy to guarantee the reduction of energy consumption.[40]

Among the measures mentioned above are the shutdown of electric ovens, the disconnection of air conditioning equipment, and the rationalised use of lighting, such as stopping water and fuel pumping.[41] In this last case, it is essential to highlight the establishment as an exception in the cases of water and fuel supply to the population. Resolution 152 safeguards these two essential services and is therefore not subject to strict energy consumption control measures at peak demand times.

Another relevant element of Resolution 152 is Article 15. In anticipation of the entry into force of Decree-Law 345,[42] the Ministry of Energy and Mines regulated the promotion of renewable energy sources and the efficient use of energy[43] in the following way:

---

[37] Cf. Article 2. Ministerio de Energía y Minas (2018).

[38] Cf. Article 3. Ministerio de Energía y Minas (2018).

[39] Cf. Article 11. Ministerio de Energía y Minas (2018).

[40] Luis Cordova et al. (2022), p. 13.

[41] Cf. Article 11 (3). Ministerio de Energía y Minas (2018).

[42] Cf. Article 21.1 "State legal entities have a "Programme for the development, maintenance and sustainability of renewable sources and efficient use of energy", with a scope of five years, hereinafter "Programme", which responds to the directives set out in the previous article, and includes the goals to be achieved, the necessary human and financial resources, among others, and a timetable for its implementation." (Own translation) Consejo de Estado (2019).

[43] Following the entry into force of Resolution 152, this regulatory body was complemented by Resolution 124 of the Ministry of Energy and Mines of 2019. The purpose of Resolution 124 was to improve energy management, efficiency, and conservation, as well as the implementation of Energy Management Systems in entities with high energy consumption in the Cuban economy. Therefore, these new regulations became applicable to state and non-state legal entities; to commercial companies with one hundred percent (100%) Cuban capital; and to foreign investment modalities. In this way, the Ministry of Energy and Mines took charge of regulating the energy consumption of these entities in order to guarantee energy availability for the rest of the national energy demand and the stability of the Cuban energy sector. Undoubtedly, the regulation of these

Article 15
The entities shall keep the "Programme for the Development, maintenance and Sustainability of Renewable Sources and Efficient Energy Use" updated with a scope of five (5) years, following the provisions of the legislation in force. (Own translation)[44]

As of this regulation, the entities subject to control under Resolution 152 must outline their projections concerning the exploitation of renewable sources and the promotion of energy efficiency. The elaboration of the programme mentioned above and its implementation has a dual impact on the satisfaction of energy needs that is later strengthened by Decree-Law 345. The dual impact is given in two dimensions: energy availability and supply sustainability.

Implementing renewable energy sources in the so-called "entities" implies increased generation capacity. This increase ensures a part of the energy supply necessary to satisfy the needs of the Cuban population. Added to this is the added value of the sustainability dimension. This dimension is achieved by exploiting "inexhaustible" energy carriers and by using a clean or environmentally friendly generation process. In this way, part of the entities' budget defined in Article 2 of Resolution 152 is oriented towards satisfying the national energy demand.

9.7 Decree-Law 345/2019, Opening a New Horizon for the Right to Energy

From Article 3, Decree-Law 345 provides instructions to the legal system and its subsequent implementation to a series of essential elements for the satisfaction of each of the elements of the content of the right to energy. The first focuses on using distributed generation as the second source of energy generation in the country. In this sense, subparagraph a) impacts all the elements of the right to energy as shown by Figure 9.1.

Distributed generation has a leading role in generating energy in the country. It has been implemented as a backup plan for the national energy system, but distributed generation contributes to energy access in contexts where access to the grid is not available. In turn, distributed generation decreases energy losses and, therefore, decreases generation costs. This condition contributes to energy affordability for end users.

It also contributes to energy reliability as a backup means in the event of climatic contingencies. Thus, it contributes to the satisfaction of basic energy needs, as well as to energy needs for productive purposes that contribute, in turn, to satisfying other basic needs such as food.

---

high consumers is beneficial for the satisfaction of the Cuban population's energy needs, especially in contexts of energy crisis such as those still facing the country in 2023. Ministerio de Energía y Minas (2019b).

[44] Cf. Article 15. Ministerio de Energía y Minas (2018).

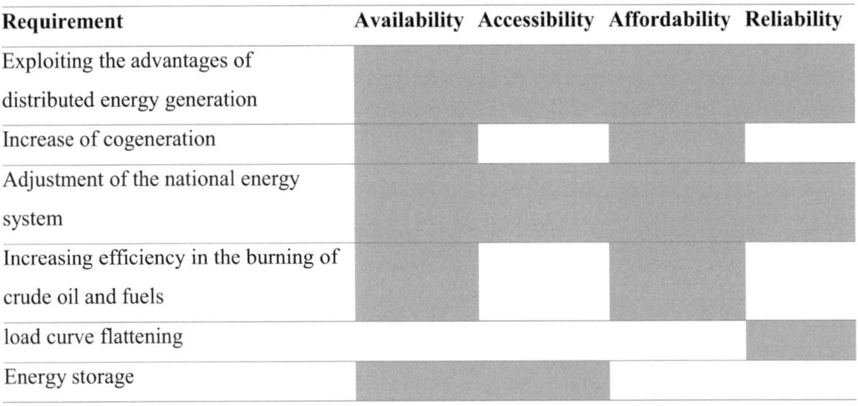

Fig. 9.1 Article 3: indicators assessment in fulfilling the right to energy

Another provision of Article 3 is the promotion of energy polygeneration. Through cogeneration and trigeneration, the simultaneous generation of electricity, heat and/or cooling is achieved with a single energy carrier, thereby increasing the energy generated by the energy sector. In turn, this reduces generation costs by obtaining different forms of usable energy, which can reduce the consumption of imported fuels.

In addition to the above, paragraph c) calls for the need to adapt the electricity system. Such adequacy implies the capacity of the energy system to adapt to the increase in energy demand to satisfy it. In turn, it implies that the energy sector must overcome the obstacles to satisfy the energy needs of 100% of the population and, therefore, access to energy. In addition, measures must be implemented to guarantee energy affordability, for which energy and technological sovereignty are essential. Finally, the adequacy of the energy system implies energy reliability through greater energy resilience.

The other three requirements established by Article 3 are the increase of fuel combustion efficiency, the load curve flattening of the national electricity system and the use of energy storage technologies. Implementing the first requirement ensures higher energy availability with lower fuel consumption through more efficient power generation. This implementation, therefore, benefits energy availability and affordability by reducing generation costs.

The load curve flattening implies stabilising energy demand by reducing peak energy consumption. It contributes to energy reliability by avoiding voltage variations and power outages. Last but not least, the call in Article 3 for the implementation of energy storage systems benefits energy availability and accessibility. This complement offers backup in multiple circumstances by guaranteeing access to energy that was generated before the advent of such adverse scenarios.

Another consequence of Legislative Decree 345 linked to the right to energy is the energy transition. Thus, at the regulatory level, incentives for foreign investment in developing the renewable energy sector are created to guarantee energy supply. The transformation of energy systems through the transition to sustainability implies technological changes, the implementation of new infrastructures, institutional work, investments, the creation of support mechanisms, and the integration of renewable energy sources into the energy sector.

In this context, energy auctions have become a mechanism to promote sustainable energy development. However, implementing this type of practice requires, among other elements, the implementation of a legal framework, the design of an institutional framework, and the development of infrastructures and human resources, for which foreign investment plays a fundamental role.

For that reason, the Ministry of Energy and Mines has shown great interest in studying the energy auction schemes implemented globally to define the most viable implementation in Cuba and the elements that should be included in the legal framework. As a result of the above, in early 2022, a call was launched to construct solar-photovoltaic parks with a generation capacity of 900 MW,[45] and new energy auctions are still ongoing.[46]

Related to the above emerges another implication of Decree-Law 345 in the realisation of the right to energy. It refers to the promotion of energy sustainability. By promoting the participation of renewable sources in the national energy matrix, Cuba pursues the fulfilment of the 2030 Agenda and, in this way, guarantees energy supply with a reduction in greenhouse gas emissions. Such a reduction is significant, considering that the energy sector greatly impacts CO_2 emissions into the atmosphere.[47]

Another of the provisions aimed at promoting the generation of renewable energy sources are the regulations relating to state-sector investments. Based on the planning of the economy as a principal component of the economic and social development management system, the Cuban state has the potential to organise economic activity.

[45] Delgado Triana et al. (2022) and Mendes (2022).

[46] Shetty (2022) and Sánchez Molina (2023).

[47] According to the International Energy Agency, following regional analysis, energy-related CO_2 emissions grew by 0.9% in 2022, equivalent to 321 Mt for a new record high of 36.8 Gt. IEA (2022).

Article 19

"The state directs, regulates, and controls economic activity by reconciling national, territorial, collective, and individual interests for the benefit of society.

Socialist planning is the system's central component for directing economic and social development. Its essential function is to plan and guide strategic development, providing for the appropriate balance between resources and needs." (Own translation)[48]

In this sense, Decree-Law 345 entrusts state legal entities with creating programmes for the development, maintenance and sustainability of renewable sources and the efficient use of energy. These programmes determine an increase in installed generation capacity from renewable sources that contributes to the realisation of the right to energy. This result is achieved by providing state assets to guarantee energy availability to meet the energy needs of Cuban society.[49]

Consequently, based on Decree Law 345, Resolution 123 of the Ministry of Energy was issued. This normative body developed the regulations of Chapter IV of Decree Law 345 (Articles 20, 21, 22 and 23)[50] regarding the development of renewable energy sources in the top management organisations, the business systems of provincial and municipal administrations, and budgeted entities. Resolution 123 implemented renewable energy sources mandatory on a cost-benefit country basis.[51] Such regulations consistently follow the provisions of the existing Resolution 152 of 2018 of the Ministry of Energy and Mines.[52]

In turn, Article 8 of Decree-Law 345 assumes a revolutionary wording by opening the energy sector to energy democracy.

Article 8

"Natural and legal persons may acquire equipment that uses renewable sources and others that allow the efficient use of energy, and, if required, to avail themselves of bank credit, following the principles for granting credit established in the legislation in force." (Own translation)[53]

The exercise of energy prosumerism has been a practice that has been spreading in different regions of the world as a means of empowerment through the active participation of people in the energy sector, given the multiplicity of benefits

---

[48] Cf. Article 19. Constitución de la República de Cuba (2019).

[49] Cf. Article 4.1. "State legal entities shall include in their economic plan, in accordance with the provisions established for this purpose and the directives issued under Article 20 of this Decree-Law, investments for the installation of equipment and means that use renewable sources and those that promote the rational and efficient use of energy." (Own translation) Cf. Articles 5, 6, 7, 20, 21, 22 and 23. Consejo de Estado (2019).

[50] Cf. Article 20, 21, 22 and 23. Consejo de Estado (2019).

[51] Cf. Para. 1. Ministerio de Energía y Minas (2019a).

[52] Cf. Article 15. Ministerio de Energía y Minas (2018).

[53] Cf. Article 8. Consejo de Estado (2019).

involved.[54] For this reason, Decree-Law 345 is at the height of its time, allowing a diversification in energy generation to guarantee availability and accessibility as elements of the content of the right to energy by authorising the exercise of energy prosumerism to, in turn, promote the transition towards renewable energy sources.

Article 8 authorises natural persons to acquire renewable energy generation technologies. For this purpose, the possibility of using bank loans is envisaged. Although the position taken by the legislator is very advanced, the legal and economic reality does not ensure the effectiveness of such a postulate.

9.8 Regulatory Development of the Decree-Law 345/2019

In that context, also in 2019, the Central Bank of Cuba issued Instruction 6 on granting bank loans to natural persons to acquire specific equipment that uses renewable energy sources.[55] The granting of bank credits for exercising energy prosumerism would allow the holders of the right to energy through renewable energy sources to meet all or part of their energy needs. However, Instruction 6 limits the potential for this type of practice. This instrument only declares eligible applications for credits to purchase water heaters and solar photovoltaic systems. This restrictive approach constitutes a limit to exploiting other renewable energy sources, such as wind energy.

At the same time, the credits granted, although they can cover up to 100% of the value of the equipment, are quoted in Cuban pesos. This quote makes this credit partially inoperative for importing renewable generation technologies. Therefore, borrowers must look for offers in the national market, where the production of this type of technology is in the development process, making it challenging to achieve the objectives of Decree-Law 345.

However, as of Resolution 141 of the Ministry of Domestic Trade issued in 2019, the procedure for commercialising equipment using renewable sources and efficient energy use is legally established. This resolution directly impacts energy accessibility as it aims to develop infrastructure for energy generation. For this reason, the Corporación Copextel S.A., the Grupo Empresarial de Logística (Gelma) and the companies Comercializadoras y de Servicios de Productos Universales are authorised to commercialise this type of technology. For this purpose, the described bank credits were conceived within Instruction 6 of the Central Bank of Cuba.[56]

---

[54] The European Union is a pioneering region in the creation of regulatory frameworks to promote energy prosumerism. Since the 2018/2001 and 2019 Directives, these regulatory frameworks have been strengthened. These directives are not the first precedents regarding the exercise of energy prosumerism, given that since the creation of the internal electricity market by Directive 90/547/EEC, different associated figures have been conceived.

However, with the evolution of the European regulatory framework, the legal regulation of energy prosumerism has been perfected and so has its implementation. Luis Cordova et al. (2023).

[55] Banco Central de Cuba (2019).

[56] Ministerio del Comercio Interior (2019).

Article 15 of Decree-Law 345 reflects the commitment of the Ministry of Energy and Mines to energy production by consumers, which is the approach taken legally concerning the holders of the right to energy in Cuba. In this context, Decree-Law 345 reinforces the exercise of energy prosumerism through the possibility of selling surplus energy produced to the National Electricity System. To this end, it provides for the purchase of surpluses by the Unión Eléctrica as the sole transmitter, distributor, and marketer of electricity in the country.

Article 15.1
"The Ministry of Energy and Mines promotes the production of energy by consumers, including the residential sector, based on the use of technologies that take advantage of renewable energy sources for self-supply and the sale of surpluses to the National Electricity System.

2. Unión Eléctrica purchases all electricity generated from renewable energy sources, produced by independent producers, provided that it complies with the established technical standards." (Own translation)[57]

In addition to the self-satisfaction of energy needs, this means economic benefits for energy prosumers, which, in turn, generates environmental benefits by contributing to the reduction of greenhouse gas emissions by the national energy sector.

Returning to another of the implications of Decree-Law 345 on the right to energy, it is essential to highlight Articles 17.1 and 2. This article states the diversification of energy services through the prioritisation of the use of liquefied natural gas.

Article 17.1
"The Ministry of Energy y mines, to increase the efficiency y conservation of energy, has among its priorities to require y control the high vitality of the National Electricity System. Efficiency y energy conservation is among its priorities to demand y control, which is a high vitality of the National Electricity System.

2. It also prioritises the use of Liquefied Natural Gas in the completion of existing capacities, with combined cycles, as an alternative for diversifying the structure of fossil fuels." (Own translation)[58]

Such an initiative positively impacts the realisation of the right to energy through diversification of access. In this scenario, liquefied natural gas is a viable alternative for satisfying energy needs such as cooking, water heating and others. The availability of this energy carrier is an alternative solution to electricity service interruptions to safeguard the right to energy in contexts of energy crises.

---

[57] Cf. Article 15. Consejo de Estado (2019).

[58] Cf. Article 17.1 and 2. Consejo de Estado (2019).

Decree-Law 345 formulations and the implementation of its regulations at the normative level have numerous implications for the right to energy. In this way, the Cuban government's political will regarding energy security and sovereignty has been crystallised in a regulatory framework, creating incentives for the nation's sustainable energy development and access to energy. To this end, at the legal level, priority has been given to increasing the participation of renewable energy sources in the national energy matrix. In addition, the implementation of power purchase agreements has allowed the generation capacity to be contracted in photovoltaic solar parks.

To complement Decree-Law 345 regarding the exercise of energy prosumerism, in 2021, several regulatory bodies issued by the Ministry of Energy and Mines and the Ministry of Finance and Prices were put into force. These regulations were focused on facilitating the importation of technologies linked to the use of renewable sources for energy generation by natural persons. In this sense, it is essential to highlight Resolutions 208 and 206 issued by the Ministry of Energy and Mines.

Resolution 208 aimed to approve the import of technologies that generate or operate with renewable energy sources, their parts, and pieces without establishing quantity limits for importing equipment, parts, and fundamental pieces.[59] In conjunction with Resolution 208, Resolution 206 was issued, which authorises the import of photovoltaic systems by natural persons.[60]

Resolutions 322 and 319 of the Ministry of Finance and Prices were added to these two resolutions. The first of these resolutions exempts the following from customs duties: non-commercial imports: solar heaters; photovoltaic pumps; small wind turbines; geomembrane biodigesters; biogas motor pumps; solar lighting and solar air conditioning systems, as well as the fundamental parts and pieces of this equipment.[61] In this way, this legal instrument constitutes an incentive to import this type of technology that contributes to the right to energy.

Implementing Power Purchase Agreements represents another energy legal framework initiative to promote energy access. For this reason, Resolution 242 of 2021, issued by the Ministry of Energy and Mines, was put into effect. This resolution offers another alternative for the satisfaction of the right to energy through the commercialisation of installed generation capacity, but it also aims to raise funds for investment in the development of generation from renewable energy sources.[62] Despite the novelty of this initiative in the Cuban context, its benefits are limited due to its impact on energy affordability. These limitations are due to the payment system established in Resolution 242.

In Resolution 242, the tariffs for contracting this type of energy supply are established in freely convertible currency (MLC). Using MLC has resulted from the monetary reorganisation process developed in 2021, which has impacted every

[59] Ministerio de Energía y Minas (2021b).

[60] Ministerio de Energía y Minas (2021a).

[61] Ministerio de Finanzas y Precios (2021).

[62] Ministerio de Energía y Minas (2021c).

sector of Cuban society. The need to obtain foreign currency for the sustainable energy development of the country forced the Ministry of Energy and Mines to establish tariffs on the Power Purchase Agreements in MLC, which has a negative implication on the affordability for the holders of the right to energy.

This negative implication is because the currency in circulation in the country is the Cuban peso, which is not an exchangeable currency in the formal exchange market. For this reason, people's ability to pay for these types of contracts has been eliminated. However, the commercialisation of installed photovoltaic power is an alternative for those with the necessary financial resources to cover part of their energy needs in this way, although this is still a small sector of the Cuban population.

However, the Cuban government's continued concern about guaranteeing energy affordability is worth noting. Such concerns are reflected in the electricity services subsidy maintained in Cuba, which is up to a monthly consumption of 500kWh.[63] Despite the effects of the monetary order on the Cuban economy and the effects of the global energy crisis, Agreement 8957 of the Council of Ministers maintains a system of tariffs according to consumption ranges, which, although they penalise excessive electricity consumption, promote the affordability of the electricity service.[64]

9.9 Law 150/2022 "Law of the Natural Resources and Environment System"

Another element that affects the realisation of the right to energy in Cuba is the energy-environment interaction, which is why another law with implications for the right to energy is Law 150 of 2022. This law, known as the Law of the Natural Resources and Environment System, was passed on 8 June 2022.[65] As of its entry into force, this law updated Cuba's legal-environmental system, replacing its predecessor, Law 81, "Law on the Environment".[66]

Based on the premise that energy, from an environmental regulatory perspective, is assumed to reduce energy consumption and the consumption of natural resources to reduce the energy sector's environmental impact,[67] Law 150 adopts the energy transition within its regulatory body. In this way, Law 150 promotes energy development based on environmental sustainability, and, once again, the Cuban legal system reinforces energy sustainability to satisfy the right to energy. In this sense, it makes the bodies, agencies of the Central State Administration, national entities,

[63] Alonso Falcón et al. (2020).

[64] Consejo de Ministros (2020).

[65] Asamblea Nacional del Poder Popular (2022a).

[66] Asamblea Nacional del Poder Popular (1997).

[67] Drnas de Clément (2016), p. 5.

and government bodies at the national and territorial levels responsible for the following:

> Changing the energy matrix by improving energy efficiency and the widespread introduction of renewable energy sources, in a way that is conducive to less greenhouse gas-intensive development. (Own translation)[68]

9.10 Resolution 54/2018 "Indications for the Organisation and Implementation of Consumer Protection in the Internal Trading System"

A constitutional consequence that impacts the implications of the Cuban legal framework is Article 78.[69] This pronouncement regarding the right to consume quality goods and services is aligned with Resolution 54 of the Ministry of Domestic Trade, which came into force in 2018. This normative instrument establishes guidelines for consumer organisation and enforcement in the country. Although it is focused on the internal trade system, it defines a consumer in its Annex I as:

> a natural or legal person, who acquires, uses or enjoys, as a final recipient, goods and services of any nature, retail end user or beneficiary.[70]

Referring to services of any nature opens the framework for including energy services as a subject of regulation.

This body of law declares principles such as respect for consumer rights, consumer education, information, and dissemination; ethical performance and social responsibility of the supplier; transparency and professionalism; prevention and continuous improvement. It also establishes the rights and obligations of consumers, which is a step forward in consumer protection.

Although Resolution 54 was a step forward in consumer protection in Cuba, the assumption of the right to energy within consumer law limits its protection. Given the generic nature of Resolution 54, the understanding, regulation, and protection of the holders of the right to energy is truncated. In this sense, it does not include the protection of all the elements that make up the content of the right to energy. In addition, there is a deficient definition of vulnerable consumers, including disabled people, children, pregnant women, and older people.

This definition leaves out energy consumers in situations of energy poverty and vulnerability, given that no indicators are established to determine the existence of this type of situation from an interdisciplinary approach with multifactorial origins. Another shortcoming of this regulatory instrument is that it does not regulate the setting of

---

[68] Cf. Article 103, para. e). Asamblea Nacional del Poder Popular (2022b).

[69] Cf. Article 78. Constitución de la República de Cuba (2019).

[70] Ministerio del Comercio Interior (2018).

energy tariffs and prices in a way that promotes energy services affordability. Nor does it recognise or promote the creation of organisations to represent consumers.[71]

9.11 Conclusion

After assessing the Cuban legal system in the "light" of the right to energy, regulatory successes and failures stand out as conclusions. The first of these successes is implementing a set of legal norms with a high degree of implication in the realisation of the right under study. Among these implications is the existence of rules aimed at achieving the availability, accessibility, affordability, and reliability of energy services.

Added to this is the priority the legal system gives to the energy transition to guarantee energy security and sovereignty, which positively impacts the realisation of the right to energy. In addition, promoting energy democracy initiatives is a new step forward of its kind, which contributes to the self-satisfaction of the energy needs of the holders of the right to energy.

Despite the national legal system's successes in achieving the right to energy, many shortcomings become regulatory challenges. The most important issue is the non-constitutional recognition of the right to energy, which negatively affects its legal protection and the delimitation of its meaning and scope. In turn, the absence of constitutional recognition means that the content of the right to energy can only be safeguarded by other rights. In addition, many of the incentives created for promoting energy democracy are rendered ineffective by the current legal and economic conditions. Another shortcoming is the qualification of the holders of the right to energy as consumers since the protection offered to them is limited.

Considering the strengths and weaknesses of the Cuban legal system, it is necessary to determine the legal bases that should support the future recognition of the right to energy. As it is a right that has not yet been recognised in Cuba, its bases must be coherent with the Cuban legal system.

References[72]

Alonso Falcón R, Figueredo Reinaldo O, García Acosta D, Rodríguez Martínez K, Carmona Tamayo E, Carmenate R (2020) Modifican tarifas eléctricas para el sector residencial y precios del gas licuado de petróleo. Cubadebate, La Habana. http://www.cubadebate.cu/noticias/2020/12/28/modifican-tarifas-electricas-para-el-sector-residencial-y-precios-del-gas-licuado-de-petroleo/#anexo-1474615. Accessed 3 Mar 2025

Asamblea Nacional del Poder Popular (1997) Ley 81 'Ley del Medio Ambiente'. Gaceta Oficial No. 7 Extraordinaria de 11 de julio. Gaceta Oficial de la República de Cuba, La Habana. https://

[71] Luis Cordova and Rodríguez Rivero (2023).

[72] All links to the cited websites were operational as of 3 March 2025.

www.gacetaoficial.gob.cu/sites/default/files/extraordinaria_7_del_1997__0.pdf. Accessed 3 Mar 2025

Asamblea Nacional del Poder Popular (2022a) Acuerdo IX-129/2022. Gaceta Oficial No. 58 Ordinaria de 8 de junio. Gaceta Oficial de la República de Cuba, La Habana. https://www.gacetaoficial.gob.cu/sites/default/files/goc-2022-o58_0.pdf. Accessed 3 Mar 2025

Asamblea Nacional del Poder Popular (2022b) Ley 150 'Del Sistema De Los Recursos Naturales Y El Medio Ambiente'. Gace, Cuba. https://www.gacetaoficial.gob.cu/sites/default/files/ley_150_del_sistema_de_los_recursos_naturales_y_el_medio_ambiente.pdf. Accessed 3 Mar 2025

Asamblea Nacional del Poder Popular (2022c) Ley No. 151: Código Penal. Gaceta Oficial No. 93 Ordinaria de 1ro. de septiembre de 2022. Gaceta Oficial de la República de Cuba, La Habana. https://www.gacetaoficial.gob.cu/sites/default/files/goc-2022-o93_0_0.pdf. Accessed 3 Mar 2025

Banco Central de Cuba (2019) Instrucción 6. Gaceta Oficial No. 95 Ordinaria de 28 de noviembre. Gaceta Oficial de la República de Cuba, La Habana. https://www.gacetaoficial.gob.cu/es/instruccion-6-de-2019-de-banco-central-de-cuba. Accessed 3 Mar 2025

Comité Ejecutivo del Consejo de Ministros (1998) Decreto No. 260: Contravenciones personales de las regulaciones del Servicio Eléctrico. Gaceta Oficial No. 60 Ordinaria de 11 de diciembre. Gaceta Oficial de la República de Cuba, La Habana. https://www.gacetaoficial.gob.cu/sites/default/files/GO_O_060_1998.rar. Accessed 3 Mar 2025

Consejo de Estado (2019) Decreto Ley 345 "Del Desarrollo de las Fuentes Renovables y el Uso Eficiente de la Energía". Gaceta Oficial No. 95 Ordinaria de 28 de noviembre. Gaceta Oficial de la República de Cuba, La Habana. https://www.gacetaoficial.gob.cu/sites/default/files/goc-2019-o95.pdf. Accessed 3 Mar 2025

Consejo de Ministros (2020) Acuerdo 8957. Gaceta Oficial No. 68 Extraordinaria de 10 de diciembre. Gaceta Oficial de la República de Cuba, La Habana. https://www.gacetaoficial.gob.cu/sites/default/files/goc-2020-ex68.pdf. Accessed 3 Mar 2025

Constitución de la República de Cuba (2019) Gaceta Oficial No. 5 Extraordinaria de 10 de abril de 2019. Gaceta Oficial de la República de Cuba, La Habana. https://www.gacetaoficial.gob.cu/sites/default/files/goc-2019-ex5.pdf. Accessed 3 Mar 2025

De Cores CA, Cal JM (2007) El concepto de interés público y su incidencia en la contratación administrativa. Revista de Derecho de la Universidad de Montevideo 6(11):131–140. http://revistas.um.edu.uy/index.php/revistaderecho/article/download/882/1094. Accessed 3 Mar 2025

Delgado Triana Y, Luis Cordova JG, Milian Gómez JF, Fariñas Wong EY, Lorenzo Yera B, Sánchez Fernández A (2022) Energy auctions: an alternative for energy investment in Cuba. Oil Gas Energy Law 5. https://www.ogel.org/article.asp?key=4057. Accessed 3 Mar 2025

Drnas de Clément Z (2016) El Derecho Ambiental y el Derecho de la Energía, ¿paradigmas compatibles o contrapuestos? Academia Nacional de Derecho y Ciencias Sociales de Córdobam Córdoba. https://www.acaderc.org.ar/wp-content/blogs.dir/55/files/sites/55/2022/04/ZDIDARNEnerg20161.pdf. Accessed 3 Mar 2025

Figueredo Reinaldo O, Rodríguez Martínez K, Carmenate R (2021) Robo de: Apuntes sobre una estafa conocida. La Habana, Cubadebate. http://www.cubadebate.cu/especiales/2021/06/07/robo-de-electricidad-apuntes-sobre-una-estafa-conocida/. Accessed 3 Mar 2025

García de Enterría E (1975) El control de los poderes discrecionales de la administración. Revista de Derecho Público (17):81–96. https://revistaderechopublico.uchile.cl/index.php/RDPU/article/view/35203. Accessed 3 Mar 2025

IEA (2022) CO2 emissions in 2022. Global energy, vol 62. https://www.iea.org/news/global-co2-emissions-rebounded-to-their-highest-level-in-history-in-2021. Accessed 3 Mar 2025

Le Riverend J (1974) Historia económica de Cuba. Editorial Pueblo y Educación, La Habana. https://books.google.be/books/about/Historia_económica_de_Cuba.html?id=jp6xAAAAIAAJ&redir_esc=y. Accessed 3 Mar 2025

Luis Cordova JG (2022) Regulación jurídica de la energía en Cuba: valoración crítica para su perfeccionamiento. In: Correa AM, Núñez DPV, Oseguera DJR (eds) Reflexiones sobre

Derecho Público, vol III. Editorial UNIJURIS, La Habana, pp 164–180. https://www.researchgate.net/profile/Andry-Matilla-Correa/publication/369356237_2022-2_Matilla_Correa_A_Viteri_D_y_Romero_D_J_Coord_Reflexiones_sobre_Derecho_Publico_III/links/6415c7a5a1b72772e40a7ea8/2022-2-Matilla-Correa-A-Viteri-D-y-Romero-D-J-Coord-Re. Accessed 3 Mar 2025

Luis Cordova JG, Rodríguez Rivero DL (2023) Energy consumer in the Cuban legal system: towards comprehensive protection. J World Energy Law Bus 16(4):309–319. https://academic.oup.com/jwelb/advance-article/doi/10.1093/jwelb/jwad010/7206380. Accessed 3 Mar 2025

Luis Cordova JG, Dueñas Rodríguez A, Byttebier K, Delgado Triana Y (2022) Energy and law. A critical approach to the Cuban context. Glob Jurist 22(2):413–432. https://www.degruyter.com/document/doi/10.1515/gj-2021-0085/html. Accessed 3 Mar 2025

Luis Cordova JG, Byttebier K, Delgado Triana Y (2023) Decentralized energy generation for sustainable energy development in EU. Eur Energy Environ Law Rev 32(4):164–176. https://kluwerlawonline.com/journalarticle/European+Energy+and+Environmental+Law+Review/32.4/EELR2023010. Accessed 3 Mar 2025

Mendes JK (2022) NTPC invites bids from developers to build 900 MW solar PV park in Republic of Cuba. Construction Week. https://www.constructionweekonline.in/projects-tenders/ntpc-invites-bids-from-developers-to-build-900-mw-solar-pv-park-in-republic-of-cuba. Accessed 3 Mar 2025

Mexico Suprema Corte de Justicia, Universidad Nacional Autónoma de México Instituto de Investigaciones (2009) Expropiación, amplitud del concepto de utilidad pública y limitaciones a la propiedad privada. Ciudad de México. https://www.worldcat.org/title/expropiacion-amplitud-del-concepto-de-utilidad-publica-y-limitaciones-a-la-propiedad-privada/oclc/499444070. Accessed 3 Mar 2025

Ministerio de Energía y Minas (2017) Resolución 92 'Reglamento para el servicio de gas licuado de petróleo a la población'. Gaceta Oficial No. 55 Extraordinaria de 7 de diciembre. Gaceta Oficial de la República de Cuba, La Habana. https://www.gacetaoficial.gob.cu/sites/default/files/goc-2017-ex55.pdf. Accessed 3 Mar 2025

Ministerio de Energía y Minas (2018) Resolución 152 'Manual de Inspección a los Portadores Energéticos'. Gaceta Oficial de la República de Cuba, La Habana. https://www.gacetaoficial.gob.cu/sites/default/files/goc-2018-ex61.pdf. Accessed 3 Mar 2025

Ministerio de Energía y Minas (2019a) Resolución 123. Gaceta Oficial No. 95 Ordinaria de 28 de noviembre. Gaceta Oficial de la República de Cuba, La Habana. https://www.gacetaoficial.gob.cu/sites/default/files/goc-2019-o95.pdf. Accessed 3 Mar 2025

Ministerio de Energía y Minas (2019b) Resolución 124. Gaceta Oficial No. 95 Ordinaria de 28 de noviembre. Gaceta Oficial de la República de Cuba, La Habana. https://www.gacetaoficial.gob.cu/sites/default/files/goc-2019-o95.pdf. Accessed 3 Mar 2025

Ministerio de Energía y Minas (2021a) Resolución 206. Gaceta Oficial No. 67 Extraordinaria de 28 de julio. Gaceta Oficial de la República de Cuba, La Habana. https://www.gacetaoficial.gob.cu/sites/default/files/goc-2021-ex67.pdf. Accessed 3 Mar 2025

Ministerio de Energía y Minas (2021b) Resolución 208. Gaceta Oficial No. 69 Extraordinaria de 30 de julio. Gaceta Oficial de la República de Cuba, La Habana. https://www.gacetaoficial.gob.cu/sites/default/files/goc-2021-ex69.pdf. Accessed 3 Mar 2025

Ministerio de Energía y Minas (2021c) Resolución 242. Gaceta Oficial No. 111 Extraordinaria de 30 de diciembre. Gaceta Oficial de la República de Cuba, La Habana. https://www.gacetaoficial.gob.cu/sites/default/files/goc-2021-ex111_0.pdf. Accessed 3 Mar 2025

Ministerio de Finanzas y Precios (2021) Resolución 322. Gaceta Oficial No. 69 Extraordinaria de 30 de julio. Gaceta Oficial de la República de Cuba, La Habana. https://www.gacetaoficial.gob.cu/sites/default/files/goc-2021-ex69.pdf. Accessed 3 Mar 2025

Ministerio de Finazas y Precios (2015) Resolución 1034: 'Procedimiento del cálculo para el pago del impuesto sobre los servicios en lo referido a la trasmisión de energía eléctrica al sector residencial nacional y extrajero'. Gaceta Oficial No. 51 Ordinaria de 25 de noviembre de 2015.

Gaceta Oficial de la República, La Habana. https://www.gacetaoficial.gob.cu/sites/default/files/go_o_51_2015.pdf. Accessed 3 Mar 2025

Ministerio de la Industria Básica (2009) Resolución 64: Procedimiento para la atención a las reclamaciones por daños ocasionados a la propiedad de clientes reesidenciales y no residenciales, por anormalidades en el suministro de energía eléctrica. Gaceta Oficial No. 010 Ordinaria de 26 de marzo. Gaceta Oficial de la República de Cuba, La Habana. https://www.gacetaoficial.gob.cu/sites/default/files/go_o_010_2009.pdf. Accessed 3 Mar 2025

Ministerio del Comercio Interior (2018) Resolución No. 54 'Indicaciones para la organización y ejecución de la protección al consumidor en el sistema de comercio interno'. Gaceta Oficial de la República, , La Habana. https://www.gacetaoficial.gob.cu/sites/default/files/goc-2018-ex26_mincin.rar. Accessed 3 Mar 2025

Ministerio del Comercio Interior (2019) Resolución 141. Gaceta Oficial No. 95 Ordinaria de 28 de noviembre. Gaceta Oficial de la República de Cuba, La Habana. https://www.gacetaoficial.gob.cu/es/resolucion-141-de-2019-de-ministerio-del-comercio-interior. Accessed 3 Mar 2025

Ministro de la Industria Eléctrica (1975) Reglamento del Servicio Eléctrico. Gaceta Oficial de la República de Cuba, La Habana. https://www.unionelectrica.cu/wp-content/uploads/2018/11/ley-electrica.pdf. Accessed 3 Mar 2025

Poder Ejecutivo (1938) Ley de Minerales Combustibles. Gaceta Oficial de la República de Cuba, La Habana

Poder Ejecutivo del Consejo de Ministros (1975) Ley 1287 'Ley Eléctrica'. Gaceta Oficial de la República de Cuba, La Habana. https://www.unionelectrica.cu/wp-content/uploads/2018/11/ley-electrica.pdf. Accessed 3 Mar 2025

Redacción Digital (2020) Se combaten en Cuba ilegalidades en el consumo de electricidad. CubaSí. https://cubasi.cu/es/noticia/se-combaten-en-cuba-ilegalidades-en-el-consumo-de-electricidad. Accessed 3 Mar 2025

Sánchez Molina P (2023) Cuba to hold 60 MW solar tender. PV Magazine. https://www.pv-magazine.com/2023/06/12/cuba-to-hold-60-mw-solar-tender/. Accessed 3 Mar 2025

Shetty S (2022) ISA floats tender for 1150 MW solar project in Cuba. Solarquarter. https://solarquarter.com/2022/08/11/isa-floats-tender-for-1150-mw-solar-project-in-cuba/. Accessed 3 Mar 2025

Thomson H, Day R, Ricalde K, Brand-Correa LI, Cedano K, Martinez M, Santillán O, Delgado Triana Y, Luis Cordova JG, Milian Gómez JF, Garcia Torres D, Mercado C, Castelao Caruana ME, Pereira MG (2022) Understanding, recognizing, and sharing energy poverty knowledge and gaps in Latin America and the Caribbean – because conocer es resolver. Energy Res Soc Sci 87:102475. https://linkinghub.elsevier.com/retrieve/pii/S2214629621005624. Accessed 3 Mar 2025

Chapter 10
Theoretical-Legal Elements for the Recognition of the Right to Energy in Cuba

10.1 Introduction

The constitutional recognition of the right to energy in Cuba, as a fundamental right, is an imperative necessity as the maximum legal guarantee of its realisation. The absence of such recognition means that the Cuban legal system does not provide sufficient mechanisms for the protection of the right under study. This means that even the legal-social transcendence of affectations related to what this research defines as the right to energy is not appreciated prima facie.

This is related to the fact that, according to the Constitutional Rights Protection Chamber of the People's Supreme Court of Cuba, the social-legal transcendence established in Article 5.3 of Law 153 is still an undetermined concept in Cuban legal reality and practice.[1] Given the lack of constitutional recognition of the right to energy, the determination of the theoretical-legal bases on which it should be based in order to sustain its recognition is a matter of vital importance.

An example is appeal number 11 of 2023 before the Constitutional Rights Protection Chamber of Cuba's People's Supreme Court. This appeal aimed to restore the right to adequate housing, given the absence of constitutional recognition of the right to energy and its legal delimitation. In this sense, this appeal for protection sought to reestablish the public electricity service, which was declared admissible by the mentioned Constitutional Rights Protection Chamber.[2] Although motivated by the severe impact on family life for its adequate development, this decision was closely linked to the impact on what is defined in this investigation as the right to energy.

---

[1] Sala de Amparo de los Derechos Constitucionales (2023).

[2] Sala de Amparo de los Derechos Constitucionales (2023).

J. G. Luis Cordova, *Theoretical and Legal Dimensions of the Right to Energy*, Economic and Financial Law & Policy – Shifting Insights & Values 9, https://doi.org/10.1007/978-3-032-33252-3_10

This situation simply results from the legal-constitutional system's omission of the right to energy. For this reason, the elements that should underpin the right to energy in Cuba will be developed below at a theoretical level and as a theoretical-legal basis: its conceptualisation, the principles that should inform it, its subjects, its content, and its legal regulation and guarantees.

10.2 Towards a Right to Energy in Cuba, Between Its Concept and the Shortcomings of the Cuban Legal System

Determining the theoretical-legal basis of the right to energy in Cuba, it is necessary to start from the following premise: this right is a human right in the formation process to which the Cuban legal system does not grant it the status of a fundamental right through express recognition on the Cuban Constitution. This premise imposes boundaries on the conceptual delimitation of a right that, despite satisfying fundamental needs, is not considered a fundamental right in the Cuban Constitution of 2019. For this reason, the theoretical contributions of this research will be determined, in part, by the characteristics of the Cuban legal system.

The conceptual approach to what should be understood by the right to energy in Cuba is based on the operationalisation of the earlier definition in this research.[3] To this end, the following operational variables are identified: availability, accessibility, affordability, and energy reliability.[4] In this sense, energy is defined by its double dimensionality as energy services and energy sources. Following the analysis of the Cuban constitution and the national legal framework, several normative elements affect each identified operational variable in the "light" of the right to energy.

In the area of variable energy availability, from the constitutional provisions of 2019 to infra-constitutional norms, such as the Law on Combustible Minerals, the state declares itself sovereign over the energy resources under its jurisdiction. This constitutional declaration is also based on the international legal system, starting with Resolution 1803 of the United Nations General Assembly on permanent sovereignty over natural resources.[5] In this way, the Cuban state ensured the exploitation of natural energy resources, regardless of their nature, to satisfy the national energy demand.

---

[3] Cf. already supra, Sect. 5.3.2.

[4] Luis Cordova (2025), pp. 1–3.

[5] Permanent sovereignty over natural resources is considered an element of the right to self-determination of states, which is exercised in the interest of national development and the population. For this reason, states are entitled to grant concessions in accordance with national legal frameworks to investment capital, without prejudice to their right to nationalise, expropriate or reacquire the rights granted for reasons of public utility, security, or national interest, against payment of the corresponding compensation. In turn, any violation of permanent sovereignty over natural resources is considered contrary to the UN Charter. UN General Assembly (1962).

Unquestionably, energy availability, as a fundamental premise for the realisation of the right to energy, depends on the availability of both non-renewable and renewable energy resources. In this sense, the Cuban State ensures, under the socialist ownership of all the people, the natural resources within the exclusive economic zone of the Republic of Cuba under the principles of inalienability, indefeasibility and non-seizability. Without prejudice to the above, energy availability is safeguarded, given that it provides for the transfer of other types of rights over natural resources following the economic and social development of the country.[6] In this way, energy availability can be favoured through foreign investment in energy generation.[7]

In turn, energy availability in Cuba encompasses the control of the energy demand of the state sector in the time intervals of highest consumption. This control contributes to reducing energy demand to ensure that energy generation can satisfy the energy demand of the holders of the right to energy.

In addition to the above, energy availability in the Cuban context benefits from the generation of energy from renewable sources, which, although it is still a growing sector, guarantees that part of the national energy demand is satisfied through renewable sources. This results in an increase in generation capacity and, consequently, in energy availability.

Another element that, at the regulatory level, defines energy availability and gives way to accessibility as a second operational variant of the concept of the right to energy is the exercise of energy prosumerism. While the regulatory conception of this type of initiative impacts energy democracy, it contributes to obtaining economic income. However, much more importantly, it contributes to obtaining a new type of income for people by self-satisfying their energy needs.

The exercise of energy prosumerism, as provided for in the Cuban legal framework, promotes energy availability and access to energy. This second element is vital, especially for the fraction of the Cuban population that still does not have access to the central electricity distribution network. In this sense, at the regulatory level, mechanisms have been established to develop energy generation infrastructures based on renewable sources aimed at both the holders of the right to energy and all economic sectors.

At the same time, despite the normative conception of energy prosumerism, guaranteeing energy accessibility is still the state's responsibility, and the business system has been created for this purpose. This responsibility is reflected in developing transmission and distribution networks to guarantee the country's electrification, especially in the most difficult-to-access areas.

---

[6] Cf. Article 23. Constitución de la República de Cuba (2019).

[7] In September 2023, 18 project opportunities for foreign investment were found to be open. These business opportunities, although still limited in view of the energy crisis in Cuba, open up the spectrum for foreign investment ranging from wind power generation, solar photovoltaic, installation and operation of bioelectric power plants to oil exploration. The total amount of the aforementioned project opportunities is around 1.5 billion dollars. Ministerio del Comercio Interior e Inversión Extranjera de Cuba (2023).

Concerning energy affordability, several elements characterise this operational variable in Cuba. In this sense, the state's interest in guaranteeing energy affordability through the establishment of subsidies that, despite being mainly focused on fossil fuels, reduce the economic impact of satisfying the energy needs of the holders of the right to energy on their assets. Despite the harmful effects of maintaining such subsidies on the national economy, part of the state's budget is used to guarantee affordable energy services to boost the country's economic and social development. Therefore, such subsidies can be seen as a supplement to wages.

However, regarding the exercise of energy prosumerism, energy affordability is an element that still constitutes a challenge for energy policy and regulation. This challenge is linked to the current functioning of the national economy, which means that the acquisition of infrastructure for energy generation by the holders of the right to energy is still limited. Despite the credit and tax advantages the Cuban legal system provides, the self-satisfaction of energy needs in Cuba is far from reaching its true potential due to economic conditions, among many others.

Reliability, as the fourth operational variable of the concept of the right to energy, is one of the variables that, at the regulatory level, is characterised by a lower level of reinforcement. In this context, few normative references regulate responsibility for the reliability of energy services. The obsolete Electricity Act and its regulations are particularly relevant in this respect. Attributing such responsibility to the now-extinct Central State Administration bodies is an element that affects the assurance of energy reliability in determining the obligated subjects.

The Cuban legal system leaves many gaps in recognising and protecting the right to energy. For this reason, protecting its holders is an unresolved issue for the jurisdictional bodies that must decide where the right to energy could be violated. For this reason, it is necessary to determine the principles in force in the Cuban legal system that should inform the right to energy to ensure effective protection.

10.3 Essential Principles that Should Inform the Right to Energy

The essential general principles that inform the right to energy have been discussed above.[8] The observance of these principles must be considered to fully fulfil the right to energy in Cuba. Each offers precise instructions to the legal system to regulate the specific aspects of the right to energy to ensure its recognition, protection, and guarantee as a human right.

Nevertheless, it is crucial to explain how the specific principles for the future recognition and configuration of the right to energy in Cuba should be conceived. To this end, the principles of energy security, energy justice, economic efficiency and environmental sustainability will be analysed.

[8] Cf. already supra, Sect. 6.2.

The principle of energy security in Cuba must be considered an essential principle of the right to energy because of its close interrelation with the content of this right. From the outset, the mandate of this principle should be aimed at guaranteeing the satisfaction of everyone's energy needs. Although some authors consider that it involves the energy demand of society and industry,[9] energy security is a principle of the right to energy and seeks to guarantee energy availability to cover the energy needs of the entire Cuban population.

A second mandate of the energy security principle is accessibility. It is not enough for the Cuban energy sector to develop the necessary conditions to generate sufficient energy to satisfy the needs of the Cuban population. Mechanisms must be created to guarantee access to energy. These mechanisms imply strict observance of the universality of energy services given the fundamental needs they satisfy. Access to energy implies full access to energy, which means that there are no periods when energy needs cannot be satisfied once they appear.

Energy affordability encapsulates the third mandate of the principle in question. This mandate encompasses the economic affectation of the holders of the right to energy concerning the satisfaction of energy needs. This aspect of the energy security principle extends from energy policy to energy payments. Therefore, energy policy must promote legal, economic and infrastructure development measures.

Such measures should analyse the economic impact of energy prices and tariffs. On the one hand, they should ensure that the economic impact derived from satisfying energy needs does not affect the satisfaction of other fundamental needs. On the other hand, energy needs should not be partially satisfied due to affordability issues if this results in a deterioration of a dignified life.

Finally, the availability, accessibility, and affordability of energy are not enough if they are unreliable. Reliability, as the last element of the energy security principle, implies that energy services must be secure. This security includes the stability of these services, the absence of risk to people and their property and the uninterrupted supply.

Energy justice is the second specific principle that should underpin the right to energy. This principle encompasses the fair distribution of energy in Cuba. This principle implies equitable access to energy regardless of the context. In particular, fair distribution becomes a maxim irrespective of any discrimination. Energy needs are not exclusive to a specific population sector, so there should be no differences or privileges within the Cuban population. For this reason, the fair distribution of energy is aligned with equity and equality as principles of the Constitution of the Republic of Cuba of 2019.

The second component of the energy justice principle is identifying vulnerable groups. The identification of population groups in situations of energy vulnerability or energy poverty is an essential step towards the eradication of such phenomena. Under the constitutional premise of social justice, the Cuban legal system must

[9] Cf. Pan (2020), p. 2; Vine (2012), p. 401; Dannreuther (2010), p. 152.

establish diagnostic, treatment, and feedback schemes to fight against energy vulnerability and poverty as factors that threaten human life beyond the legal sphere.

Energy justice in Cuba must contemplate the configuration of processes and procedures to guarantee access to information, popular participation in public energy administration, and defence mechanisms in the face of violations of the right to energy. Such processes and procedures should be based on empowering the holders of the right to energy against those obliged to carry it out or third parties who impede its peaceful enjoyment.

This path brings us to the fourth sphere of the principle of energy justice. In the event of an infringement of the right to energy, the creation of restoration mechanisms is required. In this sense, they include the restoration of the affected services and compensation for the damages and prejudices that the harm caused to the holder of the right to energy may have produced. The configuration of restoration mechanisms, although it is the last element analysed, closes the cycle of the principle of energy justice, and if it does not occur, it will result in the non-realisation of the right to energy due to illegitimate damages.

Economic efficiency is Cuba's third essential principle of a future right to energy. This principle plays a significant role in Cuba's development. Efficient management of scarce economic resources is the only way forward if the nation's energy sovereignty is to be achieved.

Economic efficiency must have both a financial and an energy aspect. The financial aspect pursues energy investment based on economic cost-benefit criteria. These criteria imply strategic investments that maximise socio-economic benefits to satisfy the energy needs of the Cuban population.

The energy aspect includes the efficient management of energy resources. Given the energy sector's dependence on imported fossil fuels and the scarcity of this type of energy resource in its natural state in Cuba, energy efficiency must be a priority. Optimising efficiency in energy generation, transmission, and distribution must be a principle of economic efficiency. An example of this is energy losses. Although it is impossible to avoid energy "losses", i.e., transforming useful energy into non-useful energy, reducing energy losses contributes to optimising available energy resources.

Economic efficiency also encompasses energy consumption. As promoted in the past through the Energy Revolution, the promotion of energy efficiency in energy consumption should be an essential pillar of the principle of economic efficiency. The commercialisation of equipment with higher levels of energy efficiency would contribute to the reduction of energy consumption and the reduction of fossil fuel consumption. On this basis, the principle of economic efficiency encompasses every aspect of the legal-energy relationship, focusing on optimising resources. This principle is strongly linked to energy affordability by reducing the total costs of energy generation.

Environmental sustainability is the last of the essential principles that must inform the right to energy. This principle leads to energy generation from renewable sources, and then the energy transition must set the tone for the country's energy development. Increasing the renewability of energy generation is an essential issue for preserving the environment and tackling climate change. To this end, the principle of environmental sustainability must be reflected in the national energy policy through short-, medium- and long-term planning.

Such planning will establish the path towards Cuba's energy sovereignty through a near-zero-emissions generation model. However, it is essential to emphasise that, although this is the path to follow, the fundamental nature of energy needs means that they cannot be sacrificed for the sake of the energy transition. Therefore, the Cuban Energy Policy and its regulatory framework must move towards a clean energy generation system without compromising the rest of the principles which should inform the right to energy in Cuba.

However, the Cuban constitutional legal system contains specific guiding principles for the right to energy. For this reason, the essential principles that must be considered in the legal system for the realisation of the right under study will be explained below. In this sense, three essential principles that inform the right to energy in Cuba are identified. These principles, as optimisation mandates,[10] are human dignity, interdependence of rights and solidarity. The latter is configured from the perspective of energy solidarity.[11]

To begin the analysis, we start with human dignity as the supreme principle determining the Cuban legal system from Article 1 of the Constitution of the Republic of Cuba of 2019.[12] In this regard, the Cuban constitutional system follows the trend that many countries assume dignity as the core of constitutional precepts to establish limits to conduct or actions that may violate it.[13] This trend has a long tradition in international human rights law, especially since the Universal Declaration and the preamble of the San Francisco Charter, where human dignity became the underlying basis of human rights.[14]

Human dignity, as a principle, is integrated into the right to energy since only the right to energy can be the conduit for protecting the energy needs of human beings as fundamental needs.[15] Such an attribution to the right to energy responds to the fact that, as a socio-economic right by nature, its realisation determines existence in conditions of dignity.[16] Beyond any simplistic vision, the principle of human dignity must inform the right to energy in Cuba. This principle is vital for protecting the right to energy in the Cuban legal system, which has no express recognition and insufficient protection mechanisms.

The second of the principles that should inform the right to energy in Cuba is the interdependence of rights. Given its non-inclusion in the catalogue of fundamental

---

[10] Optimisation mandates are defined, as described by Alexy, as "norms that order something to be done to the greatest extent possible, within the existing legal and real possibilities". (Own translation) Velasco Gutiérrez (2013), p. 10; Alexy (1993), pp. 139–141.

[11] Cf. Andoura (2013), Talus (2021), Iakovenko (2021) and Kaschny (2023).

[12] Cf. Article 1. Constitución de la República de Cuba (2019).

[13] Ojeda Bello (2019), pp. 84–85.

[14] Tonetto and Guerra (2020), p. 122.

[15] Sin-Hang Ngai (2012), p. 605.

[16] Bombaerts et al. (2020), p. 51.

rights in the 2019 Cuban Constitution, this essential principle should inform the right under study. This principle originated in the Vienna Declaration and Programme of Action and[17] is a dynamic principle of interpreting and applying the rights recognised in the Constitution of the Republic of Cuba of 2019.[18] The principle of interdependence means that the right to energy is informed, reinforced, and nurtured by the fundamental rights declared by the constitutional legal order. In this way, the right to energy is integrated into the unity of purpose of constitutional protection of the holders of fundamental rights in Cuba.[19]

The application of interdependence, as an informing principle of the right to energy, is one of the solutions or alternative ways of the Cuban legal system to guarantee the implementation of the Constitution of the Republic of Cuba of 2019. The structuring of fundamental rights offers a protective umbrella that would be incomplete without the realisation of the right to energy. Rights such as the right to adequate housing, education, health, and work require energy for the realisation of their respective contents.

For that reason, interdependence constitutes a foundation with constitutional origins capable of motivating jurisdictional decisions in Cuba, where the right to energy is violated. However, the courts of justice are bound by a narrow plexus of fundamental rights that includes the above-mentioned and others and, in turn, excludes the right to energy. This context is why merely applying interdependence as a principle only partially solves this problem.

The harm to what this research defines as the right to energy damages the realisation of other fundamental rights that depend on this right. For this reason, interdependence, as an informing principle of the right to energy in Cuba, is based on avoiding risks and damage to the rest of the constitutionally recognised fundamental rights, especially those of a socio-economic nature, that may cause violations of the right under study.[20] In this way, the consequences of non-recognition of the right to energy are minimised, and partial protection of its holders is achieved.

In addition to the above, progressivity is the third principle that should inform the right to energy in Cuba. After its constitutional recognition as a fundamental right, its progressive nature is imposed as a conquest within the legal system. The principle of progressiveness reinforces the recognition of the right to energy by imposing limits on the possible and eventual disregard of its content and the progress achieved in its realisation.[21] To that is added the positive obligation of the state to improve the protection and content of the right in question.[22]

---

[17] World Conference on Human Rights (1993), p. 3.

[18] Porter interprets interdependence as a dynamic principle of interpretation and application of human rights since, through it, the norms that recognise these rights and the content of each one of them "(…) inform, reinforce, nurture and grow together in response to human rights claims emerging from human experience." Porter (2020), p. 302.

[19] Porter (2020), p. 302.

[20] Neves-Silva et al. (2019), p. 5.

[21] Espina Molina (2007), p. 261.

[22] Suprema Corte de Justicia de la Nación (2019), p. 199.

The principle of progressivity reinforces the right to energy as a right of a socio-economic nature. However, it should be emphasised that this principle in no way implies the postponement of the right to energy for an indefinite period of time, but rather the legal regulation of the path to be followed and the stages to be completed in order to achieve the full satisfaction of the content of the right to energy.[23] Through the aforementioned principle, the State is obliged to move forward expeditiously and effectively in the full realisation of the right under study. This obligation includes the prohibition of regressivity or irreversibility,[24] which involves the prohibition of deliberate measures that entail the worsening of the level achieved in the enjoyment of the right to energy.[25]

It follows from the above that the principle of progressivity, as a guiding principle of the right to energy in Cuba, entails two types of obligations. The first of these is the positive obligation to promote the progressive and gradual realisation[26] of the right mentioned above, and the second is the negative obligation of regression in the levels achieved in its realisation.

In this context, the principle of progressivity is constituted as a principle of legislative interpretation. This function is integrated into public policy-making and legislative processes in such a way that they are aligned with the constitutional norms that recognise the right to energy and the infra-constitutional norms that develop it in order to avoid decreases in the progress achieved. For this reason, the principle of progressivity radiates the political and normative evolution of the right to energy in such a way as to promote its gradual and progressive realisation and to prohibit any regression in the protective conquests achieved.[27] Hence, the vision of Díaz Muñoz, based on the arguments of Courtis,[28] is reflected in the above-described proscription of regression of results in terms of the consequences of a public policy and normative regression in terms of the content of a given legal norm.[29]

What has been described so far, with respect to the principle of progressivity, presents the progressive conception of progressivity and gives rise to operational progressivity that includes two key elements that seek to safeguard the advances achieved in terms of the right to energy. The first of these elements is the right of complaint, demand, or petition, which grants prohibition of regressivity to the holders of the right to energy to claim for violations of the right to energy.[30] The second element is justiciability, which will be explained as a basic guarantee of the right to energy in Cuba.[31]

---

[23] Stinco (2019), p. 54.

[24] Toledo Toribio (2011), pp. 2–3.

[25] Montejano Hilton (2016), p. 118.

[26] Comisión Nacional de los Derechos Humanos (2022), pp. 38 and 64.

[27] Díaz Muñoz (2019), pp. 3–4.

[28] Courtis (2006).

[29] Díaz Muñoz (2019), p. 4.

[30] Galdámez Zelada (2008), p. 148.

[31] Cf. infra, Sect. 10.6.

The fourth principle in Cuba, which entails the right to energy, is energy solidarity. Solidarity, as a principle of an economic-social nature,[32] finds its support in several of the postulates of the Constitution of the Republic of Cuba of 2019. This principle has been associated with the fundamental principles of the legal-constitutional order, constitutional duties, and the exercise of municipal autonomy.[33] However, in doctrine, solidarity has been qualified as energy solidarity.

As a principle, energy solidarity has its antecedents in EU law and case law.[34] As a general principle of European Union law, this principle aims at cooperation between Member States to accelerate the energy transition, considering the existence of an internal energy market. This reality would imply that the progress of that purpose in each state will benefit the rest of the member states in terms of energy security, affordability of energy and an increase in energy availability, issues that determine the realisation of the right to energy.

Despite such a context in the European Union, the principle of energy solidarity assumes a different dimension in Cuba. As a developing country with limited availability of energy resources, extreme energy dependence and an unstable energy system, the principle of energy solidarity must become a pillar for the realisation of the right to energy. In this sense, the energy solidarity principle arises from the interaction of principle number two of the 2030 Agenda: Leave No One Behind[35] and energy justice.

In Cuba, the principle of energy solidarity is based on the integration of constitutional premises such as dignity, humanism, equity, equality, well-being, and individual and collective prosperity.[36] Based on the above, the principle in question pursues the universality of the right to energy through the protection of all people, especially those in circumstances of vulnerability or energy poverty.

In this sense, the principle of energy solidarity involves multi- and interdisciplinary studies to identify indicators to determine the existence of vulnerability and energy poverty. Such studies aim to create reinforced protection systems for holders of the right to energy in such situations. These reinforced protection systems are, in addition to creating and regulating mechanisms, to assist people in vulnerability and energy poverty to contribute to energy affordability.

Energy solidarity also includes the rational and conscious use of energy by promoting energy saving as a factor to be considered for reducing demand. This

---

[32] Ministerio para Transición Ecológica (2019), p. 76.

[33] Cf. Articles 1, 47, 90 (l) and 169. Constitución de la República de Cuba (2019).

[34] Cf. European Council (2022), Boute (2020), Iakovenko (2021) and Talus (2021).

[35] Principle two: Leave no one behind represents the commitment of the Member States of the United Nations to the eradication of poverty, discrimination, and exclusion. It also aims to reduce inequalities and vulnerabilities of people. Therefore, this principle of the 2030 Agenda focuses on lifting barriers constituted in legal frameworks, public policies and social practices that prevent people from accessing services, resources and opportunities and, therefore, undermine the realisation of their rights. United Nations (2015).

[36] Cf. Article 1. Constitución de la República de Cuba (2019).

principle implies a fundamental link of human society[37] that includes the joint commitment of all subjects of the right to energy to its full realisation. For this reason, energy solidarity must be a fundamental pillar of energy policy and regulation in Cuba to guarantee the content of the right to energy in an inclusive manner, without discrimination of any kind and under conditions of full equality.

The principle of energy solidarity encompasses the development of sufficient and diversified generation capacity to meet the energy needs of the holders of the right to energy. It guides the creation of resilient energy systems through risk assessment and management mechanisms, as well as coping with contingencies in such a way as to ensure uninterrupted and reliable energy services. Such situations include climate-related phenomena, energy crises, infrastructure breakdowns, and other phenomena that pose a potential risk to realising the right to energy.[38]

Finally, the principle of energy solidarity includes the realisation of the right to energy in a way that guarantees the equitable satisfaction of energy needs, regardless of the prevailing conditions in each temporal and spatial context. Although in Cuba, the right to energy does not have the status of a fundamental right, this does not eradicate its condition as a human right and, therefore, the importance of its full enjoyment by its holders. Based on the above, it remains essential to determine who should be the subjects of the right to energy in Cuba from a critical perspective for the sake of the future improvement of the Cuban legal system.

10.4 Subjects of the Right to Energy

As discussed above, the Constitution of the Republic of Cuba of 2019 does not expressly recognise the right to energy. Despite the disaggregated protection that the Constitution offers to the right to energy through the spheres of protection of other fundamental rights, it is article 78 that has the most significant implication for protecting the right to energy. This article covers goods and services of multiple natures, including energy carriers and energy services.

The formulation of Article 78 places the right to energy in the scope of Consumer Law. Although adopted by many countries in Latin America and the Caribbean, as well as in the European Union, this trend has a series of limitations that affect the protection of the holders of the right to energy as subjects to be analysed in the first part of this section. Based on the Cuban regulatory framework, the holders of the right to energy in Cuba are protected as consumers with an object of consumption that is susceptible to intangibility: energy.[39]

Despite the above, in Cuba, there is no regulatory framework aimed explicitly at protecting energy consumers, so they are subsumed under the general consumer

[37] Parra Cortés (2018), p. 63.

[38] Rodríguez (2018), p. 30.

[39] Luis Cordova and Rodríguez Rivero (2023).

protection regulations. Although Law 697 on Consumer Protection was passed in 1960, the passing of the years meant that it became obsolete and out of step with Cuban reality around 2000.[40] However, it was not until 2018 that a lower-ranking law came into force to regulate consumer protection in Cuba.

Thus, Resolution 54 of 2018, issued by the Ministry of Domestic Trade, came into force. This normative body entered the Cuban legal system to establish the indications related to the organisation and execution of consumer protection in Cuba, which have a high implication in the legal regime of energy consumers.[41]

Despite the above, this approach suffers from multiple limitations in the comprehensive protection of the holders of the right to energy. Among them is the marked sectoral nature of Resolution 54.[42] To this is added the enforceability of the rights attributed by the regulatory body itself, given that, by assuming the right to energy as part of Consumer Law, they would only be enforceable against the service providers as the only obligated parties. This consequence creates a dilemma with the regulatory system of the Cuban energy sector.

After identifying the energy consumers who are the active subjects of the law under study in Cuba, it would be appropriate to identify the duty-bearers. The characterisation of the Cuban legal framework for the energy sector allows for identifying two duty-bearers related to the type of energy service they provide.

Concerning electricity services, Unión Eléctrica is the only wholesale marketer that took on this responsibility in 1988 on behalf of the now-extinct Ministry of Basic Industry.[43] The second duty-bearers in the case of the gas service, by normative definition, are the companies and business units of the Unión Cuba-Petróleo, subordinated to the Ministry of Energy and Mines, which are responsible for providing the service mentioned above.[44] From the above, a series of obligations emerge which, regulated with greater or lesser precision, safeguard the realisation of the right to energy in Cuba.[45]

Even though the subjects identified from the analysis of the legal framework of the energy sector in Cuba, it is necessary to argue who should be the subjects of the right to energy in Cuba. In this sense, the Cuban legal system offers an unfinished approach to recognising and regulating the subjects of the right to energy, which restricts its protection. Regarding the holders of this right, taking as a premise its character as a human right, any approach that circumscribes this condition to a

---

[40] Tabares Neyra et al. (2020).

[41] Ministerio del Comercio Interior (2018).

[42] Resolution 54 focuses primarily on the activity of commerce and those related to the sale of goods, gastronomy, technical and personal services, and accommodation. For this reason, energy is only subsumed under the activity of commerce, with the consequence that the progress of Resolution 54 is limited in the energy field by taking such a general approach to consumer protection. Luis Cordova and Rodríguez Rivero (2023).

[43] Ministerio de la Industria Básica (1998).

[44] Ministerio de Energía y Minas (2017).

[45] Cf. infra, Sect. 10.5.

specific group and, therefore, excludes the rest is a misguided approach. All human beings should normatively be considered holders of the right to energy.

The consequence of the above is that even the condition of citizenship as a determining condition of the legal status of the individual armed with rights exercisable against the State, duties, and guarantees[46] is still insufficient. Restricting the status of the holders of the right to energy in Cuba will always result in a lack of protection. For this reason, the right to energy cannot be restricted to a select group but must be a fundamental right declared universal by the Cuban constitutional legal system.

Based on the above, limiting responsibility for the realisation of the right to energy to the duty-bearers mentioned above is insufficient. The Cuban state cannot exempt itself from its responsibility for the realisation of the right to energy as a premise for human dignity. However, it is essential to emphasise that, without assuming an exemption from such state responsibility, granting concessions to third parties to create material guarantees of the right to energy is a viable strategy. These concessions are relevant if they positively impact the right to energy fulfilment.

All of the above declare it incompatible with converting a relationship that, by nature, should be justifiably fundamental under the simple formula of a consumer relationship. This approach limits the protection of the right to energy. The simplistic qualification of energy consumers would only empower the holders of the right to energy to demand the obligations that make up the content of this right vis-à-vis energy service providers and exempt States as the real duty-bearers.

Adopting a human rights approach to the right to energy and, in turn, its conception as a fundamental right is the only possible solution to guarantee its realisation legally. However, to do so, it is essential to determine the responsibilities that must integrate the content of the right to energy in the Cuban legal system.

10.5 Content of the Right to Energy

Considering the lack of recognition and regulation of the right to energy in the Cuban legal system, the elements that should make up its content will be delimited below. The theoretical development of the content of the right to energy in Cuba will be based on the aspects previously described in this research[47] and the leading legal norms that impact them. For this purpose, a critical approach is adopted concerning the strengths and weaknesses of the Cuban legal system.

The starting point is availability as a fundamental premise for the realisation of the right to energy, which is linked to the generation of sufficient energy to satisfy the energy needs of the holders of this right.[48] Three main elements emerge from the

---

[46] Cardona Ospina et al. (2015), p. 108; Prieto Valdés (2019a), p. 12.

[47] Cf. already supra, Sect. 10.1.

[48] Jones and Dodds (2017), p. 23.

above: energy generation, sufficiency, and energy needs. The interrelation of these three aspects guarantees the existence of energy availability.

Each of the mentioned elements adopts specific characteristics in the Cuban context. As a developing country with an energy matrix dependent on fossil fuels and the limited availability of these resources in the national territory, Cuba must base energy generation on a decentralised energy matrix with a gradual increase in the participation of renewable energy sources. This path implies that, in the immediate future, basing energy availability on generation from renewable sources is a reality that could jeopardise the sufficiency of generation. Despite the growing need to drive the energy transition for environmental and economic reasons, this cannot imply that sufficient energy generation will be affected.

Generation adequacy is linked to the energy needs of the holders of the right to energy. For this reason, sufficiency is determined by these needs. This need means that the Cuban energy sector must evolve so that energy generation meets the energy needs of the holders of the right to energy. However, through energy literacy strategies, conscious consumption and energy saving must be promoted, mainly when energy is generated from non-renewable sources.

As part of energy availability, the State must also promote the implementation of energy democracy initiatives. Although these initiatives have implications for increasing installed generation capacity as a complement to the energy system, they also impact the other three elements that comprise the right to energy. Promoting this type of initiative must be effectively integrated into the Cuban legal system, considering the prevailing economic reality. For this reason, financial incentives for exercising energy prosumerism must be strengthened, as well as the availability and access to technologies based on renewable sources in the national context.

This path leads to the second element of the content of the right to energy: accessibility. This second element, the responsibility of the duty-bearers of the right to energy, must be conceived incrementally.[49] For this reason, the right to energy in Cuba must have a gradual character, backed by the constitutional principle of progressiveness contained in Article 41 on the Cuban state's recognition and guarantee of human rights.[50]

The conception of the right to energy as a fundamental right in the national legal system starts from a baseline based on universality. This baseline ensures that the basic needs of the holders of the right under study are met.[51] This obligation serves as the basis for the prohibition of disconnection and compels duty-bearers to seek alternative solutions to suspend energy services. From this baseline, two further incremental levels are traced in which duty-bearers must ensure the realisation of the right to energy to meet production needs and the needs of modern society.[52] To progressively develop energy accessibility, a timeline with short-, medium- and

[49] International Energy Agency (2020); Hesselman et al. (2017), pp. 9–10.

[50] Cf. Article 41. Constitución de la República de Cuba (2019).

[51] Practical Action (2010, 2013, 2014).

[52] Cf. already supra, p. 125.

long-term objectives must be established to allow for evaluation and feedback on this process.[53]

Accessibility also involves the State's obligation to guarantee the necessary conditions for the exercise of energy prosumerism. This obligation implies the development of a legal framework for this type of initiative that allows the individual or community practice of energy needs self-satisfaction. To this end, energy solidarity must be established as a guiding principle to promote inclusive access to energy without leaving anyone behind. In addition, effective mechanisms must be created to enable access to technologies that, in turn, become gateways to energy generated from renewable sources.

As a third element, affordability establishes the obligation of duty-bearers of the right to energy to establish, maintain and modify the energy price and tariff regime in a way that does not compromise the economic capacity of the right holders under study. This obligation implies that such prices and tariffs cannot jeopardise or compromise the ability of the holders of the right to energy to meet their other basic needs. For this reason, energy policy and regulation must establish fair mechanisms for setting prices and tariffs, guaranteeing their publicity.

In turn, procedures and indicators should be established at the policy level to measure energy affordability accurately. Such indicators, with a robust socio-economic character, may include the ratio of energy costs to household income, average energy consumption, living costs, and the number of people without access to energy, among many others.[54]

This third element also involves the creation of protection mechanisms for sectors involved in the context of energy vulnerability or poverty. To this end, the conceptual frameworks of both phenomena and the indicators for their identification must be regulated. Such indicators must be designed based on interdisciplinary work to guarantee a comprehensive approach to the conditions that generate them, the ways to reduce their effects and their reversal.

Among the mechanisms recognised by the legal system, the following can be regulated: the establishment of subsidies,[55] social tariffs,[56] the creation of flexible payment systems, and financial support, among others. The appropriate design of the regulation and oversight of these mechanisms contributes to protecting energy-poor or vulnerable sectors.

The fourth aspect of the content of the right to energy is reliability. This element implies the responsibility of duty-bearers for the continuity and quality of energy services, as well as access to information.

---

[53] The progressive implementation of the right to energy, as a socio-economic right, implies irreversibility. This involves the prohibition of regressivity with respect to the progress achieved at the three levels of energy access. In this way, the increase of satisfied energy needs is ensured without the threat of setbacks at the regulatory level and in the objective reality for the holders of the right to energy. Cf. Stinco (2019).

[54] Cf. Lin (2018) and Deller (2018).

[55] Singh and Ru (2022), p. 18340.

[56] Duran and Condorí (2022).

Continuity of supply implies promptly meeting energy needs whenever they arise.[57] Continuity, therefore, means uninterrupted energy services.[58] Such uninterrupted energy services lead to the permanent operation of energy generation, transmission, and distribution as a prerequisite for reliability. For these reasons, the duty-bearers of the right to energy must ensure the design and operation of a resilient energy system capable of facing contingencies of different natures. All the above elements aim to guarantee adequate and safe energy services operation at any time.[59]

On the other hand, the quality of energy services, without entering a technical debate, implies the stable operation of these services. Such stability of energy services encompasses the absence of variations that threaten the satisfaction of energy needs or could pose a risk or damage to the assets of the holders of the right to energy or their physical integrity.[60]

Access to information is another aspect that integrates the responsibility of reliability as an obligation of the duty-bearers of the right to energy. This aspect, related to the right to information, includes the obligation to provide truthful, objective, and timely information[61] regarding energy services. In this context, duty-bearers are responsible for making information relevant to the right to energy accessible.

Such information includes the powers vested in the holders of the right under study, mechanisms of the legal protection of such powers, energy consumption, processes of tariff formation and energy prices, billing of energy services, and shaping of the energy mix, among others that, by their nature, concern the realisation of the right to energy. In this way, access to information promotes transparency in the context of energy services.

The realisation of what has been described as the content of the right to energy requires tools to ensure its effective realisation. Such tools are integrated into the legal system and must be enforced. For this reason, this research will now analyse the guarantees that must underpin the right to energy in the Cuban legal system.

10.6 Basic Guarantees of the Right to Energy

Guarantees for the realisation of fundamental rights are a vitally crucial element. Such is the case of the right to energy, whose system of guarantees must ensure its enjoyment and defence, considering that its absence or injury would imply an imbalance between the subjects of the right under study.[62]

[57] Gonzáles Prada (2019), p. 138.

[58] Gordillo (2013), p. 401.

[59] Couder (2015), p. 28; Baarsma and Hop (2009), p. 1378.

[60] Cf. Arellano Martínez et al. (2012), p. 34.

[61] Cf. Article 52. Constitución de la República de Cuba (2019).

[62] Cf. Prieto Valdés (2020), p. 224.

Constitutional recognition is necessary as a superior guarantee of any fundamental right in the legal and political order.[63] In this sense, it is understood that rights, considered fundamental rights, do not have a static character, so the Constitution becomes a means of giving and receiving.[64] For this reason, given the fundamental needs that the right to energy satisfies, its first guarantee must be the attribution of its character as a fundamental right by the Cuban constitutional legal system through its express recognition.

The constitutional recognition of the right to energy is integrated as a "guarantee of the guarantee", which implies the requirement of further development and instrumentation for the satisfaction of its iusfundamental content.[65] In this sense, a system of guarantees must be articulated to ensure and protect the holders of the right in question for its enjoyment. Such a system of guarantees comprises two levels: a normative level and a material level.

As mentioned above, based on the principle of constitutional supremacy, the normative level will be governed by the constitutional norm that recognises the right to energy. Based on the configuration of this constitutional norm, a legal subsystem must be established in development norms, which regulates the elements of the right to energy to establish its principles,[66] its subjects (active and passive),[67] its content[68] and guarantees.

Because of the above, the legal framework of the right to energy includes the security of energy supply as a guarantee, in the first instance, of a normative nature and, in the second instance, as a guarantee of a material nature.[69] At the normative level, the security of energy supply implies the conception of the legal framework for energy that regulates the exploration, generation, distribution, storage and commercialisation of energy in Cuba.

At the material level, this guarantee implies the creation, maintenance, and development of the national energy system in such a way as to guarantee the complete satisfaction of the content of the right to energy. Such material conditions also imply the commercialisation of technologies based on renewable sources, especially those aimed at implementing energy prosumerism.

Another of the guarantees that must underpin the right to energy is the prohibition of disconnection. This guarantee has an eminently normative nature and safeguards the protection of the holders of the right to energy. This normative guarantee

---

[63] Prieto Valdés (2022), p. 44.

[64] Prieto Valdés (2016), p. 175.

[65] Prieto Valdés (2019a), p. 6; Prieto Valdés (2019b), p. 55.

[66] Cf. already supra, Sect. 10.3.

[67] Cf. already supra, Sect. 10.4.

[68] Cf. already supra, Sect. 10.5.

[69] According to Prieto Valdés, material guarantees are "material situations that are necessary so that rights can be realised or enjoyed, since without the right and without conditions that favour its enjoyment, it remains a dead letter, a simple legal enunciation without imperativity". Prieto Valdés (2016), p. 171.

includes the regulation, in the first instance, of the obligation of duty-bearers to satisfy the basic needs of the holders of the right to energy.

From this obligatory baseline, the regulation must provide, by legal mandate, the progressiveness of the right to energy to satisfy the rest of the levels of access to energy. Similarly, the legal system must establish the non-regression[70] of the right to energy. In this context, non-regressivity implies that the norm sanctions the regression of the advances obtained in the energy access levels.

Once the above has been regulated, the Cuban legal system must contemplate the justiciability of the right to energy as a fundamental right.[71] To this end, only once recognised as a fundamental right will the right to energy enjoy autonomously privileged judicial protection through an expeditious, concentrated and preferential procedure.[72] In this way, the holders of the right under study are empowered to appeal to the competent jurisdictional body through the corresponding appeal in case of violations of the right to energy. The effective protection of this right is an essential guarantee of protection against arbitrary action.

In this context, it is important to analyse Law 153, "On the Process of Protection of Constitutional Rights".[73] However, the effectiveness of implementing these mechanisms for judicial protection of the right to energy will be limited to a considerable extent by their constitutional recognition. Such recognition, in Cuba, will always be the starting point for protecting the right to energy as a fundamental right.

Following the analysis of how the Cuban legal system affects the elements of the content of the right to energy, such as availability, accessibility, affordability, and reliability, two other legal norms should be analysed, given their relevance. The first is Law 153, "On the Process of Protection of Constitutional Rights", and Resolution No. 54 of the Ministry of Domestic Trade regarding the indications for the organisation and execution of consumer protection in the domestic trade system.

The fact that the right to energy is not included in the catalogue of fundamental rights recognised by the Cuban Constitution limits its protection.[74] Although Constitutional Article 99 establishes the effective protection of fundamental rights, its application is truncated by not recognising the right to energy. For this reason, the justiciability of the right to energy is an element of its content that has no clear legal backing in Cuba.

---

[70] Cf. Agudo Zamora (2017).

[71] The justiciability of socio-economic rights, such as the right to energy, is gaining growing support as an increasing number of arguments advocate for its legal enforceability. Thus, through justiciability as a guarantee of rights of this nature, the minimum guarantee of the right to energy is pursued to protect its full enjoyment and enjoyment for the full development of the human personality. For this purpose, the normative delimitation of the content of the right to energy is required to eliminate the possible vagueness of its future constitutional guarantee. Cf. already supra, Sect. 10.5. Cf. Pachot (2010), p. 30.

[72] Pérez Gutiérrez and Hierro Sánchez (2019), p. 191.

[73] Cutié Mustelier and Mondelo Tamayo (2019), p. 158.

[74] Cf. already supra, Chap. 8.

Article 1
"This Law regulates the process for the courts to hear claims concerning the violation of the rights enshrined in the Constitution of the Republic in the event of damage or harm suffered by individuals, caused by State bodies, their directors, officials or employees, due to the improper action or omission of their functions, and by private individuals or non-State entities, following the provisions of Article 99 of the Constitution, except for those provided for in Article 6 of this Law." (Own translation)[75]

When analysing Law 153, "On the Process of Protection of Constitutional Rights", from Article 1, because of the constitutional mandate of Article 99, only violations of the rights enshrined in the Constitution will be subject to jurisdictional jurisdiction.

However, in this author's opinion, a contradiction arises with Article 2 when it is declared that, in:

> Conflicts arising from the violation of constitutional rights, the normative provisions are interpreted in the way that most favour the individual and respect for human dignity, following the values and principles enshrined in the Constitution (…) to guarantee the effective judicial protection of rights, without prejudice to respect for (…) the international treaties in force for the Republic of Cuba. (Own translation)[76]

Following the analysis previously carried out in this research,[77] it was illustrated how the principles and values of the Constitution of the Republic of Cuba of 2019 underpin the need for a fundamental right to energy in Cuba, which is why they all have an impact on the interpretation of the normative provisions to favour the holders of the right to energy. Added is the reference to guaranteeing effective protection by observing international treaties with binding force for Cuba.

In this context, the need to make the right to energy justiciable can be based on the Convention on the Elimination of All Forms of Discrimination against Women.[78] Although this international treaty does not take a comprehensive approach, it constitutes a basis to request the effective protection of the right to energy as a human and fundamental right.

Another element that should be highlighted from a critical stance is Article 5.2 of Law 153. Based on this normative pronouncement, even if the right to energy were to have express constitutional recognition, judicial protection would not prosper if there were other means of protection. In this way, the justiciability of the right to energy remains as a residual means of protection after using the rest of the protection mechanisms, which include administrative remedies.[79]

However, as an exception to the above, Article 5.2 provides that the court may hear amparo proceedings if the right claimed is of legal-social importance and

[75] Cf. Article 1. Asamblea Nacional del Poder Popular (2022).

[76] Cf. Article 2. Asamblea Nacional del Poder Popular (2022).

[77] Cf. already supra, Chap. 8.

[78] Organización de Naciones Unidas (1979).

[79] Cf. Article 5(2). Asamblea Nacional del Poder Popular (2022).

requires urgent and preferential action. For such an assessment, the court must evaluate "the legal-social significance of the alleged violation, the possible irreparability of the violation and of the damage or harm caused, if the protection of the constitutional right is delayed, and the situation of vulnerability of the injured party, among other circumstances of a similar nature". The above would make the justiciability, in the first instance, of the right to energy subject to the discretion of the court, which could delay the duration of the damages that could derive from the violation of the aforementioned right.[80]

Based on the above, the system of basic guarantees that must underpin the right to energy in Cuba comprises normative and material guarantees. The first of these guarantees is the constitutional recognition of the right to energy, followed by the normative development of its legal subsystem. From this, the following guarantees can be deduced: security of supply, the prohibition of disconnection and the justiciability of the right to energy.

10.7 Conclusion

The theoretical and legal elements developed in Chap. 6 of this research were considered to establish the theoretical and legal elements that should underpin the recognition of the right to energy in Cuba. These elements were adapted to the Cuban legal system, including the Constitution of the Republic of Cuba of 2019 and its complementary norms. Based on this process and the operationalisation of the concept of the right to energy, it was found that, even though the right to energy is not expressly recognised in the Cuban legal system, it responds to the availability, accessibility, affordability, and reliability of energy. However, the Cuban legal system still has ample room for improvement.

In addition to the above analysis, the theoretical foundations of the principles that should underpin the right to energy have been added. These principles were adapted to the political, legal, and economic reality to form a solid foundation for the realisation of the right to energy. Beyond the general human rights principles, there are specific principles of the right to energy (energy security, energy justice, economic efficiency, and environmental sustainability). Furthermore, human dignity, interdependence, progressivity, and energy solidarity are established as essential constitutional principles in Cuba.

This framework led to the identification of the subjects of the right to energy according to the current legal framework (energy consumers and energy service providers) without losing sight of the need for a universal right to energy in Cuba, where the state should be legally obliged to guarantee the realisation of the right under study.

---

[80] Cf. Article 5.3. Asamblea Nacional del Poder Popular (2022).

To continue substantiating the theoretical-legal elements that should support the recognition of the right to energy in Cuba, the obligations that form part of the content of the right mentioned above were developed in depth. These obligations were developed in depth. In this sense, energy availability must include energy generation, sufficiency, and energy needs. For its part, accessibility is analysed based on the constitutional principle of progressiveness, which insists on promoting energy prosumerism as a complementary alternative to satisfy energy needs. At the same time, affordability orients the creation of fair price and tariff formation mechanisms and the creation of protection mechanisms for people in conditions of vulnerability and energy poverty. Finally, energy reliability is based on continuity of supply, quality of energy services, as well as access to information and transparency in energy services.

This research proposes four basic guarantees to ensure the effectiveness of the obligations that make up the content of the right to energy. As a starting point, it argues the need for constitutional recognition of the right to energy. To this recognition, security of supply is added as a guarantee at a normative and material level, with the prohibition of disconnection and justiciability as a secondary guarantee.

References[81]

Agudo Zamora M (2017) El principio de no regresividad de los derechos sociales en el ordenamiento constitucional español. Revista de Derecho Político (100):849–879. https://revistas.uned.es/index.php/derechopolitico/article/download/20720/17219/0. Accessed 3 Mar 2025

Alexy R (1993) Teoría de los Derechos Fundamentales. Centro de Estudios Constitucionales, Madrid. https://www.academia.edu/41432948/TEORIA_DE_LOS_DERECHOS_FUNDAMENTALES_ROBERT_ALEXY. Accessed 3 Mar 2025

Andoura S (2013) Energy solidarity in Europe: from independence to interdependence. https://institutdelors.eu/wp-content/uploads/2020/08/energysolidarity-andoura-ne-ijd-july13.pdf. Accessed 3 Mar 2025

Arellano Martínez A, Mireles Huerta D, Samayoa Castillo RJ (2012) Calidad de la Energía. In: Mejora de la confiabilidad en el edificio Valdés Vallejo de la UNAM. Universidad Autónoma de México, pp 34–61. http://www.ptolomeo.unam.mx:8080/jspui/bitstream/132.248.52.100/288/5/A5.pdf. Accessed 3 Mar 2025

Asamblea Nacional del Poder Popular (2022) Ley 153 'Del Proceso de Amparo de los Derechos Constitucionales'. Gaceta Oficial No. 74 Ordinaria de 15 de julio. Gaceta Oficial de la República, Cuba. https://www.gacetaoficial.gob.cu/sites/default/files/goc-2022-o74.pdf. Accessed 3 Mar 2025

Baarsma BE, Hop JP (2009) Pricing power outages in the Netherlands. Energy 34(9):1378–1386. https://doi.org/10.1016/j.energy.2009.06.016. Accessed 3 Mar 2025

Bombaerts G, Jenkins K, Sanusi YA, Guoyu W (2020) Energy justice across borders. In: Bombaerts G, Jenkins K, Sanusi YA, Guoyu W (eds) Energy justice across borders. Springer International Publishing, Cham. https://link.springer.com/10.1007/978-3-030-24021-9. Accessed 3 Mar 2025

[81] All links to the cited websites were operational as of 3 March 2025.

Boute A (2020) The principle of solidarity and the geopolitics of energy: Poland v. Commission (OPAL Pipeline). Common Mark Law Rev 57(3) https://www.ssrn.com/abstract=4094556. Accessed 3 Mar 2025

Cardona Ospina RA, Rodríguez Torres DA, Bonilla Sánchez G (2015) Del concepto de ciudadanía: una aproximación teórica. Revista Temas (5). https://dialnet.unirioja.es/descarga/articulo/5894361.pdf. Accessed 3 Mar 2025

Comisión Nacional de los Derechos Humanos (2022) La progresividad de los derechos humanos. Políticas públicas, actores e instituciones. Ciudad de México. https://produccion.siia.unam.mx/Publicaciones/ProdCientif/PublicacionFrw.aspx?id=631965. Accessed 3 Mar 2025

Constitución de la República de Cuba (2019) Gaceta Oficial No. 5 Extraordinaria de 10 de abril de 2019. Gaceta Oficial de la República de Cuba, La Habana. https://www.gacetaoficial.gob.cu/sites/default/files/goc-2019-ex5.pdf. Accessed 3 Mar 2025

Couder J (2015) Energy security, including power reliability. Literature review, with a focus on the impact of energy efficiency on energy security in the EU. Antwerp. https://www.researchgate.net/publication/298352053_Energy_Security_including_Power_Reliability_Literature_review_with_a_focus_on_the_impact_of_energy_efficiency_on_energy_security_in_the_EU. Accessed 3 Mar 2025

Courtis C (2006) Ni un paso atrás. La prohibición de regresividad en materia de derechos sociales. Editores del Puerto s.r.l., Buenos Aires. https://www.cels.org.ar/web/wp-content/uploads/2006/08/Ni-un-paso-atras.pdf. Accessed 3 Mar 2025

Cutié Mustelier D, Mondelo Tamayo JO (2019) La ponderación de derechos Constitucionales. Realidad y perspectivas en el escenario judicial cubano. In Claves para la interpretación de la Constitución cubana de 2019, edited by Carlos Manuel Villabella Armengol and Leonardo B. Pérez Gallardo. Santiago de Chile: Ediciones Jurídicas Olejnik. https://vlex.cl/vid/ponderacion-derechos-constitucionales-realidad-1016870370. Accessed 3 Mar 2025

Dannreuther R (2010) Energy security. In: Peter Burgess J (ed) The Routledge handbook of new security studies. Routledge Taylor & Francis Group, Oxon. https://www.routledge.com/The-Routledge-Handbook-of-New-Security-Studies/Burgess/p/book/9780415539333. Accessed 3 Mar 2025

Deller D (2018) Energy affordability in the EU: the risks of metric driven policies. Energy Policy 119:168–182. https://doi.org/10.1016/j.enpol.2018.03.033. Accessed 3 Mar 2025

Díaz Muñoz ES (2019) El principio de progresividad en el derecho colombiano: revisión teórico-jurídica. Criterio Libre Jurídico 16(2):1–13. https://revistas.unilibre.edu.co/index.php/criterio-juridico/article/view/6405. Accessed 3 Mar 2025

Duran RJ, Condorí MA (2022) Alcance de la Tarifa Social sobre los hogares en situación de pobreza energética de la Argentina urbana en el periodo 2016–2018. Estudios Socioterritoriales. Revista de Geografía (29):075. https://ojs2.fch.unicen.edu.ar/ojs-3.1.0/index.php/estudios-socioterritoriales/article/view/1539/1321. Accessed 3 Mar 2025

Espina Molina MV (2007) El principio de progresividad de los Derechos Humanos. Revista De Derecho Público (112):261–266. https://www.corteidh.or.cr/tablas/r26575.pdf. Accessed 3 Mar 2025

European Council (2022) Council Regulation (EU) 2022/2577: laying down a framework to accelerate the deployment of renewable energy. Official Journal of the European Union. https://eur--lex.europa.eu/legal-content/EN/TXT/PDF/?uri=CELEX:32022R2577. Accessed 3 Mar 2025

Galdámez Zelada L (2008) La progresividad en la jurisprudencia de la Corte Interamericana de Derechos Humanos. Revista de Derecho (Coquimbo) 15(1):139–158. https://www.redalyc.org/pdf/3710/371041322006.pdf. Accessed 3 Mar 2025

Gonzáles Prada C (2019) El principio de continuidad en la prestación de servicios públicos de telecomunicaciones. Revista de Derecho 18(1):129–154. https://revistas.udep.edu.pe/derecho/article/view/1609. Accessed 3 Mar 2025

Gordillo AA (2013) Teoría General Del Derecho Administrativo. Tratado de Derecho Administrativo y obras selectas, vol 8. Fundación de Derecho Administrativo, Buenos Aires. https://www.gordillo.com/pdf_tomo8/tomo8.pdf. Accessed 3 Mar 2025

Hesselman M, Tirado-Herrero S, Smith M, Antepara I, Bajomi A, Barrella R, Cao U, Chatterjee S, Cuerdo T, Dobbins A, Frigo G, Fuller S, Feenstra M, Gouveia J, Guyet R, Kizilcec V, Lennon B, González I, Robić S, Robinson C, Smilevska N, Varo A, Yoon H, Živčič L (2017) Moving forward on the right to energy in the EU. https://www.engager-energy.net/wp-content/uploads/2022/02/ENGAGER_Right-to-Energy-Toolkit_FINAL.pdf. Accessed 3 Mar 2025

Iakovenko M (2021) A need for clarification of the energy solidarity principle: what can be learned from the General Court's judgment in the OPAL case? J World Energy Law Bus 14(1): 38–48. https://academic.oup.com/jwelb/article/14/1/38/6146759. Accessed 3 Mar 2025

International Energy Agency (2020) Defining energy access: 2020 methodology. https://www.iea.org/articles/defining-energy-access-2020-methodology. Accessed 3 Mar 2025

Jones O, Dodds PE (2017) Definitions of energy security. In: Steinberger-Wilckens R, Dodds PE, Kurban Z, Abad AV, Radcliffe J (eds) The role of hydrogen and fuel cells in delivering energy security for the UK. H2FC SUPERGEN, London, pp 32–45. https://discovery.ucl.ac.uk/id/eprint/10087004/. Accessed 3 Mar 2025

Kaschny L (2023) Energy justice and the principles of Article 194(1) TFEU governing EU energy policy. Transnatl Environ Law:1–25. https://www.cambridge.org/core/journals/transnational-environmental-law/article/energy-justice-and-the-principles-of-article-1941-tfeu-governing-eu-energy-policy/AD5833BF76187FE0E475E52BA8CECB08. Accessed 3 Mar 2025

Lin J (2018) Affordability and access in focus: metrics and tools of relative energy vulnerability. Electr J 31(6):23–32. https://www.sciencedirect.com/science/article/pii/S1040619018301489#:~:text=This%20work%20will%20focus%20on%20the%20consumer%E2%80%99s%20household,most%20appropriate%20to%20measure%20the%20%E2%80%98affordability%E2%80%99%20of%20energy. Accessed 3 Mar 2025

Luis Cordova JG (2025) The right to energy and the data protection and privacy rights: towards a coherent enforcement under EU law within the energy transition. Eur J Risk Regul: 1–15. https://doi.org/10.1017/err.2025.30. Accessed 3 Mar 2025

Luis Cordova JG, Rodríguez Rivero DL (2023) Energy consumer in the Cuban legal system: towards comprehensive protection. J World Energy Law Bus 16(4):309–319. https://academic.oup.com/jwelb/advance-article/doi/10.1093/jwelb/jwad010/7206380. Accessed 3 Mar 2025

Ministerio de Energía y Minas (2017) Resolución 92 'Reglamento para el servicio de gas licuado de petróleo a la población'. Gaceta Oficial No. 55 Extraordinaria de 7 de diciembre. Gaceta Oficial de la República de Cuba, La Habana. https://www.gacetaoficial.gob.cu/sites/default/files/goc-2017-ex55.pdf. Accessed 3 Mar 2025

Ministerio de la Industria Básica (1998) Resolución 2079. Gaceta Oficial de la República de Cuba, La Habana

Ministerio del Comercio Interior (2018) Resolución No. 54 'Indicaciones para la organización y ejecución de la protección al consumidor en el sistema de comercio interno'. Gaceta Oficial de la República, Cuba. https://www.gacetaoficial.gob.cu/sites/default/files/goc-2018-ex26_mincin.rar. Accessed 3 Mar 2025

Ministerio del Comercio Interior e Inversión Extranjera de Cuba (2023) Proyectos por Provincia. Cartera de Oportunidades de Inversión Extranjera. https://inviertaencuba.mincex.gob.cu/es/sectores/energetico/. Accessed 3 Mar 2025

Ministerio para Transición Ecológica (2019) Estrategia Nacional Contra la Pobreza Energética 2019–2024. Madrid. https://www.miteco.gob.es/es/prensa/estrategianacionalcontralapobrezaenergetica2019-2024_tcm30-496282.pdf. Accessed 3 Mar 2025

Montejano Hilton ME (2016) El Principio de Progresividad en los Tratados Internacionales de Derechos Humanos. ARS Iuris (51):111–138. https://revistas-colaboracion.juridicas.unam.mx/index.php/ars-iuris/article/view/34179/31151. Accessed 3 Mar 2025

Neves-Silva P, Martins GI, Heller L (2019) Human rights' interdependence and indivisibility: a glance over the human rights to water and sanitation. BMC Int Health Hum Rights 19(1):14. https://bmcinthealthhumrights.biomedcentral.com/articles/10.1186/s12914-019-0197-3. Accessed 3 Mar 2025

Ojeda Bello Z (2019) El derecho a la protección de datos personales: bases teóricas para su regulación jurídica en Cuba. Universidad de Oriente

Organización de Naciones Unidas (1979) Convention on the elimination of all forms of discrimination against women. Oficina del Alto Comicionado para los Derechos Humanos. https://www.ohchr.org/en/instruments-mechanisms/instruments/convention-elimination-all-forms-discrimination-against-women. Accessed 3 Mar 2025

Pachot K (2010) A propósito del carácter fundamental de los derechos económicos, sociales y culturales: Una mirada desde la doctrina comparada y la experiencia del ordenamiento jurídico cubano. Estudios constitucionales 8(1):13–42. http://www.scielo.cl/scielo.php?script=sci_arttext&pid=S0718-52002010000100002&lng=en&nrm=iso&tlng=en. Accessed 3 Mar 2025

Pan K (2020) Energy security and 'big stick' legislation. SSRN Electr J 37(5):607–625. https://www.ssrn.com/abstract=3671131. Accessed 3 Mar 2025

Parra Cortés LV (2018) Exigibilidad política y jurisdiccional de los derechos sociales. Universidad Carlos III de Madrid. https://e-archivo.uc3m.es/rest/api/core/bitstreams/9f5ba481-8d4e-4051-a464-1c8b62ae3b99/content. Accessed 3 Mar 2025

Pérez Gutiérrez I, Hierro Sánchez LA (2019) Por una plena protección judicial y constitucional. Universidad De La Habana (289):187–206. https://revistas.uh.cu/revuh/article/view/2450/2161. Accessed 3 Mar 2025

Porter B (2020) Interdependence of human rights. In: Research handbook on economic, social and cultural rights as human rights. Edward Elgar Publishing. https://china.elgaronline.com/view/edcoll/9781788974165/9781788974165.00024.xml. Accessed 3 Mar 2025

Practical Action (2010) Poor people's energy outlook 2010. Practical Action Publishing, Rugby. http://admin.indiaenvironmentportal.org.in/files/poor-peoples-energy-outlook.pdf. Accessed 3 Mar 2025

Practical Action (2013) Poor people's energy outlook 2013: energy for community services. Practical Action Publishing, Rugby. https://infohub.practicalaction.org/server/api/core/bitstreams/77b6c4b0-1053-48c9-b08c-861ac90d587b/content. Accessed 3 Mar 2025

Practical Action (2014) Poor people's energy outlook 2014: key messages on energy for poverty alleviation. Practical Action Publishing, Rugby. https://www.ourenergypolicy.org/wp-content/uploads/2014/06/poor.pdf. Accessed 3 Mar 2025

Prieto Valdés M (2016) Las garantías constitucionales de los derechos fundamentales y la Constitución de 1976. In: Correa AM (ed) La Constitución cubana de 1976: cuarenta años de vigencia, vol 17. Unión Nacional de Juristas de Cuba, La Habana. https://cuba.vlex.com/vid/garantias-constitucionales-derechos-fundamentales-647584885. Accessed 3 Mar 2025

Prieto Valdés M (2019a) La Constitución cubana de 2019: nuevos contenidos y necesidades. Universidad De La Habana (289):0–1. https://revistas.uh.cu/revuh/article/view/2403/2120. Accessed 3 Mar 2025

Prieto Valdés M (2019b) Las novedades de la Constitución Cubana aprobada el 24 de febrero de 2019. Revista 'Cuadernos Manuel Giménez Abad' 17:53–66. https://dialnet.unirioja.es/descarga/articulo/6967545.pdf. Accessed 3 Mar 2025

Prieto Valdés AL (2020) Garantías judiciales y propuestas para la defensa de los derechos constitucionales: Cuba, 2019. Universidad De La Habana (289):223–234. https://revistas.uh.cu/revuh/article/view/2453/2163. Accessed 3 Mar 2025

Prieto Valdés M (2022) Algunas consideraciones sobre el artículo 99 constitucional y el proceso garantista de los derechos. Revista Cubana de Derecho 2(1):42–55. https://revista.unjc.cu/index.php/derecho/article/view/109/181. Accessed 3 Mar 2025

Rodríguez V (2018) Seguridad energética: análisis y evaluación del caso de México. Serie Estudios y Perspectivas (179):1–133. https://repositorio.cepal.org/server/api/core/bitstreams/7b0b428a-070e-49cb-815d-baf161c92a0f/content. Accessed 3 Mar 2025

Sala de Amparo de los Derechos Constitucionales (2023) Sentencia No. 14

Singh S, Ru J (2022) Accessibility, affordability, and efficiency of clean energy: a review and research agenda. Environ Sci Pollut Res 29(13):18333–18347. https://doi.org/10.1007/s11356-022-18565-9. Accessed 3 Mar 2025

Sin-Hang Ngai J (2012) Energy as a human right in armed conflict: a question of universal need, survival, and human dignity. Brooklyn J Int Law 37(2):579–622. https://core.ac.uk/download/pdf/228597477.pdf. Accessed 3 Mar 2025

Stinco J (2019) El principio de progresividad en materia de derechos fundamentales. Ab-Revista de Abogacía 3(5):49–62. https://publicaciones.unpaz.edu.ar/OJS/index.php/ab/article/view/539. Accessed 3 Mar 2025

Suprema Corte de Justicia de la Nación (2019) Principio de progresividad de los derechos humanos. Derecho Global. Estudios sobre Derecho y Justicia 4(12):199. http://derechoglobal.cucsh.udg.mx/index.php/DG/article/view/260. Accessed 3 Mar 2025

Tabares Neyra LM, Kautzmann Torres A, Pérez Cuevas CM, Balari ER, Sánchez Legrán F, Cabrera Trimiño GJ, Gutiérrez Guerra I, Rey Hernández J, Letamendi Castro L, Ojeda Rodríguez NC, Tamayo Pineda N, Cárdenas Travieso O, Ruiz Legido O, Gutiérrez Castillo OW, Calves Hernández S (2020) La Protección de los Derechos de los Consumidores. Una Necesidad Real para Cuba Hoy. Edited by Ana Molina González. Syria Studies 7 (1). La Habana: Editorial Universitaria: 183. http://scielo.sld.cu/scielo.php?script=sci_arttext&pid=S2308-01322019000200016#:~:text=El%20art%C3%ADculo%20aborda%20el%20tema%20de%20la%20protecci%C3%B3n,no%20materializaci%C3%B3n%20de%20estos%20derechos%20en%20el%20pa%C3%ADs. Accessed 3 Mar 2025

Talus K (2021) The interpretation of the principle of energy solidarity. A critical comment on the opinion of the advocate general in OPAL. The Oxford Institute for Energy Studies, Oxford. https://www.oxfordenergy.org/wpcms/wp-content/uploads/2021/04/Insight-89-The-interpretation-of-the-principle-of-energy-solidarity-.pdf. Accessed 3 Mar 2025

Toledo Toribio O (2011) El Principio De Progresividad Y No Regresividad En Materia Laboral. Derecho y cambio social 8(23):1–12. https://dialnet.unirioja.es/descarga/articulo/5500749.pdf. Accessed 3 Mar 2025

Tonetto FF, Guerra S (2020) La protection de la dignité humaine comme point de convergence entre pa constitutionnalisation et l'internationalisation du droit. Revista de Direitos e Garantias Fundamentais. Sociedade de Ensino Superior de Vitoria 21(3):119–140. https://sisbib.emnuvens.com.br/direitosegarantias/article/view/1823. Accessed 3 Mar 2025

UN General Assembly (1962) Resolution 1803 (XVII): 'resolution on permanent sovereignty over national resources'. United Nations. https://documents-dds-ny.un.org/doc/RESOLUTION/GEN/NR0/193/11/PDF/NR019311.pdf?OpenElement. Accessed 3 Mar 2025

United Nations (2015) Leave no one behind. 2030 Agenda. https://unsdg.un.org/2030-agenda/universal-values/leave-no-one-behind. Accessed 3 Mar 2025

Velasco Gutiérrez Y (2013) La dignidad humana como valor, principio y derecho en la jurisprudencia constitucional colombiana. Criterios 6(2):81–130. https://revistas.usb.edu.co/index.php/criterios/article/view/2006. Accessed 3 Mar 2025

Vine M (2012) Energy security, oil and the transport sector - is Australia's policy adequate, reliable and affordable? Environ Plann Law J 29(5):401–414. https://www.academia.edu/16522810/Energy_security_oil_and_the_transport_sector_is_Australia_s_policy_adequate_reliable_and_affordable. Accessed 3 Mar 2025

World Conference on Human Rights (1993) Vienna Declaration and Programme of Action. UN office of the High Commissioner for Human Rights, Vienna. https://www.ohchr.org/sites/default/files/vienna.pdf. Accessed 3 Mar 2025

Chapter 11
General Conclusions

11.1 Conclusions and Contributions to the State of the Art

The research contained in this book answers the scientific question: What essential theoretical-legal elements should underpin the right to energy in Cuba to sustain its recognition and configuration?

In order to answer this scientific question, the general objective of this research was to lay the foundations of the essential theoretical and legal elements on which the right to energy must be based, recognised, and configured in Cuba. This objective has been developed by three specific objectives, which in turn respond to the central scientific question of this research. Each of the specific objectives outlined was developed throughout the book as a contribution to the state of the art on the right to energy.

The first specific objective was developed in three stages. The first stage was the study of the historical background (economic, social, political, etc.), which was mainly developed in Chaps. 2, 3, 4 and 7. The contribution to the state of the art of the right to energy, based on the development of the second specific objective, is evidenced in the initial phase of the research through the analysis of the global context and later the Cuban national context.

Considering the above explanation, the contributions to the state of the art are summarised in the systematisation of the essential theoretical elements that underpin the recognition and configuration of the right to energy from a doctrinal, legal, and comparative approach. This systematisation includes the analysis of human history from each of its energy phases. The organisation of such a systematisation by phases made it possible to understand the causes and conditions that generated the birth and evolutive process of the right to energy through a structured organisation of pre-existing historical knowledge.

After a critical evaluation of each of the historical phases of humanity, the indispensability of energy for human survival and development and for the existence of

J. G. Luis Cordova, *Theoretical and Legal Dimensions of the Right to Energy*, Economic and Financial Law & Policy – Shifting Insights & Values 9,
https://doi.org/10.1007/978-3-032-33252-3_11

human dignity was established. However, the satisfaction of energy needs in each historical phase has been characterised by extreme dependence. Despite the fact that the first energy sources used were renewable and free, the increase in energy needs associated with the development of processes, relations and means of production led to a "dead end".

Each of humanity's energy phases has increased our dependence on non-renewable energy sources. This dependence marked the beginning of today's so-called energy market, where suppliers took the reins thanks to the spread of neoliberalism. However, humanity is now embarking on a new path towards energy sovereignty through the energy transition as an alternative to guarantee the realisation of the right to energy.

In the second stage of the systematisation developed under the first specific objective, relevant international and regional (European Union, Latin America, and the Caribbean) legal instruments and constitutional norms were analysed. This part of the systematisation made it possible to identify the main normative background of the right to energy.

The international analysis was developed chronologically to facilitate an understanding of the evolution of the right to energy in the international legal order. As a result of this analysis, it was found that the right to energy is an evolving human right whose recognition and formulation are still in the process of gestation.

Despite that context, the Convention on the Elimination of All Forms of Discrimination against Women has set an important precedent with binding force in the recognition of the right to energy. However, while the assessment of the remaining binding international legal instruments concludes that the right to energy is not explicitly recognised, the effectiveness of all of them, as well as those without binding force, depends on the realisation of what this research defines as the right to energy.

In addition to the results of the above analysis, the following findings emerge from the regional and national analysis. In Latin America and the Caribbean, at the normative level, there is a greater tendency to recognise the right to energy as a human and fundamental right. In the European Union, however, the right to energy is subsumed under Consumer Law as a consequence of the development of economic neoliberalism.

This reality is, therefore, reflected in the constitutions analysed. A further contribution to the state of the art emerges from the critical evaluation of the constitutions analysed. This contribution is the identification of four trends in the constitutional recognition and configuration of the right to energy. These trends are indirect protection, protection within the framework of consumer rights, recognition of energy as a fundamental need, and explicit recognition of the right to energy.

In the third stage, systematisation was directed towards the theoretical and legal elements that should underpin the legal recognition and configuration of the right to energy. In this way, the substantiation of the theoretical-legal elements constitutes another contribution to the state of the art, given the wide doctrinal dispersion in this area. On the basis of the above, the legal-theoretical foundation for recognising and configuring the right to energy has been established, encompassing principles, subjects, content, and guarantees to ensure its realisation.

Continuing with the implementation of the first specific objective of this research, Chap. 7 systematises the historical background (economic, social, political, and legal) of the right to energy in Cuba. As there are few academic precedents for this study and it is widely scattered, Chap. 7 organises the main historical milestones to substantiate the need for legal recognition of the right to energy in Cuba.

The first stage dates back to the period before the triumph of the Revolution, when many advances were made at the factual level about the right to energy, but many of the elements that make up its content were negatively affected. In the subjective component of the right to energy, the conclusion is that this right did not have a universal character. At the same time, elements that make up its content, such as accessibility and affordability, have been undermined.

After the triumph of the Cuban Revolution, measures were taken to transform the pre-existing reality in the energy sector. As a result, the realisation of the content of the right to energy benefited. However, the measures adopted were based on alternatives that accentuated energy dependence on external suppliers. This was partly due to the low availability of non-renewable energy resources on Cuban territory, which are still the primary resources used for energy production in Cuba.

In addition, the implementation of the US economic and financial blockade against Cuba has had an extremely negative impact on the realisation of the right to energy. The elements described so far have, among other things, provoked energy crises that have affected and continue to affect the degree of realisation of the right to energy in Cuba.

The second specific objective outlined was primarily developed in Chaps. 8 and 9. As it will be analysed below, the contributions to the state of the art significantly impact the national level. However, on an international scale, the results of achieving the second specific objective are noteworthy, given the limited literature in this field.

In pursuit of the second specific objective, the tenets of the Constitution of the Republic of Cuba of 2019 underwent a thorough critical evaluation. Following that evaluation, it was observed that constitutional efficacy hinges on the realisation of the right to energy while it lacks explicit recognition. Following this exegetical analysis, the main normative instruments within the legal framework of the energy sector and others related to the right to energy were subjected to evaluation.

As a result of this analysis, it stands out that the legal instruments analysed promote the satisfaction of energy demand, especially through renewable sources. However, the express legal recognition of the right to energy has not been included in any of the norms consulted. The right to energy is only indirectly supported through regulations such as those on consumer protection.

11.2 Theoretical-Legal Elements Should Underpin the Right to Energy

Finally, the contributions to the state of the art resulting from the development of the third specific objective, which concludes this research, are presented in Chap. 10. As will be explained below, the legal-theoretical elements are applicable at the national level in Cuba due to the theoretical, historical, and normative basis on which these elements have been developed.

In order to establish the theoretical-legal basis for the recognition and configuration of the right to energy in Cuba, its status as a human right will be taken as a starting point, without ignoring the characteristics of the Cuban legal system analysed in Chaps. 8 and 9. In the context described above, the right to energy in Cuba must be based on the general principles of human rights, the specific principles of the right to energy (energy security, energy justice, economic efficiency, and environmental sustainability) and the constitutional principles (human dignity, progressivity, interdependence, and energy solidarity).

Other legal-theoretical elements of the right to energy will be discussed. As a result of the inclusion of the right to energy within Consumer Regulation protection, the holders of this right in Cuba are the energy consumers, while those obliged to comply with it are the energy service providers. However, for the right to energy to be recognised and defined in Cuba, in accordance with its dual nature as a human right and a fundamental right, this right must (in the future) have a universal character, and the state must be considered as a duty-bearer.

Finally, the last two theoretical-legal elements are the content of the right to energy and the guarantees that ensure its realisation. The content is the core of the obligations that, if not fully met, would undermine the realisation of the right to energy. From this perspective, there are four essential obligations: availability, accessibility, affordability, and reliability.

Based on these obligations, this research has identified four guarantees that secure the right to energy. These guarantees are the recognition of the right to energy as a fundamental right in the Cuban Constitution, together with its regulation through a complementary normative framework, security of supply, prohibition of disconnection and justiciability.

11.3 Areas Yet to Explore in Future Research

Despite the scholarly contributions of this research on energy rights, there is still a long way to go. In this respect, the limitations outlined in Chap. 1 of this research highlight the way forward. In this regard, it should be noted that the academy needs to continue to mature the theory of the right to energy and that there are still many edges to be explored.

At the academic level, new knowledge is being developed from different regions of the world with unique perspectives on the right to energy. To the extent that scholarship can fill the gaps that still exist in this area of study, energy law will have a more solid foundation on which to build international legal instruments, public policies, and legal norms.

It is impossible to develop the theory of energy law without analysing other horizons. Examples include North America, the African continent, Asia, and Oceania. Each of these contexts can offer interesting experiences in the academic, regulatory, and practical fields of energy law.

Furthermore, there is a need to go beyond geographical, cultural, and linguistic boundaries and to transcend scientific boundaries. The development of the theory of the right to energy cannot be the result of a single science since its understanding and implementation depend on multiple conditions studied by different fields of knowledge. For these reasons, it is only through interdisciplinary dialogue that comprehensive results can be achieved that consolidate the theoretical core of the right to energy.

In addition to the necessary doctrinal development of the right to energy following this research, there are other areas where much work remains to be done. Doctrinal developments in this area must be accompanied by international developments in international human rights law. Civil society's demand for the recognition and protection of the right to energy must be reflected in international law, which must be based on a solid theoretical core.

At the regional and national levels, legislators and public decision-makers must use the new knowledge to design legal norms and public policies that promote the realisation of the right to energy. In addition, material guarantees must be created to support the right to energy, which, like all other socio-economic rights, requires state action for its effective realisation. This includes inter alia, the harmonious functioning of the energy sector (or market, depending on the context) in such a way that the obligations that make up the right to energy are fully met.

Although there are still many areas where action is needed by legislators, public policymakers, civil society, academics and professionals, the path towards legal recognition and protection of the right to energy is clear. The need to move forward in this mission is not a mere wish or desire but the satisfaction of fundamental needs that, beyond dignity, determine the very life of the human species.

MIX
Papier aus verantwortungsvollen Quellen
Paper from responsible sources
FSC® C105338

If you have any concerns about our products,
you can contact us on
ProductSafety@springernature.com

In case Publisher is established outside the EU,
the EU authorized representative is:
Springer Nature Customer Service Center GmbH
Europaplatz 3, 69115 Heidelberg, Germany

Printed by Libri Plureos GmbH
in Hamburg, Germany